From Label to Table

Regulating Food in America in the Information Age

———

Xaq Frohlich

UNIVERSITY OF CALIFORNIA PRESS

University of California Press
Oakland, California

© 2023 by Xaq Frohlich

Library of Congress Cataloging-in-Publication Data

Names: Frohlich, Xaq, 1979– author.
Title: From label to table: regulating food in America in the information
    age/Xaq Frohlich.
Other titles: California studies in food and culture; 82.
Description: Oakland, California: University of California Press, [2023] |
    Series: California studies in food and culture | Includes bibliographical
    references and index.
Identifiers: LCCN 2023011327 | ISBN 9780520298804 (hardback) |
    ISBN 9780520298811 (paperback) | ISBN 9780520970816 (ebook)
Subjects: LCSH: Food—Labeling—Law and legislation—United States.
Classification: LCC KF1620.F66 F76 2023 | DDC 363.19/262—dc23/
    eng/20230711
LC record available at https://lccn.loc.gov/2023011327

Manufactured in the United States of America

32 31 30 29 28 27 26 25 24 23
10 9 8 7 6 5 4 3 2 1

From Label to Table

CALIFORNIA STUDIES IN FOOD AND CULTURE

Darra Goldstein, Editor

publication supported by a grant from
The Community Foundation for Greater New Haven
as part of the **Urban Haven Project**

*For Magalí,
there are no labels for you.*

CONTENTS

ACKNOWLEDGMENTS

I teach on the history of modern intellectual property law, and one of its biggest myths is the romantic fiction of the lone author: an intellectual, researching and writing on his own, struggling to find the right words in his head. Our credit system assigns that fictive author sole ownership of his printed ideas, rendering the work other people put into the book, and into that author, invisible. Here I will try to compensate for that. This book is the product of over a decade of professional engagements and personal growth. It reflects ideas and wisdom I have drawn from a wide network of very smart people, around the world, with whom I have had the pleasure and privilege of interacting over the course of writing it, mostly from 2016 to 2022.

My studies in food and science and technology studies (STS) began at the University of Texas at Austin with Bruce Hunt. I am deeply grateful to him for being a lifelong mentor. I continued that journey at MIT in the Doctoral Program in History, Anthropology, and Science, Technology, and Society (HASTS). While in Cambridge (MA), I was awed to learn from some of the smartest people in the room. It was an honor to study with Harriet Ritvo (your seminar on "People and Other Animals" is still my all-time favorite), David Mindell, Leo Marx, Hugh Gusterson, Manuel Castells, and Steven Shapin. I thank Natasha Schüll for the title of this book and the shared interest in the shift from face-to-face to interface. I continue to reflect on the rich conversations I had with Shane Hamilton, Jenny Smith, Anne Pollock, Alex Wellerstein, Etienne Benson, Jamie Pietruska, Candis Callison, Richa Kumar, Nick Buchanan, David Singerman, and others in the graduate community there. A special thanks to my cohort: Sara Wylie, Sophia Roosth, and Chihyung Jeon. I am above all indebted to my PhD advisor, Deborah

Fitzgerald, and to my stellar dissertation committee, Susan Silbey, David S. Jones, Sheila Jasanoff, and Heather Paxson, for their detailed feedback on the thesis and all their support during and since my graduate studies.

Research for the dissertation, which was the kernel of this book, was supported by a U.S. National Science Foundation (NSF) Dissertation Improvement Grant (Award #0822876). It was very generous of Peter Barton Hutt to open his law firm's substantial archives on food law to me. Suzanne Junod White and Donna Porter were important leads for sourcing FDA materials and for contacting former administrative officials. Henry Blackburn was a friendly gatekeeper to materials on Ancel Keys and cardiovascular epidemiology. I'm grateful to all the informants listed in my Note on Primary Sources for sharing their experiences and insights into food regulation and marketing in practice.

I was pleasantly surprised when my dissertation was one of four finalists for the Business History Conference's (BHC) 2012 Herman E. Krooss Prize for best dissertation in business history. That warm welcome at BHC drew me into the world of business history and nurtured my growing interest in market studies. The BHC is a wonderful intellectual home, and I enjoy regular exchanges with Barbara Hahn, Lee Vinsel, Alexia Yates, Christy Ford Chapin, Laura Phillips Sawyer, Teresa da Silva Lopes, and others there. A special thanks to Mark Rose for insightful feedback on chapter 4 and critique of "market talk." The vibrant community of economic sociologists in France, especially Franck Cochoy, Bastien Soutjis, Martin Giraudeau, Etienne Nouguez, and Sophie Dubuisson-Quellier, have left an indelible mark on how I think about markets. I am deeply grateful to the Hagley Center for the History of Business, Technology, and Society for the Henry Belin du Pont Research Grant I received in 2012 to use their materials. The grant came at a precarious postdoc moment for me. Roger Horowitz's encouragement and guidance then, and his hard-nosed feedback on chapters of the book since, kept the project, and me, moving forward.

Writing this book began in earnest in 2016–17 when I was a fellow at the Institute for Historical Studies in the Department of History at the University of Texas at Austin, part of its yearlong theme, "Food and Drink in History." It was a true joy exchanging ideas that year with Laura Giannetti, Michelle King, and Seth Garfield, among others. I especially appreciate early feedback on the book manuscript from Rachel Laudan, and workshopping chapter 3 with Lina Del Castillo, Megan Raby, and Sam Vong at my old coffeeshop haunt, Spider House Café.

The Auburn University Department of History has been an incredible community of brilliant, supportive colleagues. I enjoyed the free-flowing fun and feedback from Elijah Gaddis, Daren Ray, Kate Craig, Heidi Hausse, and other members of our Junior Faculty (Writing) Club. Thank you, Melissa Blair, for much-needed context and comments on chapter 3 and 1960s–1970s politics. It has been my greatest joy and privilege as an educator to work with Dave Lucsko, Alan Meyer, Monique Laney, Mike Kozuh, Alicia Maggard, Diana Kurkovsky West, Jason Hauser, John

Mohr, Sadegh Foghani, and Jen Kosmin, as part of the Auburn Tech & Civ teaching team. Our weekly conversations about the history of technology, undergraduate pedagogy, and uses of the past in the present have shaped my thinking deeply.

While this book is decidedly an American study, my perspective on the U.S. benefited from substantial time abroad. I'm grateful to the Fulbright Spain Commission for a fellowship that allowed me to build ties with food law and STS collaborators in Spain, especially Fernando González Botija, Josep Lluís Barona, José Ramón Bertomeu, Ximo Guillem Llobat, Vincenzo Pavone, Ana Delgado, and others active in the Red eSCTS. Many thank yous to Ulrike Felt for inviting me as visiting professor with her STS community at the University of Vienna. Many of my research publications started as a talk at the Vienna STS seminar, and I'm grateful for feedback on my projects there from Max Fochler, Michael Penkler, Stef Schürz, and others in that community. The Korea Advanced Institute of Science & Technology (KAIST) Graduate School of Science and Technology Policy was, and will always be, an intellectual home away from home for me. I am deeply indebted to, again, Chihyung Jeon, but also Buhm Soon Park, So Young Kim, Grant Fisher, Yoon Jung Lee, Yeonsil Kang, Sungeun Kim, and everyone in the STP family for an incredible postdoc experience, and to Tae-Ho Kim and others who make my visits to South Korea so welcoming. The intellectual hospitality of Wenhua Kuo, Po-Hsun Chen, and Chia-Ling Wu left me with a deep admiration for the STS community and research initiatives in Taiwan. My thinking about food and America's place in the world were also imprinted by my visiting professorships in France and Hong Kong. I'm grateful to Pauline Barraud de Lagerie, Emmanuel Henry, and everyone at the Université Paris-Dauphine Institut de Recherche Interdisciplinaire en Sciences Sociales (IRISSO), and to Angela Leung, Izumi Nakayama, and their colleagues at the University of Hong Kong, for hosting me and providing an outsider's perspective on my American tale.

It is an exciting time to be working in the converging fields of STS and food studies. When I started, it felt like there were only a few of us. Today I benefit from a growing community of kindred spirits curious about how science and technology have changed food, and what food can teach STS. I have enjoyed collaborations, online and offline, with Susanne Freidberg, Bart Penders, David Schliefer, Mikko Jauho, Nadia Berenstein, Patrick Baur, Marc-Olivier Déplaude, Andrew Ruis, Ai Hisano, Benjamin Cohen, Christy Spackman, Helen Zoe Veit, Jonathan Rees, Bart Elmore, Hannah Landecker, Angela Creager, Claas Kirchhelle, Christine Parker, and Ashton Merck. While I never met him, reading Bill Cronon's book, *Nature's Metropolis*, in particular a sack's journey, was the spark that lit my imagination on how packaging transformed modern foodways. Finally, I'm very excited by the collegiality and energy coming out of the STS Food & Agriculture Network (STSFAN). Many thanks to Julie Guthman, Karly Burch, and Mascha Gugganig for that wonderful platform, and to Charlotte Biltekoff, Garrett Broad,

Barkha Kagliwal, Saul Halfon, and others for their incisive input there on a draft of chapter 6.

It is worth repeating my gratitude to Susan Silbey, Sheila Jasanoff, JoAnne Yates, and above all Deborah Fitzgerald for workshopping my book manuscript in the summer of 2020 and thereby helping to get it to the endgame. The book's prose was greatly improved by the exceptional developmental editing of Audra Wolfe. I'm thankful to the University of California Press staff for shepherding my book throughout its many stages of production, especially to Kate Marshall for her patience with delays caused by the convergence of COVID-19 and my new parenting identity. The critical feedback by two anonymous reviewers made the final manuscript much stronger, and I am grateful to Anne Murcott for her generous review of the manuscript, and for our ongoing conversations about all things related to food packaging. As goes the preface paradox, any errors that remain are my sole responsibility.

We often seek to partition our professional and personal lives, an effort that weighs heavily on those unable to do so well. The COVID-19 pandemic, with its lockdowns, remote Zoom classrooms and conferences, exposed the falseness of this. I owe as many personal debts as professional ones for this book. There is not space enough here to thank everyone. So I limit my thanks to family, starting with my siblings, Tom, Penny, Molly, Chovy, Honus, and Violet. My earliest memories of reading nutrition labels were from the games I played with you, comparing nutrition panels on cereal boxes to see which product "won" with the most nutrients. I'm grateful to my adopted family, Jackie, Micaela, and Miryam, for your support the past six years of writing, and to Heather Haley for being trusted extended family. My father, Cliff, made a vital, heroic final-hour contribution to the book's economy of words. Alas, Dad, the important question of whether bean waffles are edible didn't make the cut.

I have been fortunate throughout my life to have been surrounded by exceptional and accomplished women. My daughter, Magnolia, is already a force of nature. As I watch you learn how the world works, I relearn how the world works with you. My mother, Ruth, is my lifelong role model for how to be an educator, and I am grateful for your extra support these difficult past few years. And it was my wife, Magalí, who taught me purpose and hard work. Your razor-sharp mind brought clarity to my ideas and our daily conversations, your unique life experiences have transformed and bettered my worldview. It goes without saying—nobody writes a book with a newborn baby during a global pandemic without having the most dedicated and sacrificing partner. Phrases like "invisible work," "emotional labor," "care work," and "mental load" come to mind. You believed in me, and worked tirelessly to make sure I had the hours needed to finish this. To you I dedicate it.

A NOTE ON PRIMARY SOURCES

The following is a list of archives, collections, dockets, and personal papers consulted for this project. When cited in the book, I will use the following code:

AB Keys Papers	The papers of Ancel B. Keys, housed in the Division of Epidemiology and Community Health of the University of Minnesota School of Public Health in Minneapolis, MN.
CSPI Archives	The private archives of the Center for Science in the Public Interest (CSPI), at their headquarters in Washington, DC.
E Dichter Papers Litchfield Collection	The Ernest Dichter papers (Accession 2407) and the Carter Litchfield collection on the history of fatty materials, at the Hagley Museum and Library Archives in Wilmington, DE.
E Peterson Papers	The papers of Esther Peterson, 1884–1998, at the Schlesinger Library Manuscripts Collections of the Radcliffe Institute for Advanced Study in Cambridge, MA.
FDA Dockets	The FDA Docket Management Office in Bethesda, MD.
FDA RG 88	The National Archives and Records Administration (NARA) system—the Record Group 88 files for the FDA at the National Archives II at College Park, MD.
NAS FNB Archives	Committee and subcommittee files of the Food and Nutrition Board in the Biology and Agriculture

	Division of the National Academy of Sciences (NAS), located in Washington, DC.
PB Hutt Archives	The private archives of Peter Barton Hutt housed in the library of the law firm Covington & Burling LLP in Washington, DC.
PD White Papers	The papers of Paul Dudley White, D. Mark Hegsted,
DM Hegsted Papers	and Jean Mayer, housed in the Center for History of
J Mayer Papers	Medicine at Harvard University's Countway Library of Medicine in Boston, MA.
USDA NAL	The US Department of Agriculture's National Agricultural Library Special Collections in Beltsville, MD.
W Darby Papers	The papers of William Darby and Franklin C. Bing,
FC Bing Papers	at the Eskind Biomedical Library Historical Collections at Vanderbilt University in Nashville, TN.
WHCFNH Nixon Library	The "White House Conference on Food, Nutrition, and Health" series at the Nixon Library in Yorba Linda, CA.

In 2008–2009, I conducted interviews with the following former FDA staff, nutrition scientists, and others involved in the introduction of nutrition labels in the 1970s and 1990s:

BURKEY BELSER, president of design firm Greenfield Belser Ltd.

HENRY BLACKBURN, cardiovascular epidemiologist, University of Minnesota.

JOHANNA DWYER, senior nutrition scientist, Office of Dietary Supplements, National Institutes of Health (NIH).

ROBERT EARL, former American Dietetic Association representative, Nutrition Labeling Coalition.

PETER GREENWALD, director of the National Cancer Institute Center for Cancer Prevention, NIH.

D. MARK HEGSTED, nutrition scientist, Harvard University.

REGINA HILDWINE, senior director of food labeling and standards, Grocery Manufacturers Association (GMA).

PETER BARTON HUTT, senior counsel of Covington & Burling LLP.

DONNA PORTER, research specialist at the Congressional Research Service, Library of Congress.

F. EDWARD SCARBROUGH, formerly director of FDA Center for Food Safety and Applied Nutrition (CFSAN) Office of Nutrition.

VIRGINIA L. WILKENING, former staff member at FDA CFSAN.

Introduction

Food and Power in the Information Age

A consumer strolling down the grocery store aisle is awash in a sea of product information. Boxes, bags, and cans made of cardboard, plastic, or metal (with paper label wrap) are stained with yellow, red, or a rainbow of colorful ink intended to grab the attention of the passerby. Friendly, stately, or even slick company logos neatly frame bold, two-inch-tall letters spelling out the brand of the food product. Littered across the "Principal Display Panel," to use the U.S. Food and Drug Administration's lexicon for the front of a package, are phrases that tout the (implied) health benefits about the food's appealing qualities: "All Natural," "ORGANIC," "100% REAL" or "Clinically PROVEN to Help Reduce Cholesterol." The claims sit alongside more conventional marketplace puffery, like "ORIGINAL" or "AMERICA'S FAVORITE." An extended zone of food information occupies the sides or back, with summaries of the company's romanticized history, instructions on how to prepare the food, additional ways to use it as an ingredient, or strategies to incorporate the product into a daily balanced diet.

It is here, in this text-heavy zone, that the consumer discovers the conspicuously inconspicuous information panel. This is a black box bearing the modest title (in bolded lettering and easy-to-read Helvetica) "Nutrition Facts." Strikingly austere in its black-on-white math-chart display format and high-school vocabulary, the Nutrition Facts panel, with ingredients listed below, almost leaps out at the consumer by contrast with the more colorful, flamboyant product information displayed elsewhere on the package.

The present-day Nutrition Facts panel, required by the Food and Drug Administration (FDA) for all packaged food products sold in the United States, made its first appearance in the 1990s, though an earlier version had been around since the 1970s.

NUTRITION INFORMATION		
Per Serving		
Serving size = 8 oz.		
Servings per container = 2		
Calories		560
Protein		23 g
Carbohydrate		43 g
Fat		33 g
(Percent of Calories from fat = 53%)		
Polyunsaturated*		22 g
Saturated		9 g
Cholesterol* (20 mg/100 g)		40 mg
Sodium (365 mg/100 g)		810 mg

Percentage of U.S. Recommended Daily Allowances (U.S. RDA)			
Protein	35	**Niacin**	25
Vitamin A	35	**Calcium**	2
Vitamin C	10	**Iron**	25
Thiamin	15	**Vitamin B₆**	20
Riboflavin	15	**Vitamin B₁₂**	15

*Information on fat and cholesterol content is provided for individuals who, on the advice of a physician, are modifying their total dietary intake of fat and cholesterol.

Nutrition Facts

Serving Size 1/2 cup (114g)
Servings Per Container 4

Amount Per Serving

Calories 260	Calories from Fat 120
	% Daily Value*
Total Fat 6g	**20%**
Saturated Fat 5g	**25%**
Cholesterol 30mg	**10%**
Sodium 660mg	**28%**
Total Carbohydrate 31g	**11%**
Dietary Fiber 0g	**0%**
Sugars 5g	
Protein 5g	

Vitamin A 4%	•	Vitamin C 2%
Calcium 15%	•	Iron 4%

*Percent Daily Values are based on a 2,000 calorie diet. Your daily values may be higher or lower depending on your calorie needs:

	Calories:	2,000	2,500
Total Fat	Less than	65g	80g
Sat Fat	Less than	20g	25g
Cholesterol	Less than	300mg	300mg
Sodium	Less than	2,400mg	2,400mg
Total Carbohydrate		300g	375g
Dietary Fiber		25g	30g

Calories per gram:
Fat 9 • Carbohydrate 4 • Protein 4

Nutrition Facts

8 servings per container
Serving size   2/3 cup (55g)

Amount per serving

Calories	**230**

	% Daily Value*
Total Fat 8g	**10%**
Saturated Fat 1g	**5%**
Trans Fat 0g	
Cholesterol 0mg	**0%**
Sodium 160mg	**7%**
Total Carbohydrate 37g	**13%**
Dietary Fiber 4g	**14%**
Total Sugars 12g	
Includes 10g Added Sugars	**20%**
Protein 3g	

Vitamin D 2mcg	10%
Calcium 260mg	20%
Iron 8mg	45%
Potassium 235mg	6%

* The % Daily Value (DV) tells you how much a nutrient in a serving of food contributes to a daily diet. 2,000 calories a day is used for general nutrition advice.

FIGURE 1. Evolution of the FDA's nutrition label: the original 1973 voluntary "Nutrition Information" label, the 1993 Nutrition Facts label with "% Daily Value," and the present-day Nutrition Facts label with "*Trans* Fat" and "Added Sugars."

Nutrition Facts reflect a particularly American penchant for scientism, a confidence in the power of science to address society's ills. The label represents a remarkable triumph of the appearance of nutrition science in everyday life. Fifty years earlier, only diet scientists used language like "saturated fats" or "carbohydrates." Today, all prepared foods carry labels with these terms; they are commonplace vocabulary for consumers. The Nutrition Facts panel also manifests America's propensity for legalism; that is, using warning labels to solve social problems. In this sense, the FDA label represents a new paradigm for regulating food markets. Nutrition and ingredient disclosures embody a contradictory political sensibility that endorses caveat emptor—buyer beware—but also looks to a paternalistic state for public messaging on the private real estate of packaging. The Nutrition Facts panel, a mundane object that at first appears fairly straightforward, in fact encodes a complicated politics based on backstage expert decision-making. How did this legal and scientific label come to appear on millions of everyday American household products?

The standard narrative is that by giving the public better information, the FDA's Nutrition Facts panel was the government's answer to public concerns in the 1980s about the links between diet and health, and especially the rising incidence of heart disease. But the story is much older and more complicated. Why address public health concerns through food labels, specifically on commercial packaging? The origins of the FDA's Nutrition Facts panel traces back to the first half of the twentieth century, to the early years of America's packaged food economy and the rise of the FDA as a key institution regulating food markets. The growth in sales of consumer packaged goods (CPGs) and processed foods created opportunities for national and even global marketing. But packaged and processed foods also led to a perennial crisis of trust in industrial foodways: If more and more cooking and food preparation was happening backstage, by strangers, how could consumers know who to trust with making their food? If they couldn't turn to local, familiar food providers for information, how would consumers determine what made their foods good or bad to eat?

One answer was the food label. First branded manufacturers, and then government institutions, looked to the food label to replace local, interpersonal forms of trust with an impersonal, institutional form that would work in urban retailing economies. The shift from buying food from local vendors at market*places,* where consumers could sample, to buying packaged foods from grocers and supermarkets, produced a dramatic transformation in consumers' "information environment." An information environment is the totality of different sources of information, personal and impersonal, mediated and unmediated, that shape a consumer's decisions about what to buy. As Americans entered new information environments in the 1930s, producers were forced to rely less and less on face-to-face interactions to build trust. Advertising in magazines, radio, and television supplemented and ultimately displaced the direct sales approach of markets and door-to-door salesmen. Branded manufacturers touted food packaging and labels as the "silent salesmen" to which consumers could turn to distinguish quality products from cheap knockoffs.[1]

Local, state, and federal governments were pulled into these informational strategies for building trust in national markets. The FDA would become one of the most important governmental agencies for implementing rules on food labeling, from the earliest standard weight labeling and nomenclature laws to the ingredients and nutrition disclosures that are so commonplace today. Founded in 1906 as the Bureau of Chemistry inside the U.S. Department of Agriculture, initially its powers to regulate food markets were restricted almost entirely to the prevention of *mislabeling* foods. By midcentury, the FDA had grown into a powerful administrative agency overseeing markets for consumer goods, specifically food, drugs, and cosmetics. Today, the FDA oversees more than $2.7 trillion of food, medical, and tobacco products, such that FDA-regulated products account for about 20 cents of every dollar spent by U.S. consumers.[2] At times, regulators at the FDA worked within the framework of an activist state, policing and countering market abuses. At other times, FDA regulators saw their role as collaborating with market players so that their actions would not clash with specific public interests, a form of what scholars have recently called coregulation.[3] Over the course of the twentieth century, food labeling became one of the primary ways that the FDA attempted to control national food markets, even as the industry underwent dramatic transformations.

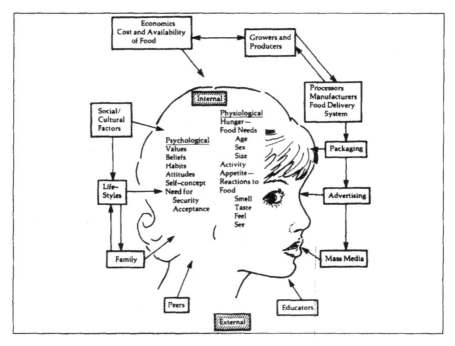

FIGURE 2. "Influences on Our Food Habits—External and Internal" diagram modeling the information environment of a typical female shopper, reprinted in an influential 1988 GAO report on food labeling. Source: U. S. GAO RCED-88-70, *Food Marketing: Frozen Pizza Cheese—Representative of Broader Food Labeling Issues* (1988), p. 12. Original: D. Wenck, B. Baren, and S. Dewan, *Nutrition: The Challenge of Being Well Nourished,* by Reston Publishing Company, Inc., a Prentice Hall Company, Reston, VA (1980), p. 24.

The result of this century of private and public efforts to build trust in packaged and processed foods is a mediated food economy: the food label has become prime real estate for shaping consumer choices. What information goes on a label? What information stays off? And how can the label best capture the equally scarce currency of a consumer's attention? These were questions experts grappled with as the FDA molded its food labeling policies. To understand why the FDA touted Nutrition Facts in the 1990s, one needs to understand the important role different groups of experts played in shaping and framing modern foodways.

HOW EXPERTS BUILT MODERN FOOD INFRASTRUCTURES

Experts shape every aspect of modern life. Yet the role of experts is often overlooked in food studies, perhaps owing to the field's commitment to foregrounding the experiences of those who have been marginalized by Big Science, Big Government, or Big Food. Writing about experts means focusing on the worldviews of powerful protagonists from business, government, and science rather than those who have been marginalized on account of their race, class, gender, or place origins.[4] Yet, by privileging experts' voices, it is not my intent to privilege their worldview.

This book describes work done by experts and expert institutions in order to look critically at the techniques and tactics expert institutions use to shape everyday life. It joins a growing literature in "new political history" that combines institutional history with social and cultural history to provide a window into what historian Meg Jacobs calls "state-building from the bottom up." Rather than taking the power of such institutions as the FDA for granted, accounts in the new political history ask how these institutions obtain and legitimate their authority.[5] Seen in this light, public and private campaigns around food labeling are part of a larger story on the contested concept of economic citizenship; that is, the rights and responsibilities of citizens as consumers in a capitalist democracy. Experts, often acting as intermediaries, navigate between top-down institutional prerogatives and the bottom-up social movements shaping America's mass markets for food.

This work required experts to interpret what issues mattered to the FDA's public as well as its institutional needs. It also required experts to "translate" between the interests of the public and the frames and constraints of governing institutions.[6] Experts developed technical rationales for their arguments for what should or should not go on the label. These rationales were grounded in culturally and historically specific "public knowledge-ways" that STS scholar Sheila Jasanoff has called "civic epistemology."[7] Experts working with the FDA on its food labeling policies were in dialogue with this changing civic food epistemology, sometimes responsive to public critiques, other times not. Food labels were part of a broader challenge for expert institutions who were concerned about how to communicate science, and in particular risk, to nonexpert publics. Would better, more informative labeling help fill what experts regularly believed to be a "deficit" in public understanding of nutrition science, or would it instead confuse or mislead the ordinary consumer?[8]

The Nutrition Facts panel is just a recent example of a long history of information devices developed by marketers, regulators, and other experts seeking to shape what consumers know about food. Long before the internet appeared, heralding an "Information Age," these communities of experts were concerned about consumers' information environments, how information about food circulated, and what they could do to shape and direct that information. This book will focus on three kinds of experts—in markets, in law, and in science—whose work helped build the modern information environments consumers depend on for food, and who in doing so sought to channel food from label to table.

IMAGINING CONSUMERS

What do consumers want? This is one of the big questions market experts mull over as they devise marketing strategies and build the market*places* where consumers get their food. Marketing, both as an everyday business practice and an increasingly arcane art, has played a growing role in framing how food is bought, sold, cooked, and eaten. Through such "market devices" as labels, trademarks, brand names, logos, mascots, and more,[9] market experts, be they economists, brand marketers, consumer psychologists, business owners, or sales specialists, hope to mold the meanings of the food they sell and thereby motivate shoppers to purchase and value their product.[10]

While officially a history of food labels, this book is also a study of how market experts have imagined consumers. The consumer is a central protagonist in histories of twentieth-century food politics, yet writing about consumers presents a problem. Whether you are a historian or a policymaker, asserting "what consumers want" quickly becomes an exercise in either projection—what *I* want a consumer to want—or metonym—what *I myself* and therefore I presume all consumers want.[11] In most narratives of public regulation, changing consumer preferences appear as a populist *deus ex machina* or a *zeitgeist* cultural backdrop. In the worst cases, consumers appear collectively as a monolithic character. While I have tried to avoid this, it remains a problem in any account that attempts to characterize the wildly diverse preferences of American consumers.

This definitional problem with consumer agency links to a bigger challenge in the history of food and agriculture: the question of "push" versus "pull" narratives. Push or supply-side narratives suggest that consumer demand for a product primarily responds to new advertising campaigns that are, in turn, typically designed to address a farm production glut. A popular example of this is the idea that our markets are saturated with corn products because corn producers successfully "captured" federal farm-subsidy programs to promote increased production and then pushed corn into new consumer markets through engineered innovations such as high fructose corn syrup.[12] Pull or demand-side narratives, by contrast, recount how producers seek to respond to an emerging consumer demand for something new; for instance, diet fads.[13] Accounts of "passive" consumers, duped by advertising and misinformation, versus "active" consumers, agents of reform empowered with information, are manifestations of these frames.[14]

Focusing on market experts as interlocutors between consumers and big market institutions offers a way to move beyond this oversimplified dichotomy. How, for instance, did experts form their impressions of consumer tastes and why consumers' tastes changed? Companies spend a fortune trying to know what the consumer wants, yet even *they* don't know. How many of us have bought a product we didn't need or want, because it was easier to buy something than to achieve the feeling or aspiration we were actually seeking? This is why companies spend a fortune trying to shape what consumers want. Experts' ideas about the consumer should be understood as a representation of the consumer, and also as an intervention into who they are. Instead of trying to speak for the consumer, or at consumers, this book explores consumers as a social construction: an idea invoked in different forms and for different purposes by different groups of experts, "cultivated" and "mobilized" through a variety of expert techniques.[15]

What power did business have to shape the consumer's sense of self?[16] One way market experts "instantiated" the consumer was as a legal or market "conceptual personae," a rhetorical device experts use to justify the actions they take. Throughout this book I describe a succession of different types of conceptual personae implied in the policies and designs of food labels: the "ordinary consumer" in chapter 2, the "informed consumer" in chapter 4, a "distributed consumer" in chapter 5, and the "rationally irrational consumer" discussed in the conclusion and common in policy circles today.[17]

A second level at which market experts shaped the agency of consumers was through their conceptualizations of "market infrastructures," the organizational and technological tissue that ties together (or separates) producers, distributors, and consumers.[18] Earlier histories of American markets described how large corporate firms, including many familiar household names in food manufacturing, vertically integrated their supply chains in the early twentieth century. The last step in this market integration was integrating the consumer. These firms invested in "mass feedback technologies," including market research and advertising, to "educate" consumers to want the goods and services companies provided.[19] In the case of packaged foods, the interface between producer and consumer was the label, which could function as either "a bridge or a barrier to communication."[20] Two key market infrastructures explored in this book are the FDA "standards of identity," introduced in chapter 1, developed over the course of the 1930s to 1960s, and informative labels, such as the FDA ingredients and nutrition panels in use since the 1970s, discussed in chapters 4 and 5.

A third way experts framed markets for consumers was through market *things*. Markets have depended on a wide variety of devices and physical things to make them work, ranging from market research focus groups and financial algorithms to shopping carts and cash registers.[21] These market things are different from theories or models because they act directly on the consumer. Foods themselves can become a "package" for a particular idea of food. For example, once certain colors or flavors were associated with quality or "freshness," companies selected, designed, and standardized foods to have those colors and flavors to create a standardized selection at the marketplace, thus by extension standardizing taste.[22] After the introduction of nutrition labeling, companies reformulated foods to be "nutritious" in a way that would be visible on the label.

The question of who counts as an expert on the consumer has itself been a moving target. Ever since Josiah Wedgewood marketed his "Queensware" porcelain in eighteenth-century England, "tastemakers"—people who decide or influence what becomes fashionable— have played a prominent role in marketing goods. Early tastemakers were often upper-class elites emulated by an aspiring middle class. This form of "conspicuous consumption" and "keeping up with the Joneses" never went away, but another type of professional tastemaker emerged with the rise of mass media and mass marketing in the late nineteenth century.[23] For much of the first half of the twentieth century, consumers looked to home economists, often women, for guidance on foods, dieting, and domestic products.[24] As new market expert professions emerged in the 1950s, adopting formal research tools from other disciplines, opportunities for women home economists diminished. Marketers' tools shifted from direct customer engagement to consumer research techniques intended to "mobilize consumers" using new models in psychology to shape consumer behavior.[25]

As food chains became more complex, market experts played a critical role in solving a core challenge at the heart of the food system: how can buyers trust where their food comes from? At the start of the twentieth century, critics of a newly emerging manufactured food economy complained of "fabricated foods," foods so packaged and processed it was difficult to assess their quality with the naked eye. They worried about a new era of market trickery they called "economic adulteration." By the 1970s, economists formalized these problems into a theory of "information asymmetry" that attributed poor market decisions to the imbalance of information between buyers and sellers. This problem of "quality uncertainty" was not just a problem for the consumer. Legitimate producers risked losing markets to competition from cheap knockoffs.[26] How could buyers and sellers establish and maintain trust in increasingly complicated food chains?

One answer to this question was to establish new infrastructures for credible sources of information, specifically the food label. The earliest examples of a modern food label can be found in seventeenth-century "patent" medicine markets, where medicines were sold in handblown bottles wrapped in labels made from handmade sheets with handprinted text. These do-it-yourself remedies foreshadowed many important features of food labeling today: branded names, such as Stoughton's drops or Anderson's pills, that identified a maker along with their (supposed) credentials as a health authority; discursive wrappers that instructed the consumer on how to use the product but also sold the buyer on the product's many benefits and trustworthy manufacture; and handheld packaging that came in a variety of shapes, sizes, and colors to distinguish the product from otherwise indistinguishable competitors. These patent medicines' manufacture and clientele, however, were fairly local by comparison to today's mass markets.[27]

In the late nineteenth century, with the expansion of railroads, market experts developed new methods of packaging and labeling to address the challenges and opportunities of marketing fresh food—particularly fruit, produce, and later milk—across long distances. These innovations ultimately gave rise to modern mass markets. Regional cooperatives of fruit growers in the American West, most famously the California Fruit Growers Exchange, or Sunkist, developed wooden shipping crates to standardize the packing process before shipment. They decorated the crates with colorful images of sunny fields to emphasize their natural regional advantages in producing better fruit than the cheaper, locally produced fruit found in eastern markets.[28] The 5-cent box of "Uneeda Biscuits," which the National Biscuit Company (or Nabisco) first sold in 1899, is widely considered to be the first nationally marketed "Consumer Packaged Good," or CPGs as the industry called them, and the beginning of branded manufactured goods in America. To highlight its innovative "In-er-Seal" packaging, which kept the crackers fresh, Nabisco used a logo to create "a visual link that connected the consumer with the manufacturer in an implicitly personal relationship."[29] The subsequent movements and countermovements in branding, standard-setting, and informative labeling that this book chronicles centered the food label as a key technology of trust that could bridge the gap of anonymous long-distance relationships in mass food markets and address pervasive anxieties about food's safety and quality.[30]

For market experts, the food label was not only a key tool for bridging the gap between producer and consumer but also a new platform for redefining what constitutes food. Packaging and processing demanded certain changes to food to facilitate scaled-up, mechanized cooking and to preserve the product for shelf stability. But the package also created the label, a new media, where consumers could access information that was not available for unpackaged foods. Was the food label just marketing hype or "puffery"? Critics certainly found them deficient: at best a reductionist statement that reflected the labeler's biases; at worst a deliberate fraud. But the new kinds of information food labels made possible created an incentive for producers to change foods to promote a particular profile on the label. Food could be redesigned to *perform* what was marketed on the label.[31]

The struggles that played out on the label among producers, market experts, and consumers attracted another set of actors: special interest groups and expert authorities who wanted to adjudicate label content. If the food label began as a market tool to advance private interests, it increasingly became the target of legal experts who believed it should serve a public good. How the FDA came to redefine the food label as a partially public platform, first through identity standards and then through informative labels, registers an important shift in what Americans expected of their political institutions concerning the regulation of individuals' choices on risk and responsibility for what they eat.

REGULATING MASS MARKETS

Why would consumers want an FDA-mandated Nutrition Facts label on their foods? How did the government get involved in dictating terms for what producers could put on their packages, or what consumers should read about food? Whose interests does the FDA speak for? Is it acting on behalf of the public as "consumer protection"? Is it colluding with or accommodating industry? Or is the FDA guided by its own kind of expert logic, following institutional commitments to rational management and administrative specialization? In short, what is the relationship of the FDA to food markets, and why does it use tools like food labels to regulate them? What does it mean, in practice, to "regulate" the wide variety of everyday activities that are implicated by the diverse product markets which the FDA oversees?

The most commonly told story is that the FDA implements rules to manage food markets because it serves a public function; i.e., it is serving the consumer. A large literature emphasizes the FDA's century-long history as a regulatory institution that protects the public's health by ensuring the safety, security, and efficacy of a wide variety of products, including foods, drugs, medical devices, biologics, and cosmetics.[32] As this story goes, the growing complexity of industrial food chains and mass markets for food, discussed earlier, and the rise of new health markets and new understandings of risk, discussed later, all evolved to create a demand for expert authorities who could aid the outgunned and underequipped consumer. The 1938 Food, Drug, and Cosmetic Act, which more than any other single piece of legislation shaped the modern FDA, was but one example of how regulators and the courts moved away from a legal culture of caveat emptor, which placed the burden of vigilance on individual consumers. The growth in size and power of administrative agencies like the FDA during the New Deal and subsequently would be one of the most significant legal developments in the twentieth century. For the five decades following the end of World War II, America's legal landscape would be characterized by these federalized, big (and distant) institutions, which were charged with giving the public a "fair deal" through their expert management of the marketplace.[33]

There was, however, a fundamental tension between the FDA's mission to address consumer needs by "protecting" consumers from businesses, and the FDA's use of expert authority to protect consumers from consumers' own (unhealthy) choices. Since the 1970s, many federal agencies have been under assault by antigovernment or "small government" political movements arguing that federal regulatory agencies are a burden on business, an infringement on individual liberties, and even a "special interest" that distorts free markets.[34] In the face of these political attacks, the FDA defended and justified its food labeling policies through claims that asserted its legal objectivity, in particular its procedural fairness, and its reputation as an expert institution built on scientific objectivity.[35] The

FDA claimed it served the consumer, even when its policies faced popular back-lash, because it blended scientific argumentation with pragmatic legal arguments about limited resources and legislative mandates.[36]

Much more was at stake in this debate than whether the FDA could speak for consumers. Food regulation entailed a wider range of work than just legislation or administrative rulemaking. Debates about the FDA's role in markets were really about who should do the work of regulation, and how it should be done. This book uses a more expansive definition of regulation to include any actions, by individuals or institutions, public or private, that are taken to determine the safety or value of food. While I focus on the FDA's food labeling activities, which centered on regulating consumerism, much of the "regulatory" work described throughout the book was carried out by market actors and even shoppers themselves.[37] At times the FDA delegated regulatory work to particular professions, establishing them as "gatekeepers" for certain markets. The creation of a product category of prescription drugs, for example, discussed in chapter 2, placed the doctor as an expert intermediary between pharmaceutical companies and the consumers of their drugs. Courts also played an important role adjudicating the public-private regulation of markets. Sometimes, private interests turned to courts to contest the FDA's authority. Other times, companies and private citizens took each other to court to litigate disputes over how markets should distribute the responsibility for risks and the rewards of a particular product.

This more expansive view of regulation helps circumvent the pervasive but misleading dichotomy of "free" markets and "interfering" government regulations. All markets involve some form of regulation. This approach also complicates another prevalent view that imagines public and private initiatives in competition with each other. Both critics and defenders of the FDA often describe a battle between private and public institutions over who should regulate markets. They disagree over how much the FDA should "intervene" in food and drug markets, or allow them to regulate themselves. Even this view, however, doesn't explain the mix of both private and public rules and modes that make up most food labels. In practice, what is more common is a hybridization of public-private governance.[38] The Ingredients and Nutrition Facts labels, though required by the FDA, are populated with information provided by the producer. These government-mandated labels sit alongside the colorful private label imagery manufacturers use to sell their product.

One significant constraint on FDA regulatory activity is the sheer scale of the mass markets the FDA regulates. In the absence of adequate resources for in-house laboratories or a large staff of enforcement officers, the FDA depends heavily on the willing participation of those businesses it regulates. In the 1950s, as I describe in chapter 2, most big food companies accepted FDA food standards so long as those regulations didn't stand in the way of their national marketing campaigns.[39] In this form of reputational interdependence, businesses used the power of their brands to control quality in supply chains, and the FDA used its reputation to force companies to comply with rules or else face the possibility of a public confrontation.[40] The FDA's scarce resources and national focus also made it particularly attuned to what Roger Horowitz has called "food chain effects."[41] Large buyers often have disproportionate impacts on how food chains are organized, which in turn shapes the choices available to smaller buyers or the end consumer. The FDA's rules tended to focus on regulating big players who would thereby shape the national markets. This meant its policies often discriminated against small operators.[42]

The FDA has also been constrained by bureaucratic pluralism, i.e., competition with other institutions that have their own regulatory frames and missions.[43] This book focuses on the FDA, but a complete history of U. S. food labeling would address jurisdictional clashes and collaborations with the Federal Trade Commission (FTC) and the U. S. Department of Agriculture (USDA), which also oversee food labeling. The FDA also interacts with the Environmental Protection Agency (EPA), charged with regulating many chemicals that end up in foods, and the Centers for Disease Control and Prevention (CDC), concerned with food-borne pathogens, food contamination, and diet-related illnesses.[44] Nor should the FDA itself be considered a unitary institution. Regulators at the FDA drew upon a patchwork of regulations with multiple and sometimes contradictory aims; as the FDA grew in staff and resources in the 1960s and 1970s, different departments and centers developed different and sometimes contradictory missions.[45] This is particularly evident in the FDA's conflicting approaches to nutrition and GMO labeling in the 1990s, as discussed in chapters 5 and 6.

The FDA's regulatory experts routinely found themselves challenged by various publics, including those they sought to protect. Most histories of the FDA describe its evolution through cycles of public scandals followed by expansion.[46] It is therefore important to pay attention to what captures regulators' attention. How do headlines, public scandals, or motivated special interests shape agenda formation and problem definition? The FDA often didn't control the political challenges that confronted it, but its power to frame those problems gave it substantial influence over the shape of food markets.

For all of the above reasons, the FDA's regulatory approach rarely develops in response to a merely technical question. Instead, the agency's policies reflect an evolving "regulatory culture," the cultural norms and attitudes of expert communities who shape, inform, or implement regulatory policies. FDA officials' viewpoints about a product might reflect the prevailing expert opinion from a certain field of medicine. They might reflect a lawyerly intuition about how the product is sold, and to whom. And these views might be shaped through interactions with special interests or elected officials. Over the years FDA staff and officials developed their own working definitions for problems that the agency faced. They used trade shorthand and jargon, naming statutory code by a statute clause number or

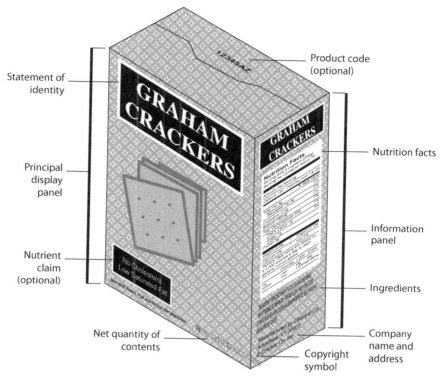

FIGURE 3. "Anatomy of a Food Label" diagram showing the information infrastructure of a food package. Source: *FDA Consumer* 28 (April 1994): 17.

a determining legal case, as well as ad hoc guidelines, such as the "jelly bean rule," discussed in chapter 2. These practices were ostensibly for professional convenience, but they also restricted discussions to specialized audiences.

The FDA's regulatory cultures emerged and changed over time. Speaking in broad strokes, I periodize the FDA's history regulating food markets into three eras: from 1880 to the 1920s, which historian Benjamin Cohen calls the "era of adulteration," when the young agency focused on chemical sleuthing of food fraud; from the 1930s to 1960s, what I call in chapter 1 the "age of standards," when a newly independent FDA developed food standards; and the "era of information," from the 1970s to the present, with the agency shifting resources away from regulating food and toward overseeing drug safety, and with food policy increasingly centered on informational regulation, including food labeling.[47] While most of this book focuses on this latter period, the transformation in the FDA's role is most visible when its history is viewed as a whole. Over the course of the twentieth century the FDA shifted from being an "activist state" rule enforcer to more of an information broker and market "umpire." This shift parallels two modes of governance that are the focus of this book: standards of identity and informative product labels.

Whether in the form of food standards or informative labels, the product label was a key FDA tool for framing markets. Labels sat at a marketing interface between producers, whom the FDA sought to regulate, and consumers, whom the agency was supposed to protect. Peter Barton Hutt, a food industry lawyer who was an FDA official in the 1970s, described advertising as "the dictionary of the labeler" to explain why promotional materials linking food to health were subject to the agency's new labeling rules.[48] The regulation of food labels created ambiguities concerning education as a public practice, deserving protection by the state, versus marketing as private practice and what came to be called protected commercial free speech. When should the FDA intervene and determine that an advertisement was inappropriate? Or when should it allow an implied health claim to remain as an acceptable form of commercial puffery? Demarcating what constitutes educating versus informing versus advertising (and deceiving) came to center on how important food was to the public's health and whether food as health was a matter of consumer protection or a marketable good.

FRAMING FOOD AS HEALTH

Food is so much more than something we simply eat to live. Food is about tradition: tying us to our family or childhood, or embodying religious meaning; food is about place: symbolizing regional identity or membership in a community; food is about economics: driven by concerns over affordability, convenience and access; food is about status: often functioning as a marker of race, class, or gender identity. Finally, food is about taste: packages of flavors and sensory stimuli we can like or dislike.

Most of this is not on the label. Instead, food labels have increasingly focused on food as a vehicle for health and nutrition. Food's reduction to health on the label involves a third category of experts who have reshaped modern understandings of food: diet scientists and nutritionists. Ever since Justus von Liebig conducted his experiments on food chemistry in the nineteenth century, scientists have sought to determine the essential nourishing elements of food. First analytic chemists and later nutrition scientists applied a reductionist approach to food, breaking it down into core elements, each with presumed health effects. Early research centered on the three primary macronutrients in foods: proteins, fats, and sugars (carbohydrates). Claims about food's vital elements quickly found their way onto food labels and into the marketing of new diets.

The marriage of marketing and new scientific ideas about food fostered two significant ideologies that still dominate food markets today: nutritionism and substitutionism. "Nutritionism" reduces food to its nutritional values and uses for health.[49] As early as 1901, home economist Ellen Swallow Richards proposed the phrase "food synonyms" to describe foods from different countries whose nutritional content and ingredients were, from the perspective of nutrition science, otherwise virtually identical.[50] The introduction of nutrition labeling in the 1970s, discussed in chapter 4, rested on this view that food could be objectively characterized as a pile of nutrients, independent of how it was produced. "Substitutionism," a belief in the interchangeability of raw materials and food ingredients,[51] was a food industry doctrine that was key to the emergence of the "plug-and-play food economy," discussed in chapter 5, and was also a crucial assumption underlying the FDA's policy of "substantial equivalence" on GMOs, discussed in chapter 6. Yet, could food's healthfulness be measured solely through the final product's properties, as scientists were apt to claim? Or was the process, how food was grown, cooked, or manufactured, also important to its wholesomeness? Debates over what the label could or couldn't say reflected these tensions.

These questions are central for the FDA because product classification is one of the key ways it regulates markets. The agency's statutory authority derives from the 1938 Food, Drug, and Cosmetic Act, which has very different standards for the three target product categories. Foods are defined as "(1) articles used for food or drink for man or other animals, (2) chewing gum, and (3) articles used for components of any such article." Drugs, by contrast, are "(A) articles recognized in the official United States Pharmacopoeia or official National Formulary . . .; (B) articles intended for use in the diagnosis, cure, mitigation, treatment, or prevention of disease in man or other animals; and (C) articles (other than food) intended to affect the structure or any function of the body of man or other animals." The parenthetical phrase "other than food" recognizes that foods also affect the structure, function, and health of our bodies, but creates a dilemma for the FDA. Indeed, the FDA's efforts since 1938 to define a clear "food-drug line" have been routinely challenged by marketers who have long used health claims on labels and advertising to sell foods, thus blurring the boundaries between foods and drugs.[52]

The FDA's task was further complicated by the fact that both popular and expert classifications for food were being turned upside down by new medical understandings of food, diet, and risk. A "chemogastric revolution" in food and medicine production in the early twentieth century turned first drugs, and then foods, into goods whose safety and other qualities couldn't easily be discerned without the help of expert science.[53] Advances in physiology and pharmacology produced a growing gap between patients' understanding of illness and cure and expert physicians' model of disease and therapeutics. When drugs targeted invisible symptoms of a disease, such as body temperature and blood pressure, patients had to take it on faith that the cure was working as the medical authority claimed.[54] Medical professional associations, chief among them the American Medical Association

(AMA), developed tools to distinguish their expert professional authority from those of drug producers, some of whom offered "magic bullets" or peddled quack treatments.[55]

This "boundary work" between conventional and alternative medicine, discussed in greater detail in chapter 2, would form an important policy backdrop to decisions about what went on and what stayed off the food label. While today most consumers take for granted the existence of "controlled substances" and "prescription drugs," these product categories reflect a marked turn away from an earlier culture that emphasized the consumer's "right to self-medication."[56] Either because these substances impaired judgment, or because a drug's risk and benefit was not self-evident, the FDA increasingly placed certain products beyond the consumer's direct reach, requiring expert intervention and consultation.

Patients might expect their medicines to be mysterious, but consumers were often surprised by the ways chemistry was transforming their food. At the beginning of the twentieth century, the chemical revolution in food generated widespread concerns about chemically "adulterated" foods and food fraud.[57] Most foods, however, remained relatively unprocessed, typically purchased at local shops that displayed their wares in bulk. Over the course of the twentieth century more and more of the consumer's budget went to precooked, processed, and packaged foods sold in self-service supermarkets. The growing use since the 1950s of "food additives," specific substances added to preserve or enhance flavor or other qualities, discussed in chapter 2, further transformed food into something that is artificially engineered and not naturally grown.[58] The industrialization and denaturing of food meant that foods were increasingly mass-produced using synthetic and purified components much like modern drugs. At what point should they be regulated as such?

Discoveries in nutrition science also changed perceptions about what was a "healthy" diet. The chemical isolation of "vitamines" in the 1910s, and the realization that such newer knowledge of nutrition could be used to remediate disease and boost health, gave rise to a "vitamania" that affected the FDA's food labeling policies. Were health tonics and supplements legitimate surplus health, or were they simply another form of fraudulent health quackery?[59]

Moreover, America was undergoing a "nutrition transition" in the first half of the twentieth century, a shift from diets and diseases of scarcity to affluent, industrial diets and problems with overeating. Just as nutritional experts were succeeding in developing public health tools for meeting basic food security, the nutrition transition and "diseases of affluence" reconfigured what was a food risk. Necessity was a shifting target. Or, as one advertising consultant colorfully put it, "in an affluent society, no useful distinction can be made between luxuries and necessities."[60]

The new sciences of food and diet posed several problems for the FDA in its efforts to make product classifications impartial and science-based. First, it is difficult to measure what a person eats, determine what constitutes their "diet," and what would happen if you were to change only one aspect of it. Is good diet and nutrition a composite of ingredients or nutritional properties, a whole food, a meal, or a lifestyle? The question of what can be "known" about a good diet according to science, partly explains the persistence of confusion in the marketplace.[61] Different studies of food, diet, and health have resulted in sometimes contradictory visions of food and eating. Public policy has had to advance on a foundation based on some degree of scientific uncertainty and contradictory evidence.

Second, any science of eating had to confront the realm of everyday experiences where everyone has an opinion. Why should consumers listen to experts about food, that most familiar of substances? Nutrition experts had to construct an "unhealthy other" in need of their services, using public platforms to chastise the uneducated or uninformed for not adopting the latest standards in food preparation and nutritional self-care.[62] Experts also had to contend with a compelling counter-rhetoric of common sense and a marketplace of competing advice. Fact-based truth claims were only one means for persuading consumers what they should eat. Diet experts sometimes found that personal rapport was more successful for building trust than scientific credentials.[63] Personal charisma, emulation, and interpersonal trust remained important in shaping food and diet markets, and experts hardly had a monopoly on them.

A third problem concerns what consumers actually want from their food. Traditionally medical treatment was, ideally, a temporary burden, while eating a daily pleasure. Negative nutrition, and socially responsible consumption more broadly, confused what eating was done in the name of healthy living and what was a joy and personal liberty.[64] Nutritionists advocated healthy eating as a counter to advertising that encouraged excessive spending or a dependence on specific health products, but marketers appropriated nutrition science to offer their own, proprietary solutions to consumers' anxieties. As discussed in chapter 2, advertisers even incorporated negative nutrition into their marketing for new diet foods, promising consumers could enjoy more of these new foods and still weigh less. If ads peddled pleasure, then nutrition scientists countered by peddling responsibility as a virtue of self-sufficiency.[65] As nutritionist Marion Nestle has well documented, by the end of the twentieth century the food industry had succeeded in co-opting diet advice and distorting food politics such that even "eat less" campaigns were used to sell more.[66] All this further complicated the FDA's attempts to distinguish foods and drugs.

At stake in all of this was the question of who should do what kinds of care work: doctors? mothers? the government? or maybe the new health food products themselves? The classification of products as foods or drugs affected regulatory tactics designed to allocate risk differently to actors in food versus drug markets. For drugs, the FDA positioned itself and medical practitioners as expert "gatekeepers" who stood between manufacturers and the consuming public. For foods, the agency focused on the food label as a market mediating device to help consumers choose wisely. As described in chapters 1 and 2, the FDA sought to keep alarming or sensational health information off food labels, to make food about "food" and not about technical matters of health. The second half of this book describes how labels ultimately made health information a feature of food, but one that was carefully regulated to ensure the information was credible.

The FDA's pivot to the food label in the 1970s, shifting the responsibility for food safety onto individuals, reflected a political realignment around managing industrial risk that scholars have described as the "risk society."[67] In markets for food and health, this new sensibility has been characterized by experts' growing preoccupation with "lifestyles"—specifically, their role in preventive medicine and health maintenance—and individuals' right to engage in risky behaviors if they assume responsibility for them.[68] The introduction of nutrition labels and health claims, discussed in chapters 4 and 5, followed this political philosophy of promoting choice and empowering self-care.

INFRASTRUCTURES FOR CHOICE IN THE INFORMATION AGE

Does anyone even read the Nutrition Facts panel? The food industry undertakes study after study evaluating how consumers interpret changes on food labels, whether labeling changes result in purchasing changes, and how new labeling designs might shape future consumption. The answer is, yes, some consumers do read Nutrition Facts.[69] Many consumers do not. This question, however, misses a larger concern: How have policies about labeling shaped consumers' food choices *even when they don't read the label*? As this book will show, labels are a central part of how experts build what I call "information infrastructures," which shape a consumer's informational environment, the context in which they make decisions about what to buy and eat.[70]

There is a paradox at the core of food labeling policies. On the one hand, it is unclear how much labels directly influence individual consumers. Labels are often thought of as a "knowledge fix," and policy debates focus on how labels affect consumer choice. The Nutrition Facts panel, however, exercises a subliminal influence that goes beyond consumer choice. Burkey Belser, chief designer of the Nutrition Facts panel in the 1990s, argued: "Convention improves comprehension. In other words, something that you see over and over and over and over again, across all media or all packaging and the like, gradually becomes iconic and gradually seeps itself in the mind so that you start to, by seeing it over again, understand it and absorb it in ways that supersede reading." Belser was highlighting the subtle, unconscious power that a product label can have when it populates products that are ubiquitous in our daily lives.[71] On the other hand, food labels play a role in regulating markets that goes beyond their function as consumer aids. Lawmakers and enforcement agencies used rules for food labeling to make companies and marketers accountable. By codifying legally binding, technical language in information tools like the Nutrition Facts panel, regulators sought to standardize industry practices. The food label became a standard reference and accounting device for the food industry's mass-marketing practices. It also became an impetus to change foods to make them more appealing on the label, regardless of whether most consumers noticed.

This book is the biography of a medium, the food label. The story behind the FDA's Nutrition Facts label serves as a vehicle to explore broader cultural questions that have shaped the food label's different uses and purposes at different phases in American history: In what ways has the marketing of food evolved since the 1930s? How does the American government engage its public, and how has this changed over time? How has nutrition science and diet advice changed, and how has this shaped modern foodways? What roles have market, scientific, and legal experts played in these changes?

The account that follows is arranged chronologically. Chapter 1 looks at the crisis in consumer confidence created by the rise of consumer packaged goods and the push from the 1930s onward to create new market infrastructures for food standards and informed selling. Chapter 2 describes how new sciences of marketing in the 1950s and 1960s, centered on diversification of product lines and niche marketing, and a new "negative nutrition" shaped the politics surrounding three product lines—vitamins, artificial sweeteners, and low-fat foods—that challenged the FDA's food standards system. Chapter 3 looks at a series of public relations crises for the FDA from 1968 to 1972, which brought previously backstage expert debates into the public limelight and generated profound disillusionment with the FDA's system of regulating foods and drugs. Chapter 4 describes how the FDA responded to this by re-centering its food policies around the informed consumer, and by using informational regulation and market devices like nutrition and ingredient labeling to shape market-based regulation. The introduction of the Nutrition Facts panel in the 1990s, described in chapter 5, marks the triumph of the new informational regulation paradigm for the FDA, and also brings expert framings of food into everyday life. Chapter 6 then examines the contrasting experience with two other important labeling movements in the 1990s: the FDA's rejection of GMO labeling under the doctrine of "substantial equivalence," and the U.S. Department of Agriculture's adoption of an official USDA organic label.

What unfolds is a history of the emergence of the "Information Age" in twentieth-century American food markets. Most people think of the Information Age as starting in the 1990s, because they associate the phrase with the popularization of the internet. Historians of technology, however, argue for a broader temporal scope for the Information Age, linking it to the evolution of information infra-structures in earlier periods.[72] The same is true for food labels. Indeed, the media-tization of food markets and marketing, especially the focus on packaging as an important form of direct-to-consumer advertising, was already underway by the 1930s. The FDA's transition from regulating food through "standards of identity," which were codified traditional recipes, to a new philosophy in the 1970s that centered on informative food labels simply accelerated the rise of the Information Age in food politics.

How do you know what you know about food and health, and how has that changed in the Information Age? Today it is less and less common for consumers to buy their food after touching it or tasting it at a marketplace, or to make decisions formed from interactions with a butcher, farmer, or knowledgeable market middleman. Our food literacy has changed. Most food is now sold at supermarkets, on the shelf and in packages. We buy food based on information, whether that information comes from the label, a magazine, diet advice, or a cookbook, or even a book like this one. This transition has changed not just our choices but also how we engage in the politics of food. How did food labels become an answer, and sometimes *the* answer, to solving the big problems in food and agriculture? The story begins at the start of the twentieth century, when a new packaged economy was transforming Americans' relationship to food.

1

An Age of Standards

Market Infrastructures

In 1939 Louise G. Baldwin and Florence Kirlin, both members of the National League of Women, published a special volume explaining the significance of the 1938 Food, Drug, and Cosmetic Act (FDCA) for consumers. Citing changes in where twentieth-century housewives obtained household goods, the women suggested that consumers faced new challenges in ensuring "the standard and quality of foods." "As a rule," they wrote, "her facility for acquiring information is limited; she has no laboratory at her disposal and is not a chemist; she cannot see through tin cans or card board packages."[1] Susceptible to a new industrial food chemistry disguising shoddy processing and poor quality, and outmaneuvered by market middlemen, the housewife portrayed by Baldwin and Kirlin was easy prey to "consumer confusion" and outright fraud.[2] She needed an ally. The government, they reasoned, had the resources to peel back the veil of America's complex industrial food system, to use food chemistry experts and laboratories to "see through tin cans" and thereby provide consumer protection.

Baldwin and Kirlin specifically identified two market tools that would help the vulnerable housewife with her shopping: food standards and informative labels. As it happened, food standards would have their day in the 1930s, while government-mandated informative labeling would not. The 1938 FDCA instituted a "standards of identity" system that the U.S. Food and Drug Administration used to regulate America's food markets. These standards mandated fixed common names (such as "peanut butter" or "tomato soup") and specified recipes with pre-approved ingredients for all mass-produced foods.

The new FDCA food standards aimed to address the growing information gap between end-consumer shoppers, like the housewife, and the business-to-business shoppers, such as large-scale wholesaler buyers and other market middlemen. When the standards were introduced, various national food manufacturers had already begun to develop voluntary food standards to facilitate their long supply chains. This reduced waste, made interchangeable ingredients feasible, and facilitated large-scale buying and selling. The FDA's standards of identity set minimum standards of quality linked to specific common named food items, thus simplifying shoppers' choices for packaged products they found at the store. Greater product uniformity improved market quality controls, including informative labeling by private producers and manufacturers.[3] The new age of standards helped end the "era of adulteration" that had plagued America's rapidly industrializing food system since the late nineteenth century.[4]

This chapter sets out to answer: Why food *standards?* Why did the FDA, Congress, and advocates for modernizing the U.S. food system in the 1930s adopt the standards of identity approach to address contemporary food problems? In looking to standards, the FDA addressed a social problem with a technical solution. In industry and engineering, trade groups commonly used standards to improve marketplace coordination or establish performance benchmarks. Historians have described the interwar period as a time when America was in "search for a modern order." Engineers believed technical standards would promote social harmony where politics and war had not. Both President Herbert Hoover's embrace of associationalism, a political movement advocating volunteerism and self-governing associations, and the New Deal's expert-led administrative state reflected a faith that rational management could solve social and political problems. For advocates of standards, the political question was whether they should be promulgated by private, often industry-led organizations, or by the state.[5] Creating product safety standards allowed the FDA to introduce a public-minded "gatekeeper" into the food production system, ensuring that the public's interests in the quality and integrity of the food supply were given voice.[6]

Making food standard was also about making food self-evident again. While this effort was partly technocratic and forward-looking, it was also nostalgic and backward-looking, authenticating food qua food.[7] The newly nationalized food economy involved new forms of chemical processing, preservation, and packaging that made it challenging for consumers seeking to identify the origins and contents of their purchases. On the face of it, food standards would help restore transparency to this system. As sociologist Lawrence Busch notes, "Standards always incorporate a metaphor or simile, either implicitly or explicitly."[8] For FDA standards, that metaphor was the traditional recipe. But what was a "traditional" industrial food? In practice, the standards of identity system never escaped this paradox. What did consumers expect from these new mass-produced foods?

The first food standards would appear within a year of the FDCA; by 1954 half of all foods purchased in America were standard foods. As the FDA scaled up its use of food standards, the new standards of identity both concealed and exposed glaring policy gaps concerning lingering cultural ambiguities about what made food wholesome.

REGULATING THROUGH FOOD FORENSICS

The 1938 FDCA was the culmination of decades of political advocacy and lobbying. Before its passage, the reigning federal food legislation was the 1906 Pure Food and Drug Act, banning the interstate traffic of adulterated or misbranded food and drug products. With its emphasis on truth and accuracy, the 1906 act incorporated age-old concerns about market fraud and food justice into newer paradigms concerning food safety and quality. The 1906 act did not establish food standards, but its insistence that a product's contents match its description informed how U. S. regulators approached food labeling for most of the twentieth century.

An important concept motivating the 1906 law was the notion of "purity" and its opposite, "adulteration." While food fraud is at least as old as cities, industrial food fraud was a particularly nineteenth-century crisis. The adulteration of milk, for example, was a recurrent concern of urban public health reformers worried about the ways industrial contamination posed a new threat to the integrity of "nature's perfect food."[9] One public scandal fresh on people's minds in the years leading up to the Pure Food and Drug Act was the Spanish-American War's "embalmed beef" incident.[10] In 1898 the Chicago Meat Trust companies shipped cheap, heavily adulterated canned meat to the U. S. Army in Cuba. The meat sickened an unrecorded number of American troops, including future president Theodore Roosevelt. The incident fueled widespread suspicion of industrial food producers, and of chemicals used in cheap, processed foods. It was this suspicion of the meatpackers and the anti-industrial language of food purity that American journalist Upton Sinclair drew upon when he published his novel *The Jungle* in 1906, chronicling the social and physical ills that a fictional immigrant family endured while working in Chicago's Packingtown. When later that year Congress passed the Meat Inspection Act and the Pure Food and Drug Act to improve food safety, but failed to implement better working conditions for workers, Sinclair famously lamented, "I aimed for the public's heart, and by accident I hit it in the stomach."[11]

Yet it wasn't always clear whether a new industrial ingredient represented chemical wizardry or deception. A telling example is saccharine, an artificial sweetener discovered in 1879 and, by the 1890s, manufactured as a sugar substitute in food and medicine. Its questionable palatability, a bitter, slightly metallic aftertaste, and reputation as a suspicious chemical substitute, attracted early regulatory scrutiny and limited its use in foods. The FDA's first commissioner, Harvey W. Wiley (1844–1930), investigated saccharine as an "adulterant" in 1908. What followed was the first direct presidential intervention in matters of federal food regulation: Theodore Roosevelt called Wiley to his office and berated him for trying to ban the chemical. Roosevelt considered himself to be diabetic, and noted that "Dr. Rixey [his personal physician] gives [saccharine] to me every day."[12] The episode calls to mind the popular refrain, 'one man's meat is another man's poison.'

Concerns about purity and invisible adulteration were a boon to emerging fields of regulatory science, scientific research motivated specifically by questions relating to regulation and public safety. From the 1880s well into the 1910s, Wiley and others spearheaded various activities providing a foundation regulating America's industrializing foodways. Many of these efforts were led by chemists, who in 1884 formed the Association of Official Agricultural Chemists (AOAC), and compiled analyses and expert opinions on "Food and Food Adulterants." Historian Aaron Bobrow-Strain, describing disputes concerning the purity of bread, notes how experts "buttressed their authority by propagating an emergency mentality."[13] Wiley attracted significant media attention when he led a volunteer group of young, healthy male government workers, known as the "Poison Squad," in self-experimentation, testing capsules of borax, formaldehyde, and other suspected common food adulterants.[14] Such was the sensation, and sensationalism, surrounding Wiley's scare tactics that another chemist dubbed it "yellow chemistry" in reference to the much-disparaged yellow journalism.[15] Wiley and other members of the USDA Bureau of Chemistry and AOAC argued that only scientific means could identify such hidden threats to America's foodways and protect the American consumer.

The 1906 Pure Food and Drug Act significantly expanded federal oversight of food and drugs, yet it was fairly limited in the enforcement powers it granted regulators. Public discussion about the legislation focused on public health and safety, especially fraud in health markets, and courts were initially conservative about applying the law to foods. The 1906 legislation required drugs to follow standards set in the United States Pharmacopoeia and the National Formulary compendia. Any variation from these standards required clear labeling of nonstandard ingredients. No similar authority was given to the USDA regarding official standards for foods—this was a gap in the 1906 legislation that regulators would seek to fill in the 1930s.

The Pure Food and Drug Act was mostly a "truth in labeling" act. By prohibiting interstate commerce in "misbranded" and "adulterated" foods, drinks, and drugs, it placed the burden on regulators to identify problem products *after* their market release. In 1913 Congress passed the Gould Net Weight Amendments to the Pure Food and Drug Act to solve the so-called "short weight problem." Manufacturers often changed the size of packages or left them half empty, thereby making consumers think they had purchased more food. The Gould amendments required all packaged foods to disclose the "quantity of their contents plainly and conspicu-ously marked on the outside of the package in terms of weight, measure, or numerical count." While barely a footnote in most accounts of twentieth-century food law, this was the first mandatory food labeling law, setting a precedent for using government-mandated information disclosures to resolve public concerns about food markets.[16]

The 1906 Pure Food and Drug Act also enabled regulators to litigate against "economic adulteration," the use of cheap substitutes that cheated consumers expecting the more wholesome authentic product. This was an extension of the government's age-old concerns about protecting a food consumer's right to a "fair" price for basic foods.[17] The concern was not food poisoning, but rather that these similar, yet cheaper quality products (e.g., saccharine) tricked consumers into misspending their money and sometimes cheapened the quality of the food sup-ply. Economic adulteration became a platform for officials to police the line between the natural and the artificial, and the authentic versus the novel.[18]

The 1906 Pure Food and Drug Act gave federal officials only limited powers to enforce the new standards for safety, so they used courts to promote their agenda, litigating against numerous manufacturers whose products posed a direct safety hazard or were labeled in some misleading way. To proactively guide industry, between 1913 and 1938, the Bureau of Chemistry published Service and Regulatory Announcements (SRAs) that included numerous guidance standards for common food products.[19] These standards were voluntary, however, not law. When industry ignored them, only courts could determine whether a particular product was ille-gal under the 1906 act.[20]

Regulators turned to analytic chemistry—specifically, the notion of "chemical purity"—to build a form of food forensics. This reflected their efforts to think like the food criminal, the *mens rea* or guilty mind, in an environment where one couldn't know all the actors involved in a food's production. In practice, Bureau of Chemistry officials targeted what might be called the usual suspects of food fraud—local or regional producers who had a history of fraudulent practices, national manufacturers who had attracted negative publicity about questionable imitation products, or cartels that prevented competition with better products. The agency's goal was to create a regulatory enforcement system that was product-based rather than process-based. To draw an analogy from courtroom language, they sought to make the evidence "speak for itself" regarding whether food was adulterated, even when witness testimony was absent.

This chemical detective work profoundly affected how the FDA was run, who it protected, and how it conceptualized food. When first created in 1862, the Bureau of Chemistry was housed inside the USDA, where its agents helped resolve pro-duction-related problems, such as product analyses to clarify tax status, or certify-ing quality control on new synthetic fertilizers. In 1927, however, the Bureau of

Chemistry was divided into two entities: the Bureau of Chemistry and Soils, and the Food, Drug, and Insecticide Administration. The division demonstrated how much the agency's food work had grown and become increasingly separate from its agriculture work. The 1930 decision to drop "insecticide" from the name reflected the FDA's increasing orientation toward food consumers.[21] Food matters related to production, such as food security, remained with other departments in the USDA, while the FDA focused on policing food safety.

These changes in regulatory practice affected how both the agency and the public assessed safety and quality, shifting the emphasis from a food's origins to its packaging. Environmental historian Ben Cohen argues that in the past a prevailing assumption underlying pure food regulation was that "pure and authentic" foods, created by natural production methods, were inherently preferable to "adulterated" foods, designed through artificial manufacturing.[22] In other words, "pure" implied something more nebulous, like today's "organic": unprocessed and wholesome. However, regulatory scientists increasingly came to define pure as a term for *chemically* pure food and uniform standards. Ironically, by defining what forms of chemical manipulation were and were not legitimate, regulators effectively established what constituted the "legal adulteration" of food.[23] Nonetheless, regulators continued to believe that "fabricated" packaged foods warranted greater oversight because there was greater potential for product manipulation. By the 1930s this view was challenged by the rise of packaged and processed foods; indeed, consumers' purchasing behavior suggested they had begun to think packaged foods were safer and even better than the natural, unprocessed foods of the nineteenth century.

PACKAGED AUTHENTICITY

Regulators' concerns with policing food fraud and holding manufacturers accountable were products of the urbanization and industrialization that transformed how Americans obtained and consumed foods. In the nineteenth century, most Americans were involved in some form of food production, often trading in kind; those who didn't make their own food shopped for it at neighborhood or urban marketplaces. By 1932 most Americans used paid wages from nonfood work to purchase food from retailers. Food markets were growing in scale, creating a network of market middlemen, including people who loaded and unloaded ships, trains, and trucks; packed and warehoused food supplies; auctioned and resold commodities; and moved food from markets to restaurants, food processors, and retail stores. The growing volume of trade created incentives to move urban wholesale markets from the city into the periphery, separating food wholesaling from end-consumer retailing.[24] This transformation was accompanied by the rise of packaged foods and the problems they posed to producers and consumers alike. How could buyer and seller establish trust, when they no longer personally knew each other, or the producer? As one home economist wrote in 1940, "Individuals, whether retailer or ultimate consumer, who have purchased industry's products have been compelled to form their judgments, to an increasing degree, on the outward appearance of merchandise. . . . Some of the most difficult problems in retailing are at least partially rooted in this lack of knowledge of the merchandise itself."[25]

Producer cooperatives, wholesalers, and chain retailers confronted this problem of trust using new, standardized approaches to packing crates and quality grading.[26] Implementing standard practices allowed companies to buy items in bulk, particularly produce, and still be assured that most of what was purchased was sellable to consumers. By the 1920s, however, many city and federal officials began expressing concern that market middlemen in these scaled-up "mass markets" passed along inefficiencies from spoilage and intermediary transaction costs to consumers in the form of high prices or poor quality foods. Public debates about the "high cost of living" motivated federal agencies such as the USDA's Bureau of Agricultural Economics to promote reforms to make markets more "modern," more compatible with new market infrastructures such as refrigeration and trucking, and easier to regulate at the regional or national level.[27] For the question of standards, this eventually prompted federal consumer advocates to consider the growing information asymmetry between producers, wholesalers, and retailers on one side, and the individual consumer on the other.

One corporate solution to the problem of trust—brand management—ultimately helped regulators as well. National manufacturers had promoted their corporate names and logos as a legal and market tool since well before 1900. For example, the Coca-Cola Company aggressively guarded its secret formula and litigated "bogus substitutes" through trademark protections on the product's name. In 1920 the Coca-Cola Company won a U.S. Supreme Court case against the Koke Company of America, with Justice Oliver Wendell Holmes Jr. writing, "the drink characterizes the name as much as the name the drink."[28] Food branding was an effective private technology promoting trust in the emerging self-service retail economy. Consumers could no longer directly question the grocer or the proprietor at the marketplace, but they could check the package, especially if it listed a brand. Brand familiarity replaced familiarity with the seller in increasingly impersonal, anonymous markets.[29]

By the 1930s and 1940s, people talked of a "Battle of the Brands." Companies invested heavily in advertising and marketing to edge out competitors. Packaging design was one front in this battle.[30] Packaging had to meet certain functional demands: first, it had to protect the contents from breakage, staleness, evaporation, leakage, or deterioration and, second, provide "convenience," i.e., be portable enough and small enough to be priced to sell.[31] There was also a revolution taking place in packaging materials and technologies. A list of packaging technologies published in a 1946 American Management Association special issue on *The Package as a Selling*

Tool offers a glimpse of how the industry was changing: "aluminum foil combined with kraft paper"; new plastic films, including "transparent sheetings" or cellophane; new electroplating methods for metal packaging; a "new one-way [nonreturnable] beer bottle"; a variety of new plastics; collapsible tubes for shaving cream and tooth-pastes; new ink products for coating and printing; and "folding boxes" to display packaging for bottled beer.[32] These new containers, wraps, and labeling materials reduced shipment costs for foods and beverages and extended shelf-life, and thus market reach. Most importantly, they provided new media for displaying and stack-ing foods, and new eye-catching tools for attracting buyers.

Packaging did more for branding than just visual selling. It transformed con-sumer trust and "attachment" to goods by creating new avenues for restoring trust diminished by impersonal supply chains, processed foods, and hidden package contents.[33] Cellophane and clear plastics were a revolutionary example of this, as they allowed consumers to inspect food through package windows or clear cello-phane wrapping. Indeed, an 1940s A&P survey found that consumers perceived "self-service meat," wrapped in cling film and displayed, to be "cleaner and less han-dled" than butcher meat, and thus believed it would "keep fresher."[34] This was par-ticularly ironic since cellophane blocked a consumer's olfactory access to foods, and "best by" or "sell by" dates were not common until the 1970s. By emphasizing visual cues over feel or smell, cellophane food packaging created a market for artificial food coloring to restore faded food to its fresh or nonprocessed ideal appearance.[35]

To manufacturers, substitution and imitations threatened brand management. Manufacturers were particularly worried about "substitution evil," that is, when grocers or retailers substituted an equivalent alternative brand for their product.[36] Building brand loyalty meant encouraging customers to insist on their brand, even when retailers didn't carry it. In their influential 1933 exposé of food, drug, and cosmetic fraud, *100,000,000 Guinea Pigs,* Arthur Kallet and F. J. Schlink describe how bakers and soda fountain shops often "remanufactured" packaged products without properly labeling the adulterated foods.[37] Producers often sought state and federal regulation prohibiting packaging and processing of ersatz imitations that led consumers to confuse the imitation and the real product, thus creating a shared interest among regulators and producers concerning food labeling standards.

Brand management and self-service retailing required a literate consumer, a housewife who read up on the products she purchased. In the 1960s the head of one supermarket chain argued the company's successful shift to self-service owed to "the increasing importance of the written word amongst an educated population." Informative labeling targeted this educated consumer, who was interested in "less talk, more print; . . . who, instead of engaging in conversation with store assistants or her peers, becomes a solitary, silent reader of innumerable printed texts on pack-ages offered for her perusal."[38] The virtue of the "silent salesman" was indeed its silence, not badgering housewives into a purchase. Consumers could take their

FIGURE 4. Packaging marketing in the 1930s and 1940s emphasized the key role of packages as "silent salesmen," particularly important in the emerging self-service retailing environment. Source: "Silent Salesmen" ad for Gardner-Richardson Co. (Middletown, OH) in *Food Industries* 18 (September 1945): 183.

time and use their own judgment. Shoppers may have trusted the printed word more than the salesman because, as stated in a 1930s marketing journal, "the printed word of advertising is less subject to falsehoods than the salesman's facile tongue."[39]

In the 1940s a consumer advocacy organization, the National Consumer-Retailer Council, Inc., developed an "Informative Selling Program" encouraging retailers to make informative labeling a central part of their self-service approach. The organization developed standard demo labels illustrating six key informational attributes of strong informative labels: What It Will Do (Performance); What It Is Made Of (Composition); How It Is Made (Construction); How To Care for It; Recommended Uses; and the Name of Manufacturer or Distributer. Sears, Roebuck & Co., for example, developed "Infotags" following this model. Informative labeling represented industry's effort to use the "force of truth" in advertising. A regional manufacturing firm president, quoted in the "Informative Selling Program" manual, noted, "I believe that facts have a definite place in advertising—and incidentally that these facts have their own particular selling appeal." The literate housewife, he said, liked informative labeling because "it is a flattering appeal, too, flattering because it recognizes the intelligence of the purchaser and supplies her with the facts she wants to know."[40] Information was a tool that manufacturers could use to build a brand's credibility. In the 1930s and 1940s, however, information did not carry the force of law.

INTRODUCING THE STANDARDS OF IDENTITY SYSTEM

Widespread interest in better market standards and ensuring consumers' access to product information led to political reform and, ultimately, to both the 1938 FDCA and the FDA's standards of identity system. Consumers were ripe for corporate manipulation. A proliferation of consumer goods without clear rules for assessing their quality and reliability had led to what economist Rexford Tugwell, member of President Franklin Roosevelt's "brain trust," called "the problem of choosing." Sociologist Robert Lynd, famous for the Middletown study of Muncie, Indiana, that he coauthored with his sociologist wife, Helen Merrell Lynd, complained: "No longer did consumer wants call production into being; rather, an interlocking network of large corporations, national advertisers, and large retail merchants manipulated consumer desires."[41] Critics of American capitalism now believed producers were pushing their products using manipulative advertising campaigns. The 1938 FDCA aimed to address this market asymmetry by introducing an architecture for FDA oversight that included new provisions for standards and premarket safety approval and enforcement.

The administrative state expanded significantly in the 1930s. Between 1933 and 1939 FDR's New Deal created dozens of new agencies, and the resulting alphabet soup of acronyms led people to call them "alphabet agencies." The FDA wasn't the FDR administration's highest political priority, as its expansion coincided with the creation of the National Recovery Administration in 1933, the Securities and Exchange Commission in 1934, and the Civil Aeronautics Board in 1938. A basic premise of the New Deal was that big business had become so organized that there was no longer an even playing field for producers and consumers. The solution was what historian Brian Balogh calls the "proministrative state": a large administrative bureaucracy managed by expert professionals working in the public interest.[42]

The FDCA's passage culminated a five-year struggle to pass food and drug legislation, and an even longer fight to expand the FDA's regulatory powers. In 1929 Stuart Chase and F. J. Schlink, authors of the best-selling *Your Money's Worth: A Study in the Waste of the Consumer's Dollar* (1927), founded Consumers' Research, a private organization dedicated to testing branded goods and publishing the results for consumers. In 1933 Schlink and Arthur Kallet published *100,000,000 Guinea Pigs*. Manufacturers concerned about maintaining the integrity of their brand identities appreciated consumer advocates like Kallet and Schlink for spotlighting the chicanery of cut-rate competitors. Many consumers, however, simply became alarmed by these accounts of producers deceiving consumers. For example, salad dressing sometimes contained cottonseed oil, a cheap substitute for other vegetable oils, and many producers swapped glucose, chemically derived from corn starch, for traditional sweeteners like cane or beet sugars, without labeling these differences.[43] Moreover, food industries disagreed about what counted as deceit. Agricultural industries, both new (corn processors and meat industry) and old (cane sugar and dairy), embraced the "pure food" movement partly to break the secrecy in manufactured foods and support full disclosure of ingredients.[44]

Consumer advocates blamed the problem on lack of government standards. FDA officials were willing to accept the blame if it might generate publicity and expand the agency's limited powers. As a public relations tool, building on the interest *100,000,000 Guinea Pigs* had created, FDA officials assembled a collection of problem products. Upon touring the exhibit, First Lady Eleanor Roosevelt dubbed it "the American Chamber of Horrors." Using cases and photos from the exhibit, Ruth deForest Lamb, the FDA's first chief educational officer, took that as the title for her 1936 best-selling book outlining the legal limitations of the 1906 act.[45]

In 1933 Senator Royal S. Copeland, a New York Democrat, introduced legislation (S.1944), which was the first attempt at a new Food, Drug, and Cosmetics Act. The bill included provisions for food labels disclosing all ingredients in order by weight; and for patent medicines and pharmaceuticals, it required stricter premarket testing and strengthened the FDA's power to regulate false advertising. The bill also placed cosmetics under the FDA's authority. It would, however, prove to be a false start. The bill foundered under withering opposition from the pharmaceutical industry and allegations that Copeland had inappropriate ties with Fleischmann's

Yeast, Eno Salts, and Phillips' Milk of Magnesia. Copeland's regular radio appearances touting unproven health benefits for these products undermined the senator's credibility with consumer advocates and manufacturers alike.[46]

Food standards were a sticking point in the 1933 legislation. By that time federal regulators had gained limited oversight powers in certain markets. A 1923 act of Congress, heavily courted by the dairy industry as a special-interest protectionist measure, defined butter and required that it contain at least 80 percent by weight of milk fat. Even more significant was the 1930 McNary-Mapes Amendment on canned fruits, establishing standards to prevent competition with deceptively substandard canned foods. This bill passed with the support of large-scale producers, who regarded minimum standards as a tool to prevent unethical competition. The canning industry was particularly invested in rooting out substandard products because of its continuing efforts to overcome consumer reservations about canned foods as a cheaper alternative to fresh foods. Because national canners were institutional buyers of produce, their purchases caused "food chain effects"; efforts to secure uniform, consistent raw ingredients for their processed products created a powerful market pressure for standardization. As a means to build credibility in national markets, by the 1930s many producers were exploring third-party certification programs, including government standards if they were voluntary.[47] Both the 1923 and 1930 acts embodied what economists have cynically called "regulatory capture," when business interests use regulation to build a barrier to competition. The acts were, however, a genuine expansion of government oversight of the rapidly growing national food market.

In 1933 the debate over standards focused on whether they should define a floor or a ceiling. The National Canners Association supported the McNary-Mapes Amendment because it created a minimum standard, a floor, but let producers decide whether to market different grades of produce, and whether to include grade information on the label. Consumer advocates, meanwhile, advocated grade labeling on canned goods as, in the words of historian Anna Zeide, "a window into the can." Industry strongly resisted this because government-issued quality standards would suggest that private market measures for quality, such as branding or price, were inadequate. Over the next few years both sides dug in over differences in what were "transparent" versus "opaque" approaches to labeling and standards.[48]

The debate over whether to adopt grade labeling or minimum standards of identity focused on what role the government should take to reduce information asymmetries between producers and consumers. It also highlighted the label's dual market role. Food labels are used as an information infrastructure tool when they serve as business-to-business (B2B) communication devices, facilitating exchanges between market middlemen. An example of this is the quality grading system the canning industry developed for its own use after the 1916 Warehouse Act.[49] Industry argued that, having developed this system, it had the right to decide how best to use it. Yet consumer advocates argued that information helping market middlemen was also useful to end consumers. Thus, labels could be a knowledge fix, empowering end consumers with information often not transparent in the end product.[50]

As often happened with food and drug legislation, a scandal over an unsafe product was the catalyst for passing the FDCA. Bills introduced in Congress each year from 1934 to 1937 had failed to pass. In the fall of 1937, however, tragedy struck. S. E. Massengill Co., a small pharmaceutical firm, took sulfanilamide, a popular treatment for streptococcal infections usually sold as pills, and created a liquid form by dissolving it in diethylene glycol. The company believed the elixir form would be popular in certain southern markets. They did not, however, test the product for toxicity, since there was no legal requirement to do so. The first shipments of Elixir Sulfanilamide went out in September. By October the American Medical Association was receiving reports from doctors about deaths related to a new sulfanilamide compound. The FDA was contacted, and what followed was an impressive detective story of nationwide sleuthing of medical markets. Over a hundred people had died, including many children. A simple toxicity test would have shown the elixir to be deadly. The FDA eventually seized supplies of Elixir Sulfanilamide under the legal technicality that it was misbranded—it should have been labeled a "solution" rather than an "elixir," because "elixir" suggested an alcoholic solution.

Journalists presented an alarmed public with a story having a clear moral: the U.S. drug market was dangerously underregulated and only the FDA's heroic efforts prevented more deaths. FDA officials used the episode to impress upon Congress the need for a long-overdue overhaul of food and drug legislation.[51] Within a year Congress had passed the 1938 FDCA, once again spearheaded by Senator Copeland. Unlike any prior regulatory act, the FDCA required drug manufacturers to test all artificial products for safety before releasing them to the market. The law established the FDA as a market gatekeeper for all new drugs sold in American markets.[52]

Public alarm over the sulfanilamide disaster meant that most political attention on the legislation centered on drugs, not foods. In addition to its requirements for premarket drug testing, the FDCA prohibited certain chemical adulterants in foods, drugs, and cosmetics, including the use of dyes made from coal tars. The final FDCA bill, however, was a much watered-down version of Copeland's initial 1933 legislation. The food and drug industries had lobbied hard to blunt the more aggressive policy provisions. Major newspapers gave the FDCA legislation little coverage, most likely because its impact on drug producers could hurt advertising revenues. The American Medical Association largely sat on the sidelines because of its general conservatism about "federal intrusion in the field of medicine" during the 1930s. Moreover, the medical profession and industry argued that, by granting certain rulemaking powers to the FDA, the FDCA challenged consumers' rights to "self-medication" or "auto-therapy," to shop around for and experiment with possible medical treatments.[53] Women's organizations, however, proved to be an effective political force pushing consumer reforms, including the passage of the FDCA. Ultimately the FDCA was a significant expansion of the FDA's powers to regulate both food and drug markets.

While the 1938 FDCA left out quality standards and ingredients disclosure, it formalized the FDA's authority to regulate the national food market by issuing minimum food standards for mass-marketed goods. The new system set identity standards as a floor. When testifying to Congress about the legislation, FDA chief Walter G. Campbell said, "The definition and standard of identity, of course, represents the very lowest level of quality at which the article is entitled to be sold under the defined name."[54] Quality standards would remain a marketing tool used at the manufacturer's discretion. Indeed, in 1939 the USDA Agricultural Marketing Service (AMS) initiated a voluntary quality standards program, better known as USDA grades, which included continuous plant inspection and the use of an AMS shield on product labels for producers purchasing this government service.[55] Even as a floor, implementing FDA food standards helped curb the proliferation of novelty brands for "fabricated" foods—mixtures or compound foods with two or more ingredients. Now there was a strong incentive for most companies to market products under the "common or usual name" of the FDA standard. The alternative, for nonstandard foods, was to list all ingredients on the label, something that was unlikely for novelty-brand companies, because of worries about revealing trade secrets on their recipes.[56]

Several changes in FDA enforcement style accompanied its emergence from the post-Depression era. The first concerned "preventive enforcement," that is, a shift away from waiting for food hazards to appear and then litigating, and toward establishing guidelines for sound industry practices.[57] The FDA's new power to set food standards emphasized this change. Second, the law created a regulatory gap between scrutiny for drugs versus foods. Drugs must be tested and found "safe," while foods just had to satisfy minimum standards. This meant that questions of product classification—whether a product was a food or a drug—became a significant issue. Third, the 1938 act emphasized "labeling" as the site where compliance or abuse would be policed. Much of the FDA's authority to regulate continued to center on what actors in the market said, what the food or drug products "purport to be," rather than on products' actual impact.[58] Products falsely representing themselves, even if they caused no direct harm, could be removed from the market as "misbranded."

The enforcement of any new law or regulation involves questions over both procedure and substance. In 1939 Charles Crawford, FDA deputy commissioner and its principal representative for the drafting of the FDCA, explained publicly how the FDA would conduct the new standards system. A Food Standards Committee would first publish a proposed standard in the U.S. *Federal Register* based on initial survey research. The FDA would give at least thirty days' notice before holding what an industry lawyer described as "an evidentiary trial-type hearing." This entailed calling witnesses, including government officials and experts, representatives of manufacturers and others in the trade, and consumers, who would be placed under oath and subject to cross-examination. Based on the hearing, the *Federal Register* would publish a finding of fact, which was open to further public comment. Then the FDA would establish a new definition and standard under the Title 21 Code of Federal Regulations, thus becoming law, but still subject to legal review in court.[59]

Holding public hearings on proposed identity standards, where both industry and consumer advocates would "have their day in court," reflected a commitment to deliberative democracy. Crawford's procedure emphasized the importance of consumer testimony in counterbalancing the direct financial interests of manufacturers, but also reflected a New Deal model of the administrative state acting as a guarantor of the public will, while embodying a faith in experts' ability to adjudicate conflicts that might arise.[60]

One key issue was what constituted a food standard. The FDA had assumed that food standards would work like "standards of purity," the voluntary food composition guidelines the AOAC and USDA had been publishing since the 1910s.[61] Under this older system, standards described a food's essential and economically important elements. A food designated as bread, for example, must include flour and yeast. Manufacturers might include other optional ingredients, but must list them on the label. A loaf of bread containing oats, for example, was still "bread," but manufacturers must acknowledge to consumers that the product also included oats. In implementing the FDCA, Crawford chose a different approach, one proposed by H. Thomas Austern, a Washington food and drug lawyer. Austern argued that incorporating the older guidelines actually lowered the standards that the FDCA was intended to strengthen. At Austern's urging, Crawford adopted a process known as "exclusive appropriation," where federal regulation assigned products common names that could only be changed by further regulation. This so-called "recipe" approach appealed to regulators because it simplified enforcement.[62]

The first standards issued by the FDA under its new system were for tomato products, published in the July 28, 1939 issue of the *Federal Register*. Just ninety-six words long, the standard of identity for "tomato juice" was "unconcentrated liquid extracted from mature tomatoes of red or reddish varieties." There was also a short description of common steps for processing tomato juice, such as draining, extracting, and straining the juice, and using heating or homogenizing to improve storage and prevent spoilage.[63] The standard for "tomato catsup," or ketchup, was more complicated and contentious, because of greater variation in how producers

Based upon the foregoing findings of fact, conclusions in the form of regulations which will promote honesty and fair dealing in the interest of consumers are hereby made and promulgated, as follows:

Regulations Under the Federal Food, Drug, and Cosmetics Act for Fixing and Establishing a Reasonable Definition and Standard of Identity for the Food Known Under Its Common or Usual Name as Tomato Juice

§ 53.000 *Tomato juice—Identity.* Tomato juice is the unconcentrated liquid extracted from mature tomatoes of red or reddish varieties, with or without scalding followed by draining. In the extraction of such liquid, heat may be applied by any method which does not add water thereto. Such liquid is strained free from skins, seeds, and other coarse or hard substances, but carries finely divided insoluble solids from the flesh of the tomato. Such liquid may be homogenized, and may be seasoned with salt. When sealed in a container it is so processed by heat, before or after sealing, as to prevent spoilage.

§ 53.005 *Yellow tomato juice—Identity.* Yellow tomato juice is the unconcentrated liquid extracted from mature tomatoes of yellow varieties. It conforms, in all other respects, to the definition and standard of identity for tomato juice prescribed in section 53.000.

It is ordered that the regulation hereby prescribed and promulgated shall become effective on January 1, 1940.

Issued this the 27th day of July 1939.

[SEAL]   HARRY L. BROWN,
          Acting Secretary of Agriculture.

[F. R. Doc. 39-2791; Filed, July 28, 1939;
              10:19 a. m.]

FIGURE 5. FDA standard for "tomato juice," one of the earliest, published in the July 1939 *Federal Register*. Source: "Regulations Under the Federal Food, Drug, and Cosmetics Act for Fixing and Establishing a Reasonable Definition and Standard of Identity for the Food Known Under Its Common or Usual Name as Tomato Juice," 4:145 *Federal Register* 3454 (July 29, 1939).

handled spicing and preservatives. Allowances were made for using dextrose (refined corn sugar) in lieu of sugar as a sweetening agent; however, over the objections of industry, this recipe did not include the preservative sodium benzoate as either a mandatory or optional ingredient. The case of ketchup proved to be a telling landmark, where the FDA's use of a standard recipe scored a long-fought symbolic victory over what it identified as a chemical adulterant.[64]

As the FDA began promulgating other standards of identity, it faced a fundamental challenge: What is a traditional *industrial* food? The 1938 FDCA called for "time-honored recipe standards." As one later critic noted, "Legislators explicitly analogized processed foods purchased in the market to their home-made counterparts."[65] Yet there were clear differences between how one bakes pies at home and how food manufacturers baked thousands of pies on an industrial scale. Companies and regulators would clash over whether definitions of conventional foods should incorporate new trends in food processing and new additives with unknown safety profiles. Public food standards hearings raised numerous questions about the scope and intent of the 1938 FDCA and the FDA standards of identity system: What were the limits to the FDCA and FDA's powers to restrict new ingredients? Would new diet science and food technology, like vitamin enrichment, be incorporated as America modernized its food? What did consumers want?

Different foods raised different concerns at the standards hearings, and attracted different public and private interests. The 1940–41 hearings on canned fruit, for example, became contentious over whether the standard would permit both sugar cane (sucrose) and refined corn sugar (dextrose) as sweetening agents in the packing medium. Secretary of agriculture, and then vice president Henry A. Wallace, who was from Iowa, staunchly supported corn sugar, whereas the sugar cane industry argued that using corn sugar deceived consumers. Both sweeteners were ultimately allowed.[66] Another debate focused on the minimum percent peanut content in peanut butter and whether the standard should include glycerin, which made peanut butter more spreadable. The hearings on ice cream featured extended discussions about the minimum percent milk fat the standards should require.[67] And so on.

While there were legal contests over specific standards into the 1960s, large manufacturers generally accepted the FDA's standards system. The federal standards created a uniform national marketplace, useful for national manufacturers scaling up production, without, at least initially, threatening most companies' ability to reformulate recipes in response to changing market tastes or the availability of ingredients.[68]

Consumer advocates saw standards as serving a pro-public and pro-consumer function because they brought clarity to the marketplace. This viewpoint was articulated by home economist Jessie Vee Coles (1894–1976). Coles, raised in Iowa, had a BS in home economics from the University of Iowa State College and a PhD in home economics from the University of Chicago. She was typical of a generation of women for whom home economics represented a path into shaping public policy. Coles was more systematic than most in articulating how both consumers and producers would benefit from stricter standards and clearer labeling. She authored three monographs on the topic: *The Consumer-Buyer and the Market* (1938), *Standards and Labels for Consumer Goods* (1949), and *Consumers Look at Labels* (1964). In *Standards and Labels for Consumer Goods*, written a decade after the introduction of the FDA's food standards system, Coles summarized why standardization was a boon to the food industry. A key step for standardization was "simplification"; there were, she argued, clear "benefits to industry of simplification" of product lines in place of an "unnecessary and uneconomical diversity of products."[69] This was because standardization was a necessary element of informative labeling, which was fast being embraced by advertisers.[70] "Although advertisers sometimes claim that the multiplicity of brands makes for freedom of choice, it may actually complicate the problem of choice. Consumers cannot try out all the brands or even a small portion of them."[71] Her conclusion: standards make mass selling possible.

The food standards hearings were also a forum where consumer advocates could rally public opinion. Ruth Desmond, a housewife and "concerned citizen," sat through a decade of standards hearings, regularly voicing her opinions about FDA rules and whether, in her opinion, they reflected the common consumer's interests. In 1959 Desmond formed the Federation of Homemakers and began publishing a quarterly newsletter for federation members. In the late 1950s and early 1960s during the peanut butter hearings, she captured headlines with her snappy critiques of company attorneys, and for arguing that peanut butter with less than 95 percent peanuts should be called "cold cream." For this she was later dubbed the "peanut butter grandmother."[72]

An open question at food standards hearings, however, was how the FDA would handle certain nontraditional foods. This gained importance in 1938 because of legal developments concerning "filled milk," i.e., any milk or cream product that was reconstituted with fats from nondairy sources, most commonly vegetable oils. Filled milk, much like margarine, had long been regulated in some states because of concerns that it could be fraudulently sold as a cheap substitute to the more expensive and natural original. This was an example of "economic adulteration" that the FDA had begun targeting in the years following the 1906 Pure Food and Drug Act. The Filled Milk Act of 1923 specifically outlawed inter-state sales of filled milk products. In 1938 a U.S. Supreme Court case tested the FDA's right to curtail these market practices. In *United States v. Carolene Products Company*, the court upheld a federal law used to seize packages of "Milnut," a con-densed skim milk filled with coconut oil, noting that there was substantial public health evidence supporting such laws. The case was important because it estab-lished a standard of review for federal agencies known as the "rational basis test." This case and the new FDCA legislation established the FDA's power to seize non-standard products, like filled milk, whenever the agency could provide a rational basis for asserting that the product undermined the public's health.

The FDCA did permit companies that created nonstandard foods to sell their products with an "imitation" label, implying they were inferior to the "authentic" standard products. Imitation products also had to list nonstandard ingredients. Courts did not always support the FDA's efforts to rid the market of such products. In 1951, in *62 Cases of Jam v. United States*, the Supreme Court rejected the FDA's arguments that "Delicious Brand Imitation Jam" was misbranded because it con-tained 25 percent fruit, instead of the 45 percent required in official jam standards. Because it was clearly labeled "imitation jam," the court ruled that any consumer

At the hearing table representatives of the fruit preserve and jelly industry, consumers, home economics specialists, and Food and Drug Administration experts presented evidence on what the standards should be. All the evidence was recorded and made available to anyone.

Beware of door-to-door sales agents who recommend high-priced food supplements as the answer to your health problems. Especially beware the agent who claims more than is stated on the label of his product. Some vitamins are harmful if you take too much for too long. It is not true that the average person needs additional vitamins if he is getting a well-balanced diet. By patronizing all departments of a modern food store we can easily supply all our nutritional needs. But if you don't feel well tell your doctor what you are eating before you pay big money for vitamins. He can tell if you need them.

FIGURE 6A. An idealized illustration of an FDA food standards hearing in a 1961 pamphlet produced by the FDA for consumers. Source: U.S. Food and Drug Administration, *Read the Label on Foods, Drugs, Devices, and Cosmetics and Household Chemicals* (FDA Publication No. 3 Rev. 3, Washington, DC, 1961), p. 11. Courtesy of the National Library of Medicine, Bethesda, MD.

FIGURE 6B. An anti–medical quackery cartoon in a 1961 pamphlet produced by the FDA for consumers. Source: U.S. Food and Drug Administration, *Read the Label on Foods, Drugs, Devices, and Cosmetics and Household Chemicals* (FDA Publication No. 3 Rev. 3, Washington, DC, 1961), p. 17. Courtesy of the National Library of Medicine, Bethesda, MD.

purchasing it understood it was an inferior counterfeit to ordinary standard jam. In 1953 the Court further articulated this imitation exception policy. The FDA seized Rich's Chocolate Chil-Zert as a misbranded imitation ice cream. Chil-Zert was a chocolate-flavored frozen dessert made from soy fat and protein that nowhere claimed to be ice cream. Indeed, the packaging claimed the opposite, clearly stating that Chil-Zert was "not an ice cream." Yet in *United States v. 651 Cases . . . Chocolate Chil-Zert* (1953), the U.S. Supreme Court sided with the FDA. The FDA's powers to create food standards implied that any substandard products resembling a food standard, even if truthfully labeled as not such, had to be labeled an "imitation."[73]

These court cases and FDA seizures established the boundaries for the FDA's authority to regulate the consumer's information environment. Courts gave the FDA wide latitude in determining what was "labeling." In 1947 the Supreme Court considered whether labeling included articles in circulation with food or drug products, not just the packaging but also informational pamphlets. In *Kordel v. United States,* the Court considered the plaintiff's argument that the FDA could not reclassify products because of promotional materials provided with them, but should instead be restricted to only information stated on the package. Kordel was a nutritionist who wrote several books and gave popular lecture tours promoting various vitamins, minerals, and herbs. In 1941 he began marketing a variety of health products. The FDA seized Kordel's products, alleging they were misbranded because circulars and pamphlets distributed to consumers by vendors, or displayed in stores alongside the products, carried misleading statements that had not been approved by the FDA. The Court ruled in favor of the FDA, arguing that the statutory phrase "accompanying such article" did not only specify physically attached items: "No physical attachment of one to the other is necessary. It is the textual relationship that is significant." This distinction between "labels" and "labeling" in the Kordel case broadened the definition of "labeling" to any source of information (e.g., accompanying pamphlet, book, shelf label, or poster) affecting how consumers might interpret a product label.[74]

While the FDCA and the courts expanded the FDA's powers to restrict certain kinds of commercial speech, the 1938 act was silent concerning what disclosures the government could compel companies to put on labels. Here industry fought to defend labels as territory best left to marketers. Industry was successful in arguing, at least in the 1930s, that more information on food labels confused consumers; for a while, FDA officials shared this view. Food standards should be simple and self-evident, and potentially confusing information, especially health-related information, should be kept to a minimum.

In 1940 the FDA moved from the USDA into the Federal Security Agency, which eventually became the Department of Health and Human Services. The move further signaled how the FDA's activities were no longer framed around agriculture and production but instead about public health and consumers. The 1938 FDCA, and subsequent court rulings in the two decades after its passage, established a new architecture of authority built on product classification and segregation, premarket testing for drugs, and standards of identity for foods. In this system the package label was more than just a product claim, subject to the low-bar test of truth-in-advertising. It was now a central component of the legal infrastructure for mass markets, and thus a key regulatory tool for controlling an economy that was scaling up.

WORLD WAR II AND THE NEW POLITICAL ECONOMY OF SCALE

The U.S.'s experience with "total war" during World War II transformed food infrastructure and policy.[75] Following World War II, professionals in the food industry marveled at wartime innovations and trends they believed would revolutionize postwar food production and sales. Willard F. Deveneau, a sales promotion manager for the National Folding Box Company, catalogued changes the food industry should consider while shifting "from gearing for war production to gearing for peacetime marketing." First, he predicted the postwar relocation of people would significantly change consumer tastes and retailing. The "forced breaking up of homes and long-established habits may mean permanent changes in the location and character of our postwar population" that "necessitate re-evaluating prewar markets." Second, he noted how innovations in packaging had been spurred by wartime "conversion packages," the provisional and ad hoc use of paper and paperboard packaging improvised to conserve materials critical to the war effort. This "forced many manufacturers, for the first time in their lives, to take an active interest in packaging as an essential part of business operations." Third, Deveneau suggested that products incorporating packaging technologies previously associated with economic hardship, such as canned foods, might experience increased sales because of their wide use and acceptance during wartime rationing. Finally, and perhaps most significantly, Deveneau described a wide variety of new foods that would soon appear in American food markets: "quick-frozen meats, fish, vegetables, fruits, and entire meals; dehydrated soups, eggs, potatoes, and other vegetables; pectin products and other foods strong in minerals and vitamins; delicacies from foreign lands, as a result of changed tastes of World War II veterans; and highly perishable tropical fruits brought in by air transport."[76]

Meanwhile, federal regulators became preoccupied with how best to regulate technology associated with "convenience" foods and how these foods reached increasingly coordinated regional and global markets. The war had ushered in what historians call "dual-use technology," technologies created for wartime use that also had peacetime adaptations.[77] Iconic examples were radar and atomic energy, but wartime research on food technology was equally significant. This is evident in the pages of *Food Technology*, the journal of the Institute of Food Technologists, which began publication in 1947. Articles described numerous new industrial food processes and analytic tests developed during the war, many of them as doctoral theses. Research funded by the quartermaster general of the U. S. Army led to significant innovations in wartime food logistics.[78] "K-rations" are probably the most famous example of a WWII dual-use food technology. These were military rations designed to be compact enough for paratroopers, yet nutritious enough to feed an army. They were a precursor to both the military's subsequent Meals-Ready-to-Eat (MREs) and what in 1950s domestic markets became known as "TV dinners."[79]

Numerous other food technologies emerged in the postwar period, prompted by wartime concerns with long-distance shipping and logistics. A patent on frozen concentrated orange juice was issued in 1948. Frozen orange juice revolutionized the Florida citrus industry, particularly after Minute Maid sponsored a *This Is Bing Crosby* radio show promoting the product.[80] Another postwar frozen food was "the Ocean's hot dog," better known as fish sticks. Prior to World War II, frozen fish was marketed mostly as a luxury item. Improvements in cold chain and flash-freezing techniques, as well as larger, sonar-equipped fishing trawlers, helped reduce costs for frozen fish and improve its quality after defrosting.[81]

Frozen concentrated orange juice and frozen fish sticks are just two examples of the ways the military worked with civilian food industries to create what one historian has called "time-insensitive foods": shelf-stable foods engineered "to make them inert and insensitive to the passage of time."[82] By one estimate, before WWII there were around a thousand processed food products on the market; after the war, anywhere from four to five thousand new processed food products could be found on supermarket shelves.[83] Processing confounded FDA efforts to make standard foods match consumers' expectations. The 1961 standards hearings for orange juice showed how new processing techniques like frozen concentrate and pasteurization allowed industry to engineer levels for juice's pulp and sugar content, or Brix, and thereby manipulate what consumers understood to be a "fresh," natural, and thus healthy drink, versus an unnatural and unhealthy "reconstituted" drink.[84] And what was the "traditional recipe" for a food that had not previously existed? What was a "standard" frozen fish stick?

All of these wartime wonders helped advance an ideology of "convenience" in postwar America. Techniques that moved foods quickly to the battlefront now saved the housewife time. Two key kitchen technologies made the convenience food culture possible: the home refrigerator and the microwave. Refrigerators began to revolutionize American foodways in the 1920s and 1930s with the introduction of the GE Monitor-Top Refrigerator, the first affordable mass-marketed refrigerator. Following World War II, ownership of household refrigerators skyrocketed, and the shelves and freezer cases of newly expanding supermarkets offered consumers ample choices for filling them. At the same time, consumers began to anticipate the possibility of reheating previously cooked foods, including precooked packaged foods, in new microwaves. The first microwave, called the "Radarange," was sold in 1946. As the name suggested, it was developed from wartime radar technology; the makers capitalized on popular interest in the radar story. A home-use microwave wouldn't appear for another decade, and microwaves wouldn't be affordable for most Americans until the 1970s. However, the microwave came to symbolize how spinoff technologies could transform the kitchen of tomorrow.

The new convenience food culture shifted the site of food preparation from the home into the factory. Advertisers heavily promoted the ease of preparing packaged, precooked foods. As one industry expert observed in 1952 in *Food Technology*: "More women than we think want basic help on the standard foods which we have taken too much for granted for years. No wonder she has gone for the packaged mixes, canned meats, macaroni-and-cheese dinners, baby foods and a score of others which cater to this demand for the pillar items built to save time."[85] As women moved out of the home and into the American workplace, advertisers reframed home cooking as a choice, or even a form of leisure that one could opt out of (if needed). Ads emphasized that convenience foods came in an all-in-one, self-contained package. This food didn't need a skilled cook. It was practically ready-to-eat.[86]

World War II also left a lasting impact on regional and global food infrastructures. The mobilization of U.S. troops and resources at a scale never previously seen demonstrated how innovations in organizational management and distribution technologies made it possible to scale up and even globalize food markets. A key component of wartime mobilization was standardization. During World War II, the U.S. government quickly became the biggest purchaser of numerous products; its product specifications fostered standardization across a variety of industries, simply as a matter of scale. Historians JoAnne Yates and Craig Murphy describe how this encouraged development of international standards after the war.[87]

These economies of scale also transformed food distribution channels. Food companies recognized that wartime mobilization and the dispersion of troops around the globe was a unique opportunity to build their brands. Coca-Cola provides perhaps the best example of global brand-building through within-firm standardization. During the war, corporate executives recognized the public relations value of supplying their beverage to homesick soldiers abroad. Coca-Cola president Robert Woodruff declared, "We will see that every man in uniform gets a bottle of Coca-Cola for 5 cents, wherever he is and whatever it costs our company." During the war the company shipped 5 billion cases of Coke to the military. To create a drink that was uniform and consistent (enough) in flavor to be familiar,

Coca-Cola had to coordinate a global supply chain and invest in regional market infrastructure. Sixty-three bottling plants were established around the world. The company sent technical observers, dubbed "Coca-Cola Colonels," to make sure they conformed to company standards. It paid off. In letters written home, soldiers told loved ones about how they tasted home in a bottle of Coke. When the war ended, Coca-Cola had an infrastructure for selling soda drinks in newly liberated or occupied foreign nations now interested in what these Americans consumed.[88] While before the war companies might have thought such globally coordinated marketing wasn't achievable, the wartime accomplishments of America's military organization now suggested otherwise. In 1946 a policy analyst at McKinsey & Company described the military's use of a large "staff form of organization" as a model for running a big company in the new postwar economy.[89]

Scale had now become an explicit challenge for the food industry to overcome and thus an opportunity for growth. Standards helped them do it. Feeding and supplying America's military around the globe had tested national manufacturers' ability to provide uniform, consistent supply chains for raw ingredients and reliable manufacturing methods for standardized packaged provisions sent overseas. Market infrastructures and food technologies, including food standards, designed to deliver packaged and processed foods meeting wartime demands, could now be employed by companies hoping to dominate national, and even global, markets for branded goods.

CONCLUSIONS

In 1946 American businesses were eager to exploit the wartime scaling-up of supply chains and postwar loosening of wartime restrictions to build a revitalized mass market economy. The rise of supermarkets seemed to embody this "trend toward self-service and mass display." Reflecting on this emerging self-service economy, Richard D. Elwell, a manager at McKinsey & Company, noted how packaging had become a top management concern because the package was a key interface between business and the consumer. "Packaging has . . . become the vehicle for providing information about your product to the customer. Your customers believe in that information and they look for it." Part of the consumer's faith in this information was attributable to the 1938 FDCA. "Previously it was, 'Let the buyer, beware,'" Elwell observed, while "today, perhaps partially as a result of that Act, customers read your statements and believe them. They look at your packaging, and believe your claims!"[90] While 1930s businesses had fought the FDCA legislation as an unnecessary New Deal incursion into markets and a threat to their private branding systems, by the late 1940s they began viewing the FDA as an important partner for building consumer trust in their products, acting as a third-party certifier to build consumer confidence.

By the 1950s one could even say that there was a "liberal consensus" for an active FDA regulating food and drug markets.[91] Big Government, with the FDA as an activist state, would work with Big Businesses, including large pharmaceutical and food manufacturers, to rationalize markets through standard-setting. In part, the liberal consensus was practical. As JoAnne Yates and Craig Murphy have argued, standardizers believed "in the long run, any standard is better than no standard."[92] Large-scale manufacturers, distributors, and retailers had already begun adopting private standards to facilitate quality assurance across national supply chains. Having the state partially assume this role, at least for minimum quality standards, boosted consumer trust and also functioned as a useful trade barrier to fraudulent competition and smaller market actors, including fringe markets.

The 1938 FDCA and the new food standards system reflected the growth of the administrative state and the role of regulatory agencies like the FDA as expert protectors of the public. Indeed, the phrase "consumer protection" first appeared in the 1950s.[93] As the FDA grew in staff size and administrative functions, its activities expanded beyond chemical sleuthing and litigation, and focused more on managing markets. Yet its reputation and authority continued to center on the idea that it was a guarantor of the public's trust. The agency was now an institutional gatekeeper for securing the safety of America's food and drug supply.

The food standards-of-identity system was a tool that, by simplifying the market into rational classifications, made it easier for regulators and businesses alike to monitor supply chains and prevent abuses that undermined consumer confidence. This process of holding FDA public hearings to build consensus for standard recipes was contentious from the start. The paradox of defining what was a "traditional" industrial food in early hearings foreshadowed future problems the FDA would have in justifying the banning of some, but not all, additives in some, but not all, foods. While FDA decisions were sometimes inconsistent, they reflected a particular regulatory culture that viewed foods as wholesome because they were whole, meaning less processed. The agency's standards sought to curb the rapid rise in industrial tinkering with food's composition. The food standards system was increasingly in conflict with the new marketing model emerging after World War II. Niche marketing, market segmentation, and a proliferation of specialty products were now supplanting earlier approaches centered on mass marketing.[94] Standards of identity implied that food was self-evident and that consumers' expectations relatively uniform. The new "consumer's republic" suggested otherwise.

For consumer advocates and regulators seeking reforms in the 1930s, setting public standards was only part of the agenda. Improving and regulating information on package labels was equally important. Ironically, the FDA's standards of identity system potentially reduced the amount of information provided to a consumer. Once a food standard was established, companies were required only to label the identity or common name of the food, not the standard ingredients it contained, many of which might be food additives that alarmed some consumers. Industry aggressively resisted the government's efforts to implement informative labels, seeking to control what it viewed as a central tool for building brand loyalty.[95] Informative labeling was, for now, seen to be a protected right of business. But FDA regulators also resisted the "more information mantra" because providing more information potentially increased consumer confusion. Indeed, because of concerns about nutrition and health quackery, the FDA increasingly restricted health information on standard foods and litigated companies marketing foods with health claims as misbranded drugs. Regulators believed that ordinary consumers didn't need such information, and those who did should talk to their doctor. A new diet food economy emerging in the 1950s and 1960s would test this position, and raise questions about how much the FDA could truly simplify America's food.

2

Gatekeepers and Hidden Persuaders

Consumer Experts

Kurt Lewin (1890–1947) was convinced that new methods and models in psychology could be used to solve important social problems, including pressing wartime concerns about how to help Americans adjust their food habits to supply shortages. Born in Prussia (present-day Poland), Lewin grew up in Germany where he trained in the Gestalt theory of psychology. The rise of Hitler and the Nazi Party led him to immigrate to the United States in 1933, where he eventually joined the Iowa Child Welfare Research Station at the University of Iowa. When the U. S. entered the war in 1941, Lewin was eager to direct his program of "action research," or applied psychology, to wartime needs. The National Research Council established a Committee on Food Habits, headed by renowned anthropologist Margaret Mead, to examine the psychological and sociocultural factors influencing food decisions. Mead commissioned Lewin to study efforts to promote the use of organ meats to relieve food shortages.[1] What he found was that the model of behaviorism, popular at the time, might explain an impulse purchase due to a flashy new package design, or disgust provoked by an unfamiliar food item.[2] But predicting whether this changed a person's food habits over time was more complicated. It required a new program of research.

Lewin's seminal 1943 paper, outlining "channel theory," reframed the usual research question of "why people eat what they eat" and instead asked "how does food come to the table and why." Borrowing concepts such as "fields" and "forces" from physics, Lewin argued that, as "food moves step by step through a channel," psychological forces governed the decision to move the food forward, or not, at each "gate." Food could reach the dinner table through different channels. Forces shaping the "Buying Channel," food bought at the grocery store, differed from

those driving food through the "Garden Channel," food grown in the family garden. In this vision of a food chain, "Food behavior is determined by the dynamics
of the food situation which includes the channels through which food comes to
the table, the gatekeeper governing the channels at the various points, and the food
ideology of the gatekeeper." The goal of the social scientist (or marketer) was to
study the decision-making of the gatekeeper, which for food was generally the
housewife, and the potential conflicting forces arising at each decision gate.[3] Channel theory suggested marketers shouldn't lecture the consumer-as-gatekeeper, but
should instead position their product campaigns in the consumer's broader informational environment. Shortly after the war Lewin died suddenly of a heart attack
at the age of fifty-seven. He never saw his new research program come to fruition.
Much of his most influential work was published posthumously in two volumes,
Field Theory in Social Science (1951) and *Resolving Social Conflicts* (1954).

Lewin's model of market channels and gatekeepers, however, created the foundation for entire schools of research in product marketing, and signaled a new
class of market experts that journalist Vance Packard would dub "hidden persuad-
ers."[4] These experts sought to shape consumers' actions in a context of large-scale,
anonymous markets. Specifically, how do marketers target key actors and influencers, those "gatekeepers" with an outsized influence over what products Americans purchased? This chapter describes how these market experts introduced new
models of consumer motivation to help businesses frame marketing campaigns
and introduce new products that could reach previously ignored or unseen "market niches" of consumers. Regulators constructed their own concept of an "ordinary consumer," in need of protection, to counter this new kind of marketing.
Who was the target of food labels: the ordinary consumer in need of protection, or
these information-seeking consumers with special niche needs and interests that
earlier mass markets hadn't met?

Heading into the 1960s, middle-class Americans were more literate and consumed more information than ever before, including information about diet and
health. But this information was often contradictory and transparently promotional. Information-savvy consumers were eager for advice on food and also cynical about the reliability of such advice. Advertisers turned to medical science and
doctors to bolster their credibility. The Food and Drug Administration and many
medical associations, in contrast, emphasized the need for expert gatekeepers for
health-related markets, seeking to shore up professional standards for drugs by
restricting health claims on food advertisements.

This regulatory debate was most pronounced for so-called "special dietary
foods," medicinal food products used by physicians to treat patients. Conceptualized in the 1938 FDCA to address a few borderline products used in special health
contexts, this classification was increasingly used by companies in the 1950s for
mass-market products. The rapid market expansion of new diet foods during that

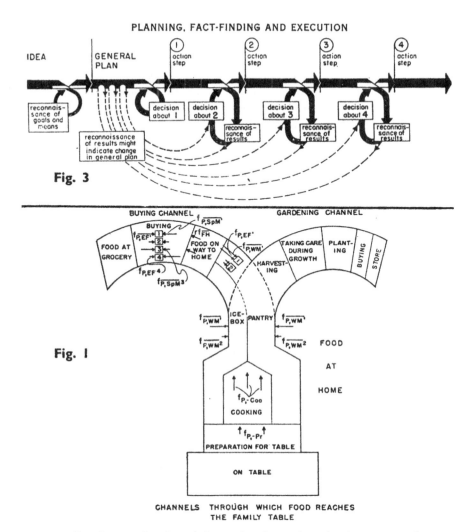

PLANNING, FACT-FINDING AND EXECUTION

Fig. 3

Fig. I

CHANNELS THROUGH WHICH FOOD REACHES
THE FAMILY TABLE

FIGURE 7. Two diagrams from Lewin's theory of marketing channels, where arrows indicate the forces pushing a product forward or backward along a "gardening" versus "buying" channel, and where gatekeepers decide based on the balance of these forces whether a food will make it to the "family table." Source: Kurt Lewin, "Frontiers in Group Dynamics: II. Channels of Group Life; Social Planning and Action Research," *Human Relations* 1, no. 2 (November 1947): 149.

decade combined two new trends: the diversification in marketing to an affluent America with a taste for novelty, including new wonder diet products, and advances in food processing technologies and food chemistry, allowing for the rapid reformulation of food recipes. Moreover, the United States was in the midst of a "nutrition transition" from an economy of scarcity to one of food abundance. This transformation had dramatic consequences for the types of illness experienced by the population, and thus the priorities of the medical profession and public health professionals in combating disease. Historian Harvey Levenstein coined the term "negative nutrition," using it to describe diet advice focused on eating less, in contrast to an earlier focus on increasing nutrition intake and, in particular, vitamins.[5] Eating less, for food companies, meant selling less. New special diet foods became their answer to the 1950s problem of the "fixed stomach," an inelastic demand for food among affluent consumers.[6] "Low cal" and "low fat" diet foods, for example, invited health-conscious consumers to continue eating without the worry. By exploiting the new science of negative nutrition, however, the new diet foods released on the market in the 1950s and 1960s challenged the FDA's food standards for food labeling and marketing. This prompted a largely backstage debate among FDA bureaucrats, medical associations, and industry representatives about dietary risk and how to "educate" the public about it.

This chapter examines the push-pull between producers attempting to sell their new diet foods and regulators attempting to govern them. In particular, it examines how companies appropriated new medical concepts into labeling and advertising campaigns. This raised questions for medical professionals and the FDA: What health information should be restricted to medical experts treating patients, and what information should be made public for mass education? How should medical associations handle profiteering from new medical knowledge, especially the market puffery surrounding diet claims? Does putting health information on food labels and in advertisements unduly burden the ordinary consumer, and does this threaten the role of gatekeepers such as the FDA and physicians? Consumer experts increasingly refashioned healthy eating not as a burden but rather as a right and privilege of health-savvy, active consumers. By the end of the 1960s, advertisers even sought to "liberate" consumers from experts by equipping consumers with the knowledge to decide for themselves. It was unclear whether food standards were protecting consumers or holding them back.

THE FOOD-DRUG BOUNDARY AND THE CHALLENGE OF "VITAMANIA"

Vitamin-enriched foods were the first of three new kinds of foods that would challenge the FDA's standards of identity system. First chemically isolated in the 1910s, "vitamines" quickly became part of what biochemist Elmer McCollum called the "newer knowledge of nutrition," which linked food chemistry to diseases of nutritional deficiencies. The discovery of diet-disease associations with food remedies initiated a new era of diet therapeutics. Beginning with cod-liver oil in the 1930s, pharmaceutical companies introduced dietary supplements that claimed to protect Americans from diets lacking in nutrition.[7]

By the 1930s, manufacturers had begun incorporating vitamins directly into processed foods, creating new possibilities for public health and new headaches for regulators. "Restoring" vitamins that were lost to a food during its industrial processing was one application of enrichment that found favor among public health professionals. An example was thiamine, or vitamin B1, linked to pellagra. By 1936 thiamine could be commercially synthesized and added to enriched bread to bring it to the same levels of thiamine found in unmilled, "whole" grain bread.[8]

In some ways vitamin supplements resembled drugs. In the 1920s and 1930s, for example, consumers purchased vitamin supplements in pharmacies, not grocery stores. Vitamin-enriched foods, however, occupied murkier ground. From the FDA's perspective, their arrival on grocery store shelves threatened to confuse consumers about the distinction between ordinary foods and drugs. The American Medical Association shared this skepticism toward marketing nutritional claims, seeing them as similar to the "quack" medical products it waged war against for nearly a century.[9] In the 1930s the AMA's Council on Foods experimented with an "AMA Seal of Approval" label for foods deemed "wholesome and [in] compli[ance] with the requirements for ingredients, composition, or nutritional values prescribed by the Council or by the government under federal food statutes." In 1943 this program was subsumed under the FDA's "special dietary foods" system, discussed later.[10] Thus, the AMA gained a degree of regulatory autonomy by forging a relationship with the FDA. This is an example of what science studies scholars call "boundary work," when experts draw boundaries of epistemic jurisdiction, such as "good" science versus "bad" science, to strengthen their authority over a field of knowledge.[11]

The issue of nutrition quackery, marketing ordinary food products and supplements as having magical health properties, became a key front for this boundary work for the FDA and the AMA.[12] These practices were so prevalent that, by the early 1960s, FDA regulators formulated a list of four common nutrition "myths." First, many quack products claimed that *all* diseases were due to improper diet. That many consumers bought this false claim was evidence of the dramatic and visible public health successes of the previous two decades. Vitamin deficiency had emerged alongside germ theory as a popular, culturally accessible explanation for illness.[13] Second, the FDA countered the notion that American foods had lost their nutritive value through "soil depletion" and the expansion of industrial farming. A third "myth" held that modern food processing techniques stripped foods of their nutritional value. Here, the FDA walked a fine line, allowing industry to use nutritional fortification to restore vitamins removed during processing, but publicly denouncing quacks who claimed this included *all* processed foods. The FDA's fourth myth concerned the relatively new scientific idea of "subclinical deficiencies" or "hidden hunger." This was the idea that nutrition deficiencies at low levels could cause mild, possibly chronic health problems without becoming a full, clinical illness. In popular marketing campaigns, the notion of subclinical deficiencies invited consumers to second-guess themselves and their doctors.[14]

The FDA's primary mode of regulating the country's foodways continued to focus on standards of identity. The prolonged hearings over bread standards are a case in point. Initiated in 1940, the bread standards hearings were suspended during the war. By this time, the mass-market bread on supermarket shelves bore little resemblance to the traditional product. According to FDA historian Suzanne White Junod, FDA officials in the 1930s and 1940s had a saying that "anyone with a new food additive or ingredient tried it first in bread."[15] The FDA had already clashed with bread manufacturers in the 1910s over the practice of using bleached flour. At that time, regulators argued that bleaching flour and then marketing the idea of "whiteness" as quality was a form of food fraud. In the 1914 case of *United States v. Lexington Mill & Elevator Co.,* the Supreme Court required the FDA to establish reasonable thresholds at which possibly toxic additives or manufacturing residues would be dangerous to health, which the agency had not done for bleaching. The result was that bleached flour was permitted.[16] But when the bread standards hearings first began in 1940, debates between regulators and industry concerned vitamin enrichment, not bleaching.

When vitamin-enrichment technologies appeared in the 1930s, the FDA and the AMA alike treated them with skepticism. They believed whole foods and a balanced diet were adequate for delivering nutrition. However, successes such as the use of iodized salt for preventing goiter, and Joseph Goldberger's campaign in the 1920s against pellagra through the use of a brewer's yeast (later discovered to supply B vitamin niacin), helped generate interest in the potential for public health programs promoting nutrients as cures.[17] During World War II, President Franklin D. Roosevelt required that the military buy enriched bread products to redress the nutritional deficiencies of army recruits. These events led both the AMA and FDA to acknowledge the public health potential of enriching basic staples.[18]

When the bread standards hearings resumed in 1948, the issue of vitamin enrichment was largely settled. Instead the hearings bogged down over disagreements about new emulsifiers used to keep packaged bread soft and "fresh," and questions about what consumers wanted. Junod describes with humor how "the question in dispute, therefore, became 'Did consumers conclude from squeezing, that a softer loaf was a fresher loaf'? All the tools of modern psychology and social science were brought to bear on the task of dissociating softness and freshness."[19] The final 1950 bread standards excluded some emulsifiers for being unnatural but allowed others derived from natural fats and oils.[20] On the matter of vitamins, the

FDA policy stated that fortifying breads with vitamins was acceptable in two specific scenarios: to restore vitamins to foods where processing removed them, and to enrich certain staple foods with vitamins deemed conducive to public health, for instance, vitamins B and D.[21]

Despite these concessions to certain forms of enrichment in certain essential foods, the FDA continued to aggressively restrict vitamin enrichment in standards-setting. Officials wanted to avoid a "horse race" toward ever higher levels of vitamins in food. FDA officials were also cautious about "fortified foods," foods enriched with vitamins they normally wouldn't have. A prominent example involved margarine, frequently fortified with vitamins A and D to make it "nutritionally equivalent" to butter. Fortifying margarine ensured that poorer consumers who bought it were getting much-needed vitamins, but also placed artificial margarine in more direct competition with the natural, more wholesome butter.

Federal courts often deferred to the FDA concerning how to interpret consumer confusion. In a 1943 lawsuit known as the Quaker Farina case, the Supreme Court considered what rights companies had in setting levels of vitamin enrichment. The concern was whether the FDA could restrict this through food standards, or whether companies like Quaker Oats could independently vary the enrichment levels based on market forces. The Court ruled in favor of the FDA: "Such [market-driven] diversity would tend to confuse and mislead consumers as to the relative value of the need for the several nutritional elements," thereby "imped[ing] rather than promot[ing] honesty and fair dealing in the interest of consumers." In other words, "diversity" in the marketplace could result in confusion which the FDA was entitled to remedy.[22] One FDA regulator at the time declared, "The new standards thus brought order out of chaos and insured that those cereal foods when sold as 'enriched' would be better designed to meet consumer expectations of benefit."[23]

Part of the FDA's concern was that consumers tended to read between the lines, often overinterpreting what was, or was *not*, stated on the labels, and were thus susceptible to implied health claims and other deceptive marketing techniques. In the Quaker Farina case, the Supreme Court noted that identity standards were "not confined to a requirement of truthful and informative labeling," but rather intended to "reflect a recognition by Congress of the inability of consumers in some cases to determine, solely on the basis of informative labeling, the relative merits of a variety of products superficially resembling each other." Thus the FDA could declare products not meeting its standards to be "imitations," even enriched foods that producers might argue were better than the standard. The agency's critics complained that this blurred the line between the FDA's clear mandate under the 1938 legislation to protect consumers from false claims, and the FDA's newer efforts to educate consumers concerning the nature of a healthy diet.[24]

This boundary between consumer protection and consumer education was problematic for the FDA. Food marketing relying on nutrition information was one means of "educating" consumers about scientific research and public health campaigns. The FDA, however, was committed to the idea that normal, healthy consumers differed from sick, vulnerable consumers. Health information, therefore, should be kept out of food marketing. In 1930 FDA Assistant Chief Paul Dunbar, addressing an audience of canners and wholesale grocers, warned, "The magic words 'health giving' are today the most overworked and loosely applied in the advertising lexicon. . . . Do you want the consuming public to get the idea that they should turn to this particular delicacy only when in unsound physical condition? Don't you want your product to appeal to the well rather than to the invalid class?"[25] Dunbar presumed that naïve consumers would read health claims as an assertion that a product was not a food, but a drug only to be consumed to restore health.

The FDA was committed to maintaining a clear boundary between "foods" and "drugs." To that end, the 1938 Food Drug and Cosmetic Act introduced a middle category of "special dietary foods" intended for use by physicians in medical treatments. In theory, special dietary products would only be available in pharmacies and doctors' offices. These products didn't require premarket testing, like drugs, but they had stricter labeling and advertising rules than ordinary foods.[26] They had to carry an information panel describing their nutritional properties (generally the quantity of vitamins). This panel was intended for patients and doctors, not for a general audience. The FDA classified vitamin supplements and fortified foods as special dietary foods, reasoning the directive would encourage manufacturers to disclose all ingredients, not just active ones.[27]

The stakes in classifying something as a food, a drug, or a "special dietary food" were huge for determining product markets and market*places*. It would have important consequences for who could sell vitamin supplements—grocers, pharmacists, or physicians—and thus which gatekeepers should aid vulnerable consumers. In the 1940s and 1950s the FDA began shifting enforcement activities more toward drugs and less on foods.[28] The establishment of America's two-tier system of over-the-counter (OTC) versus prescription drugs dramatically transformed the marketing of medicine and the relationship between patients, physicians, and the pharmaceutical industry. The creation of prescription drugs expanded doctors' role as gatekeepers and transformed the pharmaceutical industry's relationship to the medical profession. The FDA restricted all marketing on prescription drugs to physicians. Companies began aggressively targeting doctors, flooding medical journals with advertisements for new drugs or new diagnoses, and hiring drug salesmen to visit hospitals and physicians' offices.[29]

The thalidomide tragedy in 1961 catapulted concerns about drug safety to the top of the FDA's agenda. Reports of birth defects in babies whose mothers had been prescribed thalidomide to reduce morning sickness during pregnancy led to a ban on the drug's use and investigations into its safety. In 1962 Congress passed the Kefauver-Harris Amendments, formalizing the FDA's authority to require premarket approval for drugs' efficacy. Now pharmaceutical companies needed to document the appropriateness of a particular therapeutic usage, called a "therapeutic indication." Package inserts—proper use instructions and product warnings printed on paper inserts and placed inside drug packaging—became a contentious site where these claims were made and advertised.[30] The FDA was suddenly in the awkward position of regulating how drugs should be prescribed without telling physicians and physician organizations how to do their job.[31] The strengthening of rules on prescription drugs encouraged the idea that for certain products there was a need for a gatekeeper with specialized knowledge.[32]

For the FDA, the difference between foods and drugs was not just whether a marketed item was safe or risky. For a growing number of special dietary products in the gray zone between medicines and foods, the question remained: What information did an ordinary consumer need, or even want?

<h2 style="text-align:center">HIDDEN PERSUADERS AND THE
"ORDINARY CONSUMER"</h2>

The FDA's approach to segregating food and drug markets presumed that people consuming medications were a special kind of consumer, in need of protection and expert counsel, while the ordinary consumer could manage her family's food choices on her own. Similarly, the "standards of identity" system divided the envisioned food market into everyday, staple foods and a special, marginal market for dietary products and drugs. The ordinary, staple-food standards, discussed in the previous chapter, were designed for an imagined "ordinary consumer." Food manufacturers' increasing reliance on health claims in the 1950s and 1960s challenged this logic. Suddenly, it seemed, even the ordinary consumer wanted access to foods as preventive tools for public health.

"Ordinary consumer" is a legal term used by lawyers, judges, and FDA regulators to determine a reasonable enforcement standard for a given product. This concept emerged out of reforms in tort law. At the beginning of the twentieth century, the food market operated under the old common-law principles of *caveat emptor*, buyer beware, and "privity," an understanding of contract law where the warranty or responsibility for a breach in contract depends on the close relationship between the two parties, such as buyer and seller.[33] As the relationship between buyers and sellers came to involve ever longer chains of producers, distributors, and consumers, application of these principles placed enormous responsibilities on the ultimate consumer. Over the first half of the century, courts loosened these standards and held companies liable even when there was no direct contractual or product exchange between the plaintiff and the defendant. So complete was this transformation in tort law and liability that by 1960 a leading legal scholar declared the "assault upon the citadel of privity" nearly complete. Sellers of food and drink were now held in strict liability (as opposed to just liability for negligence) to the end consumer.[34]

Two important concepts affecting enforcement standards evolved out of these legal debates. The first was "the consumer expectations test," or reasonable expectations standard. This holds that a producer is only liable when a product is deemed "dangerous to an extent beyond that which would be contemplated by the ordinary consumer who purchases it, with the ordinary knowledge common to the community as to its characteristics." In the food standards hearings and legal cases on labeling, FDA and industry plaintiffs argued their positions in terms of how an ordinary consumer would receive a new labeling policy. The second concept was a recognition that "puffery," that is, extravagant promotional claims or statements of opinion and value, should not be held to the same standards of truth in advertising as factual statements about the product.[35] The FDA was thus challenged with establishing the line between acceptable puffery for the purpose of promotion, and disallowable puffery that was factually misleading.

All of this meant that enforcement required constructing what was "common sense" and determining who possessed common sense. The ordinary consumer was situated somewhere between an "overly credulous" consumer, of particular concern when regulating health products, and the "skeptical" consumer. One contemporary discussion noted that "some products by their very nature attract credulous purchasers," particularly "certain health foods and cosmetics."[36] Embedded in these discussions were social assumptions about ordinary consumers' class, gender, race, education level, and (what would come to be called) their "lifestyle."

The ordinary consumer regulators generally imagined was a middle-class, educated housewife. American workers' growing "discretionary income" caused a change in consumer expectations that included, by some accounts, "status anxiety" about "keeping up with the Joneses."[37] Several best-selling works captured this dynamic, including David Potter's *The People of Plenty* (1954), Kenneth Galbraith's *The Affluent Society* (1958), and Vance Packard's *The Status Seekers* (1959). In America's nearly "affluent society," the ordinary consumer was more concerned with food quality than price.[38] The ordinary consumer was educated enough to recognize common foods and to create a balanced diet, but also presumed to be healthy and therefore did not need to self-medicate using special diet foods.

Debates about the affluent society and markets for health foods, however, were taking place against a backdrop of changing national consumer politics. In 1962 President John F. Kennedy declared a "Consumer Bill of Rights." One right was "the right to be informed," later called "the consumer's right to know." Kennedy's comments suggested this new consumerism would be a truly democratic endeavor: "Consumers, by definition, include us all."[39] New legislation on consumer protection over the course of the decade included the Color Additive Amendment of 1960, the Hazardous Substances Labeling Act of 1960, the Fair Packaging and

Labeling Act of 1966, the Federal Cigarette Labeling and Advertising Act of 1966, and the Freedom of Information Act of 1967.[40] Food information, particularly information regarding health, was increasingly conceived as a consumer right—not just a special resource for experts. At the same time, the anticommunist atmosphere of the Cold War reoriented consumer politics "toward private acts of mass consumption."[41] These trends represented a shift away from relying on public decision-making and toward enhancing citizens' rights.

The postwar suburban lifestyle also created new social tensions that made "right to know" campaigns ripe for exploitation by advertisers.[42] National politics continued to center on what political historians call "breadwinner liberalism," post–New Deal policies promoting households headed by male breadwinners who support dependent wives and children.[43] Yet the decades after World War II saw unprecedented numbers of married women and women with children enter the workforce.[44] Newly empowered to vote with their wallets, yet lacking time for domestic pursuits, working women were vulnerable to the "attention economics" of advertising and the marketing of domestic solutions.[45] This helped fuel a new consumerism predicated on a literate, knowledgeable shopper. Advertisers, eager to extend their product lines to new consumers, saw these information-seeking shoppers as important new "niche markets" to target. The question was, how to reach them, and how to know what information they sought.

As regulators updated their standards for their imagined ordinary consumer, a new profession of market researchers were challenging old conceptions about consumers. Before WWII, marketing science was largely applied economics, and in the food industry often staffed by home economists. By the 1960s, marketers began to incorporate theories from the behavioral sciences, like those of Lewin on gatekeepers, to develop new tools for assessing consumer tastes and models for explaining consumer behavior.[46] One important approach centered on "motivation research," which involved "concept testing" through "focus groups" for different products. Ernst Dichter, discussed later, was a famous proponent, but there were others, each with their own favorite consumer test. Louis Cheskin promoted his theory of "sensation transference," the consumer's unconscious evaluation of a product based on sensory cues, especially visual appearance. Cheskin conducted "eye-movement tests" and "ocular measurements" on consumers examining product packages and advertising copy to "show the involuntary reactions of consumers to the package" and thereby "reveal the display effectiveness of the package." In his 1959 book *Why People Buy,* Cheskin asked: "How can you improve the taste [of a well-known soft drink] without changing the ingredients?" Cheskin's answer: through label design.[47]

Cheskin and Dichter exemplified a market research trend that bridged academic social sciences and business industries.[48] Their credibility rested on their use of social sciences to uncover consumers' "hidden desires" and to then build marketing campaigns exploiting Americans' "anxieties of affluence." Their methods made earlier consumer studies focused on rational decision-making seem out-of-date.[49] Indeed, in 1960 Ernst Dichter would proclaim that "rationality is a fetish of the 20th century."[50] The idea that marketers seduce consumers through desire, instead of reason, was a departure from the "pocketbook politics" and focus on rational consumption that initiated the FDA's food standards system in the 1930s, and that continued to motivate FDA regulators.

The rise of supermarkets also confounded efforts by regulators and marketers to channel consumers' food and health choices. The car transformed consumer habits and food retailing in postwar America, accelerating the decline of the central business district and the rise of satellite shopping centers. Supermarkets offered one-stop food shopping conveniently located near homes in suburbs and with ample parking. Supermarkets represented an entirely new way of selling, what industry analysts referred to as a "self-service revolution." Instead of relying on personal interaction with grocers, supermarkets allowed the consumer to move freely through the aisles and grab consumer products directly off the shelves. This created new marketing opportunities, including the use of packages as a "silent salesman" in elaborate store displays, discussed in chapter 1. In a book chapter titled "Babes in Consumerland," Packard in 1957 described women as in a trance-like state induced by all the colorful, well-stocked shelves.[51] Self-service created new challenges for marketers since they no longer had the grocer or salesman as a gatekeeper between the consumer and the product. The supermarket trade journal *Progressive Grocer* featured "traffic pattern" studies in the 1960s where store researchers shadowed particular customers and graphed the paths they traveled on a floor plan of a store.[52]

Self-service retailing also challenged the FDA concerning how to channel certain health messages to specific groups in the public. In supermarkets there was no retailer acting as a gatekeeper to ensure that special-needs consumers got the right health product. Part of the FDA's campaign against nutrition quackery and vitamania centered on partitioning the purchasing locations of foods versus drugs. From the 1930s through the 1950s, pharmacy organizations fought to keep vitamin sales restricted to pharmacies and out of supermarkets.[53] By 1965, however, super-markets surpassed drug stores in sales of diet foods.[54] In a 1953 letter to the FDA's special committee on artificial sweeteners, Commissioner Charles Crawford worried that the placement of special dietary products might suggest they were not for special consumers: "Many grocers segregate such articles and others intended for special dietary use in a clearly identified area of their stores. Other grocers intermingle such articles with staple foods and in such cases the consumer who wishes the staple article is likely to overlook differentiating labeling on the special dietary article, even when it is conspicuous."[55] These disputes centered on how to ensure that consumers received legitimate expert counseling before buying a product, or whether or not such counseling was even needed. The flow architecture of the supermarket was a direct circumvention of market gatekeepers, as it removed impediments to purchases, making it easy for shoppers to grab items without stopping to reflect.[56] Self-service promised freedom and independence—no interference from grocers or store clerks.[57] It reflected an American postwar conception of consumer independence, self-sufficiency, and affluence embodied in the new suburbia and "automobility."

But with new affluence came new afflictions, including so-called "diseases of affluence," as well as new standards for health and consumer protection. Heart disease, for example, long considered to be a disease of volition and weak willpower, in the 1950s became a symbol of the risks of indulgent living. Even as doctors concentrated on the threat of heart disease to aging men, product marketing focused on the housewife, about *her* husband's and *her* children's risk. With the new risk-based approach to illness and the growing focus on preventive medicine came marketing campaigns based on avoiding risk. Marketers built the campaigns around an ethos of "healthism."[58] Advertisements promoted the message that healthy eating was an individual's responsibility, made easier with the purchase of convenient, new diet foods. Health foods need not be limited to risk prevention or maintaining health; they were also for the healthy consumer seeking surplus health, to be even better than well.

Leading figures in advertising encouraged their clients to promote a product's health benefits, because, they argued, consumers could enjoy the benefits of affluence without the risks. Ernst Dichter (1907–1991), sometimes called the "father of motivational research," drew upon models of Freudian psychoanalysis to interpret consumers' reactions to commercial products and campaigns. Dichter showed how consumers were motivated by conscious rationalizations (e.g., affordability, healthfulness, convenience), but also by subconscious feelings and anxieties (e.g., how a product expresses one's insecurities about their social position). According to Dichter, advertisers should give the consumer "moral permission" to purchase the product by addressing deeper cultural anxieties that were acting as a barrier to purchase.[59] For example, Dichter saw a cultural divide among food consumers in the 1960s, split over their degree of faith in claims about the healthfulness of natural versus technological products.[60] In his advice to industry, Dichter rejected the FDA's rigid dichotomy of healthy "ordinary" consumers versus sick "special" consumers. In a 1957 report to Ovaltine, the Swiss malt, milk, and egg drink, he counseled them to drop advertisements targeting ill patients. "Almost everyone," he advised, "wants to be healthier and stronger than he is. Almost everyone wants to be well nourished and well fortified against illness." By associating their product with robust, active children, Ovaltine would broaden its product's appeal.[61]

Dichter's assertion that there were different kinds of consumers for different kinds of products had become the new marketing paradigm. Health was reconceived as a kind of personal taste and lifestyle rather than a medical exception. If everyone is at risk of being sick, who is an ordinary consumer? Was this puffery or medical truth?

Under Commissioner George Larrick's leadership, the FDA continued to campaign against nutrition quackery and push back against the public's enthusiasm for vitamania. Advertisers and consumers increasingly embraced the new diet food culture, but the FDA and AMA worried that a populist healthism undermined the doctor's authority to protect patients-as-consumers from market exploitation of their anxieties and lack of expert understanding of risk. Two new diet product markets, "low cal" and "low fat" foods, soon undermined that official rationale.

ARTIFICIAL SWEETNESS AND POWER

It was known as the "wasting disease." People diagnosed with it would slowly enter a semi-starved state, no matter how much they ate. Eventually it would end in either coma, infection, or starvation. Most people diagnosed with it wouldn't live longer than six years. Children under the age of ten would probably die within three. At the start of the twentieth century, diabetes mellitus was a deadly disease. Then, in 1922, Dr. Frederick Banting found that injecting the hormone insulin could produce a dramatic, miraculous reversal in children with diabetes. A year later, Banting received the Nobel Prize. The transformation of diabetes to a manageable illness also transformed the diabetic from a debilitated patient into a person who could function fairly well in society—a new population to be cared for by medicine, and a new market for special dietary treatments.[62] Soon a wide range of dietetic products appeared, low-sugar or no-sugar foods, that were specially prepared for the diabetic. These included foods with new chemical additives called "artificial sweeteners" that mimicked the sweetness of sugar without causing glucose imbalances.

In 1938 the FDA classified artificially sweetened foods as "special dietary foods," neither food nor drug. Life-or-death circumstances warranted tolerating a greater degree of risk than permitted for either standard foods or drugs being administered by a doctor. This embodied a tension in medical practice that can be characterized as a "calculus of risk." Extreme, even risky, measures might be warranted in medicine when the threat to life is high, but not when an illness is mild and non-life-threatening.

The problem for the FDA in the 1950s was that healthy consumers increasingly ignored the regulatory distinctions between food, drug, and special dietary food. The story of the diabetic exemplifies how the nutrition transition transformed American diet advice. Ordinary consumers no longer worried about wasting away; instead, they sought information on how to control their diets. Many now had the financial resources for not only adequate but "surplus" health, taking vitamin supplements as "insurance" against future health problems, or adopting the kinds of weight-managed diets that patients used.[63] In a 1961 interview Dr. Philip White acknowledged that prosperity and faddism went hand-in-hand, suggesting that modern consumers "have been conditioned by the dramatic progress of medicine . . . to believe that almost any pill, capsule or tonic is a miracle drug."[64] Producers argued that health tonics and diet fads were a kind of insurance which wealthier consumers had a right to engage in. But for the regulator, these alternative medical therapeutics threatened to water down the FDA's legal and professional standards.

The use of artificial sweeteners in foods invited particular scrutiny because of concerns related to the safety of artificial additives. Following World War II, America's food economy was awash in new chemicals, some intended for consumption and some not. New pesticides and antibiotics in agriculture and new chemicals added to foods during manufacturing caused what some historians have termed a "chemogastric revolution," and sparked a wave of new regulatory action.[65] In 1954, well before the publication of Rachel Carson's *Silent Spring*, Congress passed the Pesticide Residues Amendment, granting the FDA the authority to evaluate pesticide chemical residues that remained in foods after use in agriculture. The bill tried to assure "a proper balance" between protecting the consumer from unsafe pesticide chemicals in foods and the need to guarantee an adequate, affordable food supply.[66] The 1958 Food Additive Amendment contained a provision, which came to be known as the Delaney Clause, that adopted a stricter stance, with a zero-tolerance threshold for any food additive found to be carcinogenic.[67] Both the 1958 Food Additive Amendment and the similar 1960 Color Additive Amendment positioned certain synthetic chemical ingredients as potential adulterants, that is, something "added to" standard foods. They should therefore be tested before marketing and properly labeled.

These amendments effectively treated *new* additives much like drugs; ingredients already in use, however, could be exempted. The 1958 Food Additive Amendment authorized the FDA to identify ingredients considered "GRAS," or "generally recognized as safe," because of their previous history of use. The first GRAS list, published in the *Federal Register* in December 1958, included about two hundred substances, including two artificial sweeteners, saccharine and cyclamate. As discussed in chapter 1, saccharine first avoided being classified as an adulterant in 1908, when President Roosevelt overruled Harvey Wiley's campaign to ban it. The 1938 Food, Drug, and Cosmetic Act reclassified saccharine as a special dietary food intended for diabetics and obese patients. In 1958 it was registered as GRAS.[68]

A new sweetener, cyclamate, had been discovered in a University of Illinois lab in 1937. Subsequently Abbott Laboratories purchased its patent, intending to use it to mask the bitterness of certain drugs. In the mid-1950s, however, Abbott sought GRAS status to allow selling it in the special dietary foods market, since cyclamate was less bitter than saccharine.[69] Abbott president Ernest Volwiler nevertheless assured the FDA that the company would limit its marketing to sweetening medications or use in special dietary foods—not "foods such as would be sold in a grocery store, of course."[70]

For the FDA, the question of regulating artificial sweeteners was linked with the question of who they were for. Up until WWII, they were marketed largely to patients, especially diabetics. In the 1950s, manufacturers began incorporating artificial sweeteners into products marketed as diet aids for ordinary consumers. New manufacturing processes meant these new substances could be incorporated into familiar foods that usually weren't described as "low-calorie." New packaging technologies, meanwhile, changed how companies could market items such as packaged sweets. Candy sales had long been shaped by new packaging and processing technologies: candy wrappers made selling sticks of chewing gum and "nickel bar chocolate" possible, and molding technologies opened up the manufacture of an endless variety of lollypops and candy drops.[71] In 1957 Benjamin Eisenstadt, founder of the Cumberland Packing Corporation, designed a sugar sachet packet and started to sell saccharine as a powder mixture trademarked under the name "Sweet'N Low," which customers could use to sweeten their drinks.[72] Cyclamate also began to appear in diet sodas, like No-Cal, marketed first locally to sanitarium patients, and then regionally.[73]

In 1951 Abbott Labs rolled out Sucaryl, a product combining cyclamate and saccharine. When Sucaryl was publicly announced, Volwiler stated it would only be sold to the public in tablet form through drug stores or in bulk, powdered form to bakers and canners. Initially, Abbott did limit its marketing to diabetics and overweight patients. In the mid-1950s, however, the company launched a broader campaign to encourage Sucaryl's use in widely marketed diet products. Historian Carolyn de la Peña shows how Abbott actively educated dieters on how to incorporate Sucaryl into their recipes, publishing cookbooks that taught housewives how to "decalorize" American cooking, and glossy advertisements in a wide range of popular magazines.[74] This advertising campaign not only targeted the "final consumer" but also incorporated business-to-business (B2B) marketing directed at food processors and manufacturers who might use Sucaryl as an ingredient. Abbott encouraged food companies to include the "Sweetened with Sucaryl" logo on their products, thereby further reinforcing Abbott's promotion.[75]

The FDA viewed this as a direct evasion of its efforts to separate standard staple food products from "special dietary" foods managed through physicians. The NAS Food and Nutrition Board, the FDA's principal scientific advisory committee at the time, noted that the new sweetener had not been tested for broad, daily consumption. They felt it was one thing for diabetics to consume medicinal or special diet products with the new chemical, and quite another for otherwise healthy dieters to do so.[76]

Abbott's marketing for Sucaryl used an ambiguous language that reinforced the product's use by diabetics but encouraged its use by other consumers. For example, one ad campaign noted, "She can't (or shouldn't) use sugar-sweetened products," recognizing that not all of its customers were diabetics who must avoid sugars.[77] The Sucaryl ads played to health-conscious "alert shoppers" who would seek out products using the recognizable artificial sweetener brand. Advertisers sought to exploit a wide variety of consumer motivations for diet products. In 1958

FIGURE 8. Deliberately ambiguous language about who were the target customers for artificial sweeteners in an Abbott Laboratories Sucaryl business-to-business (B2B) advertisement, "Stop the diet shopper," in *Food Technology*, August 1955, 10.

Dichter even developed a taxonomy of dieters for targeting ads, including catego-ries like the "Deprivational Eater," the "Compromise Dieter," and the "Fun Dieter" who wanted "dieting without tears."[78]

When soda manufacturers began to release diet products in the early 1960s, artificial sweetener use expanded dramatically.[79] In 1958 RC Cola Company released Diet Rite, the first nationally marketed artificially sweetened soda. Diet Rite, like other diet colas, was at first sold as a special dietary food. In 1962, how-ever, the FDA allowed soda manufacturers to market artificially sweetened sodas without a diabetic proviso. This created a new ambiguity in policy: could soda containing both artificial and "nutritive" sweeteners use the "diet" label? The agen-cy's concern was that diabetics might purchase these "low cal" products without realizing they were inappropriate for "no cal" diabetic use. The FDA distinguished between the "technological use" of artificial sweeteners (in canned foods, to restore flavor), which did not require labeling, and "special dietary use" (in foods intended for low-calorie diets). The decision on diet sodas, and the growing clamor among physicians and industries about marketing low-fat foods, discussed later, prompted the agency to review its rules on dietary foods. On June 20, 1962, the FDA announced it would revise its standards for special dietary foods.[80]

The FDA's 1962 decision on Diet Rite opened the floodgates for mass-marketed, artificially sweetened diet products. In 1963 the Coca-Cola Company began to sell Tab Soda to diet-conscious but otherwise healthy consumers.[81] With its bright pink can, Tab was explicitly marketed to women. Abbott Labs' marketing began highlighting Sucaryl's potential value in canned fruits, diet sodas, and salad dress-ings. By 1965 one ad for Diet Rite asked, "Who's drinking all that Diet-Rite Cola? Everybody."[82] A 1967 *Supermarket News* survey identified diet foods, including low-calorie foods, as a fast-growing advertising category, and one that manufac-turers and retailers could capitalize on because of diet foods' high price markup.[83]

The FDA was fighting a two-front war on sweetness and health. Not only was it trying to regulate nonnutritive "healthy" sweeteners in traditionally unhealthy foods; it also sought to restrict the use of health ingredients, specifically vitamins, in sweets typically marketed to kids. The agency had adopted a policy, known as the "jelly bean rule," of not allowing nutritional enrichment in foods deemed to be candy. This provoked complaints from producers who felt that the rule arbitrarily enforced FDA standards concerning what was "good" or "bad" to eat. Miles Labo-ratories, for example, had just introduced its Chocks chewable vitamins for chil-dren in 1960. The company carefully designed ads to appeal to middle-class moth-ers while avoiding more exaggerated forms of nutrition quackery.[84]

The FDA policy discouraging the mixing of health-promoting but engineered ingredients with unhealthy natural ones would be tested by "fortified sugar," sweetening agents such as sucrose that had vitamins added to them. Nutrition lit-erature commonly referred to ordinary sugar as "empty calories" because of its lack of nutrients; companies began marketing fortified sugar as an easy, pleasant way to get extra vitamins into one's diet. In the 1963 lawsuit *United States v. 119 Cases . . . "New Dextra Brand Fortified Cane Sugar . . .,"* a district court noted that "the real basis of the Government's objection to the sale of fortified sugar is the notion that sugar is not a preferable vehicle for distributing vitamins and minerals." The court ruled against the FDA, arguing the FDCA "did not vest in [the FDA] the power to determine what foods should be included in the American diet; this is the function of the marketplace."[85] The explosion of fabricated foods, which broke down intuitive classes of "natural" versus "artificial," confounded the FDA's efforts to simplify markets for certain protected consumers, such as children. These problems were compounded by another front fought in the diet food wars: low-fat foods and the cholesterol controversy.

THE CHOLESTEROL CONTROVERSY AND A NEW CALCULUS OF DIETARY RISK

In December 1960 the American Heart Association (AHA) issued a report hypothesizing a direct link between high levels of dietary fat and cholesterol consumption and the risk of heart disease. There had been intense public interest in heart disease since President Eisenhower's heart attack in 1955. The 1960 report was largely a redrafting of the AHA's 1957 review paper on the so-called diet-heart thesis, "Dietary Fat and Its Relation to Heart Attacks and Strokes." This new report marked a growing consensus that levels of blood-serum cholesterol were correlated with heart attacks and strokes. Certain "diets of the affluent," generally those having more fatty foods, tended to increase unhealthy levels of cholesterol, especially in older men. For many medical researchers, the diet-heart thesis initiated a new, preventive front in the fight against heart disease. For consumers, it created an intense demand for foods low in dietary cholesterol and fat.

Food manufacturers' response to this posed a new set of challenges for the FDA. Packaging now touted foods as "low fat" or "heart healthy," raising questions about whether they should be classified as special dietary foods. More generally, the diet-heart thesis promoted a renewed movement in medicine toward prevention. Whereas some medical experts imagined a new society where all individuals exercised a measure of preventive care, because everyone is "at risk," FDA regulators clung to an older notion of the normal and the pathological. At least through the 1960s, the FDA viewed its mandate for foods as protecting "ordinary" consumers rather than "special" cases like patients.

Of particular note in the 1960 AHA report was an appendix discussing the "Different Kinds of Fat in the Diet." This mentioned the varying levels of saturated versus polyunsaturated fats in different kinds of foods, noting that saturated fats were atherogenic, promoting fatty plaques in the arteries, while polyunsaturated fats might be beneficial. The appendix even implied a hierarchy of foods that ranged from good to bad: "Poly-unsaturated fat is highest in the nonhydrogenated liquid vegetable oils; next in the lightly hydrogenated vegetable oils; then in margarines, shortenings, and lard; and is lowest in beef and dairy fat." In a move that would invite trouble with the FDA, the appendix suggested that manufacturers might consider adding labels disclosing the nature of their fat content.[86] While these statements were ostensibly directed to patients and at-risk groups, they soon became the centerpiece of marketing promotions geared for mass markets.

Manufacturers, such as Corn Products Company, the maker of Mazola oil, and Standard Brands, makers of Fleischmann's corn oil margarine, began touting foods containing polyunsaturated fats as a healthy alternative to those with saturated fats. Moreover, they positioned their products for the general public rather than consumers with special health problems.[87] Sales for margarines and low-fat foods skyrocketed. Initially the public's embrace of low-fat foods in the early 1960s had all the hallmarks of a diet fad craze. In his 1963 memoir comedian Groucho Marx panned low-fat diets as an example of how rapidly medical advice could invert common sense and even good taste. "Coronary experts" were "now frightening their patients with the terrors of cholesterol," and "rich people who used to sneer at margarine are now lapping it up as though it were worth eating."[88] The long history of dubious advertising for substitute dairy products didn't help. *American Chamber of Horrors,* for example, devoted several pages to Kraft's Miracle Whip, a legal fake mayonnaise that exploited food labeling loopholes.[89] For a long time, many consumers regarded low-fat foods as cheap, processed substitutes. Examples included processed cheese, Crisco, margarine, and filled milk. Now, customers were eager to purchase these foods as value-added, as better than the real thing.

At the FDA, officials were concerned, as always, with the possibility that manufacturers might mislead consumers. In a 1959 statement on "common food fats and oils," the FDA indicated it would regard any labeling claims, direct or implied, linking type of fat content to a preventive diet, as misbranded for products "offered to the general public." In 1961 Kenneth Milstead, assistant to the commissioner, gave a speech, "Food Fad and Nutrition Quackery," directly challenging the AHA's move to publicize the diet-heart thesis. He criticized advertisements that encouraged consumers to associate polyunsaturated fats with foods that were good to eat. Milstead stated, "Prevention and treatment of artery and heart disease is a medical problem for the medical experts. Laymen are not qualified to either recognize or treat such serious medical conditions."[90]

Milstead's comments echoed the more cautious position of the American Medical Association, which initially rejected the AHA's direct outreach to the public. When the AMA released its own report, "The Regulation of Dietary Fat," in 1962, it included the caveat: "This report is intended to serve as a guide to assist the physician. . . . It is not a recommendation for the general public."[91] The AMA took

Vitamin C is the plus in oranges.   Polyunsaturates are the plus in Mazola.

FIGURE 9. Mazola margarine advertisement comparing surplus health of vitamin C in oranges to polyunsaturates in margarines, an example of how advertisers were marketing "negative nutrition" as value added. Source: *Parade Magazine*, May 7, 1967, 10–11.

particular offense at what they characterized as a hasty and reckless way of scaring the public on an issue that called for deliberation among medical experts.

To critics, however, the FDA's 1959 statement read as foot-dragging. Jeremiah Stamler, an active proponent of the diet-heart thesis, cited a substantial literature demonstrating a relationship between elevated blood serum cholesterol and coronary heart disease. Stamler also noted that the FDA had just approved Triparanol (MER/29), a drug whose purpose was to lower blood serum cholesterol and thereby reduce the risk of heart attacks.[92] This double standard, allowing doctors to prescribe a drug to treat cholesterol levels but preventing consumers from encountering messages about cholesterol on food labels, implied that the diet-heart thesis was adequately established for doctors to act on it, but not for the lay public.

Food companies did not wait for medical professionals and regulators to settle these questions. Two days after the American Heart Association issued its 1960 report, Wesson Oil quoted the AHA statement in seven column advertisements that would appear in 205 newspapers across America. Mazola Corn Oil quickly followed suit. A September 1962 article in *Newsweek* observed, "The use of corn oil in making margarine has zoomed from 'negligible' in 1957 to 90 million pounds in 1961."[93] This boom in vegetable oil production was testimony to the popular authority that scientific organizations held, the widespread preoccupation with heart disease, and the dramatic impact these scientific reports could have on food markets and agricultural landscapes.

The diet-heart thesis was a particularly effective marketing tool for margarine, dogged by its associations with artifice.[94] Margarine had long been subject to special taxation and peculiar food composition and packaging laws because it competed with the more natural and allegedly more nutritious butter.[95] "Oleomargarine" was patented by a French chemist in the 1860s as a cheap, synthetic substitute for butter and other shortenings. Because it was often marketed aggressively and fraudulently to appear like butter, even dyed yellow, many state legislatures passed laws restricting its sale or requiring it be clearly labeled. In Wisconsin, for a time, margarine had to be dyed blue to distinguish it from butter.[96] But now marketers of margarines and cooking oils could use the new diet findings to sell artificial reformulations as better than the original.

By the 1950s, margarine producers had found ways to assuage the loudest objections of both regulators and consumers. Critics of margarine had once focused on its lack of nutritiousness, for example, citing experiments showing it lacked vitamins which milk and butter contained. By the late 1920s, however, manufacturers began adding vitamins A and D to margarine. In the 1930s and 1940s, margarine manufacturers changed their recipes, replacing industrially processed food byproducts like beef tallow with vegetable oils, especially cottonseed and soybean oils.[97] The shift was strategic, allowing margarine manufacturers to ally themselves with cotton and soybean grower associations, who had strong political clout—almost as much clout as the dairy industry. The greatest shifts in public opinion occurred during wartime, when butter shortages led governments to ease restrictions on margarine.[98] The 1950s were the first decade when consumption of margarine surpassed that of butter.

The new cholesterol craze, with its focus on different kinds of fats, encouraged margarine and vegetable oil manufacturers to differentiate their products.[99] In 1960 the Mazola company ran ads for vegetable oil in popular newspapers and magazines comparing the relative amounts of polyunsaturates in different vegetable oils. These ads built on the widespread media attention surrounding the AHA report earlier that year, reflecting both a progression in the target of marketing campaigns and a cultural shift in the notion of risk.

Initially ads emphasized the role of doctors in shaping their customers' interest in low-fat or good-fat foods, telling consumers to "ask your doctor" about these new scientific findings. To target doctors, ads ran in medical journals such as the *Journal of the American Medical Association.* Such ads might mention the "P/S ratio"—one of the common buzzwords at the time, referring to the ratio of polyunsaturates to saturated fats—or try to link familiar nutritional concepts to the newer diet science. They also exploited announcements on the latest scientific research, building implied health claims around studies showing vegetable fats, and later certain vegetable oils particularly, as being healthier than animal fats. This initial strategy exploited "diagnostic creep" by drawing doctors' attention to the new diet-heart thesis as a way of expanding the consumer market for diet products.[100]

By the end of the decade, ads now focused on a mass market. In 1967 Chiffon Margarine, one of the first soft tub-style margarines, ran an ad in *JAMA,* presumably to encourage medical professionals to use the special margarine for treating patients. But a related ad that ran in popular journals informed lay audiences that this was "what doctors are reading in their medical journals today." Such ads raised the question of whether information-seeking consumers had a right to the kind of information their doctors used. It also put FDA officials in the awkward position of arguing that freedom of information in advertising was bad because it circumvented the doctor's gatekeeper function.

The most paradigm-shifting aspect of the diet-heart thesis was its claim that healthy people today were at risk of developing heart disease in the future. A 1968 ad for Fleischmann's diet margarine made this explicit: "More and more doctors are coming to the conclusion that the best time to deal with coronary disease is thirty or forty years before it is likely to occur. That is why they are recommending good dietary habits . . . not only for the heart patient, but for the people of *all age groups.*"[101] In other words, healthy consumers, even children, should be purchasing and consuming diet foods and health-promoting food products.[102]

In the wake of the thalidomide tragedy, the FDA was especially attentive to the ways that food and drug advertising campaigns were pushing the boundaries between medical products and foods. To drive home its argument that consumers were "misled" by health claims based on the diet-heart thesis, in 1963 the FDA contracted a consumer studies firm, ARB Surveys, to poll consumers on health claims on different sources of dietary fat and cholesterol. It used this survey as evidence these kinds of advertisements misled consumers.[103] The FDA therefore rejected as inappropriate efforts to mass market vegetable oils and margarines for their health-promoting properties. A 1963 FDA publication noted, "There is no sound scientific basis for the current diet fad theory that hardening of the arteries or strokes can be prevented simply by adding unsaturated fats to the otherwise unchanged ordinary diet. TV advertising for food products is not a good source of medical advice on such matters."[104] Since most consumers were healthy, the FDA doubted they would benefit from such alarming risk information. Consumers who did require special dietary foods were (still) best directed to their personal doctor.

THE FOOD INDUSTRY RESISTS

The rapidly expanding interest in artificially sweetened and low-fat foods, and continued aggressive marketing by vitamin industry, created a large, vocal coalition of stakeholders critical of the FDA's go-slow approach to new diet foods. When the FDA released its 1962 notice revising standards for special dietary foods, it received a flood of comments from concerned industries who argued that the rules were incompatible with growing consumer demand and contemporary ideas

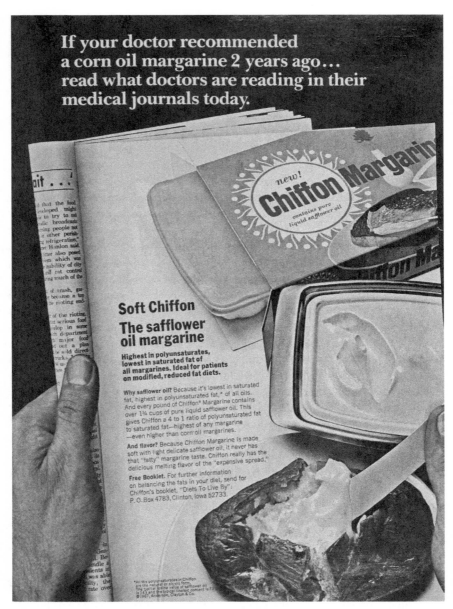

FIGURE 10. Advertisers marketing "cutting edge" diet advice directly to consumers. This ad informs consumers about the new diet marketing information their doctors are reading. Source: "If your doctor recommended a corn oil margarine 2 years ago . . .," *Better Homes and Gardens*, January 1968, 19. The advertisement it references ran in *JAMA* 199, no. 9 (February 27, 1967): 69.

in diet science. In 1964 Chief Counsel William Goodrich remarked that the proposed revision had provoked "the most voluminous—if not the best reasoned— response we have ever had on any notice of proposed rule-making." The agency had not anticipated this level of pushback.[105] The FDA's policies also created a confusing legal environment for diet food companies. In the 1963 Dextra fortified sugar case, discussed earlier, the court rejected the FDA's legal rationale for restricting vitamin use in popular products. However, in 1964 another court upheld the FDA's power to seize vitamin products with "unneeded nutrients."[106]

It was not just the FDA's vitamin policies. In 1966 a court ruled against the FDA's seizure of a safflower-based "imitation margarine," sold as Demi. Demi was designed to appeal to people concerned about cholesterol, but it didn't conform to FDA standards for margarine. The FDA argued, unsuccessfully, that it was a misbranded margarine, but the court noted that the manufacturer had clearly labeled it an "imitation margarine."[107] Companies were now seriously exploring the feasibility of marketing imitation products as better than standard ones.

In June 1966 the FDA issued its "final" standards for special dietary foods. The revised rules affected both dietary supplements and fortified foods, and low-cal and low-fat health claims involving negative nutrition. This ruling specifically prohibited any nutrition labeling or advertising language that promoted any of the "four great myths of nutrition" outlined in the FDA's campaign against nutrition quackery. These included theories about soil depletion causing subclinical deficiencies, or using foods to treat specific diseases. In what would prove an unfortunate choice of language (see chapter 3), the FDA also banned statements suggesting or implying "that significant segments of the population of the United States are suffering or are in danger of suffering from a dietary deficiency of vitamins or minerals."[108] The most important changes involved standardizing dietary supplements and restricting the number of foods that could be legally fortified with vitamins and minerals. Supplements must have a mandatory label indicating that, "except for persons with special medical needs, there is no scientific basis for recommending routine use of dietary supplements."[109] The rules, so the FDA reasoned, would tighten labeling on diet foods, providing more information (including ingredients) than ordinary standard foods, and prevent misleading claims, but companies could continue marketing their diet products in supermarkets and without a doctor's supervision.

The rules provoked a fierce negative response from industry. The American Bottlers of Carbonated Beverages asked the FDA to delay the rules on artificial sweeteners until the agency had established its standard on artificially sweetened carbonated beverages. The American Dry Milk Institute objected to the FDA's exclusion of instant breakfast products from the list of foods that could be fortified with vitamins. The International Association of Ice Cream Manufacturers said the regulations would effectively ban the sale of artificially sweetened frozen desserts

Will industry have to promote the 'imitation' as the superior product?

OR

Will federal and state regulatory agencies come to adopt the consumer understanding of 'imitation'?

Will the time come when industry is driven to popularizing the term "imitation?" . . . What would happen to butter if triangular patties now required for margarine become the superior shape?

FIGURE 11. Political cartoon in a food industry journal, *Food Processing,* satirizes the FDA's imitation label as outdated and a barrier to product innovation. Source: H. P. Milleville, "How FDA's Stand on Imitation STIFLES New Product Development," *Food Processing* 24, no. 10 (October 1963): 74.

sold to help reduce body weight. And various pharmaceutical companies complained that the vitamin standards did not reflect the current scientific thinking at the National Academy of Sciences. The comments reflected the plurality of food and pharmaceutical industry interests in special dietary foods in the late 1960s.[110]

The response to the new rules portended badly for the FDA. The objections automatically stayed the regulations, and for the next two years the agency was paralyzed by a flood of criticism. In 1968 the FDA initiated another round of standards hearings on "special dietary foods" surveying industry, medical professionals, and public officials, and covering topics including fatty acids labeling, vitamin supplements, and the adequacy of the average American's diet without fortification and special diet foods. The hearings, discussed in the next chapter, were a public relations disaster.

The FDA became the focus of an intense lobbying campaign by producers unwilling to part with their new health claims. Recently much has been made about how the food industry manipulates public institutions, transforming clear public health messages into advertisements that promote eating more, or confusing consumers about diet science.[111] The tobacco industry provides the most documented example of this kind of health sciences manipulation. Historians Naomi Oreskes and Erik Conway document how in the late 1970s tobacco industry leaders hired prominent scientists to cast doubt on the by-then crystalizing medical evidence linking tobacco smoke and cancer, and then how similar tactics were applied to numerous other industries negatively impacted by new medical research on risk.[112] Marion Nestle's in-depth study focuses on the science-distorting effects of lobbying from the food industry. Since the 1940s the food industry had been shaping public opinion and regulation by casting doubt on science, funding research, offering consulting arrangements, using front groups, promoting notions of "personal responsibility," and going to court to challenge critics and unfavorable regulations.[113] All these industry activities were used for the debates over artificial sweeteners, low-fat foods, and the FDA policies on health-claim labeling.

For example, U. S. sugar-manufacturing companies founded the Sugar Research Foundation in 1943, and in 1947 split it into two divisions: a foundation to support scientific research, and Sugar Information, Inc., focused on public education and communication.[114] Throughout the 1950s and 1960s Sugar Information, Inc., promoted sugar's "goodness" using large-spread ads in major periodicals and popular magazines. In response to Abbott Labs' campaigns promoting Sucaryl, Sugar Information, Inc., ran ads highlighting cyclamate's synthetic, chemical nature by asking questions like, "who ever heard of Sodium N-Cyclohexyl-sulfamate?" Instead, their ad argued, "sugar helps control weight naturally," implying sugar was healthy for consumers because of its role in appetite satiety and its use in reducing diets as a "spoonful of prevention." Ads described sugar as "quick energy" or invoked an "appestat" model of metabolism where "tucked away in your brain is a hunger switch" that sugar could help turn "from 'on' to 'off'."[115] Another tactic was to identify prominent diet experts, researchers whose publicity had made them "marketing influencers" or "opinion leaders," and attempt to influence their research programs. During the cholesterol controversy the Sugar Research Foundation corresponded with Mark Hegsted and other proponents of the diet-heart thesis to

FIGURE 12. While food industry recognized artificial sweeteners as a food fad, they also recognized the sugar industry's efforts to sabotage the growing market as transparently self-interested. Source: Fred Graf, "Going Her Way?" *Food Field Reporter* 32, no. 21 (November 23, 1964): 24.

discourage them from identifying the role of sugars in heart disease, and to instead focus on dietary fats. The Sugar Research Foundation deliberately sought to discredit research linking sugar to heart disease, while also funding research concerning the efficacy of reducing dietary fats.[116]

Another example was the Institute of Shortening and Edible Oils (ISEO), a trade group founded in 1934 representing U.S. refiners of edible fats and oils. Member companies included Procter & Gamble, Levers Brothers Company, Hunt-Wesson, and other major producers. The ISEO sought to shape FDA policies by lobbying scientists and scientific boards that influenced the FDA. In 1962, during debates over the AHA and AMA reports on the diet-heart thesis, ISEO representatives began to meet regularly with the AMA's Council on Food and Nutrition, both to learn from them about changing health policy, and to communicate the food industry's concerns about proposed labeling rules. At an August 1965 meeting, for example, AMA members expressed enthusiasm for informative labeling on diet-heart claims, such as the P/S ratio labels. During the meeting, however,

ISEO lawyers identified weaknesses in the labeling approach, such as how consumers might read between the lines on specific quantities, or mistake a positive declaration on a food label as a license to eat too much of the food.[117]

The ISEO's goal was maintaining the regulatory status quo. At another 1965 meeting, ISEO lawyers expressed their reservations about how labeling might influence the degree and rate of change in product reformulations. New shortening formulas were "less stable and do not perform as well," and while technology for attaining better "P/S" ratios in new diet foods would improve, "this could not be forced overnight."[118] Following the meeting, the AMA council drafted a letter to the FDA that repeated many of the ISEO's arguments. The letter argued that, if the FDA allowed fatty acids labeling prematurely, it might "disrupt the current balance between supply and demand for highly unsaturated vegetable oils" and lead to a "'fat power' race whereby each brand would strive for the highest content of polyenoic fatty acids."[119] By 1967 the dynamic in meetings between ISEO and AMA council members had shifted. AMA members were more committed to supporting fatty acids labeling, and more resistant to ISEO arguments. ISEO representatives quickly pivoted to exploring compromises: for example, allowing compositional labeling without allowing promotional claims.[120] It is difficult to measure what impact indirect industry lobbying had on the experts advising the FDA, but clearly having direct, behind-the-scenes access to these experts allowed industry groups like the ISEO to remain in step or ahead of the FDA on changing expert viewpoints.

By the late 1960s many producers of traditional foods began to consider ways to capitalize on the diet market. Dairy farmers lobbied the FDA to finalize standards for low-fat milks so that they could finally compete with companies like Carnation, whose milk-free products weren't limited by filled-milk laws preventing mixing dairy with nondairy substitutes. At the 1967 Annual Convention of the International Association of Ice Cream Manufacturers and Milk Industry Foundation, a quarter of the papers delivered concerned imitation dairy products.[121] One market test of consumer acceptance revealed a surprising open-mindedness among consumers about imitation products and linked it to consumers' experience with margarine:

> For many, it was just a step from butter to margarine; from fluid milk to powdered milks. And once the imitation milk concept was initially understood, consumers described an even more graduated development; fresh milk, canned milk, dry processed milk, dry milk with "cream" to substitute milk with the animal fats replaced by vegetable and fruit oils.
>
> We observed that attitudes toward margarine were the monitor for beliefs and expectations about imitation dairy products. If a consumer thinks margarine is healthier . . . she seemed more willing to initially accept any imitation dairy product.[122]

Recognizing that they couldn't prevent these new products from being sold, dairy trade groups urged the FDA to establish standards for milk substitutes, requiring them to match the nutritional profile of milk.[123]

A shift in FDA policy during this period was caused partly by a change in leadership. In 1966 James L. Goddard, a public health official hired from the CDC, replaced FDA commissioner Larrick. "Go-Go" Goddard, as staff called him, actively took on the pharmaceutical industry, initiating a contract with the National Academy of Sciences to review drugs approved before the Kefauver-Harris Amendments in 1962. He was the first "outside man," hired from outside the FDA for commissioner, and quickly developed a reputation as anti-industry and pro-public interest.[124] However, he expressed his pro-public views by using the language of consumer empowerment, and by ending pronouncements on "health quackery" that presumed a consumer in need of paternalistic protection. Instead, FDA officials began speaking out about consumers and consumerism. Goddard frequently emphasized that many consumers could make health decisions for themselves: "The public is considerably more sophisticated in its 'health consciousness.' . . . This is not to say, of course, that we have suddenly become a Nation of health experts, where each and every citizen is capable of diagnosing the difference between fact and fallacy."[125] By the late 1960s this sent mixed signals from the FDA concerning special dietary foods: initiatives to tighten rules about what companies could say about certain health claims, but also a growing receptiveness to informative labeling designed for diet foods in mass markets.[126]

CONCLUSIONS

Americans' food consumption habits changed dramatically in the 1960s. According to one industry assessment, in 1957, the year of the AHA's first diet and heart disease report, animal fats represented 45 percent of the total edible fats and oils consumed in food products, and the remaining 55 percent were vegetable fats. By 1966 the proportion was 67 percent vegetable fat and 33 percent animal fats.[127] Similar shifts occurred in sweeteners. A trade journal report noted that, after only a few years on the market, artificially sweetened sodas had captured 10 percent of the soft drink market; some companies like Pepsi projected this would grow to 35 percent by 1970.[128] Much of this shift occurred in production as industry adjusted its recipes in anticipation of consumer demands. But it also reflected changes in consumer purchasing patterns driven by the new marketing campaigns and popular press of scientific reports linking diet to health. By the end of the 1960s, consumers were clamoring for more information on food nutrition profiles so that health-conscious shoppers could make better decisions for themselves.

The FDA struggled to respond to these changes. The FDA's now-antiquated food standards system presumed a unified mass food market, with limited special exceptions. Regulators reasoned that most Americans ate a diet of staple, whole foods, and therefore strove to create a standards system designed for these foods. The new diet foods, however, were developed in a postwar era of market segmentation, cultivating niche consumerism and product diversification. Yet to call the confrontation between FDA policies and the new diet foods a "mismatch" is to miss the productive nature of the clash between the older regulatory system and the newer marketing of food and risk. Food companies design foods for regulatory regimes, not despite them. The new low-cal sodas and soft margarines were developed to create competitive advantage at the edges of regulatory boundaries. Food standards provided the constraints that industry sought to define its market segments. The diversification of taste by diversifying new product lines was a strategy increasingly used by companies to create demand.

One important factor affecting diversification was the widespread enthusiasm for science. By the end of the decade, news stories about the latest science of diet and healthy living were front-page material. Science shaped public policy, as media reported on what was "good to eat," and also shaped FDA policy. The 1960 AHA report, and subsequent advertising and news coverage capitalizing on the "cholesterol controversy," encouraged Americans to consume vegetable oil and margarine, forcing the FDA to eventually consider this new diet claim. Marketers drew upon the credibility of medical science to allay consumers' lingering anxieties about changing their diets. Even disagreements among medical experts about new scientific findings became an opportunity for advertisers to fashion the new diet science as cutting edge, as what your doctor was reading.

When doctors disagreed, the FDA had to decide, consistently erring on the side of maintaining the status quo. But the FDA's authority as an institution built on scientific expertise made it particularly accountable to scientific organizations. Professional associations like the AHA and AMA had considerable influence on FDA policy. As medical associations increasingly endorsed the diet-heart thesis, the FDA hesitated not because it distrusted these organizations, but because of new elements within the emerging scientific conceptualization of risk—all people are potentially at risk, not just the ill—and because of the agency's existing compartmentalization of "foods" versus "drugs." Where should the line be drawn between a reasonable, supplemental use of vitamins, and vitamin mega-dosing that raised drug-like health concerns? Did consumers benefit from new information about the diet-heart thesis, or were companies simply stoking consumer anxieties that for most consumers were hypothetical and remote? Under the FDA system, information about food was subject to everyday norms about market puffery and sensationalism. Information about drugs and health, however, should be channeled through physicians, supposedly better trained and better informed than ordinary consumers, and thus better equipped to navigate the claims about diet science, and about risk for diseases of affluence.

By the end of the 1960s, the diet food industries, consumers, and many medical experts came to see access to health information for foods as a consumer right. The new product labeling and health claims on foods invoked an older progressive concern about liberal protections on "market transparency." But they also signaled a new definition for the ordinary consumer. The new consumer could not only handle more health information but demanded it. Food and drug industries became increasingly vocal about how the FDA's food standards didn't incorporate contemporary science, and were inappropriate for diet foods. Yet consumer advocates were increasingly critical of corporate indifference to consumer rights and skeptical of the government's ability to protect or empower consumers. All agreed the FDA needed to address consumers' demands for information, but what kind of information should be on labels? Who got to see it? What kinds of claims could labels make?

While the trend in the 1960s was toward politicizing matters of food and diet, public policy debates occurred within a small community of actors. Aside from food product ads and the science reports that appeared on TV or in popular journals, labeling debates did not engage the public directly, much less invite public feedback. Indeed, "the public" in this chapter was largely consumers acting through their purchases. This would soon change, as a series of public controversies would make nutrition an urgent and visible matter of national concern. This would transform the FDA and, ultimately, bring its "standards of identity" regime to an end.

3

Malnourished or Misinformed?

Public Understanding of Science

The "ordinary consumer" who inhabited food regulators' and marketers' imaginations in the 1950s and early 1960s was well-fed, relatively well-educated, and female. Worried about her figure, her children, and her husband, she sought out diet foods, vitamins, and foods low in saturated fats. She demanded direct access to the kinds of information that would allow her to select just the right product from the shelves of her well-stocked suburban supermarket. In the early 1960s, however, this fictional, well-heeled, suburban consumer was joined by a very different kind of consumer, one who struggled to feed her children. Millions of Americans were *not* benefiting from the wondrous choices of branded packaged foods or the newfound freedoms of self-service supermarkets. For them, advertisements about new foods with new flavors or healthy options rang hollow. For these Americans, the absence of food choices, even the absence of food, defined their daily toil. In 1968, when the Citizens' Board of Inquiry into Hunger and Malnutrition in the United States published *Hunger, U.S.A.*, it propelled this mother struggling with poverty into the foreground of America's political imagination—it was a "reversal of presumption" for the country, upending assumptions about the new food economy and diseases of affluence that had governed debates discussed in chapter 2. It also challenged assumptions about the citizen-as-consumer around whom marketers and regulators built their policies.

The Food and Drug Administration's system for regulating foods was not designed for hunger. The FDA's food standards, its rules restricting colorful health claims on packaged foods with slick, glossy labels, was designed for an affluent society. In 1968, when mainstream Americans discovered there was widespread hunger in the U.S., it provoked public soul-searching about Americans' anxieties of affluence, and linked FDA policies to what had previously been considered unrelated political concerns about poverty and civil rights.[1] The liberal consensus favoring a strong government, already fracturing in the face of new lifestyles and consumer goods, began to crumble in the antagonistic politics of the time, as activists began to question the paternalistic policies of institutions like the FDA. Moreover, the reappearance of hunger proved that the New Deal's breadwinner liberalism was in crisis, foreshadowing a change in the 1970s.

In the late 1960s a series of regulatory crises embroiled the FDA in controversies about associations between epidemics of excess and scandals over scarcity, and the role of food as a vehicle for personal health. For both nutrition professionals and FDA regulators, this caused a shock of recognition regarding the changing nature of Americans' diets, consumerist values, and popular notions of acceptable risk and institutional responsibility.[2] These crises pivoted around the question of whether Americans had access to too much to eat or, rather, too little. As this attracted public attention, the clinical, neutral language of nutrition experts and FDA policymakers looked at best out of touch, and at worst cruelly indifferent to the realities of many Americans. Hunger was a subjective, moral state. Nutrition science reduced it to a clinical condition, with advice stripped of economic context. Indeed, the FDA and U.S. Department of Agriculture's food policies and standards were apparently so focused on the ordinary consumer that they failed to serve poor, hungry, marginalized consumers.

This chapter describes when, for the first time, the public directly contested the nutrition science profession's political neutrality and authority. Using media attention and strategic political framings, activists challenged what they characterized as the institutionalized forgetting of hunger. Previously, scientists who produced consensus reports or hearings on food safety and nutrition guidelines managed to keep disagreements and counterinterpretations buried in regulatory correspondences, scientific publications, or lesser-read trade newsletters reporting on the FDA food standards hearings.[3] In the late 1960s, nutritionists and other experts were suddenly called to account, testifying in public about the FDA's policies on diet and health. They found their motives scrutinized, their words broadcast on national television. The divide between consumer interests and expert interests became undeniable, with lasting consequences for food labeling.

REDISCOVERING HUNGER IN AMERICA

"In issuing this report, we find ourselves somewhat startled by our own findings, for we too had been lulled into the comforting belief that at least the extremes of privation had been eliminated in the process of becoming the world's wealthiest nation." So began *Hunger, U.S.A.*, published in 1968 by the Citizens' Board of Inquiry into Hunger and Malnutrition in the United States, a committee created by the nonpartisan coalition Citizens' Crusade Against Poverty (CCAP). The report's "startling" key finding: "Hunger and malnutrition exist in this country, affecting millions of our fellow Americans and increasing in severity and extent from year to year."[4] The report scandalized Americans who had assumed that post-war prosperity had ended extreme poverty, and helped initiate public discussions about "the other America," those left behind by America's ascendance as a global economic leader. It called into question the march-of-progress narrative that framed the notion of "diseases of affluence," and immediately shifted policies governing the nation's food and agriculture.

The problem of hunger was not "startling" to many people in 1968. In 1962 writer and political activist Michael Harrington drew attention to the forgotten, invisible poor in his explosive *The Other America*. In Washington, the book galvanized political concern about poverty, making it a focus of President John F. Kennedy's domestic agenda. President Lyndon B. Johnson's "War on Poverty," initiated in 1964 with the Economic Opportunity Act, also drew headlines to the problem of poverty, including concern about impoverished diets. The preamble of the act stated that U.S. policy aimed "to eliminate the paradox of poverty in the midst of plenty," and the act shored up America's federal social safety net, funding new programs like the Job Corps and Head Start. Yet hunger was largely framed as a secondary problem in this period. In the war on poverty, federal resources went to job creation, employing the poor to alleviate poverty, and with that hunger. The Food Stamp Act of 1964, however, targeted hunger specifically. For the USDA, the food stamps program was a significant shift in its hunger abatement strategy. Its direct commodity distribution program gave the hungry access to surplus foods, but operated outside regular commercial market channels. Food stamps meant that the poor, like ordinary consumers, could now use stamps to "purchase" familiar packaged goods at supermarkets.[5] Nevertheless, the War on Poverty was criticized for being half-hearted and always in the shadow of Johnson's more pressing political concerns, including the Vietnam War.

Civil rights leaders and grassroots activists worked to keep public and political attention on poverty.[6] Founded in 1964, the CCAP launched its "Program to Abolish Poverty in the United States in Ten Years" two years later, which, among other things, called for a universal guaranteed income.[7] By 1967 Martin Luther King Jr. and the Southern Christian Leadership Conference had shifted their focus to economic rights. King was now calling for a "radical revolution of values," including a "shift from a thing-oriented society to a person-oriented society."[8] In December 1967 King declared the Poor People's Campaign, which organized a 1968 march in Washington by thousands of poor people, followed by demonstrations at key federal agencies to protest and demand economic justice.

In spite of these efforts, antipoverty campaigns overlooked or ignored important demographics in the civil rights coalition. The male-breadwinner liberalism, embraced by most federal programs since the New Deal, left working women and minorities behind, because these programs valorized full-time, steady employment. Many women and African Americans, however, had low-income, part-time, or seasonal jobs, such as domestic servants to wealthier white women, or cheap agricultural labor during the harvest season. Policymakers and activists alike often focused on policy solutions like a universal guaranteed income instead of more mundane and pressing issues facing poor working mothers.[9]

By the mid-1960s, changes in the U.S. economy made mundane concerns, like balancing household budgets, challenging even for white consumers. Rising prices of commonly purchased goods, including beef, pork, eggs, and lettuce, placed pressure on consumers' real income, or income adjusted for inflation. This declining purchasing power contributed to a wave of supermarket picketing in 1966, encouraged by consumer activist Esther Peterson, who then served as special assistant to the president for consumer affairs. Critics tried to dismiss the boycotts as "a Ladycott," but they were effective partly because they connected urban political organizing with the political demographic and interests of suburban housewives.[10]

The civil rights movement's focus on poverty, however, faced a challenge in issue framing. The Watts Riot in the summer of 1965 shocked Americans, and made the nation's race problem undeniable. But people drew different conclusions from it. Critics of the antipoverty coalition used images of rioting African Americans as evidence of an "urban crisis," framing African American poverty as a symptom of urban social decay, not racism. This was given official credence by a 1965 government report, *The Negro Family*, by Assistant Secretary of Labor Daniel P. Moynihan. Moynihan wanted to bolster white support for antipoverty initiatives that would break the "cycle of poverty" holding African Americans down, but the report's arguments about deeply entrenched "cultures of poverty" seemed to suggest that black poverty was a self-inflicted wound. And the report's focus on higher rates of single parenthood among blacks as a key cause of poverty implicitly blamed black mothers for failing to raise responsible black citizens.[11] Quite the contrary, poor mothers, driven by need for improved service delivery of government resources, would become the core of the "mothers politics" in the war on poverty.[12]

Shifting the attention from poverty framed broadly to hunger more specifically provided political opportunities for the stalled civil rights movement.[13] Marian Wright (1939–), a lawyer and activist who later founded the Children's Defense Fund, helped steer the antipoverty coalition toward the hunger problem. In March 1967, after testifying before the Senate Subcommittee on Employment, Manpower, and Poverty about the extreme hunger she had witnessed in Mississippi, she invited senators to witness it themselves. Four committee members, George Murphy (R–CA), Joseph Clark (D–PA), Robert Kennedy (D–NY), and Jacob Javits (R–NY), did just that.[14] When they visited a deeply impoverished, predominantly black community in Mississippi and reported disturbing accounts of hunger and poverty, their visit received media attention. However, these news stories were overshadowed by more attention-grabbing headlines about the Vietnam War. But the visit did prompt investigations and hearings by Congress. And the CCAP established the above-mentioned Citizens' Board of Inquiry into Hunger and Malnutrition, chaired by Benjamin Mays, a Baptist minister and civil rights leader, and Leslie Dunbar, head of the Field Foundation, to investigate the problem of hunger in America. The CCAP's Citizens' Board published its report the following April 1968.

The CCAP 1968 report, *Hunger, U.S.A.*, helped convert growing concerns about hunger into a message that federal regulators were willing to hear. It argued that "the needs of the poor and hungry are subordinated to the concerns of large agricultural producers." That is, the USDA prioritized farm subsidies over food aid and poverty programs. One particularly effective tool was a "Geographical Distribution of Hunger in the US" map, which drew attention to "hunger counties"—U.S. counties having higher levels of post-neonatal mortality, an indicator for malnutrition. In this way the CCAP adopted a tactic "to inform and shock the public."[15] The report's tone emphasized scandal and emotion, not measured reason and statistics. Its shocking findings grabbed headlines, prompting Senate investigations and even reshaping Senator Robert Kennedy's campaign strategy. *Hunger, U.S.A.* emphasized the tragedy of economic contradictions that persisted in America, noting, "To make four-fifths of a nation more affluent than any people in history, we have to degrade one-fifth mercilessly."

Another April 1968 report, describing the failures of poverty-reduction programs to reduce hunger in children, was issued by the Committee on School Lunch Participation, a coalition of women's organizations. *Their Daily Bread* described the school lunch program as underfunded, understaffed, and fundamentally broken because many blamed children or their families for not taking advantage of it. Federal school lunch programs began during World War II as both a hunger reduction tool and a sink for U.S. farm commodities. To protect farmers, the federal government bought surplus commodities and redirected them to schools that agreed to feed needy children free or at a reduced price. The 1946 National School Lunch Act transformed these informal wartime activities of the USDA and War Food Administration into a formal federal program. In practice, however, even after two decades of operation it was not an antipoverty program. Paradoxically, communities with more resources, and arguably less need, were often more successful at implementing school lunch programs.[16]

The Child Nutrition Act of 1966, passed as part of President Johnson's war on poverty, helped the program reach more poor communities, although the civil rights movement continued to draw attention to failures at the state and local levels to adequately oversee these programs.[17] Like *Hunger, U.S.A, Their Daily Bread* mentioned this "other America," an "under-developed nation" inside America, but explicitly argued that suburbanization rendered childhood hunger invisible to middle-class Americans.[18] The release of both reports so soon after Martin Luther King Jr.'s assassination, and the days of rioting that followed, moved policymakers to act. The Poor People's Campaign, which Martin Luther King Jr. began organizing before his death, arrived in Washington, DC, in May 1968, with many carrying copies of *Hunger, U.S.A.*

In May 1968 CBS aired "Hunger in America," a documentary that catapulted these stark disparities into the national limelight. It opened by stating, "Hunger is hard to recognize in America. We know it in other places, like Asia and Africa," and then shifted to a moralistic tone, stating that "serious hunger exists in many places in the United States." In a nod to contemporary geographical, racial, and ethnic identity politics, it then offered four examples of communities hit by hunger: San Antonio, Texas, showing Hispanics; Loudoun County, Virginia, documenting "the South"; Tuba City, Arizona, a Navajo reservation; and Hale County, Alabama, showing southern black cotton growers. The documentary broadcast dramatic images of hunger and starvation in America to the television sets of millions of suburban households, challenging the nation's self-image as a land of affluence and abundance.[19] "Hunger in America" placed hunger front and center in 1968 election-year politics. But it did so by blunting the critical narratives of systemic poverty and racial disparities, central in the two reports above, and instead presenting a more sympathetic story of fellow Americans denied the American dream.[20]

Hunger had become an effective issue for the antipoverty campaign to mobilize America's sense of moral outrage. Hunger also helped civil rights advocates shake critics' framing of poverty and race as an "urban crisis." Hunger affected the poor in city ghettos and rural farming communities alike. A variety of activist organizations, dubbed "the hunger lobby," embraced hunger as yet another issue where racial disparities reflected entrenched economic discrimination and poverty. Notable examples of organizations that joined the CCAP and the Field Foundation to advocate greater attention to hunger and the need to reform the food system included the National Council on Hunger and Malnutrition, a nutrition activism organization founded by NAACP legal defense lawyer John R. Kramer; the Citizens Advocate Center, a watchdog organization founded in 1968 focused on defending Native American rights; the Community Nutrition Institute, founded in 1970 by Johnson administration USDA official Rodney Leonard; and the Food Research and Action Center (FRAC), a DC-based nonprofit antihunger advocacy center founded in 1970.[21] In what became a battleground over issue framing, they attacked those who claimed "the poor were malnourished because of ignorance, and [thus] needed education rather than direct assistance," as either being out of touch with poverty, or racist. At stake was whether to define hunger with a focus on food versus an emphasis on social inequality.[22]

The hunger crisis and the emergence of a "hunger lobby" had immediate institutional ramifications. In 1968 Senator George S. McGovern, a Democrat from South Dakota, convened the Senate Select Committee on Nutrition and Human Needs, sometimes informally called the McGovern Committee. This launched what would be the longest and arguably most in-depth congressional investigation into diet and nutrition in U.S. history. The committee would ensure that food and nutrition politics remained on the front page of the national political agenda for almost a decade, from July 1968 to September 1977.[23] Meanwhile, the FDA was mired in debates of its own. The controversy over "Hunger in America" was reshaping the conversation among FDA experts about the agency's proposed standards for special dietary foods.

DID AMERICANS NEED MORE VITAMINS?

Why had the FDA not noticed before that hunger was a problem? The answer was partly due to the way bureaucracies compartmentalize, and the limits of their power to frame policy. Since it left the USDA in 1940, the FDA had been policing food fraud and ensuring food safety, while food security and nutrition education remained concerns of the Department of Agriculture.[24] The FDA focused on markets for nutrition products, not poverty eradication. Certainly the FDA had substantial experience with vitamin science. As discussed previously, by the 1960s Americans had decades of experience with "vitamania," the widespread, enthusiastic consumption of vitamin products to solve numerous health concerns. Over those decades policymakers shifted from outright skepticism to crafting careful policies that sanctioned certain forms of vitamin-enrichment and encouraged vitamin-conscientiousness in the American diet.

One important federal program was the National Research Council's "Recommended Dietary Allowances" (RDAs), first established in 1941 for protein, energy, and eight vitamins, and, to incorporate new science, modified every few years to include additional nutrients or different recommended levels. These early dietary standards were intended to serve as a guide to "minimum," "adequate," or "acceptable" levels of a nutrient, to prevent diseases associated with nutrition deprivation. They were not meant to describe an "ideal" or "optimal" diet, although they were often used for that. Revisions of the RDAs often prompted debates as to whether they should reflect "average" levels or indicate the fact of individual variability.[25] In establishing its standards for fortified foods, such as vitamin-enriched bread, the FDA regularly consulted with the National Research Council's committee on RDAs. During the Larrick era FDA officials also invoked these standards when defending the agency's campaign against nutrition quackery, discussed in chapter 2, including when seizing vitamin products that encouraged mega-dosing or made fantastic health claims.

The increasing popularity of diet foods and health-food claims in the 1960s forced the FDA to revise its restrictive rules for special dietary foods. In 1968, after nearly two years of hedging and industry pushback, the FDA announced hearings on its proposed new regulations for foods with special dietary uses. The proposed changes covered a wide array of diet products, including vitamin and mineral supplements, fortified foods, artificial sweeteners, and foods for weight control. But its most controversial provision was a proviso requiring that all enriched foods and vitamin supplements carry a statement describing their consumption as medically unnecessary for "healthy" people. The FDA proposed the following wording: "Vitamins and minerals are supplied in abundant amounts by commonly available foods. Except for persons with special medical needs, there is no scientific basis for recommending routine use of dietary supplements."[26]

The problem was that many ordinary Americans' regular diets did not, in fact, include the vitamins and minerals they needed. In fact, the 1968 *Hunger, U.S.A.* report estimated a shocking 10 million Americans suffered from malnutrition. One challenge was how to recognize malnutrition, which was not only caused by hunger. In 1928 science writer Paul de Kruif voiced worries of a growing number of nutritionists when he wrote that there was a "hidden hunger that lets folks starve to death while they are eating plenty."[27] But measuring how many suffered this broader form of "hidden hunger" was difficult. Since the Great Depression, the U.S. Public Health Service (USPHS) had conducted surveys studying the links between diet, health, and poverty, but struggled to establish objective measures for all three, subverting efforts to assess the prevalence of malnutrition, much less the causes of dietary inadequacy. Some nutrition researchers tried to assess malnutrition by extrapolating from the USDA Bureau of Home Economics' national food consumption surveys. But this required substantial guesswork, using highly inaccurate tabulations of food eaten and RDA reference values, which critics believed resulted in grossly exaggerated numbers for malnutrition.[28] The senators' visit to Mississippi in 1967 led to Congress charging the Department of Health, Education, and Welfare (HEW), the department that included the FDA, to initiate the Ten-State Nutrition Survey run by the USPHS from 1968–70. This eventually grew into a national nutrition survey program that continues today.[29]

It was also not obvious whether hunger and malnutrition shared a common solution. Hunger was clearly associated with poverty, and thus poverty-alleviation programs might address it. Malnutrition, however, had many causes, and one was the quality of food consumers chose to eat. The U.S. had a problem with both— some malnutrition because of food access, and some because of poor dietary choices. Joseph Goldberger's campaign in the 1920s promoting brewer's yeast to address pellagra, and the use of iodized salt for preventing goiter, helped generate support for implementing food fortification campaigns to solve malnutrition.[30] They also made people aware that low-level nutrition deficiencies could cause mild, possibly chronic health problems without becoming a full, clinical illness. Awareness of "subclinical deficiencies" led otherwise healthy consumers to second-guess their diets, *and* their doctors, and marketers exploited this anxiety. It was one of the common vitamin "myths" the FDA targeted in its campaigns against nutrition quackery.[31] Yet it was unclear whether the best solution to malnutrition was to support costly government food programs providing better access to balanced diets, or to target specific health concerns by fortifying foods, while also providing more nutrition information to encourage people to make educated, healthy choices.

The FDA saw its vitamin label requirement as a compromise, necessary to combat misleading vitamin puffery. Critics derided the vitamin proviso as a "crepe label," invoking memories of the punitive crepe-paper label that the FDA pasted onto substandard products, which read, "below U. S. standard, low quality but not illegal." Indeed, then California governor Ronald Reagan referenced the proposed FDA vitamin regulations as yet another example of how an overbearing federal government was destroying the freedom of industry to run its own affairs. "If I feel better taking a little vitamin C to ward off a cold," Reagan declared, "government can keep its sticky labels off my pill bottles."[32] The FDA's vitamin proviso became the subject of repeated cross-examination at the hearings, with some experts questioning all three of the label's claims: Were consumers foolish for seeking routine use of supplements? Should vitamins only be for people with special medical needs? And were vitamins in fact adequately supplied by America's food supply?

It was clear from the start that the special dietary foods hearings would be contentious. The scale and structure of testimony gives a sense of the antagonistic, lawyerly process they entailed. At the pre-hearing conference, there were more than a hundred attorneys representing almost that many clients, each with their own particular issues. The lawyers alone nearly filled the first fifteen rows of the auditorium at the Department of Health Education and Welfare. On just the first day, May 7, FDA hearings examiner David H. Harris logged sixty-nine official appearances by participants, of which only five were consumers "who asked to take part in the hearings just for themselves." The rest were representatives of the food and drug industries.[33] Because the category of special dietary foods included a broad variety of products, and because of industry restructuring around new diet foods and supplements, industry interest groups ranged from farmer co-ops and food trade organizations to pharmaceutical companies and health food lobbyists. When the pre-hearings ended, the official number of participants had risen to 108, and the hearings examiner conservatively estimated that the record of the hearings would run to over 30,000 pages.

The question at stake in these hearings was whether America's ordinary diet was adequate, and whether industry should be encouraged or discouraged to engineer vitamins into America's food supply. Throughout the hearings Commissioner James

Goddard tried to appear impartial, yet in an early public interview he argued, "Man cannot live by vitamins alone."[34] As recently as 1961 in a "Report on Quackery," FDA commissioner George Larrick had touted the FDA for "sustaining misbranding charges against the nutritional 'big lie'—that the American food supply is impoverished and nutritionally deficient."[35] Throughout the 1960s the FDA aggressively campaigned against such claims in the vitamin supplements literature. Their efforts to introduce a crepe label on special dietary foods was a direct response to this "big lie."

To have a scandal over severe malnutrition among some Americans while the FDA argued against enriching novel foods seemed, to many, a serious contradiction, and proof that the agency was not serving the American people's best interests. In an editorial in *Nutrition Reviews,* Harvard nutritionist Fredrick Stare called for the FDA to suspend the hearings. He argued that both the "overfed" and "underfed" would benefit from industrial food fortification, writing that "those nutritional components . . . will help to prevent malnutrition among the affluent as well as the poor, for it exists among both."[36] The benefits of fortification for the poor were obvious, but the overfed, too, might benefit because it would restore minerals and vitamins to the diets of many who, because of the fast pace of modern lifestyles, had become more dependent on processed convenience and fast foods.

At the hearings, company lawyers attacked the FDA's claim that America's abundant food supply was sufficient to meet health needs. Scientists were suddenly trapped in a public debate where they did not want to appear insensitive to concerns about hunger, and a hearing where many agreed with the FDA's "foods first" policy. One dispute between two public nutrition scientists, Arnold E. Schaefer, head of the U. S. Public Health Service nutrition program, and Herbert Pollack, a nutrition researcher for the U. S. military's Institute for Defense Analyses, even made headlines in national newspapers. In his testimony on August 28, 1968, Pollack sought to discredit industry clamoring for enrichment by belittling the CCAP's *Hunger, U. S. A.* report. Pollack said the report had "no standing at all . . . as a scientific treatise" and was "a series of anecdotal statements by individuals."[37] Pollack also discredited Schaefer's USPHS's nutrition survey, which supported the claims of the hunger lobby.[38] Instead, Pollack endorsed the FDA's proposal to restrict food fortification to certain products. He opposed proposals expanding fortification, suggesting that they might open a "Pandora's box to a multitude of problems about which at the present time we know nothing."[39]

Experts in the nutrition community had mixed feelings about the politicization of hunger research. For Pollack the emotional appeals of *Hunger, U. S. A.* damaged the report's credibility, while other nutrition scientists reacted differently. One described the "Hunger in America" TV report as life-changing for him precisely because of its gripping emotional imagery: "For this author, a physician who has dealt with a great deal of kwashiorkor and nutritional marasmus [nutrition deficiency diseases] in Africa, it was eye-opening to sit in a comfortable U. S. home and to see cases of these serious nutritional diseases displayed in Texas and Arizona. . . . This program awakened in me a resolve that in the future my work . . . should also include attention to nutrition problems in the United States."⁴⁰ The scientific community split between those who saw the hunger lobby as unnecessarily politicized, and those who were awakened by the rhetoric and emotionally disturbing images.

The issue of how, precisely, nutritionists should define "hunger" and "malnutrition" came up in the FDA's hearings. At one point in December, Pollack walked out of the hearings in the middle of being cross-examined on the relevance of the *Hunger, U.S.A.* report to the FDA's policies on vitamin enrichment and supplements labeling. At his next appearance, Pollack was asked again to enumerate "all the causes of malnutrition of which you are aware." This time, he answered "everything that deviates from the so-called accepted standard," but noted a "multiplicity of causes," among them economics, could be factors. Yet Pollack, who maintained that Americans did not need vitamin enrichment, observed that it was "perfectly possible to buy a nutritionally adequate diet" on $3,000–4,000 a year.[41]

Pollack's report and testimony suggested that most Americans suffering hunger and malnutrition could achieve a healthy diet with proper training. Some nutritionists posited that Americans had simply forgotten how to be thrifty. Jean Hewitt, a home economist and regular food writer for the *New York Times,* summed up many professionals' sentiment when she wrote that inadequate nutrition was "a classless problem." Rising food costs were forcing many families above the poverty level to "trim weekly market bills." She also expressed concern about the growing reliance, among lower- and middle-class families alike, upon "convenience foods such as packaged mixes and frozen prepared dishes," rather than more economical fresh produce. In her opinion, there was "no place . . . in poverty-level budgets" for paying the "premium price . . . for a built-in maid service."[42]

Others argued education was not enough. In an *American Journal of Clinical Nutrition* editorial, several nutrition experts sought to reinfuse class politics into a critique of Pollack's testimony. "After all," they wrote, "however inadequate the nutritional education of the middle class and rich may be, they have alternatives to malnutrition."[43] They argued that if experts tackled hunger, they should look beyond just education, and factor in material constraints and class disparities. The USDA standards for the income needed to purchase a nutritionally adequate diet "completely overlook the fact that a great many people do not have the education, the freezer and pantry space, the transportation, and necessary information to carry out effective buying habits." Indeed, they saw the education argument as a ruse, noting that "many public officials and medical professionals alike frequently invoked education as an excuse to do little else for people who need food."[44]

These critics also highlighted the misconception, put forward by Pollack, that the existence of obesity among the poor showed it was possible for the poor to find adequate and even excessive amounts of food. "Most of us are hoodwinked into believing that excess weight is associated with plentiful food. It is not so simple," they argued. The hunger the poor experienced was more than just insufficient food. "Most of the people who live in the ghettos are prisoners of circumstances beyond their control. . . . They crave respite and solace," the authors explained, "from the pressing reality of their hostile existence. They often find it in calorie-cheap but caloric-high substances." A poor person "eats not merely to satisfy his body but to fill a relentless void that has drained him spiritually."[45] Although many experts dismissed these arguments, firmly believing that obesity and heart disease were diseases of affluence, not desperation, these critics were prescient. Decades later, policymakers confronted with an epidemic of obesity among the poor would struggle to make similar insights.[46]

On October 13, 1969, after 478 days of hearings, the FDA rested its case. But the special dietary hearings were now to open up for industry witnesses, cross-examinations, and redirects, which dragged the hearings well into 1970. The entire process left both nutrition scientists and government regulators drained and frustrated. At an AMA Food Nutrition Board symposium on "Food Standards," Mark Hegsted, who had advocated the diet-heart thesis throughout the 1960s, summarized nutrition scientists' conflicted feelings about the FDA's approach to regulating diet foods. He noted that due to the hearings' "tremendous cost" and "inadequate scientific base," "the general scientific nutritional community has less confidence in the Food and Drug Administration than formerly." Nevertheless, Hegsted also believed that "industry remains the most suspect." On the question of how best to proceed on informative food labeling, Hegsted was at a loss. "I suspect that it is easier to select a bad diet now than it was 25 or 40 years ago," he lamented.[47]

THE 1969 WHITE HOUSE CONFERENCE ON FOOD, NUTRITION AND HEALTH

Such soul-searching on the nature of food made for ripe political fare, and hunger was a volatile subject for the new Nixon administration. America's failure to feed all its citizens was quickly cast as a national embarrassment. Since the 1959 "Kitchen Debate" between then–vice president Nixon and Soviet premier Nikita Khrushchev, keeping the American stomach full had served as important symbolic evidence of the fruits of America's consumer-oriented capitalist economy.[48] Robert Choate, appearing at a 1969 Senate hearing, worried about how the domestic hunger scandal might affect America's campaigns against communism abroad: "I think the free enterprise system is at stake here, for it matters not how many ABMs [anti-ballistic missiles] we build if we cannot prove to the poor and hungry of other countries that we have an economic system which can take care of its own." Meanwhile, the FBI began investigating the participants of the CBS "Hunger in America" documentary, believing the hunger story to be a "gigantic conspiracy" by certain individuals hoping to guarantee the re-funding of certain poverty programs.[49]

The Nixon administration had to gain control of the hunger controversy. While the 1968 appearance of hunger in America had caught many politicians off guard, soon all parties were scrambling to reframe the problem to support their platforms. On May 6, 1969, having barely finished his first hundred days in office, Nixon sent Congress a message arguing that "the moment is at hand to put an end to hunger in America . . . for all time." He noted that hunger "is an exceedingly complex problem, not at all susceptible to fast or easy solutions." But while Nixon's comments emphasized combatting poverty, he also invoked a language of personal responsibility associated with the conservative movement: "What matters finally is what people buy with the money they have. . . . All of us, poor and nonpoor alike, must be reminded that a proper diet is a basic determinant of good health." He also raised the possibility of technological solutions, even while noting that "great advances in food processing and packaging" have "placed great burdens on those who are less well off and less sophisticated in the ways of the modern marketplace."[50]

While his message to Congress struck an unequivocally urgent tone, Nixon conveyed mixed signals on how his administration would frame the issue. On the one hand, he indicated it was a poverty issue. Many of the specific institutional goals that Nixon mentioned were to be managed by the Urban Affairs Council, established at the start of Nixon's presidency under the direction of Daniel Patrick Moynihan. Moynihan's widely debated 1965 report, *The Negro Family: The Case for National Action*, gave him greater prominence as an important scholar and political figure in the federal war on poverty.[51]

Yet Nixon's message to Congress also reflected how the administration was reframing the hunger controversy, not primarily as a failure of public antipoverty programs but rather as a call to private citizens and organizations to lift up the needy. Nixon, whose father was a grocer and merchant during the New Deal, had a deep, personal distrust of government intrusion into businesses.[52] Nixon's challenge to Congress and the public was "to make the private food market serve these citizens as well, by making nutritious foods widely available in popular forms." Nixon said that he would soon "announce a White House Conference on food and nutrition, involving executives from the Nation's leading food processing and food distribution companies and trade unions." These industry leaders would be asked to explore ways "the private food market might be used to improve the nutritional status of all Americans, and how the Government food programs could be improved." In short, the Nixon administration was choosing to frame hunger and malnutrition as a wake-up call for private innovation and involvement rather than government-against-poverty campaigns.

On June 11, Nixon announced the appointment of Jean Mayer, a Harvard nutrition scientist and well-known hunger activist, as special consultant to the White

House for its conference on food and nutrition. The White House Conference on Food, Nutrition and Health was to be a reaffirmation of "our commitment to a full and healthful diet for all Americans." What's more, the conference was to focus on malnutrition more broadly, not just hunger, because "many Americans who have enough money to afford a healthful diet do not have one." While this was only a slight adjustment of the hunger lobby's language in public debates, the shift in focus to food and nutrition, rather than hunger and poverty, was portentous.

Jean Mayer (1920–1993), a physiologist, was himself the child of two French physiologists. He gained fame during World War II as a freedom fighter for the underground Free French Forces, winning numerous decorations, including the Knight of the Legion of Honor. After receiving a double PhD at Yale and the Sorbonne, he came to Boston to work with Walter B. Cannon, where he built on Cannon's notion of homeostasis. Mayer's research focused on how exercise and food "satiety" affected the development of obesity.[53] By the time Nixon's aides picked him to run the conference, Mayer was already known as a "militant" on hunger issues. His election as chairman of the "To End Hunger in America" conference, held in Washington in October 1968, launched his national role in the hunger debate.

Mayer's framing of the White House Conference on Food, Nutrition and Health was different from the Nixon administration's. Mayer was less optimistic that novel foods or industry innovation would solve the problem—in one interview following his appointment, Mayer noted, "Special foods for the poor are not the answer. The poor should eat the same foods bought in the same stores as everybody else."[54] Here he differed from Senator Jacob Javits and other Republicans who emphasized the importance of enriched foods, and the role of private food companies, in the development and distribution of new foods.[55] This may explain why the Nixon administration assigned Dr. O. Lee Kline, a "career Fed" staff member from the FDA, to assist Mayer. One of Mayer's students later said Kline was "detailed to Mayer to control him."[56]

The three-day conference was planned for December, between Thanksgiving and Christmas, when Americans are especially attuned to hunger and charitable giving. The conference was no longer the simple private sector meeting imagined by Nixon in May. Twenty-six panels incorporated academic experts, medical doctors, representatives from agriculture and industry, and citizen representatives. In response to accusations it was not democratically representative and inclusive, it incorporated eight "task force" groups, composed of members from social action groups, women's organizations, industrial and consumer interests, professional organizations, and religious denominations. Panelists and task force members met for the week before the conference to prepare for the three-day public event.[57] Conference organizers worked hard to emphasize the diversity of attendees. They prepared a printout of all participants listed by home state to demonstrate there was representation from all fifty states. Mayer pointed out that "over 400 of the very poor themselves" would be brought in to discuss the recommendations of panels and task forces, describing these participants as "black, Mexican-American, Puerto Ricans, white, Indians, Alaskan natives, inhabitants of the Pacific Trust territories, and of our Caribbean dependencies and migrant laborers."[58] While many women were invited, few would be in a position to set the agenda. Prior to the conference one woman wrote Mayer, complaining that "in a field with a higher than average proportion of professional women," only five of the forty-nine chairmen and vice chairmen were women. Historian Hannah Leblanc has argued that conference organizers viewed women "as conduits to Mrs. Consumer, rather than as scientific experts or as community activists in their own right," despite women's groups' significant role in community organizing for the event.[59]

On December 2, 1969, Nixon convened the White House Conference on Food, Nutrition and Health, addressing nearly five thousand people at the opening plenary session. His address mirrored his administration's framing of the debate by focusing on personal responsibility and choice, stating, "The best judge of each family's priorities is that family itself, that the best way to ameliorate the hardships of poverty is to provide the family with additional income to be spent as that family sees fit." The "task of government," Nixon proclaimed, "is to enable you to make decisions for yourselves."

Highlights from different conference panels revealed the diversity of policy issues at play and suggested a shared sentiment for a need to change the nation's policies, if not agreement on what form that change should take.[60] The panel on "Traditional Foods" expressed alarm at the "significant changes in our eating patterns," including "the consumption of more snack foods between meals, more eating away from home, and greater use of convenience foods."[61] The panel's recommendations reflected its members from the meat and dairy industries, who used the platform to "dispel the confusion that surrounds the significance of fats in our national diet"—namely the recent cholesterol controversy. The Consumer Task Force attempted to counter that retrograde message with an urgently worded endorsement of informative package labels: "We need on the label a percentage break-down of the list of ingredients. This percentage information is increasingly urgent as more and more foods are processed partly or wholly." The "Food Manufacturing and Processing" panel, chaired by C. W. Cook of General Food Corp. and vice-chaired by Gordon Edwards of Kraft Co., promoted industry's alternative to the "Traditional Foods" perspective.[62] It recommended repealing the Filled Milk Act, which the panel felt was preventing innovation in the creation of less fatty and more nutritious dairy substitutes.[63] The panel also recommended repealing the Butter Act and Filled Cheese Act, thus authorizing the fortification of milks; increasing wheat, rice and corn enrichment; and allowing enrichment of chocolate products. It also recommended the "terminat[ion of] hearings on part 80.2 of proposed regulations for vitamin and mineral fortified foods," also known as the FDA special dietary foods hearings. All of these panel recommendations added to the general din of calls for reform, producing a postconference consensus for changing government policy on food distribution programs, and for improving nutrition labeling and education.

Two panels stood out for anticipating how food and nutrition policy would be framed in the years to come. First was the panel on "Adults in an Affluent Society: The Degenerative Disease of Middle Age," chaired by diet scientists Ancel Keys and Irving Page. The panel's report noted that "the poor and disadvantaged suffer from insufficient food, even outright hunger and malnutrition . . . [but] many of them of them also share the problems of the affluent—too many calories, under activity, overweight, inability to make wise food choices leading to a balanced diet."[64] Improvements in food labeling were among the possible solutions the panel offered to address this problem. It specifically encouraged changing the labeling of fatty acid content: "The Panel believes the consumer is entitled to know the content of the food he consumes." The panel also indicated industry should "make every reasonable effort to formulate and market palatable foods." While the panel's focus on overeating rather than hunger made it an outlier, its importance would grow as policies around overeating began to eclipse the hunger controversy.

The second panel of note, "New Foods: Standards of Food Identities That Simulate Traditional Foods," was chaired by Richard S. Gordon, vice president of Monsanto, and co-chaired by nutritionist Gladys A. Emerson. A third panel member, Peter Barton Hutt, an attorney from the law firm Covington & Burling, played an important role in drafting the report, and this became important when he was hired by the FDA in the 1970s. On many of the legal debates surrounding food, the panel's framing of the debates reflected a pro-industry perspective. Broadly speaking, it called on government institutions to reform regulations to let the market resolve the debates, to allow: "Freedom for industry to experiment and innovate, coupled with responsibility to consumer inquiry and Government regulation. Freedom for consumers to be informed, to inquire, and to petition; coupled with a responsibility to become knowledgeable and effective consumers." It also favored certain narrower policy reforms, such as throwing out the "jelly bean rule"—"No one type of food should be preferred over another as a nutritional carrier"—and removing caps on megadosing to let fortification be driven by the market, not the government.[65]

The New Foods panel report was substantially longer and more detailed than other panel reports, reflecting Hutt's energy and ambition as he addressed many ongoing food policy debates. Of its ten specific recommendations, especially notable were calls for an immediate food fortification program to relieve malnutrition, a policy of "truthful disclosure" requiring foods to disclose their contents, uniform food product labeling standards, and nutritional quality standards. These proposed reforms foreshadowed many policies that Peter Hutt and Virgil Wodicka would promote and implement when they moved to the FDA in the 1970s.

The White House conference report got some dutiful media coverage at the time, and subsequently was important as a reference for political lobbying and defense for institutional reforms. Immediately following the conference, however, the media gave much greater attention to incidents where the conference was disrupted by spirited protest groups and diverse social movements. Illustrative of this were strident comments made by various task force commentators on the otherwise staid scientific and industry panels. One very revealing, comparatively raw and unedited contribution to the report was the "reflections and impressions" section of the "Voluntary Action by Women" task force, listing dozens of anonymous quotes from individual task force members. To capture the frenetic and emotionally intense mood of the conference, one member contributed her impressions in prose that read like beat poetry:

> Cold people, cold people, verbose people, people not staging other people, people strutting verbally, scaring people, caring people, fighting people, and men and women. Forlorn women, women shouting, men shrugging, men talking, men explaining—more talkers than listeners. Our daily bread, but not theirs—their hunger but not ours. Scientific facts pouring from experts—flooding the rooms—drowning the uneducated. Some gentle men not listening men—and women trying, women prodding, women pushing, women helping, women seeking, and finding answers and asking more and hoping—then more and more—some bad rips mended—some cruel truths spilled over nice talk—some dark facts exposed—More talk of bread—more talk of now—keen meaning from the meaners. Some feeling of turning on—and to each other—Humility seeping through the layers of indifference. Only a start—miles to go, years to work—Starting now—no excuses, no delays, no rationalizing—Their daily bread—now.[66]

Another task force participant expressed an eagerness for results: "I have felt torn between a desire for the Conference to maximize effectiveness and the need of the kind of drama that will emphasize the need for action." Activist participants struggled with whether it was best to seek a rational, dispassionate, and productive discourse, or to hope for a powerful emotive voice that would draw attention and force real political change.

Jean Mayer put a positive spin on all this, saying "it was rather like a gigantic exercise in sensitivity training. . . . The meetings forced everyone to listen to points of view they had never listened to before."[67] But many participants were unhappy with how the conference unfolded. They especially disagreed about whether public education was a solution for hunger and poverty. A community organization report argued that "poverty, not ignorance, was the main cause of hunger and malnutrition."[68] Another problem was the disparity between how experts and ordinary people understood the issues. At the panel on "New Foods," for instance, a woman asked, "What do you mean by genetic foods?" The audience laughed, and she was told that the word she meant was "generic," not genetic. The woman

The National Council on Hunger and Malnutrition in the United States

"To assure every American family an adequate diet"

December 3, 1969

John R. Kramer
Executive Director
1211 Connecticut Avenue, N.W.
Washington, D.C. 20036
(202) 296-9135

Mr. Nixon —
You Have The Responsibility!

Yesterday, Mr. Nixon, you claimed the responsibility for the problem of malnourishment. You are responsible, Mr. Nixon.

- You are responsible for coming to this Conference grinning like Santa Claus and delivering a bundle of second-hand, useless toys: a food stamp program that won't feed very many very well; a welfare program that compels couples and individuals to face hunger on their own and offers next to nothing to families in most urban areas;

- You are responsible for making us listen to how you got thin once by opting to live for awhile on ketchup and cottage cheese and then forcing all the poor to subsist forever on the same stuff by providing them, in the distant future, no more than 27 cents per meal from both your welfare and food stamp programs combined;

- You are responsible for violating the truth-in-packaging law by leading us to believe that your speech was going to put an end to poverty-related hunger and malnutrition in America, when the only new food it delivered to the poor was the paper it was written on-- with ketchup, of course.

- You are responsible for deceptive advertising by pretending that you are stamping hunger and malnutrition as URGENT when, in fact, your only concrete suggestions were to sit tight and wait while your meager bills dribble through Congress and you lobby against stronger measures;

- You are responsible for dunning the foundations and Federal agencies for $1 million for a Conference that is strengthening your image, but not the minds and bodies of the poor, for yesterday you merely repeated what you promised us last May and still have not made good on;

M. Alfred Haynes, M.D., Ch.	Leslie W. Dunbar		Hon. Albert A. Pena, Jr.
The Rev. Ralph Abernathy	Marian Wright Edelman	Vivian Henderson	Walter P. Reuther
Doris Calloway	Jean Fairfax	Howard M. Metzenbaum	Philip Sorensen
James P. Carter, M.D.	Herman Gallegos	Martin Meyerson	The Rev. Charles S. Spivey, Jr.
Jack Conway			

FIGURE 13. Flyers such as this one from the hunger lobby circulated among participants at the White House Conference. Source: John R. Kramer, flyer, December 3, 1969, "Mr. Nixon—You Have The Responsibility!" Courtesy of the Richard Nixon Presidential Library and Museum (National Archives and Records Administration).

complained, "See? That's what I mean. You people don't tell us consumers what you're talking about. I'm confused and you're not helping us to understand with all your fancy words." Expert panelists' reliance on technical language quickly alienated and frustrated less experienced participants. Richard Hall, vice president of research at McCormick Company, was dismayed by the lack of trust between consumers and industry: "No steps have been taken, in our panel or in others I've been to, to try and bridge this problem or even discuss it."[69] Many activists complained that the intellectual breadth of the conference watered down the urgency and crisis of the hunger issue, characterizing it as "two conferences."[70]

In the weeks and months following the White House conference, people differed over whether it had met its intended goals, and what its legacy would be. Pointing to its characterization as having been "two conferences," one on hunger, the other on nutrition and consumerism, the hunger lobby argued that broadening the conference had been a tactic by the Nixon administration to defuse hunger as an issue. Nick Kotz, in his book *Let Them Eat Promises*, published the same week as the conference, quoted Nixon as saying to USDA secretary Clifford M. Hardin, "Use all the rhetoric, so long as it doesn't cost any money." Despite such criticisms, Jean Mayer defended the organization of the conference, complaining, "People have spoken too much only to others of their own type—doctors to doctors, processors to processors, consumers to consumers, poor to poor."[71]

The most visible immediate policy goals that came out of the conference were calls to expand the Food Stamps and School Lunch programs.[72] Concern over the conference and the hunger issue also helped derail many of the FDA's planned changes for labeling vitamin-enriched foods. More generally, the conference raised a food policy question, which remains today: Should farm support programs and especially subsidies be coupled to food aid programs, or should food aid be tied to welfare programs?[73] The immediate legacy of the White House conference was to shift attention from poverty alleviation to education and especially labeling, and from malnutrition to overeating. Indeed, industry found the White House conference panel reports were a useful lobbying tool for reforming the food label.[74] The uncoupling of food policy from agricultural policy became a trend that continues to the present.

THE FDA'S BITTERSWEET BAN ON CYCLAMATE

In addition to the concerns about hunger and malnutrition that motivated the White House Conference, in 1969 the FDA faced another crisis when the safety of cyclamate came into question. In 1958 the FDA had classified saccharine and cyclamate as GRAS, or "generally recognized as safe," in part because the substances were essential for diabetics' diets. Subsequently, the mass marketing of diet products exposed millions of Americans to artificial ingredients whose risk was not well understood.

Some White House Conference participants used the event to call for public scrutiny of the industry's overuse of chemical additives in food. James Turner, a public interest attorney who collaborated with Ralph Nader, wrote a separate opinion to the "Food Safety" panel report, stating that all panelists had insisted "that the chemical environment be controlled as completely as possible." Turner wanted to clarify that GRAS should not be a means for easing food additive standards.[75] On October 30, 1969, largely as a result of recommendations in the White House Conference report, President Nixon directed the FDA to assess the safety of GRAS food substances. Over the next three years, the FDA's GRAS review became a major project of its Bureau of Foods.[76] Growing public rancor over hunger and malnutrition, as opposed to the dangers of overconsumption, also encouraged FDA regulators to regard the safety of artificial sweeteners, in particular, with growing skepticism.

Ever since Abbott Laboratories decided to expand its Sucaryl market beyond diabetics to a mass public, its signature additive, cyclamate, faced scrutiny about possible negative side effects. As previously discussed, the FDA and its scientific advisory committees initially resisted the use of the "nonnutritive" artificial sweetener by otherwise healthy individuals. Those reservations reflected scientists' uncertainty concerning whether accumulative concentrations of the sweetener might have unforeseen side effects, which might not surface in small populations but could become a concern at the scale of mass markets. Even after the FDA issued a policy statement in 1962 informally accepting the additive in mass-consumed products, cyclamates were the subject of recurrent medical news stories questioning their safety. In 1964 The Medical Letter drew readers' attention to a Wisconsin Alumni Research Foundation (WARF) study suggesting cyclamate stunted the growth of rats. A Consumer Reports issue carried a copy of the message in lay terminology that received considerable press coverage. Within a year, when it emerged that WARF conducted the research under contract by the Sugar Research Foundation, most people discredited it.[77] Later in 1965 WARF researchers published an article in Nature that generated further press, but had less impact on the product's sales.[78]

Up until 1968, the FDA generally remained impartial in these inter-industry disputes over the safety of natural versus nonnatural ingredients. In 1965 an FDA review of cyclamate studies affirmed there was no demonstrated risk from use of the artificial sweetener in soft drinks and other food products. However, the agency left its official position unchanged—that is, such products were special dietary foods and thus, ostensibly, for people under special treatment.[79] In 1968 a study by FDA scientist Martin Legator showed that cyclohexylamine, a chemical precursor in the production of cyclamate that sometimes appeared in the final product, had a notably higher carcinogenic profile than cyclamate itself. This prompted renewed interest in examining whether cyclamate was safe.[80]

In April 1969 increasing media attention led Commissioner Herbert L. Ley to issue a public announcement advising "that consumers should limit their use of the cyclamates" to no more than "50 milligrams of cyclamate per kilogram of body weight per day." Recognizing that consumers would struggle to ascertain their daily consumption of a substance added to processed foods, Ley asked for the public's patience while the agency's special dietary hearings continued. Meanwhile, Ley argued that people could safely consume artificially sweetened products if they exercised a moderate amount of precaution, restricting their intake of diet soft drinks, particularly for children, for example, to no more than one or two bottles a day.[81]

Because of this uncertainty, the FDA specifically avoided the issue of safety in the special dietary hearings on artificial sweeteners. Instead, the hearing considered other issues, such as whether artificial sweeteners should be classified as food additives instead of grandfathered in to the GRAS category; whether "technological use," the use of sweeteners at low levels in canned foods for restoring sweetness, and not intended for dietetic use and health labeling, should be exempt from the standards being developed for diabetic use; and how cyclamates should be labeled. In September 1969 FDA staffer Weissenberg noted that the FDA wanted to introduce new regulations because the original label—"should be used only by persons who must restrict their intake of ordinary sweets"—implied the products were only for diabetics, whereas some new products with the label were marketed to a wider audience, yet included caloric sweeteners, and thus were not appropriate for diabetics.[82] So the hearings mostly focused on how to regulate this dual market for artificially sweetened goods, rather than face lingering questions about the sweetener's safety.

All of this changed in October 1969. Jacqueline Verrett, a career biochemist at the FDA, had been running tests of cyclamate on chicken embryos since 1966. In December 1968 Verrett shared her results internally within the FDA. Fifteen percent of the embryos she injected with cyclamate had shown visible deformities, but the agency decided that neither her nor her colleague's studies could be extrapolated to humans. On September 30, 1969, frustrated by what she later called "foot dragging" inside the agency, Verrett stated directly and emphatically in an NBC interview, "I don't recommend cyclamates for chicks, and I don't recommend it for people."[83] Commissioner Ley issued an immediate rebuttal, stating, "Cyclamates are safe within the present state of knowledge and scientific opinion available to me."

Notwithstanding Commissioner Ley's assurances, the public outcry surrounding Verrett's comments demanded a more formal response. The FDA immediately convened an ad hoc committee of the National Academy of Sciences to review cyclamate's status as a GRAS ingredient. A week later, Abbott Laboratories acknowledged funding a study that also suggested carcinogenic effects. On October 17, 1969, the ad hoc committee recommended cyclamate's removal from the GRAS list. The following day, HEW secretary Robert Finch, holding a can of Tab soda, sweetened with cyclamate and saccharine, announced that cyclamate would be provisionally banned.[84]

The seesaw nature of the cyclamate safety review prompted disagreement within the scientific community about the best approach to risk management. *The Lancet* ran an editorial noting that "never have so many pathologists been summoned to opine on so few lesions from so humble a species as the laboratory rat." Elizabeth Whelan, an epidemiologist who would become an antiregulation crusader, wrote a *Nature* editorial that characterized the wave of bans on cyclamate marching across Europe as "the cyclamate bandwagon"; she characterized Commissioner Ley's speculations on opening an investigation into saccharine as bearing the marks of "an impending witch-hunt." She also mused that banning artificial sweeteners would have the "upshot" of leading people to eat more sugar, "an outcome which there is reason to believe could be considerably more pernicious to health than any amount of artificial sweeteners in the diet."[85] Not all scientists or science reporters opposed the ban. Joshua Lederberg, a Nobel laureate in Stanford's Department of Genetics, defended the FDA's cautious actions, arguing, "The potential threat of chemical induction of cancer surely should not be taken lightly."[86] Scientists' commentaries, however, generally focused on the minimal risks being discussed and the problematic nature of relying on animal studies.

On December 11, 1969, Commissioner Herbert Ley Jr. resigned from the FDA. In accepting his resignation, HEW secretary Finch praised Ley as a "gifted scientist and a dedicated public servant," but noted that he had "coped strenuously with an unwieldy agency."[87] Ley had few positive things to say about his seventeen-month tenure with the agency. Two years later, at a congressional hearing, Ley lambasted the FDA for its close ties to industry and claimed that he left out of exasperation with an overbearing pharmaceutical industry.[88]

The cyclamate ban stood, and still stands today, despite continued appeals by Abbott Laboratories. But as discussed in the next chapter, the FDA's experience with cyclamate had significant political consequences. It led to an outside review of the FDA's GRAS standards and the procedures it used to determine which food additives were, or were not, acceptable. The cyclamate controversy also became a *cause célèbre* for those protesting what they considered to be the FDA's excessive overreaching. When the FDA sought to ban similar food items in the 1970s—in particular saccharine, then the only remaining artificial sweetener on the market—critics and industry were quick to mobilize against it.

THE LIMITS TO GROWTH AND NEW
FOOD SOLUTIONS

Following the special dietary foods hearings, the FDA backed off the unpopular "crepe label" on vitamin-mineral products. When the final rules were released in 1973, a full ten years after they had been first proposed, they were largely overshadowed by new FDA rules on nutrition labeling, discussed in chapter 4.[89] As early as

1970, when the special dietary foods hearings ended, the U.S. focus on hunger, whether at home or abroad, had evolved from discussions of the economic poverty of certain ethnic minorities to a discourse on the responsible management of populations and raising the consciousness of consumers.[90] The shift initiated a decade-long preoccupation with population and resource scarcity that would underscore the possibilities and perils of technological food solutions.[91]

On April 20, 1970, activists called for a national environmental teach-in, and millions of Americans participated in demonstrations to show their concern for various environmental issues confronting mankind. The first Earth Day marked the emergence of environmentalism but also the crystallization of a new global sensibility for personal responsibility. Alongside the new social movements mobilizing around the environment were "countercuisine" movements organized around alternative food practices and challenging the establishment food industry.[92] To politicize consumer choices, these movements infused the politics of the personal into food politics, emphasizing each individual's responsibility for the world's diet.

Concern over how to manage the world's growing population surfaced in the 1960s. In 1966 Kenneth Boulding published *The Economics of the Coming Spaceship Earth*, where he described a closure of global "frontiers" and called for an end to the "cowboy economies" of the past. Boulding argued that "the earth has become a single spaceship, without unlimited reservoirs of anything." In this new "spaceman" economy all members of the ship must work together. In 1969 in *Affluence in Jeopardy*, Charles F. Park argued that, based on estimates of lead and iron reserves, the world could soon run out of certain raw materials. Nixon, in his White House Conference opening speech, called for a "Commission on Population Growth and the American Future" and specifically mentioned the need for family planning programs. And in 1972 the newly formed "Club of Rome" published a treatise on the growing world population, *The Limits to Growth*, modeling ways that the explosion of population growth would exhaust resources. Barbara Ward and René Dubos stated this relationship directly and emotionally in their 1972 book, *Only One Earth*, arguing we had an ethical obligation to change our habits soon if we wished to care for and maintain the only home that we had.[93]

These global economic concerns problematized both notions of the affluent society and understandings of the diseases (and diets) of the affluent. A specific concern was food scarcity. In 1968 biologist Paul Ehrlich declared in *The Population Bomb*, a book comparing the world's rapidly growing population to a ticking time bomb, that "the battle to feed all humanity" had already been lost. Others characterized the battle as one where America's affluence left others across the globe behind. Thus, according to Georg Arne Borgstrom's 1965 *The Hungry Planet: The Modern World at the Edge of Famine*, if all the world's food were distributed evenly among its 3.5 billion human inhabitants, all of them would go hungry.[94]

These debates over food supply and population growth harkened back to Thomas Malthus's times, reflecting perennial arguments as to whether pessimistic projections of resources shortages spelled certain doom for society (in the form of a return to subsistence living) or whether unforeseen technological or social solutions would render those anxieties moot.[95]

This neo-Malthusian debate cast an entirely new light on the diet-heart thesis, discussed in chapter 2. Many authors linked rising levels of chronic heart disease and overeating in rich countries, particularly among the affluent, with the lack of access to food in poor communities and developing countries. Moore Lappé, for example, argued in *Diet for a Small Planet* (1971) that food shoppers' decisions at meat counters across America shaped food availability and famine around the world, since meat was an energy-intensive food product, whereas vegetarian foods were more ecological. In a 1974 *New York Times* article, Jean Mayer made a similar claim, more directly targeting Americans: "The same amount of food that is feeding 210 million Americans would feed 1.5 billion Chinese on an average Chinese diet."[96]

Challenged by the hunger scandal and the White House Conference, U.S. nutrition professionals began considering the relationship between food production, distribution, and hunger, both at home and abroad. One prospect raised in the conference and touted by some nutritionists was to use special dietary products to mitigate hunger. *New York Times* food writer Jean Hewitt wrote an article depicting the development of "low-cost, specially formulated nutritive foods" commonly used in underdeveloped countries since the end of World War II as "tests," whose lessons were not applicable to the U.S. According to the article, one of the "lessons learned" from the effort to eradicate hunger in developing countries was that it was easier to develop and produce "low-cost, specially formulated foods" than to get people to eat them. At a Senate hearing, the president of Quaker Oats opined, "The most nutritious product in the world does no one good until it is consumed."[97]

Food companies jumped on this new market for high-tech nutritive foods. They benefited from over a decade of international research efforts to create high-protein materials in developing countries, using foodstuff materials such as fish flour, oilseed flours made from vegetable oils, and soybean flour and milks.[98] New foods included Quaker Oats Company's "Incaparina," a high-protein cottonseed flour product named after the Institute for Nutrition in Central America and Panama, or INCAP, that had developed it; "C.S.M.," a corn-soy-milk mixture; and Coca-Cola's "Saci" and Monsanto's "Puma," both high-protein shakes. General Foods Corp. was preparing to market a "stable, high-protein, corn-soy-wheat elbow macaroni" in the U.S. In the fall of 1969 they test-marketed it to housewives in Alabama. The company believed it could be profitable and not just a "poor people's food"—that is, if it could avoid the stigma of the FDA's imitation label. A representative of Quaker Oats outlined a three-pronged attack on how their company would campaign on malnutrition: first, the creation of new special and enriched foods like its Incaparina; then, a person-to-person education program through "classes in the ghettos"; and, lastly, "a minority-group T.V. personality to be the poor people's Julia Child." A spokesperson for Monsanto argued that enriching food like chocolate bars, potato chips, and sodas might reduce malnutrition, given trends such as the declining numbers of people eating breakfast and increases in snacking.[99] Even the Biafra hunger crisis, gripping the attention of U.S. news viewers in 1970, was used to promote novel foods as a solution that worked abroad, and might work at home. Jean Mayer, for example, who was involved in the Biafra aid efforts, wrote a letter mentioning a product in use there with possible application in the U.S.[100] The use of fortified foods as a nutritional fix to hidden hunger in developing countries would continue for decades.[101]

What remained unclear was whether nutrition professionals could bring these tools to the U.S., into an already politically charged environment, without themselves being tainted by politics. Overwhelmed by urgent political issues, domestic and global, the public was tiring of food politics and the inanities of mundane governance, including the FDA's food standards. In July 1969 the media had fun when the president indirectly intervened in the FDA's considerations of hot dog standards. The agency was rejecting proposals allowing for a lower percentage of fat in hot dogs, while Nixon's presidential consumer advisor Virginia Knauer was arguing industry should be allowed to make products that met consumers' new demands. Nixon reportedly telephoned Knauer stating his support and famously said: "Stick to your guns, Virginia. I'm behind you 100 percent. I come from humble origins. Why, we were raised on hot dogs and hamburgers. We've got to look after the hot dog." And also, "I'm on a low cholesterol diet myself." The incident was an irresistible opportunity for jokes, with one Washington paper running the headline: "Major Administration Shift on Weenie." The joke was on the FDA. The message to the public was that the agency was wasting time and public money on something as trivial as preventing companies from making diet hot dogs.[102]

In a 1972 article, Jean Mayer reflected on ongoing debates regarding how best to frame U.S. nutrition problems for the decade ahead. Mayer noted the White House Conference was a wake-up call for the profession to address domestic problems, although he suggested that it had been willful ignorance rather than unintentional naiveté that led many nutrition scientists to ignore them. For many American scientists, he wrote, "The 'apolitical,' 'establishment-approved' character of international work was also seen by academics as more congenial than was the raising of disturbing social and political issues about our own society." That is, nutritional experts found it more difficult to work at home than abroad, where they didn't face the same political scrutiny. Mayer believed the profession should treat nutritional problems both at home and abroad, and be willing to face the inevitable accompanying social and political challenges.[103]

In the same article, in a section titled "Changing Character of Food," Mayer also suggested why the new negative nutrition, which one might say constituted an additional "limit to growth," posed a fundamental challenge for food producers and their previously harmonious relationship with the diet profession. "The food manufacturers, distributors, and retailers," Mayer noted, were "well aware that theirs is not basically a 'growth' industry." There was only so much food consumers could eat, especially if they became conscious about watching their weight. Many companies could expand new markets by selling "convenience in the form of frozen foods and packaged meals," but at a markup. "The work that was once performed by the unpaid housewife is now being done by organized labor," and this partly explained the rise in prices squeezing American consumers. Thus many consumers were "driven to find cheaper substitutes for the primary foods: meats, for instance, may be increasingly displaced by textured vegetable protein." These cheaper substitutes would only be judged acceptable, Mayer observed ruefully, if they were artificially enriched with vitamins and minerals.[104] Here, Mayer spells out the problem with many of the new foods and technical solutions that were being proposed to solve America's dietary troubles. For industry, according to Mayer, selling nutrition might simply become another tactic for whitewashing its for-profit interests in food processing and manufacturing. Mayer identified food labeling, and building a national nutrition education program, as the most promising public policy solutions to confront the trend toward unnecessary (as in unhealthy) convenience and abundance.

CONCLUSIONS

In some sense the hunger controversy simply went away. When a second White House Conference on Food, Nutrition and Health was held in 1971, the media paid little attention to it, and this time none of the activists who had highjacked the first conference protested. Conference attendees nevertheless agreed that hunger persisted in America. While hunger occupied a backseat in American food policy, concerns with global scarcity and limits to growth shaped much of 1970s politics, as would disillusionment with political institutions and their capacity to solve urgent food issues. At a World Food Conference in 1974, the United Nations adopted the term "food security," defining it as "a condition in which all people have access at all times to nutritionally adequate food through normal channels," and identifying freedom from hunger as a central policy goal. Three decades later, however, the USDA dropped the word "hunger" from its official assessments within America and deliberately replaced it with the by-then-less-politicized phrase "very low food security."[105] Even as public attention about hunger in America drifted elsewhere, the scandals of this period had several important and enduring consequences for the FDA's approach to food labeling.

Many in food studies today see this late 1960s–early 1970s period as the birth moment for contemporary political and social movements on food, diet, and health. As previous chapters show, debates over food, diet, and risk had been ongoing since at least the postwar period. What changed in 1969 was that the public became aware of what had been, at least since the Great Depression, a largely background debate among a small circle of experts. In doing so, this renewed public attention encouraged experts to listen to new voices and consider overlooked, popular sentiments on food and nutrition, thereby transforming policy conversations.

The year 1969 would be the last time in the twentieth century that "Hunger in America" was a front-page, sustained political concern.[106] As much or more than its original mission to reform antihunger programs, the 1969 White House Conference on Food, Nutrition and Health was invoked by campaigns to reform food labels. It was a shift from concern about the malnourished needy to the misinformed poor. Moreover, the whitewashing of racism (and sexism) from the conference's final policy solutions illustrates how "white ignorance" of systemic inequality and entrenched hunger can persist in the face of clear evidence demonstrating them.[107] This shift reflected both the Nixon administration's success in reframing the debate and industry's efforts to capitalize on the conference agenda. This is the irony of the controversy over hunger in America and how it shaped subsequent food labeling policy. The controversy started from a concern with "those left behind," but ultimately focused on the new challenges of the affluent society and need for novel solutions like food labeling. Once again, those left behind had been left behind.

This period also marked a turn toward a general wariness with tiresome governmental procedure. For the medical profession, arguments on the importance of personal responsibility in solving growing healthcare costs increasingly recast public health and government institutions like the FDA as needlessly paternalistic. For the public, cultural debates about eating meat versus vegetarianism, or the value of mealtime versus snacking, reflected changing food habits that redefined what was food and "nonfood."[108] From this emerged a new political order, a wave of deregulation and new policies, which caused a retooling of the FDA food labeling system, the introduction of mandatory ingredient labeling, and the first nutrition label.

4

The Market Turn

Market Devices

In the history of U.S. food labeling, 1973 marked a critical turning point. In that year, the Food and Drug Administration implemented new rules for information labels on standard foods, notably the "Nutrition Information" and ingredients panels. That was the beginning of the end of the FDA's reliance on its standards of identity system. This dramatic shift in the agency's style of regulation received little public attention, particularly when compared with the crises in food politics of 1969 described in the previous chapter. The year 1973 also saw the United States pull out of Vietnam, the Supreme Court decide *Roe v. Wade,* the public begin to learn about the Watergate conspiracies, and Arab members of OPEC proclaim an oil embargo, initiating a decade-long energy crisis.[1] The American public was understandably distracted. Thus, the FDA had more leeway than usual to develop policy reforms because most people inside the Beltway weren't paying attention.[2] Yet the FDA's changes to food labeling signaled a significant new direction in food regulation where government agencies used indirect mechanisms, such as information disclosures, to steer markets without interfering in them. The FDA's use of direct policy tools, especially food standards and ingredient bans, gave way to an "informational turn" in food policy.[3]

This chapter situates the FDA's turn toward "informational regulation" in the broader political climate and cultural context of 1970s anti-establishment backlash to government. Recent historical analysis of U.S. politics has shown that the "Reagan Revolution" of deregulation actually had its roots in 1970s politics, tracing back to the Nixon administration. Nixon's cabinet pioneered the art of devolution, that is, "transferring authority from federal government to state and local governments and from the public sector to the private sphere."[4] Yet in the 1970s, dismantling government was a cross-party platform. Critiques of the FDA and the push for a new consumerism were signs that both the left and the right had lost faith in government institutions to solve individuals' problems. The 1970s marked the end of the liberal consensus described in chapter 1; the decade ushered in what Daniel Rodgers calls an "age of fracture," where government was often seen as the problem, not the solution.[5]

In this period, antigovernment sentiment did not always translate into less government.[6] Instead, as with food labeling, it often produced a transformation in governance. The FDA's new food labeling rules embodied new ways of envisioning the state. Broadly, they embodied "regulatory reform," advocated by political actors, from Stephen Breyer to Milton Friedman, who favored modernizing New Deal agencies to make them less bureaucratic, less burdensome. Many of these reforms reflected what historian Mark Rose calls "market talk," the twin ideas that the market was or should be "free" of government, and that the market was often better than government, faster and more efficient, at solving many everyday problems.[7] For the FDA, a public health institution, reforms also reflected a new political awareness of the costs of managing risk and healthcare. The 1969 ban on cyclamate, based on studies showing only a hypothetical risk for cancer, had real, substantial economic costs. Many newly discovered dietary risks, such as the diet-heart thesis, arose from bad habits. Should taxpayers carry the cost of individuals' risky behaviors? Some policymakers argued that personal responsibility should matter as much as state action.

Informative labeling tried to thread the needle between the need for oversight of the market's uglier forms of nutrition quackery and the growing belief that individuals, rather than government bureaucrats, should decide matters concerning their own health. Put the information on the label, and let consumers decide for themselves. Public information campaigns resonated with broader social movements for information and transparency, from consumer protection movements to calls for "sunshine laws."[8] This chapter shows how the FDA's new labels fit into these broader trends. The public was fed up with government secrecy and backstage decision-making. It demanded more information.

Giving the public information, however, was not a simple story of consumer liberation or democracy ascendant. The FDA's new nutrition and ingredient label reforms gave the public more information, but also diminished the state's responsibility for dictating minimum guidelines for foods using its standards of identity system. As media scholar Michael Schudson notes, the information-sharing approach to governmental reform "affords government the least invasive action possible on some social problem."[9] In the 1973 rule changes, it transferred the means of oversight from food standards hearings to market-driven mechanisms that worked through consumer choice. The translation of political dispute into truth-in-labeling informational tools marked the beginning of an ideology of informationism that increasingly characterized food policy in the decades to come.

THE FDA IN THE AGE OF ANTI-ESTABLISHMENT

Although no one scandal or incident catalyzed the 1973 labeling changes, they were adopted against a backdrop of growing consumer activism. Media commentators and marketing analysts alike recognized the power of consumer organizations, with one author in the *Journal of Marketing* comparing the "present era of consumer unrest" to the 1900s and 1930s. As explanatory factors, the author pointed to "rising public standards of business conduct and social responsibility," sudden economic and social dislocation (including declining real incomes and purchase power), and even the appearance of new social activist organizations emerging out of the civil rights and antiwar movements.[10] These social pressures helped define the public atmosphere in which nutrition labeling was born: an atmosphere of distrust and frustration with public institutions and, conversely, optimism in pursuing private reform through market institutions.

New consumer interest groups kept issues surrounding food and diet alive even as the national policy community's interest in hunger and malnutrition waned.[11] By 1970 Ralph Nader was perhaps the most visible and media-friendly leader of the consumer advocacy movement. After his 1965 report, *Unsafe at Any Speed,* generated public concern about car safety and the need for regulation, Nader began encouraging people to organize "study groups" investigating other societal problems.[12] "Nader's Raiders," as they were called, tackled a wide range of issues, including the performance of the Federal Trade Commission (FTC), mine safety, the health hazards of air pollution, and the oversight of the food industry by the FDA. Nader's interest in the FDA began in 1969, when he testified before the McGovern Senate committee on hunger in America, discussed in the previous chapter. After testifying, Nader submitted forty-seven questions to the committee that he suggested be asked of "food manufacturers and processors." The questions highlighted popular frustration over the failure to bring enriched foods to needy populations:

(20) . . . What effect would enrichment of basic foods have on the profit of your corporation and industry in general? Why are enriched foods artificially priced higher than standardized nonenriched foods?

(32) Has your company participated in the manufacture of protein and nutrient-rich supplemental foods for use in developing countries? If so, what are these foods, and why have they not been marketed in this country? If you have not participated in this type of manufacture, why not?

(34) Is the nutritional quality of your food products a major concern of your company? How is this concern manifested in research, marketing, and advertising functions?

(46) Can you demonstrate that your convenience or processed foods contain at least the nutritive value contained in similar quantities of the foods they replace?[13]

The list signaled that Nader's Raiders had the food industry in their sights, even though it also revealed the beginning of a shift in focus: looking to food solutions rather than addressing underlying economic structures of poverty.

A key reform advocated by Nader's Raiders was the need for better consumer information programs. One powerful example was *The Chemical Feast: The Nader Report*, a 1970 exposé published by James S. Turner, a Nader's Raiders lawyer who participated in the White House Conference on Food, Nutrition and Health.[14] Turner and his team invoked the 1967 Freedom of Information Act to access information on the FDA's scientific safety review process.[15] *The Chemical Feast* chronicled how the FDA overstepped its authority in some areas while failing to provide adequate pro-consumer controls in others. It opened with cyclamates, documenting how the FDA failed to acknowledge, and perhaps even covered up, evidence of the additive's carcinogenic risks. To Turner, this suggested the FDA needed to reform its procedures for scientific safety assessment of GRAS ingredients. More generally, the report suggested that the cyclamates case reflected a systematic failure of the agency to protect the public from a flood of new and dangerous chemicals in the marketplace. A chapter titled "Hidden Ingredients" explained how the food standards system ironically obscured many of the ingredients used in standard products and created a site for industry influence in defining standard recipes.[16]

Just as damning were examples of the FDA's draconian enforcement measures on seemingly trivial issues. In a chapter on "Enforcement," Turner showed how the FDA's zeal for filing charges against individuals promoting medical quackery caused public resources to be used to prosecute, and to persecute, experts with alternative opinions.[17] Many of his examples focused on the FDA's campaigns against nutrition quackery and vitamin supplements. The discussion revealed enforcement practices that raised civil liberty questions about citizens' privacy or free speech protections, or cruel and unusual punishments for taking nonconventional health positions. The exposé also slammed the special dietary hearings, particularly the time and effort the agency spent attempting to introduce the crepe label, as evidence of bureaucratic incompetence.[18] These examples were widely cited in media reports and book reviews as evidence that the FDA's management needed reform, and also that its enforcement culture should change to reflect a new sentiment in America favoring independent and alternative cultures.[19]

Another group promoting the need for FDA reform was the Center for Science in the Public Interest (CSPI), formed in 1971 by Michael F. Jacobson (1943–) and two others from Ralph Nader's Center for the Study of Responsive Law. In 1972

Jacobson published *Eater's Digest: A Consumer's Fact-Book of Food Additives.* The book was intended to neither demonize nor defend food additives, but instead to inform the public why they were used, and to begin a dialogue about whether those uses matched public interests. In a section entitled "Standardized Foods and Food Labeling," Jacobson addressed what he called "silent labels" for "foods whose labels list none or only a few of the ingredients and additives that the food contains." Thus, Jacobson, like Turner, highlighted how the standards of identity system allowed food manufacturers to elide specific ingredients contained in their products. Writing in a more neutral style than Turner, Jacobson emphasized the need for and reasonableness of universal ingredients labeling.[20]

While CSPI's efforts attracted much less public attention than Ralph Nader's group, it became recognized for targeting consumer issues relating to diet, nutrition, and health generally, and food labeling specifically. In 1974 CSPI began publishing the "Nutrition Action Healthletter." The newsletter's wide distribution provided CSPI with a platform for spreading its views on abusive practices, whether promulgated by industry or the FDA; pressuring Congress through issue-framing; and shaming institutions into reforming or regulating egregious examples of advertisements that distorted health messages.[21] By the late 1980s, CSPI was the dominant consumer advocacy organization on most federal-level issues related to food politics, as discussed in chapter 5.

These consumer advocates attacked the FDA for foot-dragging on reform, and for being complicit when the food industry created obfuscating labels. But their aim was to improve government rules on labeling. The FDA, meanwhile, maintained that it lacked authority to require labeling. When a group of law students operating under the clever acronym of LABEL (Law student Association for Buyers' Education and Labeling) petitioned the FDA to require full ingredients labeling in May 1971, FDA commissioner Charles C. Edwards suggested a voluntary program "could provide one of the most fundamental changes in the history of food labeling in this country." In 1972 the FDA began exploring with industry possible formats for providing ingredients and "nutrient values" on a voluntary basis.[22] And food retailers, in particular progressive supermarkets, began to explore private innovations in food labeling, framing themselves as advocates for their customers in the hopes of building consumer trust and loyalty.

THE SUPERMARKET AS A CONTESTED CONSUMER SITE

In the 1970s the supermarket became a key site for debates about consumer advocacy and commercial exploitation. The supermarket had become an icon, and a metaphor for freedom of choice in American politics. From Nixon's defense of American capitalism in the "Kitchen Debate" of 1959 to calls for "supermarket banks" in the bank reform politics of the 1970s, the supermarket embodied a model of market agency where consumers could go up and down aisles and make free choices without anyone telling them what to do.[23] But interest in supermarket reform also reflected their rising role in food retailing. Most shoppers now purchased their groceries in supermarkets, and thus supermarkets became a primary target for consumer protests. In the 1970s, as the U.S. economy tightened for most consumers, supermarkets addressed economic troubles using innovations in product retailing and store layout, including offering cheaper "generic" store brands and twenty-four-hour openings.[24] To avoid negative consumer critiques and threats of government regulation, and to build a market advantage against competitors, some supermarket chains began positioning themselves as *consumer advocates* by experimenting with food labels.

Supermarkets increasingly sought to cater to what scholars call "active consumers," who actively seek out information to make decisions fitting their particular social and ethical concerns.[25] In this, they were responding to new economic theories in the 1970s that understood consumer behavior through the lens of rational choice theory and a faith in the marketplace. If properly informed, consumers would perform cost-benefit analyses to make optimal decisions for themselves. Yet experts identified concerns that limited the active consumer's ability to exercise informed choice. One problem was "information asymmetry" in markets. Economists George Stigler, in his studies on the "economics of information," and George Ackerlof, in his seminal 1970 paper "The Market for 'Lemons': Quality Uncertainty and the Market Mechanism," argued that in certain markets buyers had less information than sellers. This asymmetry invited sellers to exploit buyers by selling low-quality goods.[26] Other economic theories suggested that consumers made different kinds of decisions about food, a frequently purchased, relatively low-cost item, than more costly, less frequently purchased durable goods. In 1970 economist Philip Nelson published "Information and Consumer Behavior," describing structural differences in the return on consumers' investments in investigating products before purchase. Nelson distinguished between "search" goods, where consumers learn a lot about a good before purchase (including while shopping), and "experience" goods, where knowledge was principally gained about a product from its use after purchase.[27]

These distinctions had consequences for advertisers, including supermarkets. For experience goods, advertisers should emphasize brand and repeat the message as often as possible. But for search goods, advertisers should focus on "provid[ing] direct information about the characteristics of a brand."[28] While many food products were familiar "experience" goods, many characteristics of foods touted by health marketing were not visible to the consumer. One can't see how many calories or vitamins a food has, and it is often unclear what ingredients were used to make it. This meant healthy foods were, at some level, "credence goods," whose utility was difficult for consumers to assess before purchase. Consumers therefore had to trust the seller, or the information on the package.[29]

The challenge for supermarkets was how to convince consumers that information provided about food was credible. Many sought to position themselves as an ally to the consumer who could help rectify the information asymmetries between manufacturers and consumers. But historically, it was not at all clear that supermarkets were consumer allies. When self-service supermarkets first appeared in the 1930s, they were associated with the rise of chain stores, which came under fire in local and then national politics for being unfair competitors to locally owned mom-and-pops grocers. Chain stores also eliminated several means of consumer control of the shopping experience. Instead of a shopper's personal interaction with her local grocer, grocery chains deliberately reconfigured the shopping experience in "large, centrally managed stores that limited personal attention." They molded these new spaces of consumption to transform the housewife's role from that of an actively engaged, locally knowledgeable customer to a passive (or pacified), literate consumer.[30] At grocery stores and market stalls, a savvy shopper knew who to ask to determine the value of a product or negotiate the price down. Self-service supermarkets removed this skill from food retailing.

For decades, housewives-turned-consumer-activists relied on tactics like boycotts to pressure supermarkets, because they felt cheated. In the late 1960s a group of housewife activists dubbed themselves the "Code Breakers." The housewives knew that supermarkets had information about the age of the meat and packaged products on their shelves, but withheld that information from customers. In 1969, now operating under the name National Consumers United, the housewives descended on supermarkets with clipboards. They recorded the numbers on certain food items—bologna, bread, baby formula—and interrogated stock boys about how they knew to restock an item. The women worked on Saturdays, when their husbands were home to watch the kids. Once they had "cracked" the code on a product like peanut butter, they sabotaged old packages so that expired peanut butter couldn't be sold. Eventually, they created a codebook they offered for sale nationally by mail-order.[31] The media attention generated by the National Consumers United's codebreaking prompted more progressive supermarkets to explore introducing "open dating." With open dating in place, customers could access the same "use before" dates supermarkets were already using privately. A Nielsen report indicated that, by 1973, at least half of consumers surveyed looked for some kind of information on food packaging about food freshness or date packaged.[32]

Another area where consumer activism drove supermarket reform was with the unit pricing system. The 1966 Fair Packaging and Labeling Act required that labels show the net quantity of contents, be legible and conspicuous, and define the number of servings in terms of quantity per serving. But while the law addressed deceptive "slack fill" packaging, it did not require that manufacturers calibrate the price of a product to the quantity in the package. Consumer advocacy groups complained that producers tricked them by changing package size, but not the price. They demanded unit pricing, i.e., shelf labels providing the price per weight or per volume, making it easy for shoppers to compare prices on different packaged quantities. First Safeway, and then other supermarket chains, began to run tests of unit pricing to determine whether it was popular with customers. The results were mixed, because most consumers prioritized other product features. Its political appeal and the threat of legislation, however, led many supermarkets to adopt unit pricing. In 1970 the Commonwealth of Massachusetts passed legislation requiring unit pricing. Federal legislators pressured Safeway, the dominant supermarket in Washington, DC, to adopt it soon thereafter.[33]

Starting in 1973, stagnant wages and rising inflation, known as "stagflation," accelerated political interest in standardizing packaging rules and improving price transparency at the supermarket. So did the appearance of an important new packaging and inventory technology, the Universal Product Code, or UPC bar code. In 1974, when supermarkets began to introduce the UPC bar code on retail products, most did so for service efficiency—to make it easier to hire unskilled checkout clerks—and not to manipulate pricing. The UPC barcode sped up checkout, since clerks didn't need to look up items. But it also meant supermarkets didn't have to put price tags on individual goods. The price the computer registered at checkout could potentially differ from the price labeled on the shelf. This would undermine consumers' ability to do comparison shopping. Political lobbying by housewives, including the Code Breakers, helped to introduce item price tags to prevent this potential abuse. Initially the UPC bar code helped the political push for normalizing unit pricing. The UPC's long-term impact would be on market research, as now supermarkets could inventory all purchases at the checkout.[34]

In the early 1970s, perhaps the most heavily publicized supermarket labeling experiments involved nutrition labeling. While the FDA remained uncertain about the future of nutrition labeling, food manufacturers and retailers began to pursue private-label options. At a July 1970 Grocery Manufacturers Association meeting, FDA commissioner Charles Edwards encouraged industry to work with the agency to introduce "voluntary" nutrition labels, as a public-private joint venture. Supermarkets and many manufacturers were interested in labels that would feature proteins and micronutrients like calcium, iron, and vitamin C. Public health advocates wanted information to help consumers with calorie control, fat control, and indicated salt content. The FDA wanted uniform and consistent labels, and developed three labeling schemes to encourage industry to follow a similar approach. By October, certain trade groups, like the Institute of Shortening and Edible Oils, were holding meetings to promote this idea.[35] That same month, nutritionists working at the Consumer Research Institute, a private research center funded by the Grocery Manufacturers Association, published a survey of over eight hundred nutritionists showing strong support for nutrition labeling.[36] That fall, five supermarket chains decided to test nutrition labeling with their customers: Giant Food, Incorporated in Maryland, Jewel Company in Illinois, Kroger Company in Ohio, Consumers' Cooperative in California, and First National Store in Massachusetts.[37] The supermarkets used one or a combination of two labeling schemes proposed by the FDA, and monitored changes in customers' purchasing habits.

By far the most comprehensive and ambitious nutrition labeling experiment was undertaken by Giant Food, a progressive regional supermarket chain based in Maryland near the Washington, DC area. The experiment was led by Esther Peterson, a well-known consumer advocate hired by the company to build its consumer education program. In 1970 Peterson, who had been special assistant for consumer affairs under President Johnson, was named vice president of consumer affairs at Giant Food.[38] Peterson used the job to promote consumerism as an "asset" to retailers rather than a liability.[39] Under Peterson, Giant Food experimented with the unit-pricing system mentioned above, and also with open dating labels.[40] In September 1971 Giant Food launched its nutrition labeling program. The company's president described the labeling experiment as a partnership between consumer and business.[41]

To design its labels, Giant Food stores assembled an impressive committee of expert consultants, including Jean Mayer, James Turner, Helen Nelson (center for Consumer Affairs of the University of Wisconsin), Sidney Margolius (well-known consumer reporter), and representatives from industry, the FDA, and the FTC. The label listed the calories per household portion; grams per portion for carbohydrates, protein, and fats; and a rating on a scale from 0 to 10 for micronutrient vitamins, based on Recommended Daily Allowances (RDAs). For each product, Giant also designed a color-coded pie chart indicating the kinds of nutritional information provided. Giant initially put the labels on fifty-eight lines of its private-brand canned meats, vegetables, and carton milk. In 1972 the supermarket expanded the program and put labels on all Giant-brand foods.[42]

The Giant supermarket experiment was important as a proof of concept for the feasibility and popularity of nutrition labeling. Jean Mayer described Giant's nutrition label as the most preferable among the many being tested because "it is not promotional, and looks the least like one more advertisement," making it "much more effective to a public saturated with and tired of promotional material."[43] It also demonstrated how, as Peterson argued, retailers could become an important ally to consumers. In the supermarket economies of today, Peterson explained, "the retailer is the consumer's purchasing agent, just as I [the housewife] am the purchasing agent for my family."[44] In some ways, this was reminiscent of the 1940s idea of grocers as gatekeepers and guarantors of food quality, except now supermarkets were vendors seeking to build trust in their retail establishments through information tools.

FIGURE 14. A 1971 Giant Food flyer, "Giant Food Is Testing Nutritional Labeling,"
promoting Giant's new nutrition label by referencing "The right to be informed" from
Kennedy's 1962 Consumer Bill of Rights. Courtesy of the Schlesinger Library, Harvard
Radcliffe Institute, with permission from Giant Food, Inc.

CHANGING THE LABELS

Despite the growing popularity of private labeling initiatives, the FDA still had no
clear mandate for legally changing labeling. The 1938 Food, Drugs, and Cosmetics
Act established a three-decade precedent for defending standards of identity
through name labels rather than ingredient or nutrient declarations. The solution
to this legal impasse came from Peter B. Hutt, a lawyer at the Washington-based
law firm Covington & Burling. In 1971 FDA commissioner Charles Edwards
invited Hutt to serve as the agency's chief general counsel in charge of setting and
defending its legal positions. During Hutt's tenure, from 1971 to 1975, the FDA
introduced dramatic changes in how it established and enforced statutes—changes
that cleared the way for the agency to implement food labeling reform.

   Peter Barton Hutt (1934–) was born in Buffalo, New York, where his father
worked in retail dairy. Hutt himself worked as a milkman and at other jobs in
Hutts Dairy during the summers while in school. This personal interest in the milk
industry led him to focus most of his academic work, from Philip Exeter Academy

through Harvard Law School, on the federal government's regulation of milk. At Covington & Burling, Hutt provided legal advice to trade associations and corporate clients on a variety of food and drug topics, including labeling issues. By the late 1960s Hutt began to take a very visible position on nutrition labeling, imitation foods, and weaknesses in the food standards approach to regulating. Through his contacts with Monsanto's Richard Gordon, Hutt drafted the New Foods panel report for the White House Conference, arguing for dramatic changes in the FDA's standards of identity system—in particular, dismantling the imitation label and introducing some form of nutrition labeling.

In September 1971, at the age of thirty-seven, Hutt joined the FDA, replacing William Goodrich as general counsel. Here, Hutt turned to the New Foods panel report as the starting point for FDA food labeling reform. Hutt was one of several people joining the FDA at this time whose activities at the 1969 White House Conference shaped their agenda at the agency. Virgil Wodicka arrived in February 1970, fresh from the panel on "Food Quality," where he recommended nutrition labeling.[45] Ogden "Oggie" Johnson, a member of the "Traditional Foods" conference panel, was hired as director of the Nutrition Division (chosen over Arnold Schaefer, discussed in chapter 3, who headed the CDC nutrition survey during the Hunger debates).

Even before Hutt's arrival, Wodicka and Johnson began laying the groundwork for nutritional labeling, but faced resistance from Goodrich, who believed it was unenforceable. They recommended that FDA labeling incorporate the U.S. RDAs because "it provides an equal and fair comparison across the various products in a class and across product lines."[46] To build ties between the FDA and its potential allies, Johnson spent almost a hundred days traveling around the United States giving speeches to food and consumer groups to "[convince] them that we were on their side."[47] Yet, as the general counsel's office lacked the appetite for a fight, Wodicka and Johnson's efforts remained preliminary.

Soon after his arrival, Hutt formulated a strategy, based on ideas he had voiced at the White House Conference, for addressing the challenges of both imitation labeling and nutrition disclosures. He proposed the FDA could make labeling rules function as a voluntary exception. If companies wanted to create new nonstandard products, or use previously prohibited health claims, they must include a "voluntary" label conforming to the FDA's standards for nutrition information and ingredient lists. In other words, from now on all new foods would be treated like nonstandard foods and would have to provide more label information.

On January 19, 1973, after nearly a year of tinkering by Hutt, Wodicka, and Johnson, the FDA published its final rules on food labeling in the *Federal Register*. These rule changes were wide-ranging and significant. The proposals listed twelve separate but interrelated policy changes.[48] Three of these stood out because they marked a decided departure from the FDA's earlier food standards system: the introduction of a "voluntary" "Nutrition Information" panel; a requirement for ingredient labels on all foods, even standard ones; and a shift away from the punitive imitation label. The decision confirmed that the FDA would change its regulatory strategy from defining standards to assessing the nutritional value of foods.

Whereas the FDA previously required informational panels only on special dietary foods used under special care, now they expanded their use to cover all foods. This recognized that certain nutritional properties and health-promoting tools need not be limited to special foods. As Hutt reasoned at the 1973 background conference for the new label, "The idea of nutrient fortification is commonplace; it's almost beginning to be the rule rather than the exception, and therefore these are no longer special dietary foods, they are conventional foods."[49] Hutt and his colleagues now reasoned that, while some nutrients were of special interest to particular patients, other ingredients had a more popular appeal. The challenge was to design labeling policies that didn't confuse or interfere with these mixed uses for the nutrition label.

Recognizing public interest in the diet-heart thesis and related modified diets, the FDA now allowed companies to distinguish among the amounts of certain kinds of fatty acids in their foods. In doing so, Hutt made clear that the FDA was not taking a position on the diet-heart thesis; this was a medical controversy, for medical professionals to resolve.[50] Instead, the FDA described the new labeling policy as merely a disclosure, much like the broader nutrition labeling reforms. Fat content would appear in the nutrition information panel if the manufacturer wanted it there. By allowing this, the agency effectively reversed its prior position that such health claims had special powers to persuade and mislead ordinary consumers.

Importantly, the FDA staff characterized the nutrition label as "voluntary." Only foods that made health claims about their products, on any label or in any advertisement relating to the product's label, had to carry the standard nutrition information panel. The FDA envisioned labels as disseminating information in the market, and letting consumers decide what foods would be acceptable nutritionally.

Another change in the FDA regulations removed the exemption for ingredients labeling on foods that had a standard of identity. The new rules required that all foods carry an ingredients list, not just nonstandard or imitation foods.[51] Instead of treating standard foods as if they were traditional and self-evident, the FDA now placed them on equal footing with technological foods. Equal footing on the label, however, belied the very unequal impact that ingredient and nutrition labeling would have on the market status of whole foods versus engineered foods. Decades later, food studies critic Gyorgy Scrinis complained, "The more extensively a food is processed, the more opportunities there are for its nutrient profile to be engineered according to the latest nutritional fetish."[52] Thus, labeling processed and whole foods "equal before the law" was deceptive because it ignored the provenance of a food's ingredients and nutritional properties, and placed whole foods, which were harder to tinker with, at a marketing disadvantage when targeting consumers who sought vitamins.

There were some precedents for Hutt's new approach. In 1961 the FDA developed "Breaded Shrimp" standards of identity allowing producers to use whatever "suitable substances which are not food additives" in their breading products provided the ingredients were labeled. Another early deviation from the food standards system involved the "Orange Drink" standards proposed in 1964. Rather than set a strict standard with a minimum orange juice content, the FDA allowed orange drinks with 6 percent or more orange juice to remain on the market, provided they used standard names corresponding to the percent of juice contained. These were prototypes for the FDA shift from defining standards of identity via recipes to "characterizing ingredients."[53] In the FDA's 1972 "common or usual name" rule, which became the basis for the new ingredients labeling, the FDA combined these approaches. Like the Breaded Shrimp standard, this rule focused on setting ingredient ranges for a food's "primary ingredients," those "that have a material bearing on the price or consumer acceptance." Then, if producers labeled the percent or net weight of primary ingredients and chose a suitable standard name label for the product, they could market any novel product without restrictions. In turn, consumers could expect all foods to carry information about their basic ingredients, allowing them to make informed decisions about the product at the point-of-purchase.

Universal ingredients labeling was perhaps the most popular of the FDA's reforms. Food regulators believed ingredients disclosure solved what they referred to as Gresham's law of food recipes—if unlabeled, bad ingredients in the marketplace drive out the good. Hutt liked to explain how the labels conveyed information to consumers using his favorite dessert, cherry pie: "You can set a standard of identity and standard of quality for cherry pies, which is a long horrendous procedure; the other way of going about it is requiring on the label that the percent by weight of the cherries be labeled, so that I would have three cherry pies there and I could pick the one with the highest quality, namely the greatest amount of cherries per weight of the total pie."[54] Hutt presented ingredients labeling as an unproblematic kind of information disclosure with a certain democratic appeal. This resonated with a strand of Jeffersonian liberal individualism in American politics; the knowledgeable citizen was best suited to calculate their own risk and reward. The label situated choice with consumers, avoided inflexible and tedious hearings, and most importantly, Hutt reasoned, let the market test the strength or weaknesses of a given food recipe in terms of what consumers want.

Yet ingredients disclosure was not self-evident in every case. The disclosure of certain ingredients, subject to intense public health interest, had long raised problems for the FDA and its policies on implied health claims. One of the oldest examples of this were turn-of-the-century nomenclature battles over substitute sweeteners like "grape sugar," also known as "glucose" and "starch sugar." Different names for the same ingredient had different connotations for the public, with some names evoking chemical adulterants while others were accepted as natural additives.[55] Another example was 1970s disputes about how to label the different vegetable oils food manufacturers used in their products. There were two concerns. First, in the wake of the 1960s diet-heart controversy, certain vegetable oils, such as palm and coconut oil, were recognized as less healthy than others. Requiring disclosure for these edible oils would effectively be a negative health claim for companies still using them. Second, food manufacturers commonly swapped the vegetable oils in certain foods, like salad dressing, depending on market pricing or availability. To address this, many companies proposed the FDA permit "and / or" labeling (e.g., "contains soybean and / or cottonseed oil") in the ingredients panel.[56] Companies such as Procter & Gamble, for example, questioned whether consumers needed to know what specific kind of oil / fat was used if it was not nutritionally different from another one.[57] This question of chemical "substantial equivalence" revealed how information labels could disguise as much as they revealed about experts' assumptions about ingredients.

While Hutt and others at the FDA presented the new labeling system as an intuitive and straightforward update, it entailed a significant reconfiguration of how the agency handled food markets. The new rules did more than just provide nutrition and ingredient information to consumers. The new labeling system registered a new theory of the state and its role for the consumer, a new vision of what food is and how it should be defined, and a new philosophy of health and personal responsibility.

IMAGINING THE "INFORMED CONSUMER"

One could criticize the FDA's new rules as an expansion of governmental powers and administrative overreach. They were created by unelected staff members, not a democratically elected legislative body. While the public could submit comments on the new rules, there were no extended public hearings where public advocates could have their day in court, so to speak. To counter the view that this was regulation by fiat, the FDA sought to frame nutrition and ingredient labeling as hands-off policies, rules that primarily worked through the market and through consumer choice. Such market-oriented regulations succeeded because they were "created in the belief that putting information in the hands of the public will enable people to make informed choices that will lead to improved social outcomes."[58] They are an example of the turn to "market forces" that historian Robert Self claims realigned American democracy in this period, as the state shifted away from being a guarantor of positive rights and toward acting as a provisioner of negative rights of liberty.[59] The FDA promoted its reforms as value-neutral by capitalizing on a growing ideology of "informationism" that empowered the informed consumer as the new protagonist of enlightened governance.

One way the FDA naturalized the reach of its new rules was by emphasizing their basis in science. While the FDA sought to remove barriers to innovation in value-added foods, it still had to ensure that removing the punitive imitation label did not encourage production of cheap knockoffs. The FDA thus needed a new standard for measuring food quality that was legitimately discriminating yet could be framed as politically and economically neutral criteria. This new measuring stick was nutrition science. The agency favored nutritional measures over other methods for evaluating food because it facilitated the quantification and accountability of information, thus making FDA labeling disclosure policies procedurally fair and more politically neutral.

Indeed, the final rules in the *Federal Register* defined "inferior content" through a product's anticipated nutritional profile. Instead of scrapping the standards entirely, the FDA established nutritional standards for specific foods. Any product providing less than 98 percent of the anticipated proteins and essential nutrients for that standard food must carry the "imitation" label. Fats and calories, however, could be reduced without requiring the label. This approach effectively endorsed the ethos of "negative nutrition," but made the policy look neutral by disguising the double standard on different nutrients behind specific objective thresholds.[60]

Another way the FDA sought to present its position as neutral was by conducting consumer studies. FDA staff commissioned the Consumer Research Institute to conduct consumer surveys and tests to establish what consumers sought in a label, what they thought of different formats, and how they used them.[61] As early as December 1970 the FDA initiated consumer acceptability tests to explore different proposed label formats.[62] Ogden Johnson, the director of the FDA's Division of Nutrition, ordered staff to focus on three alternatives: (1) a numerical system listing nutrients as a function of the RDA; (2) a pictorial system incorporating symbols like stars or smiley faces to indicate the nutritional profile; or (3) a verbal system using such adjectives as "very good" or "excellent." The survey results indicated consumers' strong preference for numbers over words and pictures. The report hypothesized that consumers preferred the numerical labels for both their precision and their seriousness. As the report's author noted, "Nutrition is apparently an important subject in the mind of a consumer, and, should be approached seriously."[63]

A central characteristic of the 1973 label design was that nutrition information be a quantifiable statement of fact, not a government-sponsored advertisement or editorializing. Graphics seemed less serious and even a bit patronizing. But as historian Ted Porter showed, Americans have long exhibited a "trust in numbers." Porter describes how "quantification works as a technology of trust," substituting numerical objectivity for personal trust, in the process generating a politics of knowledge.[64] The knowledge politics here centered on which language for food most met the institutional need for objectivity and impartiality. The FDA's 1973 rules emphasized objective, quantifiable values specifically as they related to nutrition levels. Other markers of quality, such as "natural" or "organic," had no place on the new labels.[65] In an atmosphere where dairy industry and vegetable oil companies were competing against one another with conflicting data in food advertisements, numbers about nutrients, rather than statements about foods, appeared more concrete, more objective, and less politicized. If the government named a food as healthy or unhealthy, industry would argue it was an unfair attack; if, however, it named a nutrient, it was just information. This helps explain the lack of political pushback against the FDA's new labeling rules: Everyone could support a public campaign for more nutrition information. It was only when the FDA sought to tell consumers what they ought to *do* with that information that the politics crept back in.

Under the previous system of labeling, the FDA was concerned with protecting the ordinary consumer, a consumer not especially concerned with health. With the new nutrition labeling, the FDA redefined ordinary as informed—someone who might want to consider health-related information in their choices about food. Indeed, a 1975 GAO report on food labeling emphasized the FDA's statutory obligation to improve nutrition labeling, quoting the 1966 Fair Packaging and Labeling Act: "Informed consumers are essential to the fair and efficient functioning of a free market economy."[66] The FDA's interest in empowering an informed consumer was not limited to food. The agency also experimented in the 1970s with a "Patient Package Insert" label providing how-to-use and risk information for certain over-the-counter and prescription lifestyle drugs.[67] The New Deal concept of food standards, which did not carry information labels, was no longer adequate for protecting consumers' interests. The turn to information labeling reflected a different rationale: use labels to empower consumers to decide for themselves and empower companies to design "good" foods, but don't interfere with the consumer's freedom of choice.

The FDA's new administrative procedures also reflected this informational turn. Under Hutt, the FDA established regulations directly by publishing rules in the U.S. *Federal Register* instead of after elaborate, years-long public hearings. So long as the FDA addressed all submitted comments in its subsequent revised rules, the agency could make the published rules final and binding.[68] Hutt believed this allowed the FDA to circumvent public spectacles by streamlining the comments process. He also reasoned that the comments often raised scientific or technical issues not suited to settlement in trial-type hearings. Rather, they called for expert management within the FDA, where "government administrators can be trusted to exercise discretion."[69] For Hutt, this new practice was part of a larger shift in the FDA's regulatory style away from reactive regulation that responded to industry abuses and toward preventive or anticipatory regulation, providing industry guidance. As Hutt argued, "Litigation in many instances represents the failure of effective regulation."[70]

On the surface, the new labeling rules appeared to expand the FDA's powers. They were nevertheless situated within an ideological climate of regulatory thinking based on rational economics. "The market," as understood by policymakers, had come a long way from the market*place* and the physical market infrastructures that the food standards system addressed in the 1930s. Many new economic ideas in this period, including "rational expectation" models and "supply-side economics," suggested that the market was too complex to be steered by government bureaucrats, even expert bureaucrats. New economic theories, such as rational choice theory, supplanted the Keynesian model of a managed economy with a "microphysics of individual political action."[71] In this new model, the individual consumer was the locus of political organization. The government, by contrast, was a source of potentially corrupt "rent-seeking" or a manipulative "new class" of managers, experts, and professionals who dominated a suspect and overly indulgent "therapeutic state."[72] By appealing to market choice and individual choice, FDA officials could sell the new labeling rules as "lean" governance that gave citizens-as-consumers a vote, a framing that elided the many backstage decisions that FDA and industry made in determining what went on and what stayed off the label.

In the 1970s the FDA was beginning to increase its engagement with the public. In July 1972 its official magazine, *FDA Papers,* which had targeted an industry audience, was rechristened as *FDA Consumer,* with the intention to inform consumers about FDA activities and official public health concerns.[73] FDA officials saw the new nutrition labeling rules as a further opportunity for a public education program. The main feature of the FDA public campaign, "Read the Label, Set a Better Table," launched May 30, 1974, was a fourteen-minute public service announcement (PSA) that featured Dick Van Dyke in a supermarket encouraging consumers to "read the label" and explaining the new nutrition information now found on some food labels. The public service advertising spots with Van Dyke, and others with Pearl Bailey, had a limited run on television and radio. Industry and consumer groups were encouraged to reproduce the FDA's PSA, brochure, and poster, and to contact the FDA consumer affairs officer for assistance with the campaign.[74] However, the FDA's efforts on public education remained limited. Nutrition education was still almost entirely the USDA's domain, and would remain so until the late 1980s, when the FDA created the Center for Food Safety and Nutrition (CFSAN). CFSAN began developing nutrition education outreach programs and played a lead role in 1990s labeling reforms, discussed in chapter 5. Indeed, a special issue of *FDA Consumer* in 1981, commemorating the seventy-fifth anniversary of the 1906 Pure Food and Drug Act, didn't mention nutrition labeling in its histories of the FDA and recent significant milestones, despite listing "Truthful, Informative Labeling" among its core missions.[75]

When the FDA's new nutrition information label was set to become effective in 1974, Johnson, director of the FDA's Division of Nutrition, sketched out the main lingering uncertainties about the program: "The questions that keep coming back to us are: Will the consumers use nutrition labeling? Can they use it? How will they be assisted so that its use will be appropriate?" These questions would take time to answer, and at best he expected changes in consumer behavior to occur over five to ten years rather than immediately. The FDA, according to Johnson, believed that only "10 to 15 percent of the adult population on modified diets" would ultimately use the label. To promote the use of the new labels, the Department of Health, Education, and Welfare (the FDA's parent department), along with the USDA, Advertising Council, and Grocery Manufacturers Association, developed a national campaign with the simple message, "Food is more than something to eat."

Johnson had another marker of effectiveness in mind. Ultimately, he suggested, manufacturers would respond to the new transparency by ensuring "that their products are produced so that nutrition qualities are maintained."[76] That is, even if most consumers didn't understand or act upon the new labels, companies would reformulate their products for the supposed health benefit of all consumers. The irony of this observation was that it revealed the antidemocratic nature of market-driven reform. Not all consumers were informed, or wielded the purchasing power to shape corporate product design. Truth-in-labeling reforms might cater to the motivations and interests of a niche of discerning or choosy informed consumers, but would potentially have consequences for all consumers.

THE ADVENT OF NUTRITIONISM

The FDA's change of heart on the imitation label followed a decades-long battle over how best to regulate the new vitamin, low-cal, and low-fat diet products surging in popularity since the 1950s and 1960s. By the end of the 1960s, most medical professional associations had adopted some measure of support for the new diet foods as an appropriate public health tool for managing personal health. The "cholesterol controversy," for example, linking risk for heart disease, cholesterol levels, and certain fatty foods, particularly those with animal fats, had a huge impact on certain food sectors. Margarine and filled milk, once considered iconic examples of economic adulteration, were now potentially value-added health foods. Vegetable oil companies aggressively advertised their products as better for your heart than similar dairy and meat foods. The FDA's prior policies against health advertising on foods created uncertainty about whether companies could make marketing claims that their products were doctor-recommended. The new rules allowed food manufacturers to make claims through the seemingly neutral language of nutritional labeling, but they also caused the proliferation of reformulated foods and the widespread nutritionism that critics decry today.

In the last ten years food studies scholars have made various critiques of "nutritionism," broadly defined as a pervasive ideology that reduces food to its nutritional values and uses for health. This narrow framing of food as merely the sum of its nutritional components has eclipsed other broader, and in some scholars' views, better ways of understanding food as cultural and a central element of personal well-being—not just a vehicle for health. When tracing the rise of this ideology, Gyorgy Scrinis and others argue that nutritionism emerged with the industrialization of food and the marketing of processed foods in place of whole foods.[77] They identify the 1970s and 1980s as its arrival moment, and largely attribute nutritionism's rise to how the food industry captured the nutrition profession and appropriated nutrition discourse for marketing industrial foods. While the FDA presented "Nutrition Information" labels as neutral disclosures, the new system didn't differentiate between fats or calories from processed foods versus natural foods. In this way it normalized what the earlier food standards system was developed to stymie: the proliferation of non-standard, "fabricated" or processed foods. Nutritionism was a symptom of a broader political problem of informationism, in this case the idea that scientific information could replace food knowledge and practice. The nutrition information and ingredients panels, in other words, signaled a new era in food labeling.

A primary example of this transition involved filled milk, a product once reviled for its artifice. Filled milk products were dairy products reconstituted with fats from sources other than dairy cows, often vegetable oils. The dairy industry lobbied intensively against them to protect itself from competition with cheaper, often foreign sources of fats. Since the Filled Milk Act of 1923 and the 1938 Supreme Court case *United States v. Carolene Products Company,* discussed in chapter 1, interstate sales of filled milk were effectively illegal. In 1972 a district court in the case of *Milnot Co. v. Richardson* reversed that decision. The same product banned by the earlier 1938 court decision, "Milnot," a blend of fat-free milk and vegetable soya oil to which vitamins A and D were added, could now be sold as a legitimate, healthy alternative to milk. The 1972 decision, in effect, ended filled milk restrictions, opening the floodgates to imitation products so long as they could claim to be low in calories or fat.

The FDA was quick to follow this turning tide. In the 1973 labeling reforms, they included a model standard for "Mellorine," an ice cream substitute using vegetable oils, which since 1955 had to be labeled imitation ice cream. By publishing a standard for Mellorine, the FDA signaled to industry that it now encouraged non-traditional, novel, low-fat health foods. Mellorine had to be fortified with protein and vitamins to be "nutritionally equivalent" to ice cream, but could be marketed as a separate food (not unlike margarine), without facing legal challenges from ice cream producers.[78] It was a model for creating novel industrial foods with health-promoting properties.

In a 1973 interview, the FDA's Johnson explained the balance that the agency sought between old and new, between traditional and modern foods. On the one hand, Johnson was concerned about how much food people had added to their diet since World War II, specifically more meat, and how this could cause people to become "grotesquely obese." He was also concerned about "whenever a new product comes into the marketplace and displaces a traditional food that is considered a good source of nutrients," something that was increasingly a problem since so many meals were consumed outside the home. This outsourcing of cooking changed the kinds of foods Americans ate—for example, French-fried potatoes instead of "potatoes purchased fresh"—as well as Americans' awareness of what they ate. Labels weren't available for foods purchased in restaurants, where the use of "alternates or substitutes" might go unnoticed. On the other hand, Johnson mentioned soybean as a potentially beneficial new source of protein, and one that had become increasingly popular because of rising meat prices. New protein sources like soybean, Johnson argued, would have to be "labeled so that consumers know what they are" and be "nutritionally equivalent to traditional sources of protein." Ultimately, Johnson argued, nutrition labeling would meet people's "informational needs" better than older tools like the USDA's "Basic Four" Guide because it was "a mechanism to identify foods that will work for both new fabricated foods as well as the traditional foods."[79]

In 1973 the FDA's Division of Consumer Studies conducted a national survey to assess how consumers were encountering the new labels. The FDA Consumer Nutrition Knowledge Survey "consisted of 92 questions posed to 1,500 persons with primary responsibility for food purchases for their households," with participants representing "every region of the country . . . all income and education levels, ages, etc."[80] Results showed the American consumer was becoming diet conscious, with the majority of respondents indicating that "someone in their household took vitamins every day or almost every day." A similar proportion indicated that "someone in their home was trying either to lose or gain weight."[81] Respondents stated that they preferred the nutrition label to standard-recipe labels, but only about one in four indicated they actively sought out "information on the nutritional value of the food." When asked what was missing on nutrition labels, participants mentioned specific ingredients not listed on labels, such as certain preservatives or additives they were worried about. The study's architects interpreted this as a "misunderstanding of nutrition labels," because it seemed to confuse food's ingredient components with the nutritional properties of those components.[82] Another interpretation, however, was that consumers used ingredient lists as a proxy for other kinds of health concerns, such as how processed or artificial a food was.

For the FDA's new food labeling system to endure, it had to withstand legal scrutiny. Almost immediately after the rules went into effect, the Federation of Homemakers, the consumer organization led by Ruth Desmond active in the 1960s food standards hearings, brought a lawsuit against the FDA for no longer enforcing the imitation label nor promulgating new standards for substitutes. The federation's central position was nearly identical to Scrinis's critique of nutritionism decades later.

They argued the FDA had reduced imitation to merely nutritional equivalence; they noted past court cases sustaining the imposition of imitation labels based on a much broader range of factors, including "texture, smell, taste, appearance, manufacture, packaging and marketing."[83] The court, however, sided with the FDA, recognizing the agency's position that "the imitation requirement ... had unduly deterred the development of new food products," and also its more principled emphasis on nutrition equivalence as the preferred language for consumer protection.[84] Food components—ingredients and especially nutrition—would become the new axis around which "normal" and "abnormal," and "natural" and "artificial" would realign.

The Federation of Homemakers' defeat in court indicated how the status of housewife activists in food politics had changed. In her survey of twentieth-century "politics of the pantry," historian Emily Twarog describes the 1970s as "the end of an era of the citizen housewife and collective action on behalf of domestic politics." In the 1970s feminism became mainstream, and many feminists saw housewives as a vestige of an old political order.[85] Nevertheless, talk about a "family crisis" was rampant, implicating a wide range of social and political issues. Crisis talk arose from Americans' "deep anxieties about a culture of moral permissiveness" signaled by rising rates of divorce and single motherhood, sexual licentiousness, and the growing visibility of feminists and gays.[86] Historian Robert Self describes the profound realignment accompanying the end of "breadwinner liberalism," and the rise of "breadwinner conservatism," manifest in the Hard Hat Riot by workers angry over the loss of their living wage. These contests over the boundaries between public and private life presaged the "culture wars" of the 1980s and 1990s. And these contests had even more mundane manifestations, such as lamentations on the death of the family meal and the rise of snacking and processed food.[87] Subsequently conservatives reframed domestic politics as "kitchen-table politics," less about systemic reforming or food equity and more about defending "family values."[88] Housewives' associations would play a diminished role in progressive food politics, as consumer advocacy organizations, like the CSPI, gained influence, building their authority on claims about biomedicine and science rather than domestic identity.

THE ANTI-REGULATION BACKLASH

The trend toward "hands off" food governance continued even after Democrat Jimmy Carter was elected president in 1976. Carter opened his presidency stating, "One of my Administration's major goals is to free the American people from the burden of over-regulation." The end of the Civil Aeronautics Board in 1978 was the first of a series of actions dismantling New Deal regulatory institutions now seen as overly burdensome.[89] Attacks on the Environmental Protection Agency peaked in the late 1970s, foreshadowing the wave of anti-federal regulation in the 1980s.[90] Numerous industries now lobbied against the so-called "toxicity crisis" of the

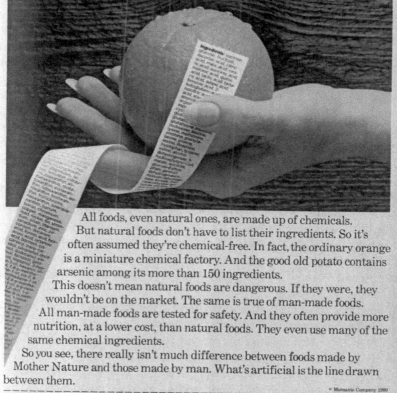

Mother Nature is lucky her products don't need labels.

All foods, even natural ones, are made up of chemicals. But natural foods don't have to list their ingredients. So it's often assumed they're chemical-free. In fact, the ordinary orange is a miniature chemical factory. And the good old potato contains arsenic among its more than 150 ingredients.

This doesn't mean natural foods are dangerous. If they were, they wouldn't be on the market. The same is true of man-made foods.

All man-made foods are tested for safety. And they often provide more nutrition, at a lower cost, than natural foods. They even use many of the same chemical ingredients.

So you see, there really isn't much difference between foods made by Mother Nature and those made by man. What's artificial is the line drawn between them.

© Monsanto Company 1980

For a free booklet explaining the risks and benefits of chemicals, mail to: Monsanto, 800 Lindbergh Blvd., St. Louis, Mo. 63166. Dept. A3NA-NY1

Name _____

Address _____

City & state _____ Zip _____

Monsanto

Without chemicals, life itself would be impossible.

FIGURE 15. Chemical companies, such as Monsanto here, respond to the "toxicity crisis" by highlighting consumers' inconsistent attitudes about what they consider to be "natural" versus "artificial" chemicals. Source: Monsanto advertisement, "Mother Nature is lucky her products don't need labels," *New Yorker* 56 (April 21, 1980): 79.

1960s and 1970s, the increased attention to chemical risks by consumer advocates and environmentalists, and battles within federal regulatory agencies over how to manage those risks.[91]

Food regulation was not immune to this anti-regulation movement. In 1979, when President Jimmy Carter, whose father had owned a peanut farm, outlined his proposal for regulatory reform, he singled out the FDA's system of identity standards as an example of poor regulation and complained: "It should not have taken 12 years and a hearing record of over 100,000 pages for the FDA to decide what percentage of peanuts there ought to be in peanut butter."[92] Carter's quip invoked the popular sentiment that some issues were too trivial or too personal to be matters for the federal state. The Carter administration did pursue some food labeling reforms. A 1975 General Accounting Office (GAO) review recommended that the FDA adopt daily percent labeling to help consumers make better decisions in food selection.[93] From 1977 to 1980 the FDA held hearings on possible revisions and drafted new proposed rules for the *Federal Register.* Ultimately, however, these proposals were shelved, a casualty of the Carter administration's general preference to let individuals, rather than government, decide.

During this time, the FDA experienced renewed challenges to its authority to regulate the food-drug line in the emerging alternative health markets. Public backlash was now buoyed by both alternative "fringe" health practitioners *and* the food additives and dietary supplements industries seeking to expand their markets. Two legislative developments substantially constrained the FDA: the 1976 Vitamins and Minerals (or "Proxmire") Amendments, and the Saccharine Study and Labeling Act of 1977.

While the 1973 nutrition labeling rules sanctioned some forms of vitamin advertising and enrichment, FDA officials remained concerned about unchecked vitamania. They continued to embrace policies centered around a so-called "food first approach," meaning that foods, rather than supplements, should be the main source of nutrition in ordinary markets.[94] The FDA continued to seek to moderate excessive levels of vitamins in foods, and to discredit proponents of "vitamin megadosing."

One of these proponents was Nobel laureate Linus Pauling, whose 1970 book, *Vitamin C and the Common Cold,* advocated using large quantities of vitamin C and other vitamins to prevent common illnesses like the cold. Of greater concern were the publications by and press attention given to Adelle Davis. For years Davis had been touting alternative diets and vitamins as cures for many illnesses. Her popularity rested on her claim that people could regain control over their lives through simple practices such as taking dietary supplements daily. In the early 1970s she received media attention for her claims that megadoses of vitamins staved off many common illnesses. She appeared on Johnny Carson's *The Tonight Show* five times during 1972 and 1973, and a 1972 *Time* magazine article dubbed her the "High Priestess of Nutrition."[95] Not only did FDA staff consider Davis's and Pauling's claims to be nutrition quackery, unsupported by science, but they also feared that, in certain contexts, megadosing might lead to poisoning. For this reason, the FDA adopted a vitamin-mineral thresholds approach that allowed legitimate enrichment while providing the FDA a tool to address extreme "promiscuous, unnecessary fortification."[96]

The new regulations on vitamin supplements provoked a fierce populist backlash, and also the attention of Congress. The passage of the 1976 Vitamins and Minerals Amendments reflected the personal zeal of Senator William Proxmire, a Wisconsin Democrat, who advocated the legislation to address the FDA's "conflict of interest" and its collusion with big pharmacy at the expense of small health-food businesses. Proxmire himself was a health enthusiast, having published a self-help book, *You Can Do It! Senator Proxmire's Exercise, Diet and Relaxation Plan*, in 1973. He had a history of clashes with the FDA.[97] In 1973 Proxmire addressed the Senate on the "hostility and prejudice" of the FDA toward small retailers of health products. In 1974, during hearings on the Proxmire bill, he claimed the FDA was "trying to play God" in setting restrictive rules on RDAs and labeling. In 1976, after two years of failed attempts, the Proxmire Amendments passed, significantly curtailing the FDA's powers with regard to vitamin supplements: "The Secretary may not classify any natural or synthetic vitamin or mineral . . . as a drug solely because it exceeds the level of potency which the Secretary determines is nutritionally rational or useful."[98] For the first time in history, Congress had moved to restrict the FDA's powers. The amendments reflected a growing political movement that reframed self-help dieting as an individual liberty, and questioned governmental agencies' authority to decide what was "sound science" or "nutrition quackery."

The Saccharine Study and Labeling Act of 1977 followed soon after the Proxmire Amendments passed. On March 9, 1977, the FDA announced its intention to ban the artificial sweetener saccharine, which studies showed caused bladder cancer in laboratory rats. Echoing the agency's reasoning for banning cyclamate eight years earlier, the new FDA commissioner, Donald Kennedy, argued in congressional testimony, "We should not allow even weak carcinogens in the environment if we can help it . . . our systems may already be overloaded." Public reaction again was fierce and swift. This time the FDA was seeking to remove the only remaining artificial sweetener on the market, a sweetener with nearly a hundred years of history. Moreover, as food studies scholar Carolyn de la Peña noted about this "saccharine rebellion," by the end of the 1970s many people had developed a weariness with alarming risk messages and a distrust of government agencies' priorities in protecting consumers. On the day of the FDA's announcement, one saccharine supporter wrote: "My life is one big cancer risk, which I am powerless to control. Surely, then, if I decide to take one further, very minor, risk of developing cancer, it must be my decision." The FDA received some 40,000 letters complaining about the ban. Consumers repeatedly noted the contradiction between policies permitting the use of tobacco products, known to cause cancer (albeit not regulated by the FDA at the time), but prohibiting a product whose carcinogenic risk for humans was uncertain and hypothetical.[99] In November 1977 Congress passed the Saccharine Study and Labeling Act, imposing a two-year moratorium against any ban on the additive, instead mandating a warning label for its risks.[100]

It is ironic that the FDA's 1969 cyclamate ban had been behind-closed-doors and unilateral, while the FDA's 1977 saccharine decision reflected a decade of institutional reform where decision-making now involved consultation with outside scientists, public comment and congressional hearings; yet it was the saccharine ban that experienced a swift political reversal.[101] One reading of the saccharine backlash was that consumers spoke, Congress replied, and the FDA was humbled. Another interpretation was that, after a decade of lobbying, regulated industries had convinced the public to be skeptical of government officials and any so-called liberal consensus.[102] De la Peña's account of the saccharine rebellion shares certain features with the tactical "market populism" promoted by businesses in the late 1960s and early 1970s as a backlash to government oversight. Corporations often disguised transparently self-interested lobbying using practices such as "astroturfing," where companies created and funded seemingly independent organizations to simulate a grass-roots political movement. Coca-Cola, for example, joined other artificial sweetener businesses to create the Calorie Control Council (CCC), which ran radio ads and newspaper pieces against the FDA saccharine ban.[103] These organizations targeted specific regulations, but also pushed back more generally against what industry saw as a threatening leftist radical movement undermining business. Businesses ran public relations campaigns attacking the government and the "liberal" consumer movement as underestimating average consumers' ability to make decisions for themselves. One advertising executive complained: "The consumer movement sees 'the typical consumer as a moron, incapable of exercising even the most elementary judgement in the marketplace.' The result was that it sought to take 'the consumer into protective custody.'"[104] These campaigns, according to historian Dan Glickman, turned "liberal" into a dirty word by the end of the 1970s. The saccharine and vitamin supplement campaigns were particularly effective in mobilizing a "sociology of attachment" to specific consumable goods. One's personal taste for things, an artificial sweetener or the promise of surplus health from a vitamin, created a seemingly spontaneous political constituency around a product.[105]

The Proxmire Amendments and the saccharine act reflected widespread hostility toward and distrust of the FDA's "meddling" with individuals' food choices: the first created an entirely new category of product, "dietary supplements," with a special regulatory status distinct from foods or drugs; the second was a direct repudiation of FDA authority to interpret risk, revealing a growing preference for using informational labels and relying on consumer choice over administrative expert discretion. Indeed, FDA commissioner Alexander Schmidt, in a 1976 speech he gave to food law professionals not long before he would be replaced by Commissioner Kennedy, recognized these populist concerns as a legitimate, perennial, even "elemental" American tradition. He compared these concerns, raised in that bicentennial celebration year, to "a somewhat more insistent assertion by the American people for less intrusive government" in 1776.[106]

The FDA's 1973 nutrition and ingredient labeling reforms weathered these assaults on the government because the labels became part of an emerging cultural movement emphasizing personal health as a form of self-actualization, and viewing risk management as a responsibility of the individual. By 1980 sociologist Robert Crawford identified a wide variety of self-help practices that reflected an ideology he called "healthism." Healthism encouraged individuals to focus on maintaining and improving health as a core value for self-development. The 1970s focus on the informed consumer and this new healthism shared two key elements. The first was a political shift toward individualism. As a social movement, healthism reinforced "the privatization of the struggle for generalized well-being."[107] It was arguably a secular example of Americans' general turning away from public pursuits in this period, and inward toward personal projects—in the words of one historian, "fantastic voyages of self-exploration"—with spiritual analogs to the rise of born-again Christians and New Age spiritual groups.[108] A second important element of healthism was how it registered a shift in the notion of dietary risk and the importance of preventive self-help medicine. In his 1980 article, Robert Crawford noted two different senses of "healthism": one entailing the extension of professional control of medicine, and a second broader sense of healthism as an "extension of the range of social phenomena mediated by the concepts of health and illness."[109] Nutrition labeling furthered this second sense, and mostly circumscribed the first. Nutrition labels encouraged consumers to use biomedical models of food, diet and risk, but without depending on doctors for advice.

The 1976 Proxmire Amendments and 1977 Saccharine Labeling and Information Act showed how previously marginal groups were now able to recharacterize what was once considered nutritional quackery as individual liberties and legitimate lifestyle differences. Nutrition labeling wrested control of diet information and counseling from doctors and handed it to consumers. For food, it represented a marketization, rather than a medicalization, of health information. It reflected a political shift in understandings of consumer protection. Under the previous labeling system the FDA focused on protecting the ordinary consumer, a consumer not especially concerned with health; with nutrition labeling the FDA redefined ordinary to include informed consumers, who might want to consider health-related information in their choices about food. This ethos of personal responsibility became an important thread in the fabric of late twentieth-century "lifestyle politics," a political identity linking personal lifestyles to self-definition, political mobilization, and, increasingly, checks and limits on government-curtailed liberties, discussed further in chapter 6. Risky behaviors were viewed as an individual's personal liberty but also a potential burden on public resources. Product bans curtailed people's fundamental right to enjoy risky business. Informative labeling, including warning labels, however, refocused attention on individual choice and revived an earlier market ethos of self-care. This call for individual responsibility reflected a broad disenchantment with government institutions in this decade, which carried into subsequent decades.

CONCLUSIONS

The FDA's embrace of voluntary nutritional labeling in 1973 changed its approach to and role in food governance. The nutrition information and ingredients labeling rules signaled the FDA's endorsement of new informational markets for food, especially diet and health information, and ended the agency's four-decade-long investment in setting food standards of identity. Indeed, the FDA grew substantially in this period, from a $5 million budget in 1955 to over $320 million in 1980, with a staff increase from less than 1,000 to over 7,000.[110] But even as policies expanded and the agency grew, this didn't quite mean "more government." Rather, the FDA's voluntary labeling system changed the structure of food markets, creating a new playing field where nutrition claims could be tested—a form of "contrived competition" in food markets.[111] In one sense, regulation here was a source of innovation.[112] Companies built marketing campaigns around the new allowances on nutrition information labeling. Thus, in 1977 the baby food company Beech Nut ran a "read the label" advertising campaign highlighting all the information consumers could find on product labels, including the nutrition and ingredients panels.[113] The number of new health foods on the market exploded in the 1980s, with other old foods rebranded for health.

Tying policy to informative labeling also represented a shift from the administrative state, or "activist state," to the state as an information broker, or "state as umpire."[114] By introducing voluntary labeling, the FDA softened the earlier system of rigid, government-mandated food standards. If standards represented FDA bureaucrats overseeing public trials and tests for defining a food, labeling fit a neoliberal ethos of personal and private responsibility for public matters and market-embedded tools for empowering the consumer. The "ideology of individual responsibility" served right-wing interests in dismantling the state and streamlining it.[115] Food labeling appropriated the anti-institutional, anti-bureaucratic message of the 1960s left, converting it to a program for small government and consumerism.[116] Informational labeling privatized and individualized the ethics of diet, health, and self-care by placing information on point-of-purchase tools, all blended in a government program promoting healthy populations through consumer protection and education. It thus exemplifies a neoliberal style of "governmentality," disposing citizens toward healthy choices that match government goals, shared and bolstered by industry.[117]

And yet: The FDA's embrace of voluntary labeling wasn't simply a turn to the right. It was highly popular with left-leaning consumer-interest organizers like Esther Petersen and Michael Jacobson. Consumer advocates and government reformers touted food labeling initiatives as examples of how the freedom of information would improve transparency and good governance. "Informational regulation" was about empowering individual responsibility, but by employing a medium that shifted citizens' agency to the realm of consumption. Thus nutrition labeling blurred the boundaries separating education, information, and advertising, and more broadly the dividing line between public and private. In the late twentieth century, it was one way that governments, particularly in the U.S., increasingly cultivated the "consumer-citizen."[118] Nutrition labeling reinforced the new business model of niche marketing, and the process by which the new health language of nutrition (and a new cult of convenience) was fragmenting and reformulating traditional understandings of food. It was the beginning of a new nutritional biosociality around dieting and lifestyle foods related to health.

What began in the 1970s accelerated in the 1980s with the Reagan Revolution. At his inaugural address on January 20, 1981, Reagan famously declared: "Government is not the solution to our problem, government is the problem."[119] When Reagan became president, the flurry of activity surrounding nutrition label reform in 1979 and 1980 came to an abrupt end.[120] The FDA's new system, based on information disclosure rather than standards, soon presented a new problem, the very problem FDA officials had feared in the 1930s through the 1950s. Consumers reported feeling overwhelmed by the volume of information, confused by conflicting claims they encountered about food and nutrition. In the 1980s this problem of information overload grew into a prominent food policy concern, and by the 1990s there would be a new period of nutrition labeling reform.

5

A Government Brand

Information Infrastructures

The 1980s and 1990s were awash in optimism about the transformative value of *information*. From cultural guru Stewart Brand's 1984 claim that "information wants to be free" to Vice President Al Gore's references to the "information super-highway," Americans embraced the democratic potential of information-sharing platforms providing more choices and greater diversity in the "marketplace of ideas."[1] That more information was equated with greater consumer empowerment shows how far people had come to naturalize the informational turn in politics, and how much Americans took for granted market-based reform. This optimism, however, was tempered by concerns that the free flow of information might cause "information overload."[2] Too much information might confuse consumers more.

As the Food and Drug Administration eased up on food-labeling rules, consumers encountered a greater variety of health claims on foods. Confusing health information was such a problem that in 1989 Louis W. Sullivan, U.S. secretary of health and human services, declared, "The grocery store has become the tower of Babel, and consumers need to be linguists, scientists, and mind readers to understand many of the labels they see."[3] The explosion of choice at the supermarket, partly due to the FDA easing food standards, increased consumer doubt and second-guessing. Steven Lubar's 1993 study of "infoculture" opened by stating, "I swim in an ocean of information." Many consumers felt like they were drowning in information—especially at the grocery store.[4]

In 1993 the FDA introduced the now-familiar "Nutrition Facts" panel to help guide consumers through the plethora of information they encountered when shopping. Between 1990, when Congress passed the Nutrition Labeling and

Education Act (NLEA) mandating a new food label, and 1993, when the Nutrition Facts panel was implemented, the FDA confronted numerous claims from consumer advocates, food producers, and other food interests groups about what information consumers needed or wanted, and how the FDA should best represent that. These debates showed how much the FDA's approach to regulation had changed since the days it sought to implement food standards for all manufactured foods. Instead of setting standards, thereby situating the FDA as an activist state directly intervening in market formation, informative labels reformulated the FDA as an information broker that nudged markets toward public policy agendas. Rather than shielding consumers from risks, the new approach attempted to manage both risk and consumers' irrational fears.

In chapter 1 I asked readers to consider why the FDA initially focused on standards. Here, I ask, why *information*? With the Nutrition Facts panel the FDA not only sought to provide more information but also to manage the flows of information about health claims. Instead of standardizing food, the FDA standardized food information. Yet control was neither universal nor absolute. The Nutrition Facts panel now appeared on millions of packages for very different types of foods, some health foods, others not. The Nutritional Facts label targeted neither an "ordinary consumer" needing protection nor an "informed consumer" pursuing healthy eating. The FDA's new label, instead, envisioned the consumer as a "distributed self," operating differently in different contexts. This new view of the consumer came about partly because new informational platforms emerged in the Information Age. For example, the Nutrition Facts label was designed on a personal computer, and the PC and people's "life on screen" exemplified how new digital platforms enabled new modes of thinking and interacting.[5] But the new realities of shopping also helped create the distributed consumer. For example, a working woman who is also mom and homemaker might look to the label for several different kinds of information about food.

The Nutrition Facts panel also reinforced what had become the dominant model of defining food. Food was no longer simply grown, nor sold to fulfill the customary recipes and traditions of housewives. Food, translated into information and coded into the FDA's black box, now became a tool for what I call a plug-and-play food economy.[6] Companies increasingly designed foods and marketing campaigns to foreground specific ingredients or nutritional qualities. This chapter explores this new food economy and what became known as "functional foods," novel foods engineered to have additional health or nutritional functions. The new food economy was also affected by parallel developments in food and agricultural biotechnology industries, where "substitutionism," discussed in chapter 6, helped shape the FDA policy of "substantial equivalence" on genetically modified foods. The new labels highlighted certain kinds of information about food, while silencing others.

THE ADVENT OF FUNCTIONAL FOODS

The 1973 changes in FDA rules on nutrition labeling reflected its openness to mass markets for diet and health food products. Indeed, in the early 1990s, FDA deputy commissioner Mary Pendergast conceded, "It is fair to say that the FDA once had a reputation for pooh-poohing the idea of taking vitamins, but that attitude is changing. We no longer disagree with anyone's desire to supplement their diet with a moderate dose of vitamins and minerals."[7] The FDA continued to worry about improper labeling, false claims, and cases of megadosing, but it substantially reduced its attention to policing vitamin and supplements markets. During the Reagan administration, FDA resources for regulating food markets were strained since Congress expanded its drug regulation powers without a corresponding budget increase.[8] The text of existing voluntary information labels, which emphasized fats and sugars, illustrated the agency's embrace of "negative nutrition." In 1984 the FDA added sodium to this list.[9] That same year Margaret M. Heckler, secretary of health and human services, wrote, "Americans, heal thyselves," in a U.S. public health services journal. This reference to the biblical warning, "Physician, heal thyself," underscored how much the Reagan administration embraced the U.S.'s new market ethos of healthism and self-help.[10]

Despite this openness to health food markets, the FDA continued to limit advertisements or label statements specifically mentioning a disease (e.g., "prevents cancer") or "structure / function" claims (e.g., "calcium builds strong bones" or "fiber maintains bowel regularity"). From the FDA's perspective, these claims directly threatened the regulatory boundary the FDA maintained between foods and drugs.

In 1984 a collaboration between the Kellogg Company and the NIH National Cancer Institute (NCI) undermined the FDA's strict policy against disease claims. A Kellogg ad for its All-Bran cereal explicitly claimed that consuming high-fiber foods reduced the risk of cancer. The ad included a generic public health message from the NCI on fiber and cancer prevention. Though critics argued this was "misbranding," Kellogg had consulted with the NCI before airing the ad. To the NCI, which had just initiated a cancer prevention awareness campaign, this seemed like a golden opportunity to expand the reach of their message.[11] This was only the first of many public-private partnerships that blurred the boundaries between advertising and public health education. Initially the FDA reacted to the Kellogg message with its usual stance against health claims on foods, then relented since NCI was also part of the Department of Health and Human Services. Shortly thereafter, FDA officials stated that the "FDA is committed to opening the door, with caution, to appropriate health claims on food labels."[12] Food products with fiber and disease claims soon flooded supermarkets.

In 1989 Kellogg introduced another new cereal named Heartwise, a multigrain breakfast flake that contained the fiber psyllium, the primary ingredient in many

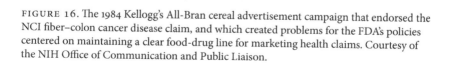

AT LAST, SOME NEWS ABOUT CANCER YOU CAN LIVE WITH.

The National Cancer Institute believes a high fiber, low fat diet may reduce your risk of some kinds of cancer.

The National Cancer Institute reports some very good health news.

There is growing evidence that may link a high fiber, low fat diet to lower incidence of some kinds of cancer.

That's why one of their strongest recommendations is to eat high fiber foods. If you compare, you'll find Kellogg's® All-Bran® has nine grams of fiber per serving. No cereal has more. In fact, ounce for ounce, no food has more. So start your day with a bowl of Kellogg's All-Bran, or mix it with your regular cereal.

GOOD SOURCES OF FIBER													
1 oz. Kellogg's All-Bran													
1 medium apple													
1/3 cup baked beans													
1 slice whole wheat toast													
1/3 cup cooked spinach													
Dietary fiber in grams —	0	1	2	3	4	5	6	7	8	9			

And for a free booklet with more preventative tips, write Box K, National Cancer Institute, Bethesda, MD 20814.

No food has more fiber than Kellogg's® All-Bran.®

FIGURE 16. The 1984 Kellogg's All-Bran cereal advertisement campaign that endorsed the NCI fiber–colon cancer disease claim, and which created problems for the FDA's policies centered on maintaining a clear food-drug line for marketing health claims. Courtesy of the NIH Office of Communication and Public Liaison.

laxatives. Because the FDA had not determined psyllium to be GRAS, or "generally recognized as safe," at the levels found in Heartwise, the state of Texas seized the product as an untested, misbranded drug, and a U.S. district court ruled in favor of the Texas attorney general's motion to remove Heartwise from the market. The court noted that the cereal's labeling, which included a heart symbol and endorsements by a hospital and heart institute, implied it was a medical cure and therefore legitimately subject to scrutiny as a drug.[13] Legal commentators focused on the fact that Kellogg's marketing emphasized psyllium as a specific additive. Kellogg thus made purified fiber, something naturally found in food, into an "active ingredient." And yet other "pure" food additives were commonly added to food. What made psyllium drug-like, while artificial sweeteners and flavors like vanillin were not?[14] The category confusion around Kellogg's Heartwise cereal was just the beginning, as companies would increasingly develop "functional foods," discussed later, to skirt this "food-drug line."

By the 1980s, even some food industries that had resisted negative nutrition campaigns discussed in chapter 2 began embracing marketing opportunities around nutrition labels. Dairy industry now manufactured and actively promoted skim or part-skim milks, cheeses, and ice creams. Supermarkets offered lean-cut packages of meats, sometimes at a premium. In 1985 the American Meat Institute and Food Marketing Institute developed a "Meat Nutri-Facts" campaign, where supermarkets could provide consumers "Nutri-Facts" cards and take-home brochures detailing nutrients and recipes for a wide variety of cuts of meat.[15] Pork producers implemented programs to adjust feed to create leaner pigs and to breed for leaner animals; they also lobbied the USDA to revise grading systems to reflect the trend toward reduction in back fat.[16] In 1987 the National Pork Board pitched pork as "the other white meat," attempting to frame pork as a healthy alternative to chicken.

Even professional health organizations now participated in health food marketing. To raise funds, in 1988 the American Heart Association marketed a "HeartGuide" seal of approval label for healthy food products. An AHA product approval unit would evaluate the nutritional content of packaged, processed foods submitted by manufacturers, and create a "Consumer Health Information Program," with a hotline for consumers. To fund this AHA program, companies would pay a $40,000 annual administrative fee plus an annual "education fee" (for advertising and promotion), prorated based on market share, that could be as great as $1 million per brand per year.

The AHA's proposed HeartGuide program encountered immediate opposition from both the FDA and industry. The FDA objected to third-party medical endorsements because they implied the product had health-promoting properties—thus the product was a drug, not a food. The agency also believed this approach implied some foods were always "good." Consumers might overindulge in those foods, whereas the agency's position was that one's health depended on total diet and lifestyle. Industry worried that the program exposed companies to legal liability: What would happen if a consumer had a heart attack after eating their AHA-approved products?[17] The AHA program also faced criticism because of its high cost—one industry representative called it "an extortion racket."[18] Nevertheless, 114 companies sought the endorsement—but HeartGuide didn't happen. The FDA and USDA killed the program, and killed other "seal" programs including those being developed by the American College of Nutrition (endorsing Mazola vegetable oil and P&G's Puritan oils) and the AMA's Campaign Against Cholesterol.[19]

Surprisingly, given the 1980s antiregulatory atmosphere, the FDA received little public or political backlash for striking down this "for-profit regulatory approach." Accompanying the growing acceptance for stricter national standards in labeling was a consensus that the nation was facing a national health crisis. The 1988 *Surgeon General's Report on Nutrition and Health* noted that two-thirds of all U.S. deaths were now attributable to heart disease, atherosclerosis, stroke, diabetes, or some form of cancer, and that our diets affected the risk for all these illnesses. The report also noted: "For most of us the more likely problem has become one of overeating—too many calories for our activity levels and an imbalance in the nutrients consumed."[20] The report strongly recommended that "food manufacturers should be encouraged to make full use of nutrition labels."[21] The report's appearance coincided with the publication of several other expert advisory reports making similar calls for diet reform.[22] The intense media attention to scientific findings connecting diet to cancer scares and heart disease served to bolster sales of healthy foods.

America's looming health crisis was just the tip of the spear for growing the market interest in dieting, novel health foods, and informative labeling. For many, healthy was more than just the opposite of sick; it was about personal enhancement, being better than well. While mainstream food producers were ramping up sales of new packaged health foods, there was a parallel, alternative movement by consumers seeking better health through more "organic" foods. This culminated in the 1990 Organic Foods Production Act and the implementation of USDA standards for organic labeling, discussed in chapter 6. Improving health was only one motivation for the eighties' "fitness craze"—slimming up could help achieve an increasingly unrealistic body image. Feminist iconoclast Naomi Wolf diagnosed Americans' obsession in the 1980s with physical perfection as a "beauty myth," elevating beauty (often disguised as health) to a super-value justifying numerous self-destructive and otherwise unhealthy behaviors and attitudes. At a time when the "working girl" was a prime subject of media attention, staying trim and looking attractive was pitched to middle-class working women as a way to avoid the masculinizing effects of full-time employment. However, marketers could also exploit those insecurities to promote new products.[23] This affected men, too. Rodale, a leader in the organic food movement, started the magazine *Men's Health* in 1986 to reach men interested in personal fitness and diets for sporty lifestyles.[24] For many reasons, consumers were willing to pay extra for foods that might help them stay healthy or support their particular lifestyle.

FIGURE 17. Political cartoon pokes fun at consumer confusion, caused by unregulated health claims, with a "food labels read" fortune teller outside a supermarket. Source: "Fortune Teller Luxor the Great," *USA Today*, July 2, 1990. © David Seavey—USA TODAY NETWORK. Courtesy of the David Seavey Collection at The Ohio State University Billy Ireland Cartoon Library & Museum.

By the end of the decade, addressing legal problems with health food marketing claims became increasingly important for the FDA. The expanding health market stimulated the agency to update nutrition labeling. Dale Blumenthal, writing in *FDA Consumer,* identified the key problems with expanding nutrition labeling: What foods should have nutrition labeling? What nutrients should the nutrition label address? Should nutrient amounts be declared according to the amount in a serving? What was the best format for the nutrition label? These questions revealed the FDA's openness to starting fresh and reinventing nutrition-labeling rules. The most difficult question Blumenthal saved for last: "Is food labeling an appropriate vehicle for disseminating health-related dietary information about specific diseases?"[25]

When Louis Sullivan, secretary of the Department of Health and Human Services, spoke at the 13th Annual National Food Policy Conference in 1990, declaring the grocery store a "tower of Babel," he stressed that the flood of health information overwhelmed consumers making food-purchasing decisions. Sullivan did not promote policies that might curb this information overload, but instead felt that too little sound dietary advice reached the public: "Vital information is missing, and frankly some unfounded health claims are being made."[26] The design of the 1993 "Nutrition Facts" label would thus be an exercise in reducing the noise and clarifying messaging about diet and health.

THE INTEREST GROUP POLITICS OF THE NUTRITION LABELING AND EDUCATION ACT

The 1990 passage of the Nutrition Labeling and Education Act (NLEA) marked a turning point in nutrition labeling reform, and its implementation stands as a remarkable demonstration of interest-group politics. As political scientist Daniel

Carpenter has observed, "The twentieth-century Food and Drug Administration was blessed and cursed with multiple publics."[27] This multiplicity sometimes made the FDA look vulnerable to multifront attacks, but also often contributed to the FDA's persistence.

For the FDA, the new label would centralize and certify nutrition information, and helped resolve the problematic distinction between food and drugs. For special interest groups, the Nutrition Facts panel became a platform for promoting lifestyle politics. For manufacturers, it was a legal instrument for ensuring uniform rules and promoting a national marketplace. For public health officials, it helped treat sick populations by encouraging individuals to act in the health interest of the population. For food technologists, the law validated a professional association's authority to determine "correct" measurement standards for very different food products. Thus the Nutrition Facts panel became a platform for each of these sometimes contradictory agendas, limiting its effectiveness for any one group, but ensuring it had a wide political mandate and numerous vested interests supporting it.[28]

In one of history's ironies, the House bill that became the NLEA was introduced the very day that millions of American kids took to the street for their annual candy saturnalia, Halloween. On October 31, 1989, Henry Waxman, a Democrat from southern California, introduced H. R. 3562 prescribing "nutrition labeling for foods, and for other purposes," thus amending the Federal Food, Drug, and Cosmetic Act of 1938.[29] The bill required that all standardized and packaged foods, with certain exceptions,[30] must display four key pieces of information: serving size; the number of servings per container; the number of calories per serving, and calories from total fat and saturated fat; and finally, the amount of total fat, saturated fat, cholesterol, sodium, total carbohydrates, complex carbohydrates, sugars, total protein, and dietary fiber per serving. The law also authorized the Department of Health and Human Services secretary, and more specifically the FDA, to require that packaged foods list vitamins, minerals, or other nutrients based upon the best scientific evidence available. The law allowed manufacturers whose products conformed to these nutrition labeling expectations to make certain health claims about their products without facing classification as a drug. The NLEA thus now allowed advertising for health-conscious food products while ensuring federal oversight of content labeling.

After the House and Senate modified the bill slightly, in 1990 it passed both houses easily, and on November 8, 1990, President George Bush signed the Nutrition Labeling and Education Act as Public Law 101–535.[31] The 1990 NLEA erased any doubts concerning whether the FDA had the authority to lead a national nutrition label and education campaign. The law directed the secretary to "carry out consumer education on nutrition labeling" and "require the nutrition information on labels to be conveyed in a manner which enables the public to readily observe and comprehend it and to understand its relative significance in the context of a total daily diet." Thus, Congress endorsed a policy permitting Americans the freedom to choose a healthy lifestyle through label literacy.

The extent of Congress's resolve to clarify food labeling was registered in the fact that the NLEA also gave the FDA authority to establish standards for defining serving sizes, whereas previously the food industry had defined serving sizes in collaboration with the U.S. Department of Agriculture. The NLEA strengthened agency officials' resolve to revise the label. Through a series of open solicitations and community outreach initiatives, the FDA hoped to initiate the largest changes in food labeling regulation since the 1938 Food, Drug, and Cosmetic Act.

The NLEA required that "nutrients be presented in the context of the daily diet." This meant that the new label would not simply display content declarations but also make recommendations. Unlike the "Nutrition Information" label of the 1970s, the Nutrition Facts panel now included "% Daily Values." This number, telling consumers how much of a given nutrient an "average" American ought to eat per day, significantly reconfigured the nutrition label as a public health tool. Although the label was intended for individualized use, Daily Values were based on population-level data. This embodied what epidemiologists call the "paradox of prevention"—when a public intervention "brings large benefits to the community [but] offers little to each participating individual." For example, encouraging U.S. citizens to eat less saturated fat might reduce a particular individual's risk of cardiovascular disease very little, while significantly reducing the incidence of heart disease at the population level. The label thus embodied the concept of collective risk—what one scientist called "treating sick populations not sick individuals."[32]

With the NLEA now in force, the FDA began its implementation. In November 1991 the FDA published the proposed new food labeling regulations in volume 26 of the *Federal Register*, and solicited feedback from the public and stakeholders. The FDA received over 40,000 written comments to the proposed rules, the largest number ever received up to that time.[33]

One group that responded was the nonprofit Center for Science in the Public Interest (CSPI), founded by Michael Jacobson in the 1970s. In the 1980s the CSPI focused mostly on low-fat-diet campaigns and consumer advocacy, blending scientific messages about diet and health with an explicitly politicized vocabulary of special-interest politics and consumerism. For such groups, the nutrition label was a platform for promoting a new kind of political health activism. The CSPI lobbied to introduce sodium labeling and ran campaigns against the use of tropical oils high in saturated fats (especially palm and coconut oils).[34] In 1989 their "Food Labeling Chaos Report" drew attention to problems caused by inconsistent food labeling policies, and offered alternative labeling tools that the CSPI had long advocated, such as pie charts and adjectival language like "good source of" or "high in."[35] CSPI publications often served both as informational pamphlets raising awareness for constituents and as reference tools for constructing a literature around advocacy issues and drawing press attention to their campaigns.

Throughout the 1980s and 1990s, CSPI used various advocacy tactics to influence governmental and corporate institutions, especially constituent surveys and write-in campaigns. In 1989 CSPI surveyed 5,715 people through its "Nutrition Action Healthletter," asking respondents yes/no and multiple-choice questions about what nutrients should be mandatory on the new label, who should determine the "serving size" (the FDA or manufacturers), and what graphical formats (pie/bar charts, percentages, and "traffic lights") were preferable.[36] In 1990 CSPI promoted a grassroots write-in campaign. The FDA received hundreds of scripted letters asking for universal labeling of nutrition facts, labels that listed "naturally occurring and added sugars separately," and clarity in using terms like "less cholesterol."[37] CSPI also organized a "Food and Nutrition Labeling Group" that included the American Association of Retired Persons (AARP), the American Cancer Society, the American Dietetic Association, and the AHA, among others. When NLEA legislation was under consideration, the group sent letters to prominent political figures supporting CSPI's positions on the nutrition label reforms.[38]

A particularly colorful example of popular mobilization around the Nutrition Facts was the National Heart Savers Association (NHSA), which was literally a one-man show. Phil Sokolof, founder and sole member of NHSA, was a millionaire Nebraska industrialist who had a near-fatal heart attack in 1966. In 1984, after the release of the NIH Consensus Conference statement on Lowering Blood Cholesterol to Prevent Coronary Heart Disease, he personally financed a national advertising campaign criticizing the food industry, especially the meat industry, and promoting the importance of a cholesterol-lowering diet. As nutrition labeling gained momentum in the late 1980s, Sokolof bought full-page ads in major newspapers with headlines like "Who Wins the War of the Labels?" and "I'm Giving Away $1 Million . . . Just to Show You How Great the New Food Labels Really Are!" These antics and his colorful statements criticizing companies like McDonald's earned him regular newspaper coverage, and helped keep the labeling reform issues visible in the media.[39]

Industry reaction to the NLEA legislation was mostly driven by self-interest. It is difficult to generalize about this because companies producing a broad array of food products, such as Kraft General Foods, had sub-departments that benefited and others that were harmed by the introduction of the label. Cereal companies, such as Kellogg and General Mills, whose products already carried the earlier nutrition label, were fairly supportive of the proposed guidelines. Their complaints were similar to those of the AMA and American Dietetic Associations (ADA) about the need for scientifically derived standards, about possible consumer confusion concerning the new Daily Values percentages, and about the precise calibration of nutrient recommendations for sugars and dietary fibers.[40] But overall these companies welcomed the new label as an opportunity to increase consumer confidence in their promotional health claims.

Generally, however, the food industry resisted mandatory labeling. Certain companies, especially those that sold snack foods, found the new mandatory guidelines onerous, particularly for products that were clearly unhealthy and not intended to balance one's diet. The Coca-Cola Company complained that the nutrition labels should only be for core dietary foods, not fringe foods like soft drinks. Coca-Cola argued consumers were cognizant of the lack of health benefits of soda, "which do not offer or purport to offer any meaningful nutritional contribution but which do provide pleasant testing [sic] refreshment."[41] While this reasoning was self-serving, Coca-Cola's complaint underscored how a standardized nutrition label might blur culturally significant, product-specific connotations between "junk food" and a "proper" meal.[42]

The U.S. Department of Agriculture (USDA) also had concerns about universal nutrition labeling. Since 1940, when the FDA left the USDA and moved into what became the Department of Health, Education, and Welfare, tensions had arisen regarding the nature and scope of their roles in managing the nation's food supply. One product of this overlapping mandate was a patchwork of jurisdictions on food labeling. The USDA's Food Safety and Inspection Service (FSIS) oversaw labeling of meat and poultry products, while the FDA oversaw all other food products.[43] In the 1970s and 1980s they began disagreeing about which agency was best suited for accumulating and disseminating nutrition information. These disputes repeatedly reached Congress, since new federal legislation could clarify their mandates.[44] The 1990 NLEA established that the FDA's Nutrition Facts label would be fairly uniform across state borders. It was still unclear whether the FDA's new label, or something like it, might also appear on the meat and poultry products regulated by the USDA.

A major sticking point between the FDA and USDA involved serving sizes. The stakes were high, because serving sizes affected every other numeric value on the Nutrition Facts panel.[45] In its initial 1990 Proposed Guidelines, the FDA suggested establishing 159 new food product categories and standard servings for each.[46] The NLEA language suggested a definition, "amount customarily consumed," which meant sizes should be based on eating habits, not recommended dietary guidance.[47] This guidance, however, did not explain how the FDA should determine a customary amount. The agency also had to decide whether to label serving sizes based on quantities "as packaged" in the food package when bought at the store, versus "as consumed" after the packaged food had been cooked. Medical associations like the AMA favored "as consumed," because the reform was intended to inform readers' consumption habits, and cooking dramatically changed a food's nutrition value.[48] Industry, and (generally) both the FDA and the USDA, favored "as packaged" because it was easier to test and wasn't affected by individual differences in cooking methods.

Meanwhile, the USDA was incorporating new serving size standards into its new Food Guide Pyramid.[49] Like the Nutrition Facts panel, the Food Guide Pyramid was intended to help consumers understand how foods they ate contributed to a healthy daily diet. While the Nutrition Facts panel provided digital information about food, using numeric referents, the Food Pyramid was an analog approach, incorporating images of food in the "Basic Four" food groups and relating proportions of each to the pyramid's visual hierarchy. The USDA determined serving sizes through a combination of *"typical portion sizes* (from food consumption surveys), *ease of use, nutrient content,* and *tradition* (of use in previous food guides)."[50] Once determined, serving sizes in the USDA Food Pyramid functioned much like the %DRVs of the Nutrition Facts panel, calibrating the proportions of foods from each group a person should eat daily. Thus, serving sizes were a crucial element of the USDA's Food Pyramid, and adopting differing serving sizes on the Nutrition Facts panel could potentially confuse consumers and undermine both education programs. These conflicts concerning serving size and jurisdiction meant that negotiations between the FDA and USDA mostly remained stalled in 1991 and 1992.

With neither side budging, and the FDA facing a "hammer clause" in the NLEA that required label rules be established by November 8, 1992, the decision had to come from the White House. FDA staff, worried the USDA might team up with the OMB and White House Council on Competitiveness, enlisted several news organizations to publicize their position.[51] After a series of White House meetings and the presidential election, President Bush ultimately sided with the FDA.[52] A version of the Nutrition Facts panel, calibrated to 2,000 calories, would appear on both the FDA's packaged foods and the USDA's meat and poultry. This was only the second time a U.S. president had intervened directly in a decision relating to food labels (the first being Teddy Roosevelt's intervention in saccharine, discussed in chapter 1).

The resolution over the new common label did not resolve tensions between food and agriculture regulators. Disagreements about standard serving sizes and contextual information like the Daily Reference Values were also arguments over whether the Nutrition Facts label was just an information tool intended to aid consumers making choices, or instead an educational tool to discipline consumer choices. USDA Extension Service state representatives complained that the FDA's label undermined their own localized nutritional measures and expertise, arguing, "By themselves, the *labels cannot educate* the consumer. . . . It would be an incredible waste of human capital and material resources to try and develop a new system of consumer education."[53] These complaints reflected a widespread feeling among nutrition specialists in the U.S. Department of Agriculture. If the new label was a stand-alone nutrition guide, these experts felt it did the job poorly and threatened to compete with their own programs and advice. These issues were never fully settled, but were instead steamrolled by the impressive media show the FDA unveiled as the 1994 industry compliance date approached.

DRAWING NUTRITION FACTS TOGETHER

More than with the 1970s Nutrition Information label, design was a central concern with the new Nutrition Facts panel. The FDA wanted its label—effectively a government message—to stand out from the colorful, corporate messages elsewhere on food packages. The FDA's attention to design, however, embraced the logic of brands, rather than merely combatting brands. The label's simple black box design would help make Nutrition Facts iconic, and its unostentatious style reinforced the label's legal impact and naturalized the scientific "facts" it presented.[54]

For assistance, Kessler turned to Burkey Belser (1947–), president of the Greenfield / Belser Ltd. design firm.[55] At the time Greenfield / Belser Ltd. worked mostly on professional services design, but had been engaged previously by the FTC to design the EnergyGuide label that is on all major appliances. Belser agreed to assist the FDA *pro bono*.[56] In an article titled "Feeding Facts to America," Belser recalled the firm's challenge as the following: "Four thousand pages of regulations had to be reduced to a few square inches, flexible enough to appear on a candy-bar wrapper or a cereal box. And the process was hampered by the byzantine maze of American politics."[57] Design would be more than just condensing. The firm sought to bend aesthetics to a purpose: to create a label projecting an authoritative aura that matched its presumed scientific and governmental mission.

Starting in 1991, working with a Macintosh computer and a fax machine, Belser and one other staff member began receiving daily comments from Congress and its constituencies, while also consulting with contacts at the FDA.[58] Along with content concerns, comments suggested various design styles for the label, including pie charts, bar charts such as a "loading bar," and variations on simply listing the nutrients. The challenge was to create a design meeting the needs of a very mixed audience. Regulators had given up their mental image of the typical American consumer as an educated, white, suburban housewife. In her place, regulators now pictured the vast diversity of people who lived in the U. S.: old and young, rich and poor, English-language learners and native-English speakers, able-bodied and visually impaired.[59]

The firm started with a slightly modified version of the 1970s voluntary label. The 1973 "Nutrition Information" label used few graphical layout elements, relying instead on spacing to separate the two main sections: above, a "nutrition information per serving" listing grams for macronutrients, and below, a "percentage of U. S. recommended daily allowances" listing percents for eight micronutrients. A dot leader on the right specified numerical values listed on the left. Besler sought to produce a table with approximately the same content, but in a tabular layout organized by "functional clusters" (macronutrients versus micronutrients). The firm used focus groups to assess different font and format styles,[60] ultimately choosing Helvetica ("black and light" Helvetica, not "bold and regular") because it was a "widely available, commonly used font."[61] They experimented with reversing the type on certain portions of the label, using a column with black background and white type, but found people tended to skip over this. To save space, the firm played with hairlines (a very thin line used to create space between elements on a printed page) and indentation of subgroups to guide reading of nutrient content. They also experimented with visual symbols for branding and aesthetic reasons, but found this sometimes sent mixed signals to the culturally heterogeneous community of U. S. shoppers. They put a black line around the panel, forming a box separating the government's space from the rest of the package.[62] And they insisted the font size be at least 8-point to ensure that the elderly and other people with vision problems could read the text.

Design decisions communicate values, and Belser and his FDA collaborators had to decide to what extent the label's design should direct consumers toward good foods and away from bad foods. David Kessler insisted that the order of nutrients should reflect their priority for health messaging, i.e., the negative macronutrients would be listed first, followed by the desirable micronutrients. But this caused disagreement between the design firm and scientists at the FDA Center for Food Safety and Applied Nutrition (CFSAN). The scientists wanted to represent the absolute value of nutrients, not their relative value. CFSAN staff objected to the firm's use of boldface for certain content—carbohydrates, sodium, and cholesterol—but not for micronutrients. The firm experimented with "prescriptive" labels, having statements like "Do not eat food high in these products, or eat foods that are high in these," as well as adjectival and street-light labels. Ultimately, they kept the percentage figures for Daily Value.[63]

The FDA announced the proposed guidelines in the November 1991 *Federal Register*, presenting seven final format candidates and six potential graphic designs for review.[64] Feedback to the FDA during this comment period revealed a strong preference for the more understated formats, in particular, favoring the 1970s *status quo* label, and what ultimately became the new label format. The agency also rejected the use of color in favor of black-and-white, as industry complained about the printing expenses associated with colored ink. To Belser, this decision proved a boon: the staid colors contrasted with the puffery elsewhere on the package.

The final version of the Nutrition Facts panel departed somewhat from the language of the NLEA legislation. The NLEA, for example, authorized the FDA to use highlighting "by larger type, bold type, or contrasting color" for elements on the panel that helped assist consumers maintaining healthy dietary practices. FDA officials were skeptical of highlighting specific nutrients, not wanting to single out specific good or bad nutrients because different users had different needs. One of

Figure 8: The Old Food Label

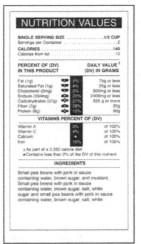

Figure 9

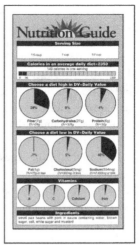

Figure 10

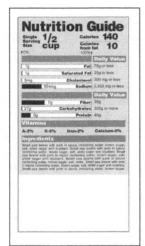

Figure 11

Figure 12

Figure 13: The New Food Label

FIGURE 18. Some of the graphic designs for the FDA's 1993 Nutrition Facts label explored by Greenfield / Belser Ltd. Source: "Evolution of the Food Label Graphic Design," in Kessler et al., "Developing the Food Label," *Harvard Health Policy Review* 4, no. 2 (Fall 2003): 21. Image credits: Greenfield / Belser Ltd, Washington, DC, with permission from Burkey Belser.

the seven potential Nutrition Facts panel formats tested did include asterisks to mark nutrients "low" or "high" relative to FDA recommended values. However, a consensus emerged from industry and nonindustry alike that such "highlighting" represented more of a marketing tool than an educational one.[65] Food companies therefore argued it should be voluntary, while consumer advocates approved it only if the FDA mandated it.[66] The American Dietetic Association requested dropping it entirely because it could confuse users about the educational mandate of the label.[67] The FDA's eventual rejection of highlighting reflected its desire to keep the nutrition-labeling panel distinct from portions of the package associated with advertising.

The black box was a triumph of clarity and economy of space over extended scientific explanation or accuracy.[68] The Nutrition Facts panel did, however, mark how public health concerns with macronutrients had triumphed over micronutrients. The two were separated by a 12-point black bar, with macronutrients situated above and given greater prominence. The use of boldface for fats embodied the public health policy effort to alert readers to the presence of unhealthy macronutrients.[69] The label's understatedness stood in stark contrast to the bright, colorful advertising on the rest of the package. The friendly, stately, and even slick company logos and slogans on the package might be in two-inch-tall lettering, or shadow bolded, with sexier font variations of serif, script, or ornamental typefaces, and accompanied by vivid, colorful illustrations and photos. But the Nutrition Facts panel would always have the same sans-serif font type, size, and black-on-white color, with a (largely) unchanging box shape on all food packages.

One further concern voiced in the feedback on proposed labels was the name of the label itself. In his early proposals to the FDA, Belser emphasized that, for branding purposes, the label needed a title. The FDA had experimented with alternative titles like "Nutrition Information Per Serving." The National Food Processors Association strongly disapproved of titles like "Nutrition Guide" and "Nutrition Values," preferring instead "Nutrition Facts" or retaining the original title "Nutrition Information."[70] In the 1993 finalized guidelines, the FDA acknowledged that the majority of comments supported retaining the former 1970s title because it was familiar to consumers. The agency chose instead to go with "Nutrition Facts."[71] The choice of an objective term, "Facts," over the more prescriptive "Guide," reflected an FDA shift toward a more moderate position on the role of labels. Criticisms from industry, the USDA, and the Bush administration had worn down Kessler's earlier enthusiasm for enforcement.

From Belser's point of view, his firm and the FDA had created "an iconic government brand, a style of labeling that *should* appear on every single type of label that the government wants to mark for consumers to pay attention to."[72] The authoritative austere design and its presence on all products, everywhere, asserted its power as a government brand.

PROMOTING NUTRITION FACTS AS PUBLIC HEALTH

On January 6, 1993, with seven permitted health claims,[73] an established % Daily Reference Value for all listed nutrients, a new Nutrition Facts panel, and standardized serving sizes for 139 food product categories, the FDA published its final food labeling guidelines in the *Federal Register*.[74] These rules went into effect February 14, Valentine's Day, and all manufacturers had to be in compliance by May 8, 1994. The USDA's compliance date for meat and poultry products was July 8. The food labeling revisions were the largest in U. S. history, requiring enormous governmental resources, with projected costs for the food industry over the next twenty years ranging from $1.4 billion to $2.3 billion. "It's been a long haul," admitted Fred Shank, director of the FDA's CFSAN. "But the greatest challenge lies ahead—in educating consumers."[75]

Over the next year and a half, the FDA undertook an unprecedented nutrition education media campaign centered on the new Nutrition Facts label. The initial campaign targets were health professionals and educators. The objective, according to Commissioner David Kessler, was to "institutionalize" messaging about the new food label by ensuring it was in home economics and health textbooks, and in materials used by nutritionists, dietitians, and health educators.[76] The USDA and FDA, working with public health organizations and food industries, also published an extraordinary variety of How-to Guides serving as educational aids explaining how the new Nutrition Facts label worked. Three million copies of *How to Read the New Food Label*, a brochure developed by the FDA and the American Heart Association, were distributed within six months of its publication. The National Food Processors Association, in cooperation with the USDA and FDA, published a ninety-two-page educator's resource guide.[77] FDA representatives also met with educators at community colleges, university extension services, and community health organizations like the Phoenix-based Concilio Latino de Salud, which focused on bilingual populations, to help them prepare short-courses and information sessions for local communities. To coordinate these efforts, the FDA and USDA established the National Exchange for Food Labeling Education (NEFLE), housed at the Food Labeling Education Information Center in the National Agricultural Library.[78]

By 1994, as the industry compliance date neared, the FDA ramped up its media efforts for a second round of ads directed at the general public. It disseminated ready-to-print articles published in hundreds of newspapers, and it released a logo featuring the agency's new slogan, "The *New* Food Label, *Check it Out!*" for organizations to include in their periodicals and health literature.[79] The media blitz reached new heights in the first week of May. Ads airing on public TV featured baseball player Roger Clemens, and children's favorite animated monkey, Curious George, who served as the label's official mascot. The FDA's new slogan was even

FIGURE 19. The NLEA and FDA Nutrition Facts rules created demand for analytic chemists organizations, such as the AOAC, and private laboratories to establish verifiable nutrient values for the thousands of new foods that would now carry a nutrition label. Source: "Lancaster Laboratories Can Help Satisfy All Your Nutrition Labeling Needs," *Food Technology,* October 1991, 87.

flashed on electronic scoreboards in Yankee Stadium and beamed from three Goodyear Blimps across the country.[80] The extraordinary media coverage was all coordinated to get across the FDA's message about the new label.

So what was the message? According to David Kessler, "It is about Americans living longer, better quality lives, and about lowering health-care costs."[81] For Kessler, Nutrition Facts took "all the dietitian's guidance and reduce[d] it to something people can use."[82] Although the nutrition content was aimed at an average (literate) American consumer, the education campaign targeted specific audiences. In a series of articles on "The New Food Label" published in 1994 and 1995, the *FDA Consumer* highlighted special dietary concerns such as diabetes and heart disease prevention. The reports also prominently featured the elderly, mothers, and minority groups, such as African Americans and Hispanics. Images of the Nutrition Facts label depicted it as a liberating force, explaining how the new label (when used in coordination with other tools such as the USDA's new Food Guide Pyramid and the U.S. *Dietary Guidelines*) helped consumers tackle dietary challenges.[83]

The Nutrition Facts panel reflected an expansion of the emerging paradigm that *all* foods have nutrition and health properties. The label was no longer voluntary. The FDA now required nutrition labels not only on foods sold and marketed for health purposes but on every packaged food in the U.S. From a sociological perspective, Nutrition Facts had a hegemonic effect, catapulting the language of nutrition science into every American household. Whether or not a consumer wanted to know the nutritional properties of foods, the label indicated that all foods have nutritional properties and the government believed this was important enough to take up space on the package.

Given the substantial federal resources devoted to developing and promoting the new label, and the intense political battles fought over who defined legitimate health claims, it was natural to ask: did people even read the label? Answering this question has sparked considerable scholarly and political dispute. On the one hand, the sheer scale of nutrition labeling suggested it was a total success. By 1997 more than 300 billion food product containers carried the label, representing around 90 percent of all food products sold in the United States.[84] The label's popularity even led to the design and adoption of a similar "Drug Facts" label for all over-the-counter U.S. drugs.[85] The USDA's Diet and Health Knowledge Survey, conducted from 1994 to 1996, suggested that 65 percent of adults used the label, and a 1999 Food Marketing Institute survey reported that 59 percent of consumers changed purchases because of information on the product label.[86]

Others, however, offered less optimistic evaluations of the label. In 1996 a spokesman for Kraft Foods, Inc., speculated that the label had probably brought few conversions to healthy diets. Instead, he imagined that health-conscious consumers who might convert still balanced other interests such as tastes and tradi-

FIGURE 20. The new Nutrition Facts label personified as a public relations spokesperson.
Source: *FDA Consumer* 29 (June 1995): 7.

tions against strictly dietary concerns.[87] A 1995 FDA study noted that "food labels have limited potential as vehicles for nutrition education or dietary advice," though it defended them as "ideally suited to be tools that enable consumers to implement dietary beliefs they already hold."[88] Many studies suggested that, while consumers read the labels, they were not reading them well.[89] One 2008 USDA study of the label's use even suggested that nutrition label readership was declining.[90] This could be because the Nutrition Facts panel was initially released as the keystone of a broader education campaign providing a set of tools to help consumers interpret nutrition information. Over time, as the FDA's attention shifted away from nutrition and toward food safety and drug approvals, funding for and attention to this public campaign ebbed.[91]

The shift to a prescriptive labeling system reflected a change in how the FDA imagined its constituents. FDA staff now recognized that their products, including labels, were consumed by a heterogeneous mix of shoppers facing a variety of circumstances. Issues such as childhood obesity, higher incidences of hypertension and diabetes among blacks and Hispanics, and an emerging awareness that obesity was often a greater problem for the working class than for the affluent, all eroded the framing of negative nutrition as a middle-class problem. By the 1990s neither the public nor public health authorities thought of cardiovascular disease as a "disease of the affluent."[92]

The label embodied these new discourses about the burden of disease, but also addressed different health concerns within a single information panel. The underlying data driving the recommendations applied to the American population as a whole rather than an individual consumer. This was illustrated by the panel's inclusion of both "Reference (or Recommended) Daily Intakes" (RDIs) and "Daily Reference Values" (DRVs). Prior to the finalization of the 1993 rules, the FDA's nutrition information was based on Recommended Dietary Allowances (RDAs), first established in 1941 by the NAS Food and Nutrition Board to address nutritional deficiencies, specifically vitamins.[93] These had been set at population-based levels "adequate to meet the known nutrition needs of practically all healthy persons."[94] The FDA's newer measure, RDIs, utilized the RDAs to determine the *average* American's *minimum* vitamin needs. This meant that Nutrition Facts labels lowered the quantity of recommended daily vitamins, in recognition that most Americans no longer experienced malnutrition—even though some people still did. The new DRVs, meanwhile, established *maximum* recommended values for macronutrient content, specifically total fat, saturated fat, cholesterol, total carbohydrate, dietary fiber, and sodium.[95] Combined as "Daily Values" (DV), RDIs and DRVs together provided recommended quantities for *all* mandatory nutritional disclosures.[96]

In effect, the label averaged consumers' needs, favoring practicality and utility over accuracy and the accommodation of individual variation. The conflict between the FDA and health and consumer-advocacy groups over the number of total daily calories in a baseline diet illustrates what was at stake. Initially, the FDA wanted to calibrate daily values to a 2,350-calorie diet, the population-adjusted mean of recommended energy allowances for persons four or more years of age. This figure, however, ignored vastly different energy needs between genders—the daily recommendation for males was around 2,500–2,700 calories, and for females 1,800–2,000 calories—and across age groups, with children ages 4 to 14 only needing around 2,150 calories. Consumer-advocacy groups like the CSPI, the AHA, and the American Dietetic Association argued that setting the figure above the needs of average women (the primary shoppers) and elderly men (a target demographic group for heart disease) encouraged overconsumption. The FDA ultimately accepted a compromise figure of 2,000 calories proposed by the ADA, because "a round number has less implied specificity."[97] As one critic later said, "Most people don't read a package as it if were a legal contract."[98] The FDA envisioned a nonexpert reader who interpreted the label's nutrition "facts" in a less precise manner, even if the use of numbers on the label evoked scientific precision.

Unlike the 1970s nutrition information label, the Nutrition Facts label was a government-endorsed recommendation, explicitly designed as an educational tool. While FDA staff recognized that many shoppers never read the label, and others were motivated to actively work through any label to find information they desired, the FDA hoped to reach a third group: moderately engaged shoppers who could be persuaded to care about their nutritional habits if this was made sufficiently convenient.[99]

By the end of the 1990s, the country's food regulators had internalized a theory, based on works by economist George Stigler and others, on how consumers seek and respond to market information. The USDA Economic Research Service, for instance, issued a 1999 report authored by Lorna Aldrich entitled "Consumer Use of Information" describing foods as "credence goods" whose qualities were difficult-to-impossible to assess either before or after purchase. The report noted that, for credence goods, the consumer cares about the "characteristics of goods, rather than the good themselves." For example, "a food is valued for taste, convenience, nutrition, status, etc., rather than for being a food," and thus "the consumer transforms the food into the characteristics."[100] Here, a substantial challenge for the consumer was the time spent in the "acquisition and consumption of both information and food." Aldrich cited research showing that, despite all the information producers and nutritional labels provided, consumers—even if they claimed otherwise—spent too little time on purchases to use much information beyond "general impressions of brands, products, and stores." By one account, "nearly half of consumers' choices were made in 1 second."[101]

Aldrich's report exemplified a new framing of food policy: a focus on the consumer of food information rather than the consumer of food. The Nutrition Facts panel now allowed the FDA to interact with shoppers in two ways. First, the label added another platform for interacting with particular "biosocial" groups, such as diabetics, heart disease patients, dieters, and other health-conscious consumers.[102] Second, the FDA label no longer targeted an "ordinary consumer" as had food standards, nor the active, "informed consumer" targeted by the 1970s voluntary nutrition information label. The Nutrition Facts panel was designed for users having multiple and variable needs: the distributed consumer. When anthropologist Bruno Latour wrote in 2005, "Even when one has to make the mundane decision about which kind of sliced ham to choose, you benefit from dozens of measurement instruments that equip you to become a consumer—from labels, trademarks, barcodes, weight and measurement chains, indexes, prices, consumer journals, conversations with fellow shoppers, advertisements, and so on," he implied a model of the consumer in a plug-and-play food economy like that envisioned by the FDA for its Nutrition Facts label.[103]

This placed a new burden on shoppers navigating the countervailing pulls of their different identities. For working moms, it was the struggle of being the "balanced woman" who had it all: to be a reliable worker, nurturing mother, and good wife.[104] The Nutrition Facts label provided information consumers needed for on-the-spot calculations facilitating self-care and self-management of diet and health. The label extended the increasingly informational experience of eating in modern America and furthered the new notion of the literate, active distributed consumer.

THE BACKLASH OF COMMERCIAL FREE SPEECH AND MARKETING FUNCTIONAL FOODS

By the late 1990s the popularity of the FDA's Nutrition Facts label had become a near fact in and of itself. In 1997 Tipper Gore awarded the FDA the Presidential Design Achievement Award for its "very useful, consumer-friendly design." Several Food Marketing Institute studies indicated that a majority of consumers were familiar with the label, and most had made decisions not to eat certain foods based on it.[105] The new label's apparent popularity trumped any pessimism about possible negative consequences. A contemporary design critic chose to describe the Nutrition Facts label simply and enthusiastically as "A Masterpiece!"[106]

Despite the food label's popularity, this mode of regulating food labels—standardizing food information—would be challenged by a broader conservative legal movement touting "commercial free speech." The concept of commercial free speech arose from a 1942 Supreme Court decision that ruled the First Amendment did not protect purely commercial advertising from government restrictions. The court recognized that, while citizens' free speech rights should be protected from government censorship, advertising was a different kind of speech that the government could rightfully regulate. In the 1976 case *Virginia State Pharmacy Board v. Virginia Citizens Consumer Council,* however, the Supreme Court partly reversed this, overruling state laws that prohibited pharmacists from advertising prescription drug prices. The court argued the state's laws weren't merely commercial regulation, but also concerned the public's interest in the "free flow of information." In 1985, with *Zauderer v. Office of Disciplinary Counsel of Supreme Court of Ohio,* the court defended the state's authority to require government-mandated disclaimers, so long as they provided "purely factual and uncontroversial information" intended "to dissipate the possibility of consumer confusion or deception."[107] These cases signaled courts would wade into regulations on advertising when acting in the interest of information-seeking consumers.

Subsequently, commercial free speech became a new legal wedge for corporate interest groups to challenge government restrictions on advertising.[108] When the FDA began promoting the 1993 Nutrition Facts label, some trade associations invoked commercial free speech to argue against the new label. For example, in 1993 and 1994 John B. Cordaro, representing the dietary supplements industry Council for Responsible Nutrition, asserted that the new FDA rules unduly limited what information advertisers could provide consumers. In one *Fox Morning News* show, Cordaro appeared opposite Michael R. Taylor, the FDA deputy commissioner for policy, and criticized the new government label. Cordaro said he was "concerned that the FDA has a very narrow interpretation of the information they believe can be allowed to consumers." He argued the 1990 NLEA was intended to provide "a free flow of information to allow consumers to know what the value of the product was," and that instead the new FDA rules had "literally choked off the flow of information to consumers."[109] Such attacks on the Nutrition Facts label were only the beginning.

The first major assault on the FDA's new health claims system was the Dietary Supplement Health and Education Act (DSHEA), signed into law by President Clinton on the eve of the 1994 "Republican Revolution" midterm elections. As with the Proxmire Amendments in the 1970s, discussed in chapter 4, trade groups lobbied Congress to "preserve the consumer's freedom to choose dietary supplements" and claimed the FDA labeling rules would take away people's vitamins. For the first time, the DSHEA legally defined "dietary supplements" as a new category, distinct from drugs or food additives. Dietary supplements were now products that did not have to pass safety or regulatory standards, and for which the burden of risk calculation rested entirely with the consumer.[110] As one industry informant noted, the DSHEA represented a direct attack on the FDA's long-standing "foods first approach"—that nutrition labeling and health claim policies should always promote the idea that foods, not drugs or supplements, were the best conveyor of nutrition.[111]

One issue in the disputes between the FDA and industry concerned the phrase "significant scientific agreement" in the 1990 NLEA legislation. While developing new food labeling rules from 1991 to 1994, FDA officials didn't want to expand the number of permitted health claims. Indeed, they initially accepted only seven of the ten health claims the NLEA explicitly authorized; this contributed to the industry backlash resulting in the DSHEA legislation. From 1993 to 1995 the FDA held a series of closed meetings discussing how best to implement the NLEA, and how to address health claims and "emerging scientific information" about food and diet. The resulting policy report, the "Keystone National Policy Dialogue on

Food, Nutrition, and Health," recommended that the FDA develop an "objective, flexible, and responsive" process for evaluating significant scientific agreement so as to move forward with approving new health claims. However, in 1997 Congress authorized companies to circumvent the FDA's rules and use health claims if other government agencies or peer institutions had issued "authoritative statements" endorsing a health claim.[112]

Thus the FDA was no longer the only arbiter for establishing what was sufficient scientific agreement for allowing new health claims in food labeling and advertising. In 1999 the Washington, DC, circuit court, in *Pearson v. Shalala*, rejected the FDA's claim that consumers face dangerous consequences when companies promoted unreviewed scientific claims in their advertisements for foods and dietary supplements. The FDA argued it was not just lack of evidence, but sometimes also the inconclusiveness of existing evidence that could lead to disallowing health claims. The court was not convinced, noting that the FDA hadn't expanded the list of ten approved health claims since the NLEA's passage in 1990, and it ruled the FDA's restrictive and "unarticulated" standard for "significant scientific agreement" created an unreasonable burden on marketers.[113]

More specifically, the court rejected the FDA's implied model of an overly credulous consumer: "[The FDA's argument is] that health claims lacking 'significant scientific agreement' are inherently misleading because they have such an awesome impact on consumers as to make it virtually impossible for them to exercise judgment at the point of sale. It would be as if the consumers were asked to buy something while hypnotized, and therefore they are bound to be misled."[114] In essence, the court ruled consumers were better judges of how health claims fit into their lifestyles than the FDA. The FDA's effort to be a central authority for standardizing health claims ran against First Amendment protections of commercial free speech. Despite the ruling, the FDA continued to police the most egregious cases where companies used disease claims to market foods. However, in 2003 the FDA again loosened oversight on health claims, stating that "consumers benefit from more information on food labels concerning diet and health." In place of the "significant scientific agreement" standard of proof, the FDA adopted a lesser "credible evidence" standard, citing the 1999 Pearson case as setting a legal precedent for this new standard.[115]

Another way nutrition facts were contested in the marketplace was the food industry's design of "functional foods." These included probiotic yogurts and fortified foods like omega-3-enriched eggs, new foods and new labels exploiting consumers' interest in nutrition facts and stretching the boundaries separating foods, dietary supplements, and drugs.[116] The phrase functional food emerged in the U. S. food industry in the early 1990s just when Congress and the FDA began rewriting food labeling laws.[117] Food industry experts believed they could market "designer foods," functional foods, and "nutraceuticals" because of public enthusiasm for so-called "superfoods" and for modifying diets to slow aging. The main challenge for industry was navigating the so-called "food-drug interface" or "food/drug line," the classification used by boundary regulators to distinguish different product categories, each having distinct safety standards and restrictions on advertising.[118] In an influential 1994 guide to the FDA's new Nutrition Facts labeling system, several authors described the 1990 NLEA rules, and rules under development by the FDA, as inflexible regulation that "discourages rather than encourages investment in . . . important advances in functional food technology," and suggested companies should carefully develop products to find strategic gaps or areas "outside the scope of NLEA health claims regulations."[119]

The food-drug interface was thus characterized as a legal lacuna caused by new food technologies that circumvented outdated legal categories for food versus drug. In short, functional foods presented what legal scholars have criticized as a "law lag" narrative.[120] In fact, functional foods were designed precisely to exist at this food-drug interface. They boasted benefits similar to those of drugs, yet were intended for a healthy, diet-conscious population.[121] Many functional foods ran afoul of the FDA's restrictions on implied health and "structure/function" claims, statements linking specific nutrients with explicit or implied claims for physiological effect (e.g., "calcium builds strong bones" or "fiber maintains bowel regularity"). Such claims gamed the FDA's nutrition labeling system, not mentioning a specific disease but suggesting health-promoting properties with clear relevance to specific disease concerns. In response, in the early 1990s the FDA introduced a new product classification: "medical foods." Ironically, this new classification attempted to recuperate the FDA's original use of "foods for special dietary purposes" that doctors prescribed to a patient, but did not intend for wider use.[122]

New food labeling and packaging strategies were also blurring the FDA's message on Nutrition Facts. Since the Nutrition Facts label's 1993 debut, marketers had experimented with front-of-package or shelf-labeling initiatives to highlight nutrition profiles for foods, focus attention on specific information on the nutrition label, or guide the consumer's overall assessment of food products. A 1992 study showed that shelf-tags, placed on shelves in supermarkets to draw consumers' attention to particular products, significantly increased market share for nutrition-tagged foods.[123] Organizations also responded to the FDA's new labeling system by renewing their efforts in third-party certification. In 1995, for example, the American Heart Association again implemented a labeling program encouraging risk-reducing diets. It developed a "Heart Check" program, where foods fitting a particular nutritional profile based on the FDA's nutrition labeling criteria could place the AHA label on the front of the package. The food industry began to develop front-of-package (FOP) labeling schemes highlighting value-added nutrients in their products—in 2002 Wegmans Supermarket introduced the "Wellness Keys"; in 2004 General Mills introduced "Goodness Corners." While these FOP labels referenced and thus arguably reinforced the importance of the FDA's Nutrition

Facts panel, they also appropriated the panel into the retailers' and manufacturers' promotional messages, turning the government brand into an extension of their own brand management and marketing campaigns.

CONCLUSIONS

As an example of informational regulation, the FDA's Nutrition Facts panel in many ways looked like a success. Since it appeared on nearly all packaged foods, it significantly reconfigured information infrastructures for food retailing and advertising. The label dramatically altered America's food supply and choices at the supermarket. Faced with mandatory, universal labeling, between 1990 and 1993 American food companies began reformulating their products to avoid startling their loyal customers with ominous information about the nutritional content (or lack thereof) of familiar foods. By 1994 consumers might have been eating the same products as previously, but were now unwittingly eating (slightly) different foods. In other words, whether or not consumers read the nutrition label, everyone was affected by its introduction.

The Nutrition Facts panel also marked the popular ascendance of nutrition science. Words that in 1945 were only used by specialized scientific experts were, in 1995, terms encountered on food packages everywhere. Even if a consumer didn't believe in dieting or calorie-counting, they probably believed in the idea of calories, that foods had them, and that some foods even had "empty calories." Listing unhealthy fats and carbohydrates at the top of the Nutrition Facts panel enshrined the idea of negative nutrition, that eating less is more, into everyday life. As advertisers embraced this new language for food, it contributed to marketing nutritionism and ideologies reducing food to health. Nutritionism, however, is a part of a broader trend in contemporary food politics toward informationism, a focus on individuals consuming food information—labels, advertisements, and books about food—while ignoring the central role that market intermediaries and expert gatekeepers play in driving what we eat.

In the 1990s, regulators embraced information as the new way to govern, by equipping consumers to govern themselves. The birth of the FDA's Nutrition Facts label fits this story neatly. When FDA commissioner David Kessler went on *Larry King Live* in 1994, he promoted the new label as a form of consumer empowerment, placing the FDA on the side of the people. After Kessler dodged a couple of King's questions referencing the polemics of the new label, the following exchange illustrated the strong association between information and democracy:

> *King*: So nobody doesn't like this? Manufacturers have settled into it?
>
> *Kessler*: It's information. It's information for consumers.
>
> *King*: You'd have to be whack to be mad at information!

Kessler: It's information you can use to affect your health.

King: Wouldn't you be kinda dumb *not* to read it?

Kessler: Well, it's up to people what they want to do.[124]

The exuberance for informational fixes obscured its many problems. In some ways the Nutrition Facts label became a victim of its own success. While the FDA promoted it as almost "self-explanatory," a "correct" interpretation of how the label could help build a healthy diet demanded substantial training. Christine Taylor and Virginia Wilkening, who both worked on designing the Nutrition Facts label, later complained, "Efforts to educate the public about the nutrition label have always struggled with virtually nonexistent funding and have come about only in limited ways, primarily as part of other public health education programs."[125] As public education campaigns for the Nutrition Facts label have dwindled, nutrition facts messages have become increasingly appropriated by private industry advertisers, whose message is ultimately to sell, not to educate.

The FDA label has also been overshadowed by a proliferation of new platforms and information environments for learning about food. Political scientist Bruce Bimber has noted one consequence of "information abundance" is that "information itself is becoming politically less institutionalized."[126] By adopting marketing and branding concepts, making regulation a matter of reputation management, the FDA reconceived government's role in markets as that of information broker. Clearly this diminished the government's role. Standards-setting placed the government at the center of market formation. Informational regulation reduced the FDA-as-information-broker to just one market player among many.[127] Nutrition Facts might be a government brand, but it had become just one brand in a sea of brands.

6

Labeling Lifestyles

Opt-Out Platforms

Can the consumer be trusted with information? In the 1990s, while some commentators welcomed the new information society, others expressed serious doubts about consumers' ability to discern good information from bad. Many leaders in consumer movements expressed a profound disillusionment with industrialization, including signature innovations of the twentieth-century American food system. Some social movements criticized modern living, pointing to nuclear waste and radiation, chemical pollution, and even the threat of genetic contamination posed by new recombinant DNA techniques, as evidence that science was remaking the world in dangerous and unsustainable ways. These movements questioned the failure of modern food marketing to embrace social and ethical issues, such as community health, environmental well-being, or the dignified treatment of workers who grow and prepare our food. Beginning in the 1980s, these groups turned to labeling and certification schemes to foster new forms of socially responsible consumption.[1]

Many experts, however, believed these movements were driven by a dangerously reactionary "anti-science" attitude, a rejection of key tenets of rational enlightenment at the core of modernization. They worried that the wrong kind of information, taken out of context or misunderstood, could mobilize the irrational fears of consumers and undermine the public good. One had to be especially careful when deciding what to put on the label.

This chapter explores different political uses of food labels in the 1980s and 1990s, happening in parallel with the Food and Drug Administration's 1993 Nutrition Facts reforms. First, the chapter examines debates over labeling risk, specifically the use of warning labels, and the concerns of risk experts about how best to manage what they regarded as the increasing politicization of risk. Second, it explores how the FDA employed a policy of "substantial equivalence," attempting to resolve a debate about risk involving genetically modified organisms (GMOs). Third, it considers the U. S. Department of Agriculture's (USDA) implementation of federal standards for an "organic" label as a contrasting case to the Nutrition Facts label.

For food labeling in the 1990s, the most significant U. S. policy developments were the FDA's Nutrition Facts panel, discussed in chapter 5, the advent of the USDA Organic label, and the FDA's policy of substantial equivalence.[2] These parallel government initiatives show that in this period food labeling was not a simple story of providing consumers with more information and greater empowerment. The same governmental agencies pushing a pro-information campaign for nutrition labeling were, in other policy arenas, expressing doubts about trusting consumers with information. In 1992, for example, the FDA chose not to recognize GMO-free labeling for foods under the rationale that GM foods were substantially equivalent to conventional foods, a decision only partially reversed in 2012.

Concerns with risk labels, debates over GM-free labeling, and the conventionalization of organic foods are all examples of "lifestyle politics," that is, the political activism around private pursuits and personal identities, including personal food philosophies and socially responsible diets.[3] Scholars have been writing about this realignment of the personal as political for decades, but haven't addressed the role that labeling played in enabling markets for these new consumer identities.[4] As early as 1990, social scientist Claude Fischler described the modern food identity crisis as the "omnivore's dilemma," observing that the modern eater's chief predicament was deciding what to eat, given the numerous options and choices available.[5] The omnivore's dilemma was a deliberate consequence of a key strategy in food marketing and retailing: more choices, more sales. This explosion of choice produced a proliferation of third-party certification schemes in food markets, which consumers experienced at the supermarket through various new "labels for lifestyles": organic, non-GM, dolphin-safe, carbon footprint, fair-trade, and animal-welfare approved, among others.[6]

This chapter examines what happened when alternative food politics were put on labels, or deliberately kept off, by market or government institutions. By the 1990s food labels were used for many purposes: as a technology of trust, to shore up consumer attachment to a brand; as a technology of transparency, to inform consumers about what they bought but cannot see; as a technology of obfuscation, to distract consumers using puffery; as a technology of regulating risk, to short-circuit resistance to industrial food by depoliticizing risk; and as a technology of lifestyle consumerism, to promote self-selecting lifestyles and self-determination. The package label's small space couldn't contain all the meanings and histories of

FIGURE 21. Examples of ethical and risk labels for foods that have appeared since the 1980s (clockwise from top left): A Greener World's "Animal Welfare Approved" certification label, Braum's Ice Cream & Dairy Store's 2007 "rBGH Free" label, NonGMO Project GMO-free certification label, California Proposition 65 warning label, NOAA Fisheries' Tuna Tracking and Verification Program "Dolphin Safe" certification label, USDA "organic" label, Fair Trade USA's "Fair Trade Certified" label, international "Radura" label for irradiated food, UK-based Carbon Trust "carbon footprint" certification label, and USDA "Bioengineered" GMO label.

the food inside. As governments, food companies, and consumer advocacy organizations increasingly turned to the food label as an interface between the consumer and macro food system policy decisions, to label or not to label became a central battleground in debates about food and agriculture.

Risk labels and lifestyle labels were a seductive market solution to political stalemate. Voluntary labeling schemes didn't threaten mainstream, conventional food production, but did allow producers to adopt socially responsible production practices and then charge a premium to consumers willing to pay for it. Much like the FDA's voluntary nutrition labeling in the 1970s, these measures resolved political problems by promoting consumer choice, transforming a "right-to-know" into a "right-to-buy."[7] Thus, for consumers with means, they provided what sociologist Ulrich Beck described as an "escape option" from the increasing hazards of the "risk society."[8] Product label campaigns offered an "opt out" solution to contentious political issues, empowering consumers to eschew lowest-common-denominator mass markets in favor of smaller, alternative "ethical" markets for selected goods. Labeling lifestyles also hastened what was arguably the logical conclusion of niche marketing: the fragmentation of the public sphere into fractious, lifestyle-specific communities of like-minded consumers with widely divergent ideas about what America's foods and foodways ought to look like.[9]

LABELING RISK

The FDA's challenges with policing the food-drug line in consumer product markets, discussed in chapter 5, were symptoms of a broader policy ailment in the 1980s: how to respond to a growing risk awareness among consumers? Public institutions, like the FDA, charged with managing risks, as well as science advisory organizations helping the FDA assess risk, struggled to keep risk assessment and management backstage given their frontstage obligations to communicate these risks to the public. Many experts feared risk was becoming a political wedge that advocacy organizations could use to unravel long-standing institutional norms separating calm, objective risk assessment and policy deliberation from emotion-laden public debates over what was politically acceptable.[10]

Policymakers' views on product labeling had evolved substantially, partly because of a growing body of social science research on the ways consumers interact with warning labels and risk. In the 1970s and 1980s the field of risk studies emerged as an area of research dedicated to understanding the apparent irrationalities of people's behavior when faced with risky decisions.[11] A key insight was the reflexive nature of risk, including situations where communicating information about risk shaped and distorted the reality of risk, sometimes leading to irrational risk-offsetting behaviors or to the "social amplification of risk." Many of risk studies' most prominent practitioners expressed concern about what one legal analyst called the "hazard of overwarning."[12] Product warnings and informational labels presupposed a rational, literate, and already-informed consumer decision-maker, a perfect reader who these scholars doubted even existed. The challenges of "miscommunicating science," "information overload," and "the public's perception of risk" undermined older policy assumptions about product labeling, and called for innovations in what would later be called "choice architecture."[13]

By the 1980s, consumers were indeed encountering an increasing number of warnings. The most famous of these were health warning labels on cigarette packages. A Surgeon General's warning had appeared on packages since 1966, but in

1984 Congress passed the Comprehensive Smoking Education Act, requiring packages and advertisements to rotate through four warnings that included language about specific diseases and health risks caused by smoking. The tobacco industry succeeded, at least initially, in using the legally mandated warning labels to reassert the limited liability of *caveat emptor*. Consumers, the tobacco industry argued in court case after court case, knew cigarettes were bad for them because it was on the label.[14] In 1988 Congress passed the Alcoholic Beverage Labeling Act, which mandated a similar warning label for alcohol products to protect pregnant women. Yet it was unclear how effective these warning labels were. Risk studies scholars believed most consumers disregarded these warnings because they read between the lines or second-guessed their meanings. The growing interest in food allergen labeling in the 1990s only compounded these concerns. "May contain" statements about peanuts and other common food allergens appeared on so many food products that it raised concerns about the potential for consumer apathy from the overuse of warning labels.[15]

Susan Hadden's 1986 *Read the Label: Reducing Risk by Providing Information* provides a good example of how risk studies experts addressed the problems of information labeling. Susan G. Hadden (1945–1995) was a public policy analyst who regularly testified before House and Senate committees on informational regulation for chemicals in consumer products. Her book describes how information, by its nature, is a "public good": once "available to some, it is difficult to prevent it from being used by others." For this reason, for many products there is little incentive for private interests to provide "socially optimal" amounts of information for consumers.[16] Hadden therefore supported making the FDA's nutrition labeling programs mandatory for all foods. She saw two problems with the FDA's voluntary approach to nutrition labeling in the 1980s. First, manufacturers rapidly incorporated nutrient disclosures into their advertising campaigns and product comparisons, blurring the line between merely informative disclosures and disputable health promotional claims. Second, consumers were using nutrition labels as "risk labels," as guides for what to avoid rather than tools for making positive decisions about what to eat.[17] This was a problem the 1993 Nutrition Facts label didn't solve, and which resurfaced in 2002 with trans-fats labeling. Hadden thus characterized labeling policy as a trade-off between the desire to protect individual consumers' values, and the need for direct regulatory control (such as product bans), in situations where the choice to be made was too technical or the risk was collective in nature.

Not all risk studies scholars were so optimistic about informed consumers. In 1979 political scientist Aaron Wildavsky (1930–1993) authored an essay in *American Scientist*, "No Risk Is the Highest Risk of All," highlighting his concern with "an overcautious attitude toward new technological developments" that he worried would "paralyze scientific endeavor" and even make society potentially less safe. He argued "the politics of prevention" and the excesses of safety culture ignored inevitable trade-offs, including ways that reducing risks could introduce new ones.[18] One of Wildavsky's main concerns was how some people profited by feeding the public's increased risk consciousness. Some of these "risk-profiteers" were scientists whose research highlighted previously unseen risks, but others were activists who used fear-mongering to promote an anticorporate, and at times antiscience, political agenda.[19]

One example used by Wildavsky to illustrate how advocates of a "riskless society" could create panic was the Alar apple scare. In 1989 a CBS *60 Minutes* television special alarmed the American public with reports that trace amounts of a potentially carcinogenic chemical daminozide, known as Alar, might be found on apples children eat. The report caused panic, as parents worried they might have bought contaminated food. The scare figured prominently in the promotion of organic labeling, discussed later, and it also was widely cited in policy circles as a cautionary tale. Experts subsequently decided the trace amounts posed little to no risk. For Wildavsky, it served to show how a single scientific study on a product's risk could receive disproportionate media attention. Wildavsky complained this kind of "popular epidemiology" was just "an exercise in producing anger, not knowledge." He disparaged the precautionary principle, becoming a popular tool in European environmental law, as nothing more than "a marvelous piece of rhetoric."[20]

In the late 1980s, policymakers' worries about overly anxious food consumers were so pervasive that a spokesman for the Institute of Food Technologists compiled a list of common causes, explanations, and solutions for what he called "food neophobia," published in the journal *Food Technology*. He described recurrent questions, many viewed by food scientists as already settled by science or just simply absurd, that audiences regularly asked him at public workshops: "Are irradiated foods radioactive? Is MSG bad for you? Does sugar cause criminal behavior? Is it true that Twinkies have a twenty-seven-year shelf-life? Is there a carcinogenic hormone injected into cows which ends up in milk?" He attributed the persistence of these concerns to several causes: consumers' all-or-nothing relation to experts; their lack of knowledge about chemistry; their "I saw it on TV so it must be true" impressionability; and a desire for absolute certainty that clashed with scientists' tendency to "chase zeroes" and highlight "detectable" and "minuscule amounts." The author encouraged his food industry readers to engage the public by "maintain[ing] perspective," "sort[ing] sense from nonsense," and communicating accurate information at all times. But "perhaps the most needed action," he argued, was to "take 'Chicken Little' to court," to litigate public interest groups who incited a public panic until they apologized publicly for doing so. He gave the example of the Alar apple scare, and concluded, "Consumers end up paying a lot of money for a trivial degree of safety."[21]

Two specific policy incidents in the late 1980s illustrate how the new politics of risk directly impacted FDA policies on food and drug markets: irradiated foods and

Rank of Hazards from Eating Food

The Experts	The Public
1. Microbial safety	1. Pesticides
2. Over-nutrition	2. New food chemicals
3. Non-microbial safety	3. Chemical additives
a. Contaminants	4. Familiar hazards
b. Natural toxins	a. Fat & cholesterol
c. Ag. chemicals	b. Microbial spoilage
d. Food additives	c. Junk foods

FIGURE 22. "Rank of Hazards from Eating Food," comparing the differences between what the experts and the public worry about in food safety. Source: Fig. 1 in Ken Lee, "Food Neophobia: Major Causes and Treatments," *Food Technology*, December 1989, 63. Reprinted with permission from *Food Technology* magazine, Institute of Food Technologists.

California's Proposition 65.[22] Some risk studies scholars who argued that consumers were irrational agents, not to be trusted with certain kinds of information disclosures, frequently cited the example of consumers' ambivalence toward irradiated foods, despite scientific evidence suggesting it was safe. Irradiated foods originated during the early Cold War period, when food technologists, funded by the Atomic Energy Commission's "Atoms for Peace" program to find uses for radioactive waste, developed techniques for irradiating foods to remove foodborne pathogens, much like pasteurization. While they successfully developed a form of food irradiation that safely sanitized food without leaving it radioactive, reports in the 1950s and 1960s about the dangers of radioactive fallout from nuclear testing created a strong negative association that proponents of food irradiation were unable to overcome.[23]

The FDA revived interest in food irradiation when it published new rules in 1985 and 1986 allowing industry to use food irradiation for products labeled with the Radura symbol and the statement, "treated with radiation" or "treated by irradiation." Various food industry, consumer, and technical interests formed the

Coalition for Food Irradiation in 1985 to promote the benefits of the process, especially for fresh spices and produce.[24] But would consumers accept irradiated foods? Some in industry proposed alternative wording, such as "electronically pasteurized," to overcome consumer resistance, but consumer-interest groups repeatedly mobilized against such proposals. Over the next decade, researchers in risk studies used food irradiation to test their theories of risk perception and consumer acceptance. Most studies noted consumer ambivalence, not outright rejection, and attributed it to the fact that food irradiation was an unfamiliar technology. Studies also tended to ignore or conflate consumers' broader rejection of nuclear technology, for political or environmental reasons, with more specific anxieties about safety. All agreed, however, that for a subsection of the population concerned about natural foods and having "antitechnology attitudes," the "treated with radiation" label was a nonstarter. This made marketing labeled foods difficult.[25] Irradiated foods came to serve as a lesson for how, with some new technologies, industry would have to fight labeling.

A second policy concern was the California ballot initiative on "Proposition 65." In 1985 David Roe of the Environmental Defense Fund, Carl Pope of the Sierra Club, and Barry Groveman, an environmental prosecutor, authored a ballot initiative titled, "Safe Drinking and Toxic Enforcement Act." The act stringently limited the discharge of carcinogenic chemicals into the state's drinking water and required businesses to provide warning labels or signs whenever their activities or products exposed people to toxic environments. The statute placed the burden on manufacturers to prove that discharged chemicals did not pose a "significant" danger. The labeling clause in "Proposition 65," as it came to be known, particularly frightened industry since it required the following statement to be included on any chemically risky goods: "WARNING: THIS PRODUCT CONTAINS A CHEMICAL KNOWN TO THE STATE OF CALIFORNIA TO CAUSE CANCER." The ballot initiative was approved by California voters in 1986 and went into effect in February 1988.

The Proposition 65 statute quickly became the object of attacks by industry critics who claimed it was not "sound science." They argued that the statute was ineffective as a tactic to improve "information economics," since it didn't provide the consumer with adequate information about specific risks, and might even confuse consumers if the statement appeared for some toxic chemicals (named in the ballot) but not others.[26] Industry concerns about the California ballot initiative coalesced into a lobbying effort at the national level for "preemption," a legislative approach allowing more permissive or favorable federal laws to override more stringent and variable local laws. Indeed, this was a motive for some in industry to support the 1990 NLEA, discussed in chapter 5, hoping that it would preempt the California labeling law. Lobbyists argued that initiatives like Proposition 65 posed a threat of patchwork regulation, requiring industry to tailor its products to fifty different jurisdictions.[27] But industry concerns about Proposition 65 labeling proved to be overblown; the warning statement appeared on so many products and was so ubiquitous that the public largely ignored it.

Some consumers looked for and cared about these risk labels; others, however, did not. The growing pull of lifestyle politics indicated potential market opportunities (at least for some) from risk labeling, not just liabilities. Yet risk-warning fatigue, and a feeling across the political spectrum that government was out of touch with people's lifestyles and personal liberties, affected the politics of food labeling for the FDA in the 1980s and 1990s, and the government's attempts to enforce even mundane food rules.[28]

In 1991, for example, FDA commissioner David A. Kessler had two thousand cases of a leading brand of orange juice, Citrus Hill Fresh Choice, seized because it was falsely labeled as "fresh." Kessler intended to send a message that the FDA was tough on "the din of mixed messages and partial truths on food labels in this country."[29] HIV / AIDS activists, however, used the incident to critique the agency's priorities. One activist complained, "Dr. Kessler could be a hero, but he's looking at orange juice, isn't that a joke?"[30] Even where the stakes were clearly significant, such as the classification for safety purposes of foods versus drugs, the clash between expert legal classifications and popular lay classifications created an environment ripe for ridicule that undermined the agency's authority to control misleading or dangerous health claims. Lifestyle politics converged with the sentiment that, where risk was concerned, government should get out of the people's business. Nowhere was the disconnect between the public's and the FDA's view of food more striking than on the issue of genetically modified organisms (GMOs) and GM labeling on foods.

OBSCURING RATHER THAN INFORMING

Recombinant DNA technology, and its use in foods via GMOs, raised many issues for food politics: the challenge of making risk decisions about food and environmental safety based on scientific uncertainty; the need to engage the public when deliberating on those risk decisions; the ethics of patenting life, including corporate "biopiracy" of many traditional foods and medicines; the wisdom of encoding pesticide- and fertilizer-dependency into the genetic makeup of food crops; and whether rich import countries are justified in dictating these decisions to the poor export countries that grow food.[31] For many scientists tired of an increasingly hardened public rejection of *all* GM foods, the GMO debate has come to symbolize the same neophobia and irrational reaction to new biotechnologies that had accompanied food irradiation. For FDA regulators, the advent of GMO foods prompted a new strategy, "substantial equivalence," that attempted to settle lingering political divisions by sidelining labeling altogether.

One of the earliest ways a new biotechnology enters agriculture, and by extension the food system, is through animal feed and pharmaceuticals.[32] This was the case for GMOs, in the form of recombinant bovine somatotropin (rBST), also known as recombinant bovine growth hormone (rBGH). Bovine somatotropin is a hormone that increases milk production in dairy cows. While animals produce some of it naturally, recombinant DNA techniques made it possible to produce large quantities of rBGH in genetically engineered bacteria, allowing the commercial use of rBGH to enhance milk production. In 1984 Monsanto and several other multinational companies requested approval in the U.S. to sell milk produced in test trials for rBGH. In 1986 the FDA granted the companies' request, ignoring social debates about the unfair advantage rBGH would provide large farmers over small ones, as well as animal welfare concerns. The milk was sold—unlabeled—so companies could recoup research costs while awaiting broader approval for rBGH's use in mass markets. By the late 1980s and early 1990s, however, evidence accumulated suggesting a number of hidden costs from long-term use of rBGH.[33]

Activists in both the United States and Europe mobilized against approval in mass markets. In the U.S. the FDA dismissed these criticisms, citing a growing body of studies that rBGH posed no harm. In 1993 the FDA approved rBGH as safe for human consumption. In 1996 an appellate federal court overturned a Vermont law requiring milk produced by rBGH to be labeled as such. The court argued the state government was infringing on producers' constitutionally protected "commercial free speech." With access to the market assured, U.S. milk producers began using the hormone. Consumers reacted with indifference. A subsequent USDA Economic Research Service report attempting to explain this somewhat surprising outcome drew two conclusions. First, it indicated American consumers by and large trusted their regulatory institutions. Second, the absence of reports of harm from rBGH after its approval in mass markets became a reinforcing mechanism for its public acceptance.[34]

In Europe, by contrast, legislators put a moratorium on rBGH's use because it created a socioeconomic hardship for Europe's dairy farmers, already struggling with an oversupply of milk production. In a move that would become a trend for U.S.-Europe trade standoffs over the next decade, the U.S. turned to the World Trade Organization (WTO), who ruled the European embargo was an illegal form of economic protectionism.[35]

The difference between the rBGH debate in Europe and the U.S. was indicative of larger cultural and regulatory differences in response to GMOs. As early as 1997 the European Union required labeling of all GM foods, which the U.S. protested. Several member countries passed temporary moratoriums on the release of live GMOs, effectively preventing GM crop production and substantially slowing research, and in 2000 the E.U. followed suit with a de facto moratorium on live-release GMOs. In the U.S., meanwhile, regulators not only permitted the use of GMOs without disclosure but actively blocked attempts to label products as GMO-free.

Beyond its significant impacts on food producers and global trade in agriculture, the growing divide between GMO-friendly and GMO-opposed countries sparked debate about the relationship between risk and consumer behavior.[36] Social scientists, policymakers, and politicians wanted to know: What was driving the debate? How much were protests on GMOs about moral problems posed by the technology, or about broader political concerns, such as top-down globalization threatening regional identity and autonomy? And did policymakers owe it to the public to listen to their concerns? The debate drove a major shift in the field, as many scholars in science and technology studies rejected the idea that public skepticism about new technologies resulted from ignorance or fear. Instead, these scholars reversed the question, asking whether it was science policymakers misunderstanding the public, not the public misunderstanding the science. Advocates of GM crop technologies wanted to frame the GM debate as one of public misunderstanding and irrational fears, but critics of GMOs increasingly argued consumers had a right to choose what they ate, to determine what they personally felt was or was not a reasonable risk, and that the food industry couldn't circumvent public choice.

Many of the first-generation GM foods, approved in 1994 and placed on the market in 1996, were producer-oriented products, designed to address farmers' concerns about crop management with a technological fix rather than appeal to consumer concerns about food quality. Monsanto developed GM "Roundup Ready" soybeans, rapeseed (canola), and corn so the company's Roundup herbicide only killed undesirable weeds, without negatively affecting the crop plant. Several biotech companies developed GM "Bt crops" for cotton, potato, and maize, named for *Bacillus thuringiensis* bacteria that naturally produced a protein toxic to many insect pests. All of these crops were widely used in animal feed or processed foods: while few American consumers would encounter GM-based corn or soybeans firsthand, they routinely consumed them in cereals, snack foods, baked goods, soft drinks, dairy products, and even some processed meats, whether they realized it or not.

The early market success of first-generation GMOs in U.S. agriculture is indicative of how U.S. agriculture in the 1980s and 1990s was being restructured by two trends: "productivism" and "substitutionism." The first, productivism, was the belief that producing more food should be the primary goal of agricultural innovation, even if technology adoption entailed intensive capital investments as well as environmental and social costs for rural communities or consumers generally. Political activist Jim Hightower attributed the productivist mentality to vertical integration in the agro-food industry, arguing that it redirected "nature's plan" to conform to the demands of industrial processing and mass marketing, rather than helping resource-strapped farmers protect their rural livelihoods and communities.[37] A 1980s farm crisis, prompted by high interest rates and oil prices, accelerated farm debt from land and equipment purchases, furthering the consolidation of small family farms by large agribusinesses. These large-scale farmers primarily sold to large-scale institutional buyers and agricultural processors, not to small-scale food retailers like local restaurants or food markets. They therefore focused on producing large quantities of commodities with small profit margins. New technologies, including GM crops that supported pesticide use and insect resistance, helped large farmers efficiently manage large-scale fields. What the consumer wanted was a secondary consideration, often reduced to a simple metric: price.

GM foods also reflected a logic of "substitutionism" that had been deeply entrenched in the American food processing industry for decades. In their 1987 analysis of emerging agricultural bio-industries, sociologists David Goodman, Bernardo Sorj, and John Wilkinson argued that the increasingly mechanized industrial manufacture of foods meant that "the rural form of [food] and its constituents could then be modified and obscured, facilitating its treatment and presentation as an industrial product." Increasingly a food's taste, perishability, or "identity" arose more from an industrial process or a manufacturer's brand than its basis in rural production. The eventual outcome was a substitution whereby the value-added component of an agricultural product was replaced by a nonagricultural, synthetic product.[38] This describes a plug-and-play food economy, where different steps in food production and different components in food were easily modified and exchanged to create a flexible mass-production process for marketing endless novelty.

The biotechnology industry's first-generation GMOs reflected this supply-side logic. The industry further reduced agricultural crops to, as Goodman, Sorj, and Wilkinson put it, "the status of biomass, differentiated [only] by their chemical composition."[39] Substitutionism would be most effective for producers if consumers didn't care, or didn't know, where or how the food was made, so long as it was cheap and healthy. For the biotech industry, it was therefore important that no process-based information about whether bioengineering was used to make a food ingredient should appear on the label.

The first genetically modified food to be sold in the U.S. where the product itself was the modified plant was the Flavr Savr tomato, developed by Calgene, a small biotech firm. The Flavr Savr tomato was designed by anti-sense DNA recombination, where the undesirable trait, in this case a gene for a protein that speeds up the tomato ripening, is inserted backwards, essentially negating or decreasing that trait's expression. A Flavr Savr tomato took seven to ten days longer to ripen than a conventional tomato. This potentially offered value added for both crop transporters, allowing for longer storage time, and consumers, because the longer ripening time increased the tomato's flavor. Calgene planned to market the Flavr Savr as *better* for consumers, and therefore requested the FDA apply greater scrutiny to their product to build consumer confidence in it. In 1994 the FDA approved it, and Calgene heavily promoted it at supermarkets and in magazines.

The Flavr Savr tomato, however, ultimately failed on the market. Public opposition to GMO foods, spearheaded by vocal GM critic Jeremy Rifkin (1945–), a political activist who ran the nonprofit organization Foundation on Economic Trends, certainly contributed to its failure. But Calgene also failed to solve more fundamental problems with its business model, including producing the tomato at a cost that didn't offset the expense of R&D and patenting litigation.[40] For larger biotech companies, the spectacular demise of the Flavr Savr tomato confirmed that consumers weren't worth the effort and expense of GMO research and development. Rather, they should continue to focus on more dependable buyers: farmers.

Calgene's attempt to use Flavr Savr's GMO status as a marketing tool was unusual for an industry that generally preferred to keep GM information backstage, among producers and away from consumers. In 1992 the FDA issued a "Guidance to Industry," explaining how it intended to regulate modified foods under the Coordinated Framework for the Regulation of Biotechnology, newly announced by Vice President Dan Quayle. The framework reflected heavy lobbying by the biotech industry, especially Monsanto, an American agrochemical and agricultural biotechnology company.[41] GM foods would be regulated like normal hybrid plants with minimal safety oversight, unless a protein produced by the introduced genes was allergenic, or substantially different in chemical structure and function from conventional food proteins. In those situations it would be classified as a food additive. Thus, most new GM foods would be GRAS, or "generally recognized as safe" and acceptable for the U.S. market.[42]

This became a key rationale for genetically modified foods: if they weren't substantially chemically different from their non-GM equivalents, they should be labeled the same without reference to the GM production process. A year later the Organization for Economic Co-operation and Development (OECD), an international institution that set global standards and internationally harmonized guidelines for industry, declared this the "substantial equivalence" principle.[43] The U.S. policy of not labeling "substantially equivalent" GM products posed an immediate challenge to European countries. Because the U.S. government and exporters like Archer Daniels Midland and Cargill considered GM soybeans substantially equivalent to unmodified soybeans, requests in 1996 by European Union governments to segregate soybean products shipped to Europe were ignored, making it nearly impossible for them to label GM soybeans.

One very vocal advocate of substantial equivalence was Henry I. Miller (1947–), who served as the founding director of the FDA Office of Biotechnology from 1989 to 1994. Trained as a medical doctor, Miller began working for the FDA in 1979. He later boasted he was "instrumental in the rapid licensing of [rDNA-synthesized] human insulin and human growth hormone." Miller was the FDA representative on the Recombinant Advisory Committee throughout the 1980s. Before, during, and after his time at the FDA, Miller was a strident critic of government regulations on biotechnology and what he considered to be the public's hypersensitivity to biotechnological risks. After leaving the FDA, Miller joined a conservative think tank, the Hoover Institution, and continued to be a vocal proponent of GMOs and a critic of efforts to regulate them. When movements to introduce GMO-labeling picked up in Europe and the U.S., Miller argued strongly this would not be "in the best interest of consumers." In addition to creating a burden on producers that translated into costs for consumers, Miller attributed the push for labeling to "ideological opponents" who wanted to increase consumer anxiety. He echoed risk studies scholars from the 1980s, arguing, "The consumer views the technologies that are most regulated to be the least safe ones. Heavy involvement by government, no matter how well intended, inevitably sends the wrong signal."[44] In other words, the less a product is regulated and the less information provided, the better for public trust.

Even as the FDA pushed for regulating GM organisms based only on their "end product," another peer government agency decided genetic engineering warranted special oversight. In 1994 the U.S. Environmental Protection Agency (EPA) introduced "process-based" guidelines that required companies to seek an EPA permit for any large-scale release of a GM pesticide plant. Unlike the FDA, the EPA was treating new GM plants with added pesticide properties as *not* substantially equivalent to just the pesticide, which was already approved. GM crops using familiar pesticides would still require environmental safety review by the EPA. The different policies by the FDA and EPA partly reflected different stakes in the risks being assessed. The FDA was considering health risks from foods derived from GM crops. The EPA was concerned about potentially irreversible ecological damage caused by releasing GM plants into the environment. If a GM food proved risky, the FDA had recourse to a recall; the EPA did not. But the EPA's process-based approach also reflected differences in regulatory cultures and the two agencies' different standards on what was an acceptable risk. Having grown weary of consumers' recurrent distrust of new food technologies, many at the FDA were increasingly dismissive of any anti-GM food opinion. The EPA's policies elicited fierce criticisms from Miller, who derided the agency's efforts to create "additional experiments of the kind performed in the 1970s . . . to assess the risks of rDNA-modified organisms as a category" as "scientifically unsound."[45]

For the 1990s and 2000s the FDA adopted Miller's position, not that of the EPA. Regulators asserted a "may contain GMOs" or "GM-free" label could invite irrational and unnecessary suspicions. The U.S. contested the European Union's 1997 labeling requirement as an unfair trade barrier, but the World Trade Organization (WTO) rejected this claim. In 2006 the WTO overturned Europe's ban on GMOs, citing a lack of scientific evidence for safety concerns. However, the WTO's protections on labeling indicated it accepted Europe's appeal to consumer sovereignty. European consumers had a right to information on GMOs if their governments sought to require it. The WTO decision reflected an increasingly common market compromise favoring lifestyle politics. Labels privatized risk. Labeling allowed companies to continue selling products and made it the consumer's choice, and problem, as to what risks were acceptable.[46]

For almost a decade this was the uneasy settlement: GM labeling in Europe, while in the U.S. "GMO-free" labeling was prohibited. As more Americans learned about European consumers' apprehensions, however, American consumer advocacy organizations succeeded in reopening the GM-labeling question. In 2010 the Non-GMO project started a product verification program where foods not genetically modified could carry its label with a butterfly logo. In 2012 a coalition of hundreds of organizations launched a "Just Label It" campaign, petitioning the FDA to require mandatory labeling. In May 2013 a California state ballot initiative to require GMO labeling almost passed. And in 2014 Vermont passed the first mandatory state GMO food labeling law, with other states considering similar measures. Also, more and more branded manufacturers and retailers began using "rBGH free" and "GM free" labels, despite federal policies against it, partly in response to "name and shame" campaigns by anti-GM activists and partly to cater to concerned consumers.[47]

In 2016 Congress passed, and President Obama signed, a law regulating GMO labeling and mandating disclosure of genetically engineered ingredients. Yet the new law was hardly a victory for proponents of labeling. Instead, it illustrated how labeling can be used to mute or minimize awareness for certain risks, and doesn't always amplify them.[48] Producers were allowed to use a scannable QR code, a machine-readable image made up of black and white squares, in place of a label declaration on the food package, arguably disguising the disclosure.[49] Unless the food consumer scanned the QR code with their smartphone, they might never learn whether the food contained GM ingredients. Indeed, as if to confirm that U.S. policies on GM labeling sought to obscure rather than inform, in 2020 the FDA and USDA Agricultural Marketing Service implemented a new food disclosure standard whereby GM foods were labeled "bioengineered" or "derived from bioengineering," instead of more familiar "may contain GMOs" or "GM-free" labels.

THE MAINSTREAMING OF AN ALTERNATIVE FOOD MOVEMENT

When consumers buy "organic," what are they looking for? Organic foods are defined principally by how they are made, that is, by the use of organic gardening and farming techniques and by the absence of certain agricultural technologies. Unlike the Nutrition Facts label, which discloses contents, the organic label specifies a production process. At the same time, the word "organic" carries connotations of wholesomeness. It suggests something "natural," meaning "in harmony

with nature," and "whole," as in not artificially processed, and certainly not contaminated with unnatural chemicals.[50] Because the term is holistic, it is difficult to
define. Advocates of organic do not seek to disentangle human health, environmental health, and cultural practices, but instead emphasize their interrelatedness.
In this sense, the Organic label is the antithesis of Nutrition Facts. Organic inte-
grates and synthesizes diverse elements of good living with health, while Nutrition
Facts seek to separate out health qualities in food, ignoring where those qualities
come from and how that nutrition is eaten. The two labels engender different
food-as-health products. Nutrition Facts leads to tinkering with functional foods,
while organic evokes the older purity-versus-contamination ideology of the early
twentieth-century pure food movements.

Because organic labeling sells difficult-to-measure qualities, including a production history not directly accessible to the consumer, organic foods are a classic
example of a credence good. Credence good labels function as a seal of trust, much
like a brand, between the buyer and third-party certifier. Insofar as the consumer
trusts the certifying institution, it trusts that the product is "virtuous" as labeled.
The consumer's embrace of a credence label like organic is a strategy for escaping
information overload by trusting a filtering mechanism, and an example of what
sociologist Andrew Szasz calls the "inverted quarantine," an "individualistic
attempt to barricade one's self from looming noxious threats" by restricting one's
diet.[51] The push for the USDA to certify organic foods in the 1990s is an interesting
example of the trade-offs in institutionalizing a social movement and mainstreaming an alternative food ideal. It was also an example of how labeling lifestyles
transformed ideals into consumerism.

In the U.S., the organic movement is usually traced to Jerome I. Rodale (1898–
1971). In 1940 Rodale started an organic farm. Two years later he began publishing
a magazine, *Organic Farming,* which taught readers how to garden with organic,
nonintensive techniques, such as composting. Rodale and his adherents actively
disparaged the "chemical farming" approach celebrated in conventional agriculture after WWII, including the use of chemical pesticides and synthetic fertilizers.
They sought more harmonious, natural techniques that restored nature instead of
battling it. In 1950 Rodale started another magazine, *Prevention,* which focused on
health, because he wanted to emphasize the connections between human health
and the environment. A key feature of Rodale's advocacy was his savvy blend of
niche consumerism with populist appeals to common sense. As historian Andrew
Case put it, Rodale's marketplace environmentalism "did not require a PhD or
peer-reviewed results to gain entry." "Green consumerism" foregrounded personal
choice over public health. This gave organic farming a democratic appeal, but also
encouraged marketing claims that exploited people's health anxieties.[52]

For much of the second half of the twentieth century, most commentators and
food policy experts regarded organic farming and food as an anti-establishment

fad. Indeed, in his 1967 book, *Walk, Do Not Run, to the Doctor,* Rodale boasted, "I believe I am America's No. 1 food faddist."[53] Advocates of organic foods, including Rodale himself, were often targets of the 1950s AMA-FDA campaigns on nutrition quackery discussed in chapter 2. From 1964 to 1968 the Federal Trade Commission (FTC) took Rodale and Rodale Press to court for making "false statements and representations in advertising . . . concerning diet, disease, and the health of mankind."[54] The FTC lost the case, but other establishment experts and institutions continued to campaign against organic food fads. Harvard nutritionist Frederick Stare and epidemiologist Elizabeth Whelan published numerous diatribes casting organic foods as a health lifestyle hoax. In 1974 the FDA prohibited any claims that "organic" and "natural" foods were better for your health. A 1977 *Newsweek* article claimed organic and natural food movements were turning Americans into "nutritional hypochondriacs."[55] Despite such efforts by conventional food and agriculture institutions, or perhaps because of them, organic foods and farming continued to grow in popularity, particularly as prominent counterculture restaurants began to advertise their commitment to organic produce and foodways.

Geographer Julie Guthman describes how different social and cultural movements came to embrace the organic farming movement. In the 1960s, various counterculture movements promoted organic farming: those interested in community-building through food cooperatives; groups who formed back-to-the-land communes seeking self-sufficiency; and members of the emerging environmental movement, who criticized productivist farming's nonsustainable use of pesticides and artificial fertilizers.[56] In the 1970s, because of its growing popularity and because of now-diverse interests in organic practices, numerous organizations began developing a key tactic to promote standards of organic farming: certification programs. The first to establish organic certifications was the California Certified Organic Farmers program (CCOF), founded in 1973, but by the early 1980s third-party certification programs and regional associations had proliferated. Because organic certification was decentralized, a label reflected the values and politics of its certifying organization, rather than adherence to any consistent set of practices. Conflicts between certifying agencies about specific ingredients or processes were common, creating problems for producers of mixed-ingredient organic foods.[57]

The Organic Foods Production Act (OFPA), passed by Congress in 1990, transformed the organic movement into a mainstream consumer option. The OFPA called for the USDA to develop consistent, uniform standards, and to establish a National Organic Standards Board to oversee these standards. The legislation passed partly in response to the 1989 Alar apple scare, when panicked shoppers desperately sought foods uncontaminated with the presumed carcinogen. Meryl Streep, speaking on behalf of the environmental nonprofit Natural Resources Defense Council, encouraged Americans to support organic farms.[58] Familiar proponents of organic, including Rodale Press, happily used their media platforms to promote organic food as the solution to the presence of toxic chemicals in agriculture.[59] Following the Alar scare, and in the absence of regulations defining "organic," many food processors put organic labels on their products. In this context, the growing organic food industry became motivated to accept USDA oversight because its leaders feared that "organic" would soon seem as empty and toothless as "natural."

Historically, the USDA opposed organic farming practices, viewing them as anti-tech and a pseudoscience. However, in 1980, after receiving numerous requests for information, the USDA compiled a report on organic methods that had been tested and proven to be useful. The report signaled a thaw in the USDA's hostile approach to organic farming. By 1989, when the Alar scare occurred, the USDA was receptive to overseeing organic standards.

The implementation of the 1990 OFPA and the USDA "Organic" label posed a problem for both consumers and organic farmers: exactly what defines something as organic? Is a product's organic status determined just by production standards, or is it about something more?[60] The 1990 OFPA was designed to encourage a market for packaged organic foods, which contradicted the spirit of "whole" foods in earlier organic farming. The OFPA had a proviso for processed organic: product could be labeled organic only if more than 50 percent of the ingredient weight (minus water) was from organic ingredients. Otherwise the product could not be labeled as organic, but individual ingredients could be labeled as such in the Ingredients panel. The law's provisions for heavily processed foods particularly irked the segment of the organic movement that equated organic foods with healthy living. Thus nutrition scientist Joan Dye Gussow criticized the 1990 OFPA for focusing too narrowly on production methods and ignoring the food product. She illustrated this criticism with the hypothetical ironic example of an organic Twinkie.[61] Was it organic if it was junk food? While organic may have evoked broad ideals about a return to natural and authentic foods, USDA-certified organic paradoxically created a market for organic *convenience* foods.

Even when it came to production standards, the USDA's initial 1997 proposed guidelines allowed categories of products and product ingredients that surprised organic activists: GMOs, irradiated foods, and sewage sludge used as fertilizer. Outraged, organic food organizations mobilized their memberships and consumer base to write negative letters. The USDA received 275,000 public comments, the largest ever received on a labeling proposal, and quickly reversed course on these three technologies.[62] The result was that, once the labels hit the shelves in 2002, many consumers viewed the organic label as an assurance of what a food did *not* contain. The USDA Organic label, for example, became a proxy for consumers seeking non-GMO products. Indeed, in 1999 Secretary of Agriculture Dan Glickman said there was no need to label GM-free food in the U.S. because the USDA organic label would guarantee this.[63] Similarly, the organic label worked as a "voluntary ban" or "opt out" for pesticides.

The USDA Organic label unquestionably compromised important principles of earlier regional and local certifying associations, but this observation fails to understand how labels function. Label certification organizations had to make judgment calls and adapt policies to incorporate broad ideals about what is "organic" or "fair trade," or as with the case of the FDA's standards of identity, what is "customary." But the label functions as a technology of trust in those organizations' commitments and practical interpretations of the ideal. By ceding management of the organic label to a national board and the USDA, proponents invited certain compromises and sacrifices in exchange for extending the organic brand. What were those compromises? The USDA failed to embrace certain features of earlier organic movements. Although it was a production-based label, USDA Organic ignored community and social justice concerns with farming, including the equitable treatment of labor. The onerous certification process discouraged many smaller organic farms from entering the program, and in this way the USDA Organic label shed organic farming's earlier "small is beautiful" spirit. And, of course, organic certification criteria focused strictly on enforceable production standards, ignoring whether some packaged and processed foods violated the spirit of organic foods.[64]

Ultimately, the USDA Organic label opened the way for large-scale "organic agribusiness," disparaged by one food writer in 2001 as the "organic-industrial complex."[65] The USDA organic label demonstrated both the opportunities and limits of a "marketplace environmentalism" that used the consumer marketplace as a tool for environmental action.[66] While it may be an exaggeration to say organic was "co-opted" by the USDA and industrial farming, the national certification program did create separate paths for American agriculture. Without fundamentally threatening establishment farming, the organic label provided an "opt out" option from conventional agriculture for the discerning, affluent consumer. Julie Guthman argues that this "conventionalization" of organic transformed it from a social movement of ideals into a price premium upgrade option at the supermarket.[67] As the authors of a 2001 book, *Living Organic: Easy Steps to an Organic Family Lifestyle*, noted, "Today you can buy organic food without adjusting your lifestyle."[68]

CONCLUSIONS

In the first decades of the twenty-first century, consumers' embrace of "natural" foods was as much a rejection of high-tech, industrial foodways as it was an embrace of a romanticized, albeit ahistorical view of traditional foods.[69] The FDA's attempts to respond to this consumer trend through regulatory action became a highly choreographed exchange between "objective" informative disclosures and "subjective" value attributes. In developing the Nutrition Facts panel and the doctrine of substantial equivalence for GMO-based foods, the FDA embraced scientific objectivity. Facts believed to be science-based and salient to health would go on government-mandated disclosures, and information considered to be inherently subjective or political was relegated to credence labels and private branding. By this logic, the reader of the FDA's Nutrition Facts panel didn't need to know whether a food was processed or "natural" to evaluate its healthfulness: they could simply look at the ingredients. By contrast, the introduction of the USDA Organic label presumed consumers trusted the certifying institution to maintain a semblance of the nebulous standards they sought in organic food. This was politics, not science. Meanwhile, risk labels continued to generate heated arguments about whether food labels are tools of transparency or obfuscation. Do labels hide more than they reveal?

Different labels targeted different market strategies and imagined consumers. The FDA's Nutrition Facts label was an information infrastructure for mass markets, seeking to standardize the flow of health claims for a busy, "distributed consumer." USDA Organic, by contrast, was a one-size-fits-all label for a credence good, a guarantor of trust for consumers seeking an alternative to mass-marketed industrial foods. Lifestyle labels like USDA Organic also became a market "escape option" and a political opt-out for the conscientious consumer. Those who were exasperated with reforming the food system through public deliberation and politics could now buy their way into a more virtuous private one.[70] Labeling risk, or its absence, transformed political contests over how to reform the food system into private, personal choices for consumers (who could afford it).

The wide variety of political uses for labels in recent decades has muddied the signal sent by any one label. Consumers read different labels to cross-check and challenge the claims on other labels, a consequence of what historian Paul Duguid describes as the multiplicity of voices in food chains.[71] The FDA's food labeling policies focused on the informative panel as a conduit of science-based information, intended for rational calculation. But lifestyle labels demonstrated what advertisers and brand marketers have long known: the label is a technology of trust and consumers read (and second-guess) the information there, looking for more than just facts. Consumers have an emotional relationship to food and therefore to the food label.[72] Drawing upon new theories in behavioral economics, discussed in the conclusion, policymakers have increasingly framed food labeling policies for the "rationally irrational" consumer, whose purchases reflect emotional drives and impulses but are nevertheless patterned and predictable.

Conclusion

The Informational Turn in Food Politics

In 2002 a new food scare hit. *Trans* fats were suddenly found to be even worse than saturated fats for causing cardiovascular disease and possibly numerous other health issues. *Trans* fats—fatty acids chains with *trans* chemical bonds—were partially hydrogenating liquid vegetable oils that became solids at room temperature. Scientific concern about the possible risks of trans fats wasn't new. The Center for Science in the Public Interest had been advocating labeling trans fats since the mid-1990s.[1] Widespread concern only emerged after a 2002 Institute of Medicine report stated that "the only safe intake of trans-fats is zero." Media coverage drew attention to a wide range of products—Crisco, many packaged baked goods, and most commonly used margarines—which carried trans fats. Soon McDonald's restaurants and then Frito-Lay snack foods announced they were removing trans fats from their products. By the end of 2002, nutritionists, science writers, public health officials, and indeed nearly everyone was advising consumers to avoid trans fats when possible.

The Food and Drug Administration appeared to be on top of the issue. In 1999 it had solicited feedback on proposed guidelines for trans-fat labeling. By 2003 the FDA published final rules that, beginning in January 2006, the nutrition panel must disclose trans fats. This was the first addition to the Nutrition Facts label since its introduction in 1994, and the last change for a decade.

In some respects the trans fat scare of the 2000s was analogous to the 1960s cholesterol scare discussed in chapter 2. A scientific study identified a potential food risk or correlation; other scientific studies generated supporting evidence; the concern became credentialed as scientific organizations and then governmental institutions created policies and issued public health guidelines; this spawned news headlines that brought about a consumer panic, prompting the food industry to reformulate its foods. Both scares invited public moralizing over the social ills of America's affluence and the nutrition establishment's failure to anticipate the threat. In the 1960s the threat was abundance, and the feeling that the "conventional wisdom" of old-school nutritionists should give way to a new vanguard of negative nutrition. In the 2000s the threat was novel foods, and the suspicion that the diet-heart thesis establishment had oversold low-fat food solutions.[2] In both the 1960s and 2000s the food industry worked backstage to have its cake and eat it too. Initially lobbying the FDA to delay trans-fat labeling, by 2002 industry had developed reformulated products marketable with "0 grams *trans* fats" labels on the front panel of the package, as permitted under the new FDA rules. Trans-fats labeling was a victory for all: the FDA updating its public health tool to reflect new diet science, consumer interest groups providing more information to their constituents, and companies showing they can accommodate changing consumer demands. Indeed, when the FDA banned trans fats in 2015, it was essentially certifying what was already a market fact. Labeling had succeeded in driving out the bad ingredient.

The story of trans-fat labeling illustrates how America's foodways had become a plug-and-play food economy, with the food label as the principal interface between consumer and producer. Throughout the twentieth century, food markets and market infrastructures dramatically changed how we get food. Self-service retailing and packaged foods recreated the shopper as a reader instead of someone who samples foods prior to purchase. This has changed how shoppers assessed food claims, making them more dependent on informational sources. Humorist Andy Rooney wryly remarked, "The two biggest sellers in any bookstore are the cookbooks and the diet books. The cookbooks tell you how to prepare the food and the diet books tell you how not to eat any of it."[3] His witticism captures the irony in how Americans have come to "read" food more than they "eat" it. Americans read articles or books about food and dieting, watch television or YouTube videos about food and cooking, while spending less time actually growing, cooking, and savoring food.[4]

HOW HAVE FOOD POLITICS CHANGED FROM THE 1930s TO PRESENT?

This book focuses on a market device, the food label, and an institution, the FDA. It describes a broad transition in the FDA's regulatory approach, from setting food standards to standardizing information through informative labels, thus embracing an "informational turn" in food politics.[5] Across this broad transition we can see several related transformations: new tactics used for governance, a new role for the state in regulating markets, an evolving image of the ideal consumer, a change in identity politics for food public policy, and a change in what we understand food to be.

The FDA's change in tactics for managing food markets reflected the increasingly abstract and impersonal nature of food markets over the course of the twentieth century. As Michael Schudson observed, "It is only in the world where so much of our knowledge comes secondhand that it makes sense to think of consumer decisions as arising from an 'information environment.'"[6] When the FDA began implementing a new food standards system in the 1930s, simplifying the market by reducing options still seemed like a reasonable approach for managing an increasingly diverse and national food system. Many consumers still purchased foods from local grocers they knew personally. The rise of suburban supermarkets serving a new market protagonist, the literate shopper cut off from traditional community, created an information vacuum that product labels and packages were used to fill. Product labels were part of the new "disclosure culture" that touched several social issues of relevance to the FDA, including new medical and diet science ideas about being "at risk," a new legal approach to contributory responsibility in tort law, and marketing that promoted endless novelty for diverse lifestyles.[7] Since the 1970s the FDA has increasingly used food labels to affect public policy, preferring to regulate markets indirectly by requiring product disclosure, rather than more directly interfering by banning foods or ingredients.

This tactical change caused a corresponding change in the role of the state in the marketplace. The food standards system cast the FDA in the role of a New Deal activist state, characterized by command-and-control paternalism but also by direct consultation through public hearings. Informative food labeling transformed the FDA, at least in the context of health messaging, to the role of information broker, employing market-based nudges through informative disclosures and indirect information solicitation from the public. This change in governance style exemplified the backlash to liberal government that began in the 1970s but was consecrated in the 1980s.[8] In the 1980s, technology balkanized the public square. First cable news and later the World Wide Web ensured that no single media institution could "control the narrative" of events sufficiently to create consensus.[9] Just as some historians argue that the 1945–73 period of liberal consensus was a "long exception," a short-term detour from the *laissez-faire* individualism of American history, I argue that the FDA's demarcation of a clear food-drug line was an aberrant form of market regulation embedded within a longer history of largely unregulated health products and claims.[10] The FDA has been reduced to an information provisioner with a diminished role concerning what it can do to promote public health.

The evolving policies on food labels reflect a change in how experts imagined the consumer. In the 1950s the food standards system, justified by the state function of consumer protection, focused on the "ordinary consumer." In the 1970s the voluntary nutrition label discussed in chapter 4 focused on "informed consumers"

and was justified by a belief that markets met the needs of and rewarded knowledgeable citizens. The 1990s Nutrition Facts panel was intended to be an extended
cognition aid for the "distributed consumer." More recently policymakers have
embraced "choice architecture" and built food policy around a "rationally irrational consumer" who acts on emotions and irrational behaviors but in predictable
ways. These "nudge" policies are justified by substituting a libertarian paternalism
that protects individual choice and lifestyles for the much maligned, old-fashioned
liberal paternalism. While I have connected these changes to specific time periods
and labeling policies, there have always been a variety of competing consumer
standards invoked to justify or criticize FDA policies. In 2002 this question about
what consumer standard is most appropriate surfaced when the FDA published a
"Guidance for Industry," stating their standards would no longer strive to protect
the "ignorant, unthinking and credulous" and instead adopted a "reasonable person" standard. The earlier consumer standard originated in 1910 when a circuit
court of appeals noted: "The law is not made for the protection of experts, but for
the public—that vast multitude which includes the ignorant, the unthinking and
the credulous, who, in making purchases, do not stop to analyze, but are governed
by appearances and general impressions." A century later the FDA had decided
this was too paternalistic. While consumers weren't expected to be experts, individuals would "perceive their own best interests."[11]

One striking change in food politics concerns who shows up to the fight, particularly what kinds of public interest groups and activists seek to represent the
public. Identity politics has changed from "domestic politics" centered on homemakers to "lifestyle politics" centered on biosociality and shared risk.[12] This is most
clearly registered by the disappearance from food politics after the 1970s of the Federation of Homemakers, and women's and housewife associations, replaced by a
new breed of public interest groups, like the Center for Science in the Public Interest
(CSPI). This was partly a change in social labels. "Housewife" became politically
unfashionable in the 1970s.[13] Advertisers continued to put mother to work in com-
mercials; however, in the 1980s, food ads began appealing to mom by drawing on
biomedical arguments about nutritional healthiness. The change from domestic
politics to lifestyle politics reflected a change in the gender and class of the presumed consumer, and a departure from food for family or community toward a
more individual-centered politics of eating. It also reflected a change in where
"good" food was made: from homemade to factory processed, from the housewife
as productive homemaker to the working woman as just one kind of consumer.

Finally, the shift from standards-setting to informative labels changed what we
understand food to be and what we expect it to do for us. Food changed from a
"wholesome" whole and "authentic" product to one that is designed with interchangeable parts, emphasizing novelty and transcendental properties. This change
paralleled the new paradigm of risk for diet and health described in chapter 2:

from a model of health where people are either ordinary or sick, to one where everyone is at risk and must consider risk factors when determining diet. It is tempting, when analyzing the rise of nutrition labeling, to attribute the new risk paradigm to a rise in "nutritionism" and the biomedicalization of food in our increasingly healthist society.[14] One could draw a direct line from Ellen Swallow Richards's conceptualization of "food synonyms" in 1901 to Henry Miller's arguments about "substantial equivalence" in 1991. I argue that it is the other way around. The biomedicalization of food is symptomatic of a broad shift in the production and consumption of food: the increase in anonymous food prep and marketing that promotes a plug-and-play food economy. Food is known less for the work that went into making it, its provenance, and instead, as Benjamin Cohen writes, "our connections to the land tend to be mediated through the label on the shelf" so that we "trust the label, not the farmer."[15] Policymakers now take this change for granted, and increasingly envision policymaking as an art of "choice architecture" and "nudging" consumers instead of protecting consumers and safeguarding their foodways.

"NUDGEOLOGY" AND IMAGINING THE "RATIONALLY IRRATIONAL CONSUMER"

In 2008 legal scholar Cass Sunstein and behavioral economist Richard Thaler published their highly influential policy treatise, *Nudge*, advocating a benevolent form of governance they called "libertarian paternalism." *Nudge* combined Sunstein's decades-long advocacy of policy reform centered on information design or "choice architecture" with Thaler's insights on human nature drawn from behavioral economics. Policymakers indirectly nudged people toward social goals by framing their everyday decisions so that they would default to desired outcomes. For food scholars, *Nudge* is particularly interesting because it opens with the thought experiment of designing a school lunch cafeteria. The imagined local policymaker, a school's food service director, is encouraged by a supermarket management consultant to design the layout of the school lunch line buffet like a supermarket floor plan, that is, by putting highly desirable items like dessert last and less popular items first. The school cafeteria policymaker must decide which organizing principle should motivate her design: a random neutral order, or prioritizing healthy eating, prioritizing foods kids tend to pick, or maximizing the school's profits? According to Thaler and Sunstein, by doing this she becomes a "choice architect," "nudging" kids toward the school's policies without directly telling them what to eat.[16]

In some ways this science of nudge-ology exemplifies the informational turn in politics. Indeed, some experts reframed the persistent problem of information overload as a challenge not of too much information but rather of attention scarcity, adopting the term "attention economy" and envisioning marketers as "attention merchants."[17] Choice architecture could cut through the consumer's information clutter and decision fatigue, without threatening the sacred role of choice. Adding to *Nudge*'s influence on policy was the fact that President Obama chose Sunstein to head the Office of Information and Regulatory Affairs from 2009 to 2012.

A central trope in *Nudge*, however, was its critique of economists' imagined conceptual personae of the "Econ," the "*homo economicus*" individual with a genius-like capacity for rational calculations. Thaler and Sunstein argued that real people, or "Humans," weren't so rational as Econs, although thanks to the "emerging science of choice," namely behavioral economics, Humans *were* predictable.[18] *Nudge* sought to displace the rational-actor Econ in market models with a "rationally irrational consumer."[19] In some ways this reflected a natural cycle, from rational to irrational and then rational again, in how consumer experts had modeled the consumer since the 1930s. The appearance of these models around 2008 also reflected a public crisis in information. The 2008 economic crisis had shattered faith in markets and models of rational actors.[20]

Food studies provide various examples concerning this loss of faith that modern food information environments steer consumers toward sound choices. In his 2007 book *Good Calories, Bad Calories,* journalist Gary Taubes used "informational cascades" to explain how the diet-heart thesis became nutrition dogma. Information cascades occur when an early endorsement of a claim gradually, through repeated citation, becomes a self-referencing scientific truism, even if the original claim wasn't true. Attributing the diet-heart thesis's success to information cascades evoked a pessimistic view of the consumers' information environment.[21] Nutrition marketing and consumer behavior expert Brian Wansink received media attention for his experiments demonstrating "mindless eating." His most widely cited experiment was with a bottomless bowl, showing that eaters take visual cues from the size of what they eat, and that these cues could be manipulated to make them eat more. Another experiment demonstrated that putting a nutrition or health label on a product, even an unhealthy one, caused consumers to believe it was healthier. Recently, Wansink's studies were found to be faulty, debunked by other researchers in the broader reproducibility crisis in social sciences. But they show how researchers at the time were questioning the reliability of consumers to easily navigate industrial foodways.[22] Even the concept of "food deserts," promoted around 2008 as one explanation for America's obesity epidemic, challenged the idea that consumers have equal access to choice in food markets.[23] The phrase referred to areas where consumers had limited access to supermarkets, and thus depended on convenience stores and fast food which afforded poor nutritional options. That there were food deserts suggested that changing people's information environments and choice architecture wouldn't help some Americans eat better.[24]

Former FDA commissioner David Kessler provided the strongest argument against the rational consumer model. In a 2009 book, *The End of Overeating,* he argued that industry engineered foods to take advantage of our biological hard-wiring, so that junk foods would trigger addiction much like an illicit drug. Drawing upon brain scans and neurological models, Kessler painted a bleak picture of consumer willpower, and argued that governments needed more than labeling to correct our obesogenic environment.[25] Yet while left-leaning policy analysts promoted government intervention, the right backlash against overbearing food governance continued. Though not focused specifically on food, conservative journalist David Harsanyi's angry 2007 diatribe on the "nanny state" got media traction partly because audiences could relate to his irritation with "priggish moralists" that he called "Twinkie Fascists."[26]

THE POLITICS OF TRANSPARENCY AND AUTHENTICITY

The rise of technocratic solutions to America's food information crisis was met by an active contingent of public intellectuals and advice gurus advocating a return to food simplicity and common sense. The nostalgic foodieism of journalist Michael Pollan in his 2008 eater's manifesto, *In Defense of Food,* was evidenced by food rules shirking expert jargon and appealing to reader's intuition. His advice to "[not] eat anything with more than five ingredients, or ingredients you can't pronounce," would have frustrated food technologists weary of a public unfamiliar with basic organic chemistry terms for even traditional cooking. His rule, "Don't eat anything your great grandmother wouldn't recognize as food," was panned by food historians for romanticizing past generations' "authentic" diets and transforming food activism into self-satisfied foodie consumerism.[27] Such criticism did little to slow Pollan's popularity and influence in food policy.

The currency of authenticity in food politics was both an old feature of dietetics, rejecting expertise in favor of rhetorics of personal charisma and relatability, and also a very modern preoccupation with industrial foodways, with a direct line from the pure food movements of the turn of the twentieth century up to contemporary organic food movements.[28] Psychologist Barry Schwartz's 2008 diagnosis that too many choices increased shoppers' anxiety concerning a "paradox of choice," echoed the 1949 arguments of Jessie V. Coles favoring the "benefits of simplification" that standardization provided. Schwartz used the modern supermarket as the paragon of this problem, calling for a "voluntary simplicity" movement because "we have too many choices, too many decisions, too little time to do what is really important."[29] As if seeking to exploit this, there is a growing food industry interest in "clean label" foods, designed to be or at least appearing to be "simple" by having few ingredients listed on the Ingredients panel. Historian Nadia

Berenstein noted, however, that "clean" can be misleading, too, because it suggests more authentic but doesn't truly mean less artificial or more natural.[30]

Perhaps no word has gained more traction among food activists than "transparency." Transparency, alongside "traceability," describes catch-all solutions to a wide variety of food concerns, including government reforms and market-based mechanisms. Every generation has its adherents who believe that exposing ugly truths will somehow solve them. Hawthorne's *The Scarlet Letter*, Emile Zola's "J'Accuse . . .!," Teddy Roosevelt's "muckrakers," and the 1966 Freedom of Information Act are all variations on this theme.[31] The "push to know" parallels the expansion of a backstage to production and its masking using modern marketing trends to sell seamless, packaged end products. Moving procedures backstage and making them "opaque" to consumers is often a deliberate feature of the industrial food chain.[32] Advocates of transparency believe greater transparency empowers consumers. Yet modern food systems are so complex that we are ultimately dependent on backstage architects and experts who make decisions for us. There is no escape from the classic governance concern: *Quis custodiet ipsos custodes?* Who will watch the watchers?[33]

The informative food label emerged out of these trends as an informational fix. More information on labels is a technical solution to problems caused by a market of anonymous relationships. Historians of technology call this "solutionism," the idea that a technological fix will work independent of the users and producers it depends on. Read-the-label campaigns rely on "informationism," the belief that informational fixes can solve policy problems, because, if properly informed, Americans will make "correct" decisions.[34] Here I outline how labeling, rather than liberating readers from experts, actually makes them more dependent on experts.

THE LOGIC OF LABELING

Labeling is often seen as a tool of empowerment. The appeal of read-the-label campaigns is considerable. Regulators like labels because they make producers accountable: the product must be what it is "purported to be." Producers seek third-party certification labels, such as USDA Grade labels, to build consumer trust in their brand and confidence in their marketing claims. They also sometimes support risk labels as an opportunity to unload responsibility onto the consumer, caveat emptor, or create alternative markets for risk-free alternative products, such as "GM free" or "o trans fats." Health experts see the label as a knowledge fix, a tool for educating consumers on nutritionally "correct" understandings of food. And for lifestyle movements, such as those discussed in chapter 6, labeling campaigns offer a positive agenda, a way to create value added from a social movement, a welcome change from what are often negative campaign strategies of marching, boycotting, and protesting the conventional food system. Informative labels also resonate with a fundamental value of liberal democracies—that knowledge will set you free.

This book documents how the shift to labeling, however, hasn't solved problems so much as transformed them. Reading food is different from eating food, and the growing reliance on food labels to solve consumer problems has caused new problems common to most read-the-label campaigns, what I call here the "logic of labeling."

Labels individualize solutions

There is often a mismatch between public problems that are collective in nature, such as community health based on population-level statistics or social and environmental factors, and interventions centered on individual behavior. One limitation of labels as a policy tool is that they work through individualized actions, shopping choices, that only aggregate as statistical market data on consumer purchases. Food and eating are often social in nature, a fact highlighted by anthropologists and food studies scholars who emphasize the importance of commensality. Labels, however, are designed, tested, and rationalized for individuals, a form of methodological individualism that ignores the social nature of eating.

Labels are a public-private infrastructure

Is the food label intended as a space for education, marketing puffery, or "neutral" product information? Or all of the above? Recent movements in socially responsible consumption have blurred the boundaries between public and private interests. There are numerous examples, such as the National Cancer Institute seal on Kellogg's cereal or the American Heart Association's Heart-healthy logo (see chapter 5), where nonprofits or government institutions promoted public education messages on private platforms. While the Nutrition Facts panel was conceived as a way the FDA's "government brand" could occupy part of the product label, in practice nutrition facts were easily folded into the marketing objectives of food and beverage producers. This is because product labels are ultimately a market tool, and advertisers, too, seek to educate the consumer. As marketers appropriate science, long seen as a public good, into promotional messages about food, the view of science as impartial and objective is replaced by the view that diet science is merely an extension of the food industry's "he said she said" marketing tactics.[35]

Read-the-label campaigns will always be a market-based, political "opt out"

Labels target market niches of motivated consumers, providing a class-based "opt out" for political reform. There is a risk that food reformers advocating consumer-driven reform are merely preaching to the choir. This is arguably what happened with organic foods: ethical-minded consumers opted out of conventional agriculture without reforming it (see chapter 6). And having their virtuous option, they were less motivated to advocate that virtue for all. Indeed, labels divide groups as much as they unify them. If all foods were ethical—hormone-free, for example—there would be no need to label them as such. Labeling movements leave some citizens behind. This was the case for cigarette warnings. Once labeled, tobacco companies argued there was a presumed assumption of risk by smokers who continued to use the product. Responsibility for long-term health risks was unloaded on the smoker.[36]

Labels are an emotional tool

Food labels don't simply inform, they sell, and they do so by evoking consumer aspirations.[37] When Berkey Belser argued that label information supersedes reading, that Nutrition Facts work as a form of branding, he was describing the affective power of familiarity. Even though Nutrition "Facts" emphasize a science-based model of diet, it is not just science. The desire for rational self-control common in dieting, such as calorie-counting, is an emotional condition. In the hands of diet food advertisers, it becomes a powerful persuasive trope.[38] Other value-added labels, such as organic or fair trade, not only empower the ethical purchaser, they also gratify their sense of self-worth. When labels become opt-out tools from mainstream products, they also create a moral platform for judging less conscientious consumers.

Labels are not simply about transparency, but a translation

A common critique of labels is that they are a reduction of the full range of information that a food embodies. Gyorgy Scrinis criticized "nutritionism," for example, by arguing nutrition labels reduce food to its nutritional components and properties. This presupposes that labels are a window into the product which, if designed properly, would be "transparent." In reality, labels are what market sociologists describe as "performative," an articulation of the thing which, through its articulation, makes it so.[39] Information labels are not merely a reduction, but rather a translation of physical aspects of a food into visual or digital representations, which may then cause the producer to physically reshape the food.[40] History suggests that food companies will game any food labeling system. Once nutrition information appeared on the food label in the 1970s, producers created foods that made that labeling information appealing. Food became "nutritional." Indeed, using *information as obfuscation* is a much more common problem posed by labeling than reductionism. Consumer confusion is often produced. Sociologist Bastien Soutjis's research on the introduction of digital labeling of GMOs in the U.S. in the 2020s provides a good example of this. While digital labeling ostensibly offers more information to consumers, in practice many industries use it to bury information in complicated interfaces.[41]

Trust is not only about proof, it is relational

While the label is intended to equip the consumer to make personal choices, one never escapes the influence of experts backstage who frame the label before a consumer ever has the chance to choose. Ultimately labels are a technology of trust in a society of anonymous relationships. The introduction of nutrition labels was a form of disintermediation, a shift from face-to-face to interface, where informative labels replaced expert gatekeepers. This reconfigured what we meant by "active consumer." With food market*places,* it was a consumer who boycotted in front of the store or haggled over price. Consumers knew their seller and whether or not they could trust them. Today an active consumer is someone who reads and whose subsequent purchase choices are interpreted for consumerism impact. Analysis displaces taste.[42] The shift from mediator to medium is a shifting of responsibility for those doing the work of informing and deciding, from doctors in medical markets and grocers in food markets, to consumers reading the Nutrition Facts and drug package inserts.

Labels are never read in isolation

Labels are embedded within a broader informational environment. This lesson carries certain corollaries. Information environments must be produced and maintained, which usually involves either public or private institutional resources. Participation in information environments is unequal. Food infrastructures create differences in people's ability to participate, actively or passively, in market politics. There are operating costs and participation thresholds incurred if you make read-the-label part of your political solution. This raises certain unavoidable questions: Is there adequate consumer literacy and purchasing power? How effective are interpretative communities at promoting and translating label information into knowledge that consumers can use? This is not meant to be an indictment of labeling campaigns—the 1994 Nutrition Facts panel was not a doomed public health initiative. However, its success depended on investing resources in a broader, community-based public education campaign translating nutrition "facts" into achievable and personalized healthy "values."[43] This did not happen. Private marketers swooped in, filling the vacuum left by the absence of such a campaign.

Scholars who study the use of labels for political mobilization observe that labels usually favor "delegation" rather than consumer empowerment.[44] Susan Hadden recognized this in 1986 when she wrote, "It seems ironic that a program to control risks through information provision, thereby maximizing individual freedom, entails increased government responsibility in areas ranging from overseeing the quality of laboratory tests to formulating a progressive educational curriculum." Writing with a prescience that almost anticipates the crisis of faith in experts in recent decades, Hadden predicted, "One characteristic of the information age will be the increased interdependence of people, each of whom has specialized technical information that others will not be able to assess for themselves."[45] A more cynical take on the logic of labeling is that labels are not just a market opt-out from more direct, sustained political reforms, but a burden on consumers, and especially mothers, who become responsible for "precautionary consumption routines" to read up on and weigh the cost benefit of what's on the label.[46] Labeling campaigns cannot replace good governance. The citizen-consumer, agent of "boycotts" and "buycotts," should not replace the citizen as the beneficiary of political reform.

INFORMATIONISM FEEDS RESTLESS CONSUMPTION

This book describes how FDA policies intended to protect the American consumer shifted from focusing on foods, standardizing foods in markets, to focusing on information, provisioning consumers with information about food. In making this shift, the FDA succumbed to informationism. The faith in labeling as *the* solution comes from the mistaken belief that information liberates consumers from interfering governments or markets. Labels offer a false promise of delegating authority and responsibility to consumers. Better food labeling alone does not remove the need for market oversight. Devices like the food label increase, not decrease, consumers' dependency on expert mediators who determine what goes on or stays off labels. The information age is populated with experts, including institutions like the FDA, who seek to shape information environments where food decisions are made. Public policy should focus on how to build trust in these institutions and experts, not how to circumvent them.

Information environments change. This book focused on informative labeling as a new media and a new twentieth-century market regulatory tool, but soon printed-on-packaging food labels may seem passé. Indeed, other scholars are already studying how digital labeling and online platforms are reshaping food con-sumption and health.[47] It is likely that FDA efforts to centralize the meanings of Nutrition Facts will be even further undermined as consumers move onto online platforms characterized by decentralized information environments. Even the idea of controlling separate marketing "channels," each with a distinct push or pull on consumers—what gatekeeper theorists have studied since Lewin in the 1940s—has given way to the "convergence culture" of smartphones. Market experts now promote "contextual commerce" with its "frictionless cross-channel shopping experience" that seamlessly blends digital and physical buying.[48] These information environments for future foodways will look quite different from those described here. This book seeks to provide a toolkit for future scholars analyzing them. Its critiques of informational fixes and the "More Information" mantra of informationism are likely to hold true even for food in the future.

Consumers in the twenty-first century arguably have access to more food information, more books, articles, websites, videos, and documentaries, than ever before. As twentieth-century foodways moved increasingly out of sight, the consumer lost touch with how food is made, who makes it and where it comes from. To replace this, the market has offered up a proliferation of information devices to fill the void. And yet, paradoxically, this has left consumers even less satisfied. Food scandals and scares generate new labels, but also new anxieties about what's not labeled, leading to what some call "restless consumption."[49] We are starving for knowledge about our food on a full stomach of information. This is because regulation is relational, and the reliance on simple information fixes ignores this. If you do not trust the people who produce your food, a food label, no matter how informative, will never paper over that.

CHRONOLOGY

Selected events in the history of regulations governing food labeling in America, 1900 to 2020.

1902–1903   Harvey Wiley and volunteer "poison squad" at USDA draw attention to widespread use of questionable chemicals in processed, packaged foods.

1905   American Medical Association (AMA) sets a policy prohibiting "patent medicine" ads in its journal, *JAMA*, pressuring drug manufacturers to avoid medical and nutrition "quackery" that challenged the food-drug line.

1906   Pure Food and Drug Act bans the sale of "misbranded" foods.

1913   Gould Net Weight Amendment requires all packaged foods to disclose the "quantity of their contents plainly and conspicuously marked on the outside of the package in terms of weight, measure, or numerical count."

1923   Congress passes legislation defining a butter standard, the first legislation to create a food standard.

   Filled Milk Act outlaws interstate sales of "filled milk" products, any milk or dairy product that is reconstituted with fats from nondairy sources, most commonly vegetable oils.

1930   McNary-Mapes Amendment establishes minimum standards on canned fruits to prevent competition with deceptively substandard canned foods.

1933   FDA's *American Chamber of Horrors* exhibit draws attention to common forms of "economic adulteration" and packaging fraud in American food markets, raising concern about the need for new food regulation.

1938   Food, Drug, and Cosmetic Act (or FDCA) authorizes FDA to establish food standards of identity for all mass-produced foods, and creates a category of "special dietary foods" for use by physicians.

1939	FDA issues its first food standards for tomato products in the July issue of the *Federal Register*.
	USDA Agricultural Marketing Service begins its voluntary quality grade–labeling program (e.g., "U.S. Grade A"; "USDA prime beef").
1941	National Research Council Food and Nutrition Board establishes "Recommended Dietary Allowances" (RDAs), updating them every few years thereafter. The 1968 edition would be used for establishing levels for later FDA nutrition labels.
1947	In *Kordel v. United States*, the Supreme Court rules FDA has the right to extend its regulations on food labels and packages to any "accompanying such article" or "labeling" that might shape a consumer's understanding of the label.
1958	Food Additive Amendment authorizes FDA to identify "generally recognized as safe" or "GRAS" ingredients considered to be historically safe for use in food. It contains the "Delaney Clause," which adopts a zero-tolerance threshold for any food additive found to be carcinogenic.
1959	FDA recalls tainted cranberries, which test positive for a toxic weedkiller, weeks before Thanksgiving, raising public alarm about chemicals in food.
1960	Color Additive Amendment defines "color additive" and requires FDA to evaluate their safety in food, and also includes a Delaney Clause for carcinogens.
	American Heart Association report on "Dietary Fat and Its Relation to Heart Attacks and Strokes" initiates years of "cholesterol controversy" and a boom in low-fat and low-cholesterol food products.
1961	FDA and numerous medical associations hold a Congress on Medical Quackery, which includes a campaign against nutrition quackery promoting vitamania.
1962	Kefauver-Harris Amendments, passed in part as a response to the thalidomide tragedy, establish FDA's power to enforce premarket approval for drugs, increasing the significant difference in enforcement standards for food and drug markets.
	President Kennedy proclaims the "Consumer Bill of Rights," including the "right to be informed" and the "right to choose."
	FDA proposed to revise its "special dietary foods" standards to accommodate the growing diet food market. Strong industry complaints led to no rules being established.
1966	Fair Packaging and Labeling Act of 1966 sets rules on all consumer goods to prevent deceptive "slack fill" packaging sizes, requiring product labels to show the net quantity of contents, be legible and conspicuous, and define the number of servings in terms of quantity per serving.

FDA publishes final proposed rules on "special dietary foods," but renewed industry objections lead to these rules being stayed.

A Surgeon General's warning appears on all packages of tobacco products, indicating its risk to consumer health.

1968   Citizens' Board of Inquiry into Hunger and Malnutrition in the United States publishes *Hunger, U.S.A.* report, initiating several years of public debate.

FDA begins its public hearings to revise standards for "special dietary foods."

1969   White House Conference on Food, Nutrition and Health draws attention to federal food programs, and also to the need for reforming food and nutrition labeling.

FDA removes cyclamate's GRAS status, because of concerns under the Delaney Clause about it being a carcinogen, effectively banning the use of cyclamates in food.

1970   FDA ends the public standards hearings on "special dietary foods." Final rules won't be released until 1973.

Supermarkets start to introduce unit pricing—shelf labels that provide the price per weight or per volume.

FDA introduces a "Patient Package Insert" label, one of the first for prescription drugs, providing how-to-use and risk information to consumers for oral contraceptives.

1971   Giant Food Supermarket launches its highly publicized and popular nutrition-labeling program.

1972   Supermarkets adopt "open dating" of food (e.g., "Best if Used Before" or "Sell By") in response to pressure from consumer groups.

FDA rechristens *FDA Papers,* its official magazine, to *FDA Consumer,* making it a platform for public outreach.

In *Milnot Co. v. Richardson,* the Supreme Court overrules the Filled Milk Act of 1923 and allows the sale of "filled milk" healthy alternative products to regular milk.

1973   FDA publishes its final rules on food labeling in the *Federal Register.* The new rules introduce a voluntary "Nutrition Information" panel, require ingredient labels on all foods, and move away from using the "imitation" label on substandard products.

California Certified Organic Farmers program (CCOF) is the first to establish third-party organic certification in the U.S.

1974   Supermarkets introduce the Universal Product Code (UPC) to facilitate stock inventory and product checkout at the register.

1976   Vitamins and Minerals (aka "Proxmire") Amendments restrict FDA's authority to classify natural or synthetic vitamins or minerals as drugs, which carry stricter safety standards and premarket approval.

1977   Senate committee releases *Dietary Goals for the United States,* also known as the *McGovern Report,* which endorses the new diet science of "negative nutrition," recommending Americans avoid excessive intake of certain nutrients linked to chronic disease. These goals would become the foundation for the later USDA Food Pyramid and FDA Nutrition Facts label.

Saccharine Study and Labeling Act imposes a moratorium on any FDA ban of saccharine, restricting FDA's power to remove this food additive even if it were found to be a potential carcinogen and violate the Delaney Clause.

1984   FDA adds "sodium" to the list of nutrients on the voluntary "Nutrition Information" panel.

Kellogg's All-Bran collaborates with the National Cancer Institute on an advertising campaign linking fiber consumption to reduced risk of colon cancer. It opens the floodgates for other companies to make "disease claims" (e.g., "fiber reduces risk of cancer") and "structure-function claims" (e.g., "calcium builds strong bones") on foods that undermined FDA's food-drug line.

1986   California voters pass the Proposition 65 ballot initiative, which, starting in 1988, requires any chemically risky products to carry a carcinogen warning label.

FDA grants approval to sell milk produced in test trials for rBGH without labeling.

1988   *Surgeon General's Report on Nutrition and Health,* along with the 1989 National Research Council's *Diet and Health: Implications for Reducing Chronic Disease Risk* report, draws attention to a national health crisis caused by overeating and recommends better use of nutrition labeling.

Alcoholic Beverage Labeling Act mandates a warning label for alcohol products to protect pregnant women.

Dutch NGO Max Havelaar establishes the first modern "fair trade" label. Other fair trade organizations establish similar independent certification and labeling programs.

1989   Alar apple scare generates widespread concern about industrial farming and interest in organic foods.

Animal Welfare Institute obtains first USDA-approved "animal welfare" label for pigs raised to roam free on pastures and without routine use of antibiotics.

1990   Nutrition Labeling and Education Act (or NLEA) authorizes FDA to require nutrition labeling on all mass-produced foods, define serving sizes, set definitions for specific health-related labeling terms (e.g., "healthy"), and approve select health claims on foods.

Organic Foods Production Act (or OFPA) authorizes USDA to develop consistent, uniform standards for a "USDA organic" labeling program, and to establish a National Organic Standards Board to oversee these standards.

Dolphin Protection Consumer Information Act regulates the definition of private "dolphin safe" labeling on tuna cans.

1991   FDA seizes a leading brand of orange juice because the agency argues the juice was falsely labeled "fresh," initiating a discussion of how to define common labeling terms like fresh and "natural."

USDA releases its Food Guide Pyramid as a public educational tool for federal dietary recommendations.

FDA adopts a policy of "substantial equivalence" for GM foods. If the end-product wasn't substantially chemically different from non-GM equivalents, they would be labeled the same without reference to the GM production process.

1993   FDA publishes its final rules in the *Federal Register* for post-NLEA food labeling, including the "Nutrition Facts" panel with "Daily Values" percentages of a recommended average 2,000-calorie total daily diet. The new rules would become mandatory for most foods by mid-1994.

1994   Dietary Supplement Health and Education Act (DSHEA) defines "dietary supplements" as a new category, distinct from drugs or food additives, and therefore such supplements do not have to pass FDA safety assessment or regulatory standards.

2002   National Organic Program begins to implement the USDA program for certifying "USDA organic" foods.

Wegmans Supermarket introduces the "Wellness Keys" private front-of-package (FOP) labels that reference side-panel Nutrition Facts. Other supermarkets and manufacturers follow suit with similar programs over the following decade.

FDA adopts a lesser "credible evidence" standard on health claims for foods, replacing its previous, stricter "significant scientific agreement" standard of proof.

Farm Security and Rural Investment Act requires retailers to provide country-of-origin labeling (e.g., "Product of USA") for fresh beef, pork, or lamb. In 2008 Congress expands it to include some fresh fruits, nuts, and vegetables. A 2015 World Trade Organization ruling prompts Congress to repeal the law for beef and pork.

2003   FDA publishes final rules requiring a new line on the Nutrition Facts panel disclosing "trans fats." The rules become mandatory in 2006.

2004   Food Allergen Labeling and Consumer Protection Act requires clear labeling for the eight most common food allergens.

2006   U. K. organization Carbon Trust introduces the first carbon labeling program with the "Carbon Reduction Label."

2010   Non-GMO Project, an NGO, starts a third-party product verification program where foods not genetically modified can carry its butterfly logo.

2016   FDA finalizes rules for the new Nutrition Facts label, which increase the focus on total calories, update serving sizes, and require an additional line disclosing "added sugars." The new label would become mandatory in 2020.

Congress passes a GMO labeling bill that requires food companies to disclose GMOs, but doesn't require that they use a GMO label on packages.

Grocery Manufacturers Association starts the "Smart Label" initiative, where consumers can use QR codes on food packages to access more information about a product digitally.

2018   USDA releases final GMO labeling rules implementing the 2016 legislation. GM foods will be labeled "bioengineered" or "derived from bioengineering." The rules would become mandatory in 2022.

NOTES

INTRODUCTION

1. Susan Strasser, *Satisfaction Guaranteed: The Making of the American Mass Market* (New York: Pantheon Books, 1989).

2. US FDA, "Fact Sheet: FDA at a Glance," November 2021, https://www.fda.gov /about-fda/fda-basics/fact-sheet-fda-glance, last visited April 5, 2022.

3. Marian Garcia Martinez, Andrew Fearne, Julie A. Caswell, and Spencer Henson, "Co-regulation as a Possible Model for Food Safety Governance: Opportunities for Public-Private Partnerships," *Food Policy* 32, no. 3 (2007): 299–314; Edward J. Balleisen, "The Prospects for Effective Coregulation in the United States: A Historian's View from the Early Twenty-First Century," in *Government and Markets: Toward a New Theory of Regulation*, ed. Edward J. Balleisen and David Moss, 443–81 (New York: Cambridge University Press, 2009); Ashton Wynette Merck, "The Fox Guarding the Henhouse: Coregulation and Consumer Protection in Food Safety, 1946–2002" (PhD diss., Duke University, 2020).

4. Recent works that focus on the history of experts shaping food culture and modern foodways include Carolyn de la Peña, *Empty Pleasures: The Story of Artificial Sweeteners from Saccharin to Splenda* (Chapel Hill: University of North Carolina Press, 2010); Tracey Deutsch, *Building a Housewife's Paradise: Gender, Politics, and American Grocery Stores in the Twentieth Century* (Chapel Hill: University of North Carolina Press, 2010); Carolyn M. Goldstein, *Creating Consumers: Home Economists in Twentieth-Century America* (Chapel Hill: University of North Carolina Press, 2012); Charlotte Biltekoff, *Eating Right in America: The Cultural Politics of Food and Health* (Durham, NC: Duke University Press, 2013); Helen Zoe Veit, *Modern Food, Moral Food: Self-Control, Science, and the Rise of Modern American Eating in the Early Twentieth Century* (Chapel Hill: University of North Carolina Press, 2013); Anna Zeide, *Canned: The Rise and Fall of Consumer Confidence in the American Food Industry* (Berkeley: University of California Press, 2018); Ai Hisano, *Visualizing Taste: How*

Business Changed the Look of What You Eat (Cambridge, MA: Harvard University Press, 2019); Amy Bentley, *Inventing Baby Food: Taste, Health, and the Industrialization of the American Diet* (Berkeley: University of California Press, 2019); Helen Tangires, *Movable Markets: Food Wholesaling in the Twentieth-Century City* (Baltimore: Johns Hopkins University Press, 2019); Lisa Haushofer, *Wonder Foods: The Science and Commerce of Nutrition* (Oakland: University of California Press, 2022). See also several recent edited volumes: Angela N. H. Creager and Jean-Paul Gaudillière, eds., *Risk on the Table: Food, Health and Environmental Exposure* (New York: Berghahn Books, 2021); Benjamin R. Cohen, Michael S. Kideckel, and Anna Zeide, eds., *Acquired Tastes: Stories about the Origins of Modern Food* (Cambridge, MA: MIT Press, 2021); Heather Paxson, ed., *Eating beside Ourselves: Thresholds of Foods and Bodies* (Durham, NC: Duke University Press, 2023).

5. Meg Jacobs, *Pocketbook Politics: Economic Citizenship in Twentieth-Century America* (Princeton, NJ: Princeton University Press, 2005), 7.

6. On this idea of expert "translation" in consumer markets, see Goldstein, *Creating Consumers.*

7. Sheila Jasanoff, *Designs on Nature: Science and Democracy in Europe and the United States* (Princeton, NJ: Princeton University Press, 2007), 249.

8. On critiques of the "deficit model" of public understanding by scholars in STS, see Stephen Hilgartner, "The Dominant View of Popularization: Conceptual Problems, Political Uses," *Social Studies of Science* 20, no. 3 (1990): 519–39.

9. Franck Cochoy, "A Sociology of Market-Things," in *Market Devices*, ed. Michel Callon, Yuval Millo, and Fabian Muniesa (Malden, MA: Wiley-Blackwell, 2007).

10. On market intermediaries, see Regina Lee Blaszczyk, *Imagining Consumers: Design and Innovation from Wedgwood to Corning* (Baltimore: Johns Hopkins University Press, 2002); Franck Cochoy, "Another Discipline for the Market Economy: Marketing as a Performative Knowledge and Know-How for Capitalism," in *The Laws of the Markets*, ed. Michel Callon, 194–221 (Malden, MA: Wiley-Blackwell, 1998).

11. For an interesting exploration of this practice of averaging out consumers, see Michael S. Kideckel, "The Search for the Average Consumer: Breakfast Cereal and the Industrialization of the American Food Supply," in *Acquired Tastes: Stories about the Origins of Modern Food*, ed. Benjamin R. Cohen, Michael S. Kideckel, and Anna Zeide, 117–32 (Cambridge, MA: MIT Press, 2021).

12. "Capture" refers to the theory of regulatory capture, which argues that the public-interest agenda of regulatory institutions is easily diverted toward private interests through corporate lobbying. Michael E. Levine and Jennifer L. Forrence, "Regulatory Capture, Public Interest, and the Public Agenda: Toward a Synthesis," *Journal of Law, Economics and Organizations* 6 (1990): 167–98. For the example of corn subsidies, see Michael Pollan, *The Omnivore's Dilemma: A Natural History of Four Meals* (New York: Penguin, 2006).

13. My term "pull narrative" here is a little different from "pull marketing." Pull marketing is about building brand loyalty to keep the customer coming back instead of going to a competitor.

14. On narratives of consumer defeatism versus consumer triumphalism, see Lawrence B. Glickman, *Buying Power: A History of Consumer Activism in America* (Chicago: University of Chicago Press, 2012), 206–7.

15. On "mobilizing," see Peter Miller and Nikolas Rose, "Mobilizing the Consumer: Assembling the Subject of Consumption," *Theory, Culture and Society* 14, no. 1 (1997): 4. On "cultivating" consumers, see Frank Cochoy and Alexandre Mallard, "Another Consumer Culture Theory: An ANT Look at Consumption, or How 'Market-Things' Help 'Cultivate' Consumers," in *The SAGE Handbook of Consumer Culture,* ed. Olga Kravets, Pauline Maclaran, Steven Miles, and Alladi Venkatesh, 384–403 (Thousand Oaks, CA: Sage, 2018). See also Marie-Emmanuelle Chessel and Sophie Dubuisson-Quellier, "Chapter 4. The Making of the Consumer: Historical and Sociological Perspectives," in *The SAGE Handbook of Consumer Culture,* ed. Olga Kravets, Pauline Maclaran, Steven Miles, and Alladi Venkatesh, 43–60 (Thousand Oaks, CA: Sage, 2018); Goldstein, *Creating Consumers.*

16. Jeffrey Sklansky, *The Soul's Economy: Market Society and Selfhood in American Thought, 1820–1920* (Chapel Hill: University of North Carolina Press, 2002), 240–41. See also James Block, *A Nation of Agents: The American Path to a Modern Self and Society* (Cambridge, MA: Belknap Press, 2002).

17. On conceptual personae, see Gilles Deleuze and Felix Guattari, *What Is Philosophy?*, trans. Hugh Tomlinson and Graham Burchell (New York: Columbia University Press, 1996). The concept of the consumer has changed over time. Perhaps the most significant shift was from "customer" to "consumer," the latter a conceptual foil to "producer" that registered a shift in markets from a "regular and continuing relationship" between local purchaser and supplier to a "more abstract figure in a more abstract market." Raymond Williams, *Keywords: A Vocabulary of Culture and Society* (New York: Oxford University Press, 1985), 78–79.

18. For an excellent historical account of the evolution of market infrastructures in America, see Tangires, *Movable Markets.* A prevalent version of this mode of imagining consumers is the "supply chain" or "food chain," which depicts the "end" consumer as the last step in a journey a product travels, from farm to fork. Shane Hamilton, "Analyzing Commodity Chains: Linkages or Restraints?," in *Food Chains: From Farmyard to Shopping Cart,* ed. Warren Belasco and Roger Horowitz, 16–28 (Philadelphia: University of Pennsylvania Press, 2009).

19. The classic work in this vein is Alfred D. Chandler, *The Visible Hand: The Managerial Revolution in American Business* (Cambridge, MA: Belknap Press, 1993). On market research as a "feedback technology," see James R. Beniger, *The Control Revolution: Technological and Economic Origins of the Information Society* (Cambridge, MA: Harvard University Press, 1986), 20. See also Goldstein, *Creating Consumers.*

20. Ernest Dichter, *Packaging, the Sixth Sense?: A Guide to Identifying Consumer Motivation* (Boston: Cahners Books, 1975), 10–11.

21. Cochoy, "A Sociology of Market-Things."

22. On the artificial flavor industry, see Nadia Berenstein, "Designing Flavors for Mass Consumption," *Senses and Society* 13, no. 1 (2018): 19–40. On how the food dye industry changed food, see Hisano, *Visualizing Taste.*

23. Blaszczyk, *Imagining Consumers.*

24. Goldstein, *Creating Consumers,* 9–11.

25. Miller and Rose, "Mobilizing the Consumer."

26. On "quality uncertainty" see Lucien Karpik, *Valuing the Unique: The Economics of Singularities* (Princeton, NJ: Princeton University Press, 2010), 26–27.

27. Thomas Hine, *The Total Package: The Secret History and Hidden Meanings of Boxes, Bottles, Cans, and Other Persuasive Containers* (Portland, ME: Back Bay Books, 1997), 46–55.

28. William Cronon, *Nature's Metropolis: Chicago and the Great West* (repr., New York: W. W. Norton, 1992); Steven Stoll, *The Fruits of Natural Advantage: Making the Industrial Countryside in California* (Berkeley: University of California Press, 1998); Douglas Sackman, *Orange Empire: California and the Fruits of Eden* (Berkeley: University of California Press, 2005). See also Susanne Freidberg, *Fresh: A Perishable History* (Cambridge, MA: Belknap Press, 2009).

29. Quote from Jennifer M. Black, "The 'Mark of Honor': Trademark Law, Goodwill, and the Early Branding Strategies of National Biscuit," in *We Are What We Sell: How Advertising Shapes American Life . . . And Always Has*, vol. 1, ed. Danielle Sarver Coombs and Bob Batchelor (Westport, CT: Praeger, 2014), 266. Sea also Mira Wilkins, "The Neglected Intangible Asset: The Influence of the Trade Mark on the Rise of the Modern Corporation," *Business History* 34, no. 1 (1992): 66–95; Diana Twede, "The Birth of Modern Packaging: Cartons, Cans and Bottles," *Journal of Historical Research in Marketing* 4, no. 2 (2012): 248; Strasser, *Satisfaction Guaranteed*.

30. Karin Zachmann and Per Østby, "Food, Technology, and Trust: An Introduction," *History and Technology* 27, no. 1 (2011): 1–10.

31. By "perform" here I am referring to arguments in economic sociology on the "performativity" of markets. See Michel Callon, ed., *The Laws of the Markets* (Malden, MA: Wiley-Blackwell, 1998).

32. Important histories of the FDA include: Oscar E. Anderson, *The Health of a Nation: Harvey W. Wiley and the Fight for Pure Food* (Chicago: University of Chicago Press, 1958); Charles O. Jackson, *Food and Drug Legislation in the New Deal* (Princeton, NJ: Princeton University Press, 1970); Mitchell Okun, *Fair Play in the Marketplace: The First Battle for Pure Food and Drugs* (DeKalb: Northern Illinois University Press, 1986); James Harvey Young, *Pure Food: Securing the Federal Food and Drugs Act of 1906* (Princeton, NJ: Princeton University Press, 1989); Daniel P. Carpenter, *Reputation and Power: Organizational Image and Pharmaceutical Regulation at the FDA* (Princeton, NJ: Princeton University Press, 2010); Benjamin R. Cohen, *Pure Adulteration: Cheating on Nature in the Age of Manufactured Food* (Chicago: University of Chicago Press, 2019); Jonathan Rees, *The Chemistry of Fear: Harvey Wiley's Fight for Pure Food* (Baltimore: Johns Hopkins University Press, 2021); Suzanne [White] Junod, "Chemistry and Controversy: Regulating the Use of Chemicals in Foods, 1883–1959" (PhD diss., Emory University, 1994); Barbara Resnick Troetel, "Three-Part Disharmony: The Transformation of the Food and Drug Administration in the 1970s" (PhD diss., City University of New York, 1996); Clare Gordon Bettencourt, "Bread and Butter Policy: Food Identity Standards in the United States, 1938–2022" (PhD diss., University of California–Irvine, 2022). Recent journalistic accounts of the FDA include Phil Hilts, *Protecting America's Health: The FDA, Business, and One Hundred Years of Regulation* (Chapel Hill: University of North Carolina Press, 2003); Deborah Blum, *The Poison Squad: One Chemist's Single-Minded Crusade for Food Safety at the Turn of the Twentieth Century* (New York: Penguin Press, 2018).

33. Jessica Wang, "Imagining the Administrative State: Legal Pragmatism, Securities Regulation, and New Deal Liberalism," *Journal of Policy History* 17, no. 3 (2005): 257–93.

34. For an early STS study of this political turn as it played out in the Environmental Protection Agency, see Sheila Jasanoff, "Science, Politics, and the Renegotiation of Expertise at EPA," *Osiris* 7 (1992): 194–217.

35. Criticisms of this large administrative state have described how the accumulation of regulations over the course of the twentieth century has resulted in a nearly autonomous state ruled by experts or career public officials through complicated calculations or arcane procedures independent of the public will. Theodore M. Porter, *Trust in Numbers: The Pursuit of Objectivity in Science and Public Life* (Princeton, NJ: Princeton University Press, 1996); Michael Power, *The Audit Society: Rituals of Verification* (Oxford: Oxford University Press, 1997).

36. Stated more succinctly, "Any institution that is going to keep its shape needs to gain legitimacy by distinctive grounding in nature and in reason." Mary Douglas, *How Institutions Think* (Syracuse, NY: Syracuse University Press, 1986), 112. On the problem of expert institutions in democracies, see Sheila Jasanoff, *The Fifth Branch: Science Advisers as Policymakers* (Cambridge, MA: Harvard University Press, 1994).

37. Regulating food labels, for example, delegates the responsibility for healthy choices and work of safe cooking to consumers, in contrast to regulation directed at food safety oversight of production methods, such as that used by the USDA and CDC. See Timothy D. Lytton, *Outbreak: Foodborne Illness and the Struggle for Food Safety* (Chicago: University of Chicago Press, 2019); Saul Halfon, *Measuring Food Risk and Danger at the US Department of Agriculture*, 10th International Conference in Interpretive Policy Analysis, July 8–10, 2015, https://ipa2015.sciencesconf.org/conference/ipa2015/pages/IPA_2015_Paper_Refs.pdf.

38. Lytton, *Outbreak,* 238, 334–35.

39. On reputational interdependence, see Lytton, *Outbreak,* 237.

40. Carpenter, *Reputation and Power.*

41. Roger Horowitz, *Kosher USA: How Coke Became Kosher and Other Tales of Modern Food* (New York: Columbia University Press, 2016).

42. See, for example, Heather Paxson, " 'Don't Pack a Pest': Parts, Wholes, and the Porosity of Food Borders," *Food, Culture and Society* 22, no. 5 (2019): 657–73.

43. Claas Kirchhelle, "Between Bacteriology and Toxicology: Agricultural Antibiotics and US Risk Regulation (1948–1977)," in Creager and Gaudillière, *Risk on the Table.*

44. On relevant histories of the EPA, see Sarah A. Vogel, *Is It Safe?: BPA and the Struggle to Define the Safety of Chemicals* (Berkeley: University of California Press, 2012); Jasanoff, *Fifth Branch.* On histories involving the CDC, see Claas Kirchhelle, *Pyrrhic Progress: The History of Antibiotics in Anglo-American Food Production* (New Brunswick, NJ: Rutgers University Press, 2020); Lytton, *Outbreak.*

45. Carpenter, *Reputation and Power,* 50. For a recent critique of siloing within the FDA, see Jane Henney et al., *Operational Evaluation of the FDA Human Foods Program: A Report of the Human Foods Independent Expert Panel* (Washington, DC: Reagan-Udall Foundation, 2022), 12.

46. Historian Lee Vinsel describes regulation as a "focusing device" for the "knowledge communities" charged with implementing and enforcing it, with three classic paths by which problems become a public concern taken up by a regulatory institution: (1) "media organizations choose them," (2) "interest groups put them forward," or (3) "policymakers select them." Lee Vinsel, *Moving Violations: Automobiles, Experts, and Regulations in the United States* (Baltimore: Johns Hopkins University Press, 2019), 301, 304.

47. On the "era of adulteration," see Cohen, *Pure Adulteration.* On the "age of standards," see Bettencourt, "Bread and Butter Policy."

48. By this, FDA chief counsel Peter Hutt clarified, "What you say in advertising quali- fies and gives meaning to what is in the labeling." "Questions and Answers," *Food, Drug, Cosmetic Law Journal* (February 1973): 144.

49. On the concept of "nutritionism," see Gyorgy Scrinis, *Nutritionism: The Science and Politics of Dietary Advice* (New York: Columbia University Press, 2013).

50. Veit, *Modern Food, Moral Food*, 137.

51. David Goodman, David, Bernardo Sorj, and John Wilkinson, *From Farming to Bio- technology: A Theory of Agro-Industrial Development* (New York: Basil Blackwell, 1987).

52. Xaq Frohlich, "The Rise (and Fall) of the Food-Drug Line: Classification, Gatekeep- ers, and Spatial Mediation in Regulating U.S. Food and Health Markets," in Creager and Gaudillière, *Risk on the Table*, 297–329.

53. Suzanne [White] Junod, "The Chemogastric Revolution and the Regulation of Food Chemicals," in *Chemical Sciences in the Modern World*, ed. Seymour Mauskopf, 322–55 (Philadelphia: University of Pennsylvania Press, 1993). For a similar argument on the "pet- rochemical revolution," see Vogel, *Is It Safe?*, 16, 36–37.

54. Lewis Grossman, "Food, Drugs, and Droods: A Historical Consideration of Defini- tions and Categories in American Food and Drug Law," *Cornell Law Review* 93, no. 5 (Janu- ary 1, 2008): 1091. Drug specificity would be given further validation with the rise of gener- ics, which reinforced the idea of active ingredient essentialism and chemical reductionism, since carefully formulated branded drugs could be substituted for generic equivalents. See also Jeremy A. Greene, *Generic: The Unbranding of Modern Medicine* (Baltimore: Johns Hopkins University Press, 2014).

55. Paul Starr, *The Social Transformation of American Medicine: The Rise of a Sovereign Profession and the Making of a Vast Industry* (New York: Basic Books, 2017).

56. On prescription drugs, see Harry M. Marks, *The Progress of Experiment: Science and Therapeutic Reform in the United States, 1900–1990* (New York: Cambridge University Press, 2000). On illicit drugs, see David T. Courtwright, *Forces of Habit: Drugs and the Making of the Modern World* (Cambridge, MA: Harvard University Press, 2009).

57. Cohen, *Pure Adulteration*, 176.

58. Maricel V. Maffini and Sarah Vogel, "Defining Food Additives: Origins and Shortfalls of the US Regulatory Framework," in Creager and Gaudillière, *Risk on the Table*, 274–96.

59. Rima Apple, *Vitamania: Vitamins in American Culture* (New Brunswick, NJ: Rut- gers University Press, 1996); Harvey Levenstein, *Paradox of Plenty: A Social History of Eat- ing in Modern America* (Berkeley: University of California Press, 2003); Harvey Levenstein, *Revolution at the Table: The Transformation of the American Diet* (Berkeley: University of California Press, 2003). On the concept of "surplus health," see Joseph Dumit, *Drugs for Life: How Pharmaceutical Companies Define Our Health* (Durham, NC: Duke University Press, 2012).

60. Market consultant Louis Cheskin discussing economist John Kenneth Galbraith's arguments in *The Affluent Society*. Louis Cheskin, *Why People Buy: Motivation Research and Its Successful Application* (New York: Liveright, 1959), 309. On the "nutrition transition," see Barry Popkin, *The World Is Fat: The Fads, Trends, Policies, and Products That Are Fattening the Human Race* (New York: Avery, 2009).

61. Epidemiologists have found self-reported surveys on diet are notoriously unreliable. People forget what they ate, or they don't notice "hidden calories," such as calories from

drinks or condiments. For drugs, evidence-based medicine has adopted randomized clinical trials (RCTs) to establish what works and what is a placebo effect. Most nutrients, however, come as a "package," not in isolation. This makes it difficult to use RCTs to study the effects of a specific nutrient, except as a vitamin supplement in pill form, which is not the preferred vehicle for nutrition endorsed by most nutritionists or the FDA.

62. Biltekoff, *Eating Right in America,* 36. Here I restrict my discussion to nutrition experts, but there is a much broader literature on the expert cultivation of "good taste" for food. See, for example, Priscilla Pankhurst Ferguson, "The Senses of Taste," *American Historical Review* 116, no. 2 (April 2011): 371–84.

63. Steven Shapin, "Expertise, Common Sense, and the Atkins Diet," in *Public Science in Liberal Democracy,* ed. Peter W. B. Phillips, 174–93 (Toronto: University of Toronto Press, 2007).

64. See Glickman, *Buying Power,* 24, 250–51. On the embodied politics of the food consumer-citizen, see Annemarie Mol, "Good Taste: The Embodied Normativity of the Consumer-Citizen," *Journal of Cultural Economy* 2, no. 3 (2009): 269–83.

65. Jessica J. Mudry, *Measured Meals: Nutrition in America* (Albany: State University of New York Press, 2010); Scrinis, *Nutritionism.* On "critical nutrition studies," see Charlotte Biltekoff, "Critical Nutrition Studies," in *The Oxford Handbook of Food History,* ed. Jeffrey M. Pilcher, 172–90 (Oxford: Oxford University Press, 2012).

66. Marion Nestle, *Food Politics: How the Food Industry Influences Nutrition and Health* (Berkeley: University of California Press, 2002); Marion Nestle, *Unsavory Truth: How Food Companies Skew the Science of What We Eat* (New York: Basic Books, 2018).

67. Ulrich Beck, *Risk Society: Towards a New Modernity* (Thousand Oaks, CA: Sage, 1992).

68. On "lifestyles politics," see Nikolas Rose, *The Politics of Life Itself: Biomedicine, Power, and Subjectivity in the Twenty-First Century* (Princeton, NJ: Princeton University Press, 2006); Dumit, *Drugs for Life.* On the neoliberal politics of "responsibilization," see Ronen Shamir, "The Age of Responsibilization: On Market-Embedded Morality," *Economy and Society* 37, no. 1 (2008): 1–19.

69. As discussed in chapters 5 and 6, these consumers may read labels for many different uses. Some might use them as "risk labels," perhaps concerned with allergenicity. See Danya Glabau, *Food Allergy Advocacy: Parenting and the Politics of Care* (Minneapolis: University of Minnesota Press, 2022). Others use them for evidence of meat-derived products, such as vegetarians / vegans; for grams of protein for strength building or Keto diets; or for grams of saturated fats, added sugars, or vitamins, whether seeking weight-loss or "surplus health."

70. Xaq Frohlich, "The Informational Turn in Food Politics: The US FDA's Nutrition Label as Information Infrastructure," *Social Studies of Science* 47, no. 2 (2017): 145–71.

71. Burkey Belser, president of design firm Greenfield-Belser Ltd., phone interview with author, October 14, 2009.

72. A. D. Chandler Jr. and J. W. Cortada, eds., *A Nation Transformed by Information: How Information Has Shaped the United States from Colonial Times to the Present* (Oxford: Oxford University Press, 2000). For a broad discussion of changes in law and innovation configuring the information society, see also James Boyle, *Shamans, Software, and Spleens: Law and the Construction of the Information Society* (Cambridge, MA: Harvard University Press, 1997).

1. AN AGE OF STANDARDS

1. Louise G. Baldwin and Florence Kirlin, "Consumers Appraise the Food, Drug, and Cosmetic Act," *Law and Contemporary Problems* 6, no. 1 (Winter 1939): 146.

2. Baldwin and Kirlin's depiction of nineteenth-century homemakers reflects a fair amount of oversimplification. By the late nineteenth century, many middle-class households would have hired domestic servants, often working-class or immigrant women, to do the cooking. This created its own crisis in kitchen literacy. Ann Vileisis, *Kitchen Literacy: How We Lost Knowledge of Where Food Comes From and Why We Need to Get It Back* (Washington, DC: Island Press, 2010), 30–51.

3. Jessie V. Coles, *Standards and Labels for Consumers' Goods* (New York: Ronald Press, 1949), 154.

4. On the "era of adulteration," see Cohen, *Pure Adulteration*, 8.

5. Ellis W. Hawley, *The Great War and the Search for a Modern Order: A History of the American People and Their Institutions, 1917–1933* (Prospect Heights, IL: Waveland, 1997); JoAnne Yates and Craig N. Murphy, *Engineering Rules: Global Standard Setting since 1880* (Baltimore: Johns Hopkins University Press, 2019); Lee Vinsel, "Virtue via Association: The National Bureau of Standards, Automobiles, and Political Economy, 1919–1940," *Enterprise and Society* 17, no. 4 (2016): 809–38.

6. Here I use the term "gatekeeper" referring to Carpenter's work on the FDA, *Reputation and Power*. In chapter 2 I discuss the origins of the gatekeeper theory of markets and how it shaped FDA policies on food consumers.

7. For critiques of the persistent myth of "standard" American eating habits, see Sidney Mintz, *Tasting Food, Tasting Freedom: Excursions into Eating, Power, and the Past* (Boston: Beacon, 1997); Biltekoff, *Eating Right in America*; Donna Gabaccia, *We Are What We Eat: Ethnic Food and the Making of Americans* (Cambridge, MA: Harvard University Press, 2000).

8. Lawrence Busch, *Standards: Recipes for Reality* (Cambridge, MA: MIT Press, 2011), 10.

9. E. Melanie DuPuis, *Nature's Perfect Food: How Milk Became America's Drink* (New York: NYU Press, 2002); Kendra Smith-Howard, *Pure and Modern Milk: An Environmental History since 1900* (Oxford: Oxford University Press, 2013).

10. Edward F. Keuchel, "Chemicals and Meat: The Embalmed Beef Scandal of the Spanish-American War," *Bulletin of the History of Medicine* 48, no. 2 (1974): 249–64.

11. *The Jungle* is often given too much credit in popular accounts for driving the passage of the 1906 Pure Food and Drug Act. Much of the push for pure food legislation had already been paved by regulatory chemists like Harvey Wiley and by women's organizations well before Sinclair wrote his book. Louise Carroll Wade, "The Problem with Classroom Use of Upton Sinclair's *The Jungle*," *American Studies* 32, no. 2 (Fall 1991): 79–101; Cohen, *Pure Adulteration*.

12. James Harvey Young, "Saccharin: A Bitter Regulatory Controversy," in *Research in the Administration of Public Policy*, ed. Frank B. Evans and Harold T. Pinkett, 39–49 (Washington, DC: Howard University Press, 1975); Suzanne White Junod, *Sugar: A Cautionary Tale*, FDA website, https://www.fda.gov/files/about%20fda/published/Sugar—A-Cautionary-Tale .pdf, last visited May 12, 2022.

13. Aaron Bobrow-Strain, *White Bread: A Social History of the Store-Bought Loaf* (Boston: Beacon Press, 2012), 33, 44.

14. Blum, *Poison Squad*; Cohen, *Pure Adulteration*; Young, *Pure Food*; Rees, *Chemistry of Fear*.

15. Rees, *Chemistry of Fear*, 95.

16. Suzanne Junod, "'Proscribing Deception': The Gould Net Weight Amendment and the Origins of Mandatory Nutrition Labeling," in *Setting Nutritional Standards: Theory, Policies, Practices*, ed. Elizabeth Neswald, David F. Smith, and Ulrike Thoms, 165–94 (Rochester, NY: University of Rochester Press, 2017).

17. S. L. Kaplan, *The Bakers of Paris and the Bread Question, 1700–1775* (Durham, NC: Duke University Press, 1996); E. P. Thompson, "The Moral Economy of the English Crowd in the Eighteenth Century," *Past and Present* (1971): 76–136.

18. Historians have debated whether the central framing of the 1906 bill was consumer legislation or fair trade practice. Jackson, *Food and Drug Legislation in the New Deal*, 204.

19. Suzanne W. Junod, "Food Standards in the United States: The Case of the Peanut Butter and Jelly Sandwich," in *Food, Science, Policy and Regulation in the Twentieth Century: International and Comparative Perspectives*, ed. David F. Smith and Jim Phillips (New York: Routledge, 2000), 170.

20. Edward Eugene Gallahue, *Some Factors in the Development of Market Standards, With Special Reference to Food, Drugs, and Certain Other Household Wares* (Washington, DC: Catholic University of America Press, 1942), 98.

21. Cohen, *Pure Adulteration*, 203.

22. Cohen, *Pure Adulteration*, xiv, 9, 16.

23. Sébastien Rioux, "Capitalist Food Production and the Rise of Legal Adulteration: Regulating Food Standards in 19th-Century Britain," *Journal of Agrarian Change* 19, no. 1 (2019): 64–81.

24. Tangires, *Movable Markets*, 221.

25. Alice L. Edwards, *Product Standards and Labeling for Consumers* (New York: Ronald Press, 1940), 4.

26. Stoll, *Fruits of Natural Advantage*; Zeide, *Canned*.

27. Tangires, *Movable Markets*, 67–72. See also Jacobs, *Pocketbook Politics*.

28. Richard S. Tedlow, *New and Improved: The Story of Mass Marketing in America* (New York: Basic Books, 1990), 53–55.

29. Mira Wilkins, "When and Why Brand Names in Food and Drink?," in *Adding Value: Brands and Marketing in Food and Drink*, ed. Geoffrey Jones and Nicholas J. Morgan, 15–40 (London: Routledge, 1994). Labor organizations also briefly experimented with labeling campaigns before the 1930s. Kathryn Wish Sklar, "Consumers' White Label Campaign of the National Consumers' League, 1898–1918," in *Getting and Spending: European and American Consumer Societies in the Twentieth Century* (German Historical Institute), ed. Susan Strasser, Charles McGovern, and Matthias Just, 17–36 (Cambridge: Cambridge University Press, 2013); Dana Frank, *Purchasing Power: Consumer Organizing, Gender, and the Seattle Labor Movement, 1919–1929* (New York: Cambridge University Press, 1994), 193–246.

30. For histories of the packaging industry, see Twede, "Birth of Modern Packaging"; Hine, *Total Package*; Glenn Porter, "Cultural Forces and Commercial Constraints: Designing Packaging in the Twentieth-Century United States," *Journal of Design History* 12, no. 1 (1999): 25–43; Gary S. Cross and Robert N. Proctor, *Packaged Pleasures: How Technology and Marketing Revolutionized Desire* (Chicago: University of Chicago Press, 2014).

31. L. B. Steele, "The Responsibility of the Package in Self-Service Selling," in American Management Association, *The Package as a Selling Tool* (Packaging Series Number 19, 1946), 29. On "pick-upable," see Richard D. Elwell, "The Top Management Approach to Packaging," in American Management Association, *The Package as a Selling Tool* (Packaging Series Number 19, 1946), 6.

32. Willard F. Deveneau, "Package Design Trends and Standards," in American Management Association, *The Package as a Selling Tool* (Packaging Series Number 19, 1946), 19.

33. On the role of packaging in "attachment" theory in economic sociology, see Franck Cochoy and Catherine Grandclément-Chaffy, "Publicizing Goldilocks' Choice at the Supermarket," in *Making Things Public: Atmospheres of Democracy*, ed. Bruno Latour and Peter Weibel (Cambridge, MA: MIT Press, 2005), 648.

34. Steele, "Responsibility of the Package," 25–26. On the development of industrial "fresh" food, see Freidberg, *Fresh*.

35. Ai Hisano, "Selling Food in Clear Packages: The Development of Cellophane and the Expansion of Self-Service Merchandising in the United States, 1920s–1950s," *International Journal of Food Design* 2, no. 2 (2017): 139–52; Hisano, *Visualizing Taste*.

36. Strasser, *Satisfaction Guaranteed*, 35. See also Wilkins, "When and Why Brand Names," 20.

37. Arthur Kallet and F. J. Schlink, *100,000,000 Guinea Pigs: Dangers in Everyday Foods, Drugs, and Cosmetics* (New York: Grosset & Dunlap, 1933), 284.

38. Rachel Bowlby, *Carried Away: The Invention of Modern Shopping* (New York: Columbia University Press, 2002), 194.

39. Bowlby, *Carried Away*, 38.

40. Roger Wolcott, *Informative Selling* (National Consumer-Retailer Council, 1941), 19–29, 36, 57–58; Coles, *Standards and Labels for Consumers' Goods*, 277.

41. Lynd quoted in Jacobs, *Pocketbook Politics*, 103.

42. Brian Balogh, *The Associational State: American Governance in the Twentieth Century* (Philadelphia: University of Pennsylvania Press, 2015). See also Alan Brinkley, "The New Deal and the Idea of the State," in Fraser and Gerstle, *Rise and Fall of the New Deal Order*, 85–121.

43. Kallet and Schlink, *100,000,000 Guinea Pigs*, 208–11, 284–90; Cohen, *Pure Adulteration*.

44. Kara W. Swanson, "Food and Drug Law as Intellectual Property Law: Historical Reflections," *Wisconsin Law Review* 2011, no. 2 (2011): 355–65.

45. Ruth deForest Lamb, *American Chamber of Horrors* (New York: Farrar & Rinehart, 1936). See also https://www.fda.gov/about-fda/histories-product-regulation/american-chamber-horrors.

46. Jackson, *Food and Drug Legislation in the New Deal*.

47. On "food chain effects," see Horowitz, *Kosher USA*. On the debates among business interests over 1930s food standards, see Xaq Frohlich, "Making Food Standard: The U.S. Food and Drug Administration's Food Standards of Identity, 1930s–1960s," *Business History Review* 96, no. 1 (March 2022): 145–76.

48. Industry argued for descriptive labeling while consumer advocates argued for statements on quality. Zeide, *Canned*, 11.

49. Discussed in Zeide, *Canned*, 114. Another good examples is the Universal Product Code (UPC), discussed in chapter 4.

50. Sally Eden, "Food Labels as Boundary Objects: How Consumers Make Sense of Organic and Functional Foods," *Public Understanding of Science* 20, no. 2 (2011): 179–94.

51. Carol Ballentine, "Sulfanilamide Disaster," *FDA Consumer*, June 1981, https://www.fda.gov/files/about%20fda/published/The-Sulfanilamide-Disaster.pdf, last visited April 17, 2023. See also Jackson, *Food and Drug Legislation in the New Deal*; Carpenter, *Reputation and Power*.

52. Carpenter, *Reputation and Power*, 107–8.

53. Carpenter, *Reputation and Power*, 79; Jackson, *Food and Drug Legislation in the New Deal*, 204.

54. Wesley E. Forte, "Definitions and Standards of Identity for Foods," *UCLA Law Review* 14 (1967): 807.

55. The USDA's voluntary quality standards would develop in parallel to the FDA mandatory identity standards. They were in some ways much more visible to the public, because consumers would read the USDA seal on the labels of foods they bought. Frohlich, "Making Food Standard."

56. H. Thomas Austern, "Food Standards: The Balance between Certainty and Innovation," *Food, Drug, Cosmetic Law Journal* 24, no. 9 (1969): 132–34.

57. "Interview between: Dr. Kenneth L. Milstead, Retired Assistant to the Commissioner, and James Harvey Young, Emory University, Fred L. Lofsvold, FDA, and Wallace F. Janssen, FDA, Washington, DC, August 28, 1968, July 28, 1969, and February 4, 1982," FDA website, https://www.fda.gov/media/85948/download, last visited April 17, 2023.

58. This language of "purported to be" comes from section 403(g) of the Food, Drug, and Cosmetic Act.

59. Austern, "Food Standards," 451; Edwards, *Product Standards and Labeling*, 53–55. In 1954 the Hale Amendment modified this process, removing the requirement for public hearings if proposed standards were not contested within thirty days of being posted.

60. Wang, "Imagining the Administrative State."

61. The USDA Bureau of Chemistry published them in Circular 19. See, for example, Harvey Washington Wiley, *Foods and Their Adulteration: Origin, Manufacture, and Composition of Food Products; Infants' and Invalids' Foods; Detection of Common Adulterations, and Food Standards* (Philadelphia, 1911), 614; see also Cohen, *Pure Adulteration*.

62. Junod, "Chemistry and Controversy," 261.

63. "Regulations under the Federal Food, Drug, and Cosmetics Act for Fixing and Establishing a Reasonable Definition and Standard of Identity for the Food Known under Its Common or Usual Name as Tomato Juice," 4:145 *Federal Register* 3454 (July 29, 1939).

64. Courts would uphold the FDA standard and its implied ban of benzoate in the 1945 case *Libby, McNeill & Libby v. U.S.*, 148 F.2d 71 (2d Cir. 1945). See also Junod, "Food Standards the United States," in Smith and Phillips, *Food, Science, Policy*, 181.

65. The idea to use common recipes was set during the congressional discussion of the 1938 FDCA, where one member noted: "The government has had difficulty in holding such articles as commercial jams and preserves and many other foods to the time-honored standards employed by housewives and reputable manufacturers." H. R. Rep. No. 2139, 75th Cong., 3rd Sess. (1938). R. A. Merrill, and E. M. Collier Jr., "Like Mother Used to Make: An Analysis of FDA Food Standards of Identity," *Columbia Law Review* 74 (1974): 561.

66. R.S. McBride, "The Real Issue in the Sweetener Controversy," *Food Industries* (September 1940): 36–37. This decision closed a decades-old debate on the nomenclature of glucose as "corn sugar." Cohen, *Pure Adulteration*, 169.

67. Junod, "Food Standards the United States," in Smith and Phillips, *Food, Science, Policy*, 167–88.

68. Junod, "Chemistry and Controversy," 262.

69. Coles, *Standards and Labels for Consumers' Goods*, 157–58, 160. See Yates and Murphy, *Engineering Rules*, 84.

70. Coles would argue that "labels, advertisements, and brands are not effective as guides without the use of standards." Coles, *Consumer-Buyer and the Market*, 442.

71. Coles, *Standards and Labels for Consumers' Goods*, 82.

72. Carole Sugarman, "Peanut Butter Grandmother; Remembering Consumer Activist Ruth Desmond," *Washington Post*, October 5, 1988, E3; Merrill and Collier, "Like Mother Used to Make," 561. See also Angie M. Boyce, "'When Does It Stop Being Peanut Butter?': FDA Food Standards of Identity, Ruth Desmond, and the Politics of Consumer Activism, 1960s–1970s," *Technology and Culture* 57, no. 1 (2016): 54–79.

73. Peter Barton Hutt, Richard A. Merrill, and Lewis A. Grossman, *Food and Drug Law*, 3rd ed. (St. Paul, MN: Foundation Press, 2007), 181–82.

74. *Kordel v. United States*. 335 U.S. 345 (1948). In 1951 a district court declined to hold that a book constituted labeling even though it was circulated with certain food products and made claims that could potentially shape how the consumer understood the products. *United States v. 8 Cartons, More or Less, Molasses*, 97 F. Supp. 313 (W.D.N.Y. 1951). Yet, in 1965 a circuit court held a booklet was labeling because the vendor showed it to an undercover FDA inspector when trying to sell honey. *United States v. 250 Jars . . . "Cal's Tupelo Blossom U.S. Fancy Pure Honey,"* 344 F.2d 288 (6th Cir. 1965). As discussed in Hutt et al., *Food and Drug Law*, 99–102.

75. On the impact of WWII on food policy, see Kellen Backer, "World War II and the Triumph of Industrialized Food" (PhD diss., University of Wisconsin–Madison, 2012); Lizzie Collingham, *A Taste for War: World War II and the Battle for Food* (London: Allen Lane, 2011); Amy Bentley, *Eating for Victory: Food Rationing and the Politics of Domesticity* (Urbana: University of Illinois Press, 1998).

76. Deveneau, "Package Design Trends and Standards," 11–13.

77. Alex Roland, *War and Technology: A Very Short Introduction* (Oxford: Oxford University Press, 2016), 90–105.

78. Deborah K. Fitzgerald, "World War II and the Quest for Time-Insensitive Foods," *Osiris* 35 (2020): 1–19.

79. Herbert L. Meiselman and Howard G. Schutz, "History of Food Acceptance Research in the US Army," US Army Research Paper 37 (2003), http://digitalcommons.unl.edu/usarmyresearch/37, last visited January 15, 2020.

80. Alissa Hamilton, *Squeezed: What You Don't Know about Orange Juice* (New Haven, CT: Yale University Press, 2009), 21–23; Shane Hamilton, "Cold Capitalism: The Political Ecology of Frozen Concentrated Orange Juice," *Agricultural History* 77, no. 4 (Autumn 2003): 557–81.

81. P.R. Josephson, "The Ocean's Hot Dog: The Development of the Fish Stick," *Technology and Culture* 49, no. 1 (2008): 41–61; Junod, "Chemogastric Revolution," 326.

82. Fitzgerald, "World War II and the Quest," 3.

83. George P. Larrick, "Pure Food and Progress," *Food Technology* (October 1956): 456, as cited in Vileisis, *Kitchen Literacy,* 187.

84. Hamilton, *Squeezed,* 2009.

85. A. A. Schaal, "Consumer Trends in New Food Products for Homemakers," *Food Technology* (January 1952): 14.

86. Margaret Weber, "The Cult of Convenience: Marketing and Food in Postwar America," *Enterprise and Society* 22, no. 3 (September 2021): 605–34.

87. Yates and Murphy, *Engineering Rules.*

88. Mark Weiner, "Consumer Culture and Participatory Democracy: The Story of Coca-Cola during World War II," *Food and Foodways* 6, no. 2 (1996): 109–29; August W. Giebelhaus, "The Pause That Refreshed the World: The Evolution of Coca-Cola's Global Marketing Strategy," in *Adding Value: Brands and Marketing in Food and Drink,* ed. Geoffrey Jones and Nicholas J. Morgan, 191–214 (London: Routledge, 1994).

89. Elwell, "Top Management Approach to Packaging," 8.

90. Elwell, "Top Management Approach to Packaging," 3–4. On the postwar boom in supermarkets, see James Mayo, *The American Grocery Store: The Business Evolution of an Architectural Space* (Westport, CT: Praeger, 1993), 157–90.

91. The phrase "liberal consensus" comes from literary critic Lionel Trilling, who wrote in 1950 in a published collection of essays, *The Liberal Imagination,* that "liberalism is not only the dominant but even the sole intellectual tradition" in the United States. For a counterargument to the liberal consensus thesis, see Kim Phillips-Fein, *Invisible-Hands: The Businessmen's Crusade against the New Deal* (New York: W. W. Norton, 2009).

92. Yates and Murphy, *Engineering Rules,* 13.

93. Glickman, *Buying Power,* 266.

94. Historian Tracey Deutsch argues that segmented marketing existed before the 1940s, but was a result of the geographical segmentation of market*spaces.* After WWII, what was new was how niche marketing became a deliberate strategy of national advertising that was not tied to just local or regional geographies. Deutsch, *Building a Housewife's Paradise,* 5.

95. Coles, *Standards and Labels for Consumers' Goods,* 97.

2. GATEKEEPERS AND HIDDEN PERSUADERS

1. Alfred Jay Marrow, *The Practical Theorist: The Life and Work of Kurt Lewin* (New York: Basic Books, 1969).

2. On marketing's focus on "sense appeal" and the dominance of behaviorism in the 1930s, see David Howes and Constance Classen, *Ways of Sensing: Understanding the Senses in Society* (New York: Routledge, 2013), 140–41, 145.

3. Kurt Lewin, "Forces behind Food Habits and Methods of Change," in *The Problems of Changing Food Habits,* ed. Carl F. Guthe and Margaret Mead, NRC Report (1943), 37, 40.

4. Eugene Stivers and Susan Wheelan, eds., *The Lewin Legacy: Field Theory in Current Practice* (Berlin: Springer, 1986); Kurt Lewin and Martin Gold, *The Complete Social Scientist: A Kurt Lewin Reader* (Washington, DC: American Psychological Association, 1999); Pamela J. Shoemaker and Timothy Vos, *Gatekeeping Theory* (New York: Routledge, 2009); Kurt Lewin, *Field Theory in Social Science: Selected Theoretical Papers,* ed. Dorwin Cartwright (New York: Harper & Row, 1976 [1964]).

5. Levenstein, *Paradox of Plenty*.

6. Pollan, *Omnivore's Dilemma*, 94.

7. Apple, *Vitamania*, 18–28.

8. William B. Bradley, "Thiamine Enrichment in the United States," *Annals of the New York Academy of Sciences* 98, no. 2 (April 1962): 602–6.

9. James Harvey Young, *The Medical Messiahs: A Social History of Health Quackery in Twentieth-Century America* (Princeton, NJ: Princeton University Press, 1967).

10. On the AMA's experimentation in the 1930s with its "Seal of Approval," see Coles, *Standards and Labels for Consumers' Goods*, 559–60.

11. It is also known as the "demarcation problem." Thomas F. Gieryn, "Boundary-Work and the Demarcation of Science from Non-science: Strains and Interests in Professional Ideologies of Scientists," *American Sociological Review* 48, no. 6 (1983): 781–95; Sheila Jasanoff, *Science at the Bar: Law, Science, and Technology in America* (Cambridge, MA: Harvard University Press, 1997).

12. James Harvey Young, *American Health Quackery: Collected Essays* (Princeton, NJ: Princeton University Press, 1992); P. B. and P. B. Hutt II, "A History of Government Regulation of Adulteration and Misbranding of Food," *Food, Drug, Cosmetic Law Journal* 39 (1984): 2.

13. See Nancy Tomes, *The Gospel of Germs: Men, Women, and the Microbe in American Life* (Cambridge, MA: Harvard University Press, 1999).

14. Apple, *Vitamania*, 128; K. L. Milstead, "The Food and Drug Administration's Program against Quackery," speech delivered to Yonkers Academy of Medicine, Yonkers, New York, May 16, 1962, p. 5, PB Hutt Archives. The concept of "subclinical deficiencies" raises the prospect of invisible illnesses, which called for expert training to diagnose them. On the concern with "hidden hunger," see also Biltekoff, *Eating Right in America*, 49.

15. Junod, "Food Standards in the United States," 181.

16. *United States v. Lexington Mill & Elevator Co.*, 232 U. S. 399 (1914); Junod, "Chemistry and Controversy," 112–34.

17. Later, the enrichment of wheat with vitamin B further contributed to the declining incidence of the disease. Alan M. Kraut, *Goldberger's War: The Life and Work of a Public Health Crusader* (New York: Hill and Wang, 2004); Kenneth J. Carpenter, "A Short History of Nutritional Science: Part 3 (1912–1944)," *Journal of Nutrition* 133, no. 10 (2003): 3023.

18. Kraut, *Goldberger's War*. On how thiamine enrich bread came to be accepted in 1943, see Bobrow-Strain, *White Bread*, 110–31.

19. Junod, "Food Standards in the United States," 182.

20. Clare Gordon Bettencourt, "Like Oil and Water: Food Additives and America's Food Identity Standards in the Mid-Twentieth Century," in *Proteins, Pathologies and Politics: Dietary Innovation and Disease from the Nineteenth Century*, ed. David Gentilcore and Matthew Smith, 165–68 (London: Bloomsbury Academic, 2019).

21. Controls on vitamin labeling were still quite strict, limiting statements about enrichment to the standard product's name ("enriched flour") and prohibiting additional nutrient declarations or health claims.

22. *Federal Security Administration v. Quaker Oats Company*, 318 U. S. 218 (1943).

23. FDA RG 88, General Subject Item 1A, Food Tech, Food Standards, Nutrition Labeling, 1924–78: C. W. Crawford, "Ten Years of Food Standardization," paper delivered at the

spring meeting of the Food Industries Advisory Committee of the Nutrition Foundation, Hershey, PA, May 19, 1948.

24. Fredus N. Peters, "Industrial and Legal Viewpoints: Are Standards of Identity Assets or Liabilities in the Food Industry?," *Food Technology* 1 (1947): 583–90.

25. As quoted in James Harvey Young, "Historical Aspects of Food Cultism and Nutrition Quackery," in *Food Cultism and Nutrition Quackery*, ed. Gunnar Blix (Stockholm: Almqvist & Wiksell, 1970), 18.

26. R. B. Termini, "Product Classification under the Federal Food Drug and Cosmetic Act: When a Food Becomes a Drug," *Journal of Pharmacy and Law* 2 (1993): 1.

27. "Interviewee: William W. Goodrich, Interviewers: Ronald T. Ottes and Fred L. Lofsvold, Date: October 15, 1986, Place: Rockville, MD," FDA website, https://www.fda.gov/media/87084/download, last visited April 17, 2023.

28. Carpenter, *Reputation and Power,* 169–71.

29. Nancy Tomes, "The Great American Medicine Show Revisited," *Bulletin of the History of Medicine* 79, no. 4 (Winter 2005): 627–63; Jeremy A. Greene, *Prescribing by Numbers: Drugs and the Definition of Disease* (Baltimore: Johns Hopkins University Press, 2007). On the model of the doctor as a gatekeeper in the FDA's regulatory system, see Carpenter, *Reputation and Power.*

30. Since the late 1950s the FDA had treated package information inserts or pamphlets that accompanied drug products as a claim which required premarket testing. If companies made claims not included in the New Drug Application (NDA), the FDA would seize them. For these reasons, labels and package inserts were a central drug policy concern during the early 1960s. Carpenter, *Reputation and Power,* 165–66.

31. Greene, *Prescribing by Numbers*; Carpenter, *Reputation and Power.*

32. Harry M. Marks, "Revisiting the Origins of Compulsory Drug Prescriptions," *American Journal of Public Health* 85, no. 1 (1995): 109; Marks, *Progress of Experiment.*

33. The majority ruling in *Lochner v. New York* (1905) is a classic articulation of this older view of buyer-seller contractual law.

34. W. L. Prosser, "The Assault upon the Citadel (Strict Liability to the Consumer)," *Yale Law Journal* 69, no. 7 (1960): 1099–148.

35. As quoted in Cullen Goretzke, "The Resurgence of Caveat Emptor: Puffery Undermines the Pro-Consumer Trend in Wisconsin's Misrepresentation Doctrine," *Wisconsin Law Review*, no. 1 (2003): 172.

36. W. E. Forte, "The Ordinary Purchaser and the Federal Food, Drug and Cosmetic Act," *Virginia Law Review* 52 (1966): 1467. Court decisions from 1940s through 1970s would swing like a pendulum between standards focused on "that 'vast and unthinking' multitude who when making a purchase do not stop to analyze," in *United States v. 62 Packages . . . 48 F. Supp. 878,* 887 (W. D. Wis. 1943), as quoted in Merrill and Collier, "Like Mother Used to Make," 594, and "purchasers who are of normal capacity and use that capacity in a common sense way," in *United States v. Pinaud, Inc.* 800 F.2d 1129, known as the "ordinary person" standard. See Hutt et al., *Food and Drug Law,* 111.

37. Jacobs, *Pocketbook Politics,* 249.

38. Lizabeth Cohen, *A Consumers' Republic: The Politics of Mass Consumption in Postwar America* (New York: Knopf, 2003), 10.

39. John F. Kennedy, "Special Message to the Congress on Protecting the Consumer Interest," March 15, 1962. The American Presidency Project website, https://www.presidency.ucsb.edu/node/237009, last visited June 7, 2023.

40. Glickman, *Buying Power,* 258; Goldstein, *Creating Consumers,* 7; Emily E. LB. Twarog, *Politics of the Pantry: Housewives, Food, and Consumer Protest in Twentieth-Century America* (New York: Oxford University Press, 2017), 87.

41. Glickman, *Buying Power,* 258. See also Cohen, *Consumer's Republic.*

42. Historian Elaine Tyler May argues that new suburbanites lacked community, experiencing cultural "rootlessness," which left them without many of the traditional sources of information about food and domestic living. Many turned to scientific expertise to fill that information void. Elaine Tyler May, "Cold War—Warm Hearth: Politics and the Family in Postwar America," in Frazer and Gerstle, *Rise and Fall of the New Deal Order,"* 161–65, 167. See also Cohen, *Consumer's Republic*; Deutsch, *Building a Housewife's Paradise.*

43. Robert O. Self, *All in the Family: The Realignment of American Democracy since the 1960s* (New York: Hill and Wang, 2013). See also May, "Cold War—Warm Hearth."

44. Self, *All in the Family,* 110.

45. Weber, "Cult of Convenience."

46. V. Kumar, "Evolution of Marketing as a Discipline: What Has Happened and What to Look Out For," *Journal of Marketing* 79 (January 2015): 1–9; Cochoy, "Another Discipline for the Market Economy."

47. Cheskin also talks about how Sputnik dramatically changed American consumer psychology, making it less, not more rational. Louis Cheskin, *Why People Buy: Motivational Research and Its Successful Application* (New York: Liveright, 1959), 248.

48. Jan L. Logemann, *Engineered to Sell: European Émigrés and the Making of Consumer Capitalism* (Chicago: University of Chicago Press, 2019).

49. Goldstein, *Creating Consumers,* 270–76.

50. Indeed, Dichter declared that "feelings are facts, too." Ernst Dichter, *The Strategy of Desire* (Garden City, NY: Doubleday, 1960), 45; Katherine J. Parkin, *Food Is Love: Advertising and Gender Roles in Modern America* (Philadelphia: University of Pennsylvania Press, 2006), 31–37, 44–47. Historians of advertising have described earlier shifts like this in advertising styles, such as from "reason-why" advertising in the 1900s to "emotional appeal" advertising in magazines by the 1920s. Jackson Lears, *Fables of Abundance: A Cultural History of Advertising in America* (New York: Basic Books, 1995); Roland Marchand, *Advertising the American Dream: Making Way for Modernity, 1920–1940* (Berkeley: University of California Press, 1985).

51. Deutsch, *Building a Housewife's Paradise,* 208–9; Mayo, *American Grocery Store*; Daniel Horowitz, *The Anxieties of Affluence: Critiques of American Consumer Culture, 1939–1979* (Amherst: University of Massachusetts Press, 2005).

52. On traffic pattern studies, see Bowlby, *Carried Away,* 236–41.

53. Apple, *Vitamania,* 54–84. Self-service had a big impact on drug stores. Retailers introduced "suggestive 'pick-up' items to catch the eye and prompt impulse buying"; in particular, reminder or suggestion sellers were used to sell to people who came in for prescriptions or sodas. Steele, "Responsibility of the Package," 27.

54. Philip Nelson, "Finds Supers Lead in Diet Foods Sale," *Drug News Weekly,* September 20, 1965, 11.

55. Letter from Crawford to Williams, September 1, 1953, NAS FNB Archives, "NAS-NRC B&A: FNB, 1954: Com on Artificial Sweeteners: Ad Hoc Policy Meetings." Crawford's concern with grocers would be compounded by the rise of self-service supermarkets. Grocers had a direct and influencing relationship on their customers' choices, whereas supermarkets exercised a less personal and more indirect influence, in the form of shelf placement. Grocers acted as a visible middleman at the store, much like pharmacists, whereas supermarkets were designed to get rid of this extra personnel. Forte, "Ordinary Purchaser," 1467.

56. The invention of the shopping cart, replacing baskets, allowed shoppers to move with their hands free, unencumbered through the store, and purchase more items than they could possibly carry, making it easy to scale up purchases. Supermarket trade journals discussed ways to reorganize product inventory on the floor to decrease traffic bottlenecks or silently steer traffic to high-margin or high-profile items. Even socializing, once an important feature of shopping at markets, became a "problem" retailers needed to overcome, to prevent shopping cart blockages where neighbors parked to chat. Deutsch, *Building a Housewife's Paradise*, 199; Franck Cochoy, *On the Origins of Self-Service* (New York: Routledge, 2014), 166–98; Mayo, *American Grocery Store.*

57. Even as supermarkets promoted self-service informational environments, in the 1950s many were reintroducing meat clerks into their stores to serve as "warm experts," knowledgeable and familiar employees who "allowed the customer to feel more comfortable in their surroundings." Sara L. Wimberly and Jessica L. McClean, "Supermarket Savvy: The Everyday Information-Seeking Behavior of Grocery Shoppers," *Information and Culture* 47, no. 2 (2012): 193.

58. In chapter 4 I discuss the concept of "healthism," first coined by sociologist Robert Crawford in 1980.

59. Horowitz, *Anxieties of Affluence*, 61. Dichter's view of advertising followed the "therapeutic role" historian Roland Marchand described the advertising profession taking in the late 1930s. Marchand, *Advertising the American Dream*, 359–63. Dichter was famous for advising General Mills that its line of Betty Crocker cake-mix recipes were partly failing because of women's guilt about how easy it was. It didn't feel like cooking. His solution: instead of just adding water, have them also add in the eggs. The "egg theory" became a favorite of marketers wanting to illustrate why food advertising had to address "the homemaker's personal investment in the cake." See Laura Shapiro, *Something from the Oven: Reinventing Dinner in 1950s America* (New York: Penguin Books, 2005), 64, 75–76.

60. The psychology surrounding butter versus margarine, according to Dichter, was a good example of this. Ernst Dichter, *Handbook of Consumer Motivations: The Psychology of the World of Objects* (New York: McGraw-Hill, 1964), 51. See also Horowitz, *Anxieties of Affluence*, 53.

61. Parkin, *Food Is Love*, 163–64.

62. Chris J. Feudtner, *Bittersweet: Diabetes, Insulin, and the Transformation of Illness* (Chapel Hill: University of North Carolina Press, 2003); Martin D. Moore, "Food as Medicine: Diet, Diabetes Management, and the Patient in Twentieth Century Britain," *Journal of the History of Medicine and Allied Sciences* 73, no. 2 (2018): 150–67.

63. On "surplus health," see Dumit, *Drugs for Life,* 2012.

64. "The Fat of the Land," *Time,* January 13, 1961, https://content.time.com/time/subscriber/article/0,33009,828721,00.html, last visited April 17, 2023.

65. Junod, "Chemogastric Revolution." On the "petrochemical revolution," see also Vogel, *Is It Safe?*, 16, 36–37.

66. Bruce S. Wilson, "Legislative History of the Pesticide Residues Amendment of 1954 and the Delaney Clause of the Food Additives Amendment of 1958," in *Regulating Pesticides in Food: The Delaney Paradox* (Washington, DC: National Academies Press, 1987), 161–73.

67. Wilson, "Legislative History of the Pesticide." See also Vogel, *Is It Safe?*, 40; John Wargo, *Our Children's Toxic Legacy: How Science and Law Fail to Protect Us from Pesticides* (New Haven, CT: Yale University Press, 1998).

68. Murray D. Sayer, "Artificial Sweeteners—Their Impact on the Food Laws," *Food, Drug, Cosmetic Law Journal* (February 1966): 111–23.

69. Ernest H. Volwiler, interview by James J. Bohning, August 18, 1986, Lake Forest, IL (Philadelphia: Chemical Heritage Foundation, Oral History Transcript # 0050). Abbott Labs' expansion into vitamins in the 1920s had proved very profitable for the company.

70. Ernest H. Volwiler, "Editorial: Relationships and Similarities of the Pharmaceutical and Food Industries," *Food Technology* (November 1950): 463–66.

71. For a fascinating history of candy and changes in packaging technology and popular marketing, see Cross and Proctor, *Packaged Pleasures,* 89–129.

72. Rich Cohen, *Sweet and Low: A Family Story* (New York: Farrar, Straus and Giroux, 2006).

73. Benjamin Siegel, "Sweet Nothing—the Triumph of Diet Soda," *American Heritage* 57, no. 3 (June/July 2006), https://www.americanheritage.com/sweet-nothing-triumph-diet-soda-0, last visited April 17, 2023.

74. De la Peña, *Empty Pleasures,* 54–59, 90–93.

75. The Sucaryl ad campaign is a good example of business-to-business (B2B) marketing. JoAnne Yates, "How Business Enterprises Use Technology: Extending the Demand-Side Turn." *Enterprise and Society* 7, no. 3 (2006): 422.

76. NAS FNB Archives, 1954–1957, "Com on Artificial Sweeteners: Ad Hoc Policy."

77. *Food Technology* (August 1955): 10.

78. Parkin, *Food Is Love,* 179.

79. On the "Cola Wars," see Tedlow, *New and Improved,* 99–106, 110.

80. FDA, "Dietary Foods: Notice of Proposal to Revise Regulations," 27 *Federal Register* 5815–18 (June 20, 1962).

81. Ben McGrath, "Tab Scare," *New Yorker,* February 6, 2006.

82. Ted Sanchagrin, "Battle of the Brands: Soft Drinks," *Printer's Ink,* April 9, 1965, 21–25.

83. "Diet Foods Reaping Fat Net on Slim Ads," *Supermarket News,* August 14, 1967, 4, 10.

84. See Apple, *Vitamania,* 107. Later in the decade Miles Laboratories would partner with the popular television show, The Flintstones, to franchise a highly successful children's Flintstones Vitamins. Linda Rodriguez McRobbie, "A Brief History of Flintstones Vitamins," *Mental Floss,* October 21, 2010, https://www.mentalfloss.com/article/26157/brief-history-flintstones-vitamins, last visited April 17, 2023.

85. 231 F. Supp. 551 (S.D. Fla. 1963), as quoted in Hutt et al., *Food and Drug Law,* 233.

86. Irvine H. Page, Edgar V. Allen, Francis L. Chamberlain, Ancel Keys, Jeremiah Stamler, and Fredrick J. Stare, "Dietary Fat and Its Relation to Heart Attacks and Strokes," *Circulation* 23 (1961): 133–36.

87. Nan Ickeringill, "Food: New Margarines," *New York Times*, October 21, 1960, 37.

88. He concluded, "Last night, I had a typical cholesterol-free dinner: baked squash, skimmed milk, and gelatin. I'm sure this will not make me live any longer, but I know it's going to seem longer." Marx, Groucho, *Memoirs of a Mangy Lover* (Cambridge, MA: Da Capo Press, 1997 [1963]), 33–34.

89. Lamb, *American Chamber of Horrors,* 162–63.

90. K. L. Milstead, "Food Fads and Nutrition Quackery as Related to Dairy Products," April 10, 1962, pp. 12–15, PB Hutt Archives.

91. The AMA Council on Food and Nutrition, "The Regulation of Dietary Fat: A Report of the Council," *JAMA* 181, no. 5 (August 4, 1962): 139–57.

92. "December 21, 1960 Letter to O. L. Kline, from Jeremiah Stamler," Binder "5. Polyunsaturates3–1965," PB Hutt Archives. On triparanol and history of cholesterol lowering drugs at this time, see Greene, *Prescribing by Numbers,* 159–64; Daniel Steinberg, "An Interpretive History of the Cholesterol Controversy, Part V: The Discovery of the Statins and the End of the Controversy," *Journal of Lipid Research* 47 (2006): 1339–51.

93. "Next, a Death-Defying Diet?," *Newsweek*, September 24, 1962, 89–92.

94. Dichter, *Handbook of Consumer Motivations,* 51.

95. G. J. Stigler, "The Theory of Economic Regulation," *Bell Journal of Economics and Management Science* 2, no. 1 (1971): 3–21; R. A. Ball and J. R. Lilly, "The Menace of Margarine: The Rise and Fall of a Social Problem," *Social Problems* 29, no. 5 (1982): 488–98; R. Dupré, "'If It's Yellow, It Must Be Butter': Margarine Regulation in North America since 1886," *Journal of Economic History* 59, no. 2 (1999): 353–71.

96. Hisano, *Visualizing Taste,* 125–45; James Harvey Young, "The Fielding H. Garrison Lecture—'This Greasy Counterfeit': Butter Versus Oleomargarine in the United States Congress, 1886," *Bulletin of the History of Medicine* 53, no. 3 (1979): 407–8..

97. Helen Zoe Veit, "Eating Cotton: Cottonseed, Crisco, and Consumer Ignorance," *Journal of the Gilded Age and Progressive Era* 18 (2019): 397–421; Helen Zoe Veit, "How Crisco Toppled Lard—And Made Americans Believers in Industrial Food," *The Conversation*, December 18, 2019, https://theconversation.com/how-crisco-toppled-lard-and-made-americans-believers-in-industrial-food-127158.

98. Ball and Lilly, "Menace of Margarine"; Young, "'This Greasy Counterfeit'"; Gyorgy Scrinis, "Sorry, Marge," *Meanjin-Carlton* 61, no. 4 (2002): 108–15.

99. "Memorandum to Mr. William M. Dawson (Gann Advertising), from Irving Gilman (Institute of Motivational Research), Re: Baked Products and Packaged Cakes," E. Dichter Papers, Box 63, "Ernest Dichter Papers {{gt}} Research Reports," Folder "1373E-1374E."

100. Greene, *Prescribing by Numbers.*

101. "Is There a Heart Attack in His Future," Advertisement for Diet Fleischmann's in *JAMA* (November 4, 1968).

102. On gendered ads about motherhood, see Parkin, *Food Is Love,* 168.

103. ARB Surveys, Inc., "Public Understanding of Labeling Regarding Oleomargarine, Cooking Oils, and Related Foods," a study conducted for the FDA (New York, August 1963), PB Hutt Archives.

104. "Your Money and Your Life," *FDA Publication* no. 19, October 1963, 14.

105. He estimated that, among the 54,102 communications the FDA received, 40,000 were postcards generated by the National Health Federation, an alternative health food industry lobby group. William W. Goodrich, "The Coming Struggle over Vitamin-Mineral Pills," August 12, 1964, PB Hutt Archives, "Special Dietary Foods 2: 1964–1965."

106. *United States v. Vitasafe Corp.*, 345 F.2d 864 (3d Cir. 1965). Discussed in Peter Barton Hutt, "Government Regulation of Health Claims in Food Labeling and Advertising," *Food, Drug, Cosmetic Law Journal* 41, no. 1 (January 1986): 3–73.

107. "FDA Loses Court Test on 'Imitation Margarine' Labeling," *Food Chemical News*, May 9, 1966, 20–21. See also Hutt et al., *Food and Drug Law*, 182, on *United States v. 865 Cases . . . "Demi"* (1966).

108. FDA, "Food for Special Dietary Uses," 31 *Federal Register* 8521–27 (June 18, 1966).

109. Hutt, "Government Regulation of Health Claims," 60–61.

110. "Sebrell Says NAS Does Not Concur with FDA's Regulations on RDAs," *Food Chemical News*, May 25, 1966, 6–8.

111. Nestle, *Food Politics*; Nestle, *Unsavory Truth*; Gyorgy Scrinis, "On the Ideology of Nutritionism," *Gastronomica* 8, no. 1 (2008): 39–48.

112. Naomi Oreskes and Erik M. Conway, *Merchants of Doubt: How a Handful of Scientists Obscured the Truth on Issues from Tobacco Smoke to Global Warming* (New York: Bloomsbury Press, 2011). Their work has inspired a cottage industry for archival investigations on the role of industry finance in medical research.

113. Nestle, *Unsavory Science*, 14, 23.

114. The Sugar Association, "Our History: History of the Sugar Association," https://www.sugar.org/about/history/, last visited April 17, 2023.

115. Sugar Information published a booklet, "The Scientific Nibble," explaining how sugar could help reduce one's appetite, in *Life*, January 15, 1957, 9; "Sugar Takes Aim at Synthetics," advertisement in *Good Housekeeping*, January 1968; "The Importance of Sugar," advertisement in *Life*, April 16, 1956, 132; "Why So Many Weight-Watchers Find Sugar the Spoonful of Prevention," advertisement in *Life*, September 8, 1961.

116. In this way the Sugar Research Foundation redirected research away from sugar's role in heart disease for decades. Cristin E. Kearns, Laura A. Schmidt, and Stanton A. Glantz, "Sugar Industry and Coronary Heart Disease Research: A Historical Analysis of Internal Industry Documents," *JAMA Internal Medicine,* published online, September 12, 2016, http://jamanetwork.com/journals/jamainternalmedicine/article-abstract/2548255.

117. "Afternoon Session—August 5, 1965—Special Committee Meeting with Dr. White and Dr. Johnson—AMA," Binder "5. Polyunsaturates3–1965," PB Hutt Archives.

118. "Memorandum, Re: Summary of Meeting Held in Chicago on September 24, 1965 Between the Special Committee of the [ISEO], and the Council on Food and Nutrition of the AMA . . .," p. 3, Binder "5. Polyunsaturates3–1965," PB Hutt Archives.

119. "COPY—Commissioner Food and Drug," p. 9, Binder "6. Polyunsaturates4–1966–1967," PB Hutt Archives.

120. "Memorandum, Re: Summary of Meeting Held in Chicago on February 24, 1967 Between the Special Committee of the [ISEO] and the Council on Foods and Nutrition of the [AMA]," pp. 6–8, Binder "6. Polyunsaturates4–1966–1967," PB Hutt Archives.

121. Ken Howell, "Dairy Men Search for Solution to Non-Fat Products Competition," *Supermarket News*, October 30, 1967, 23.

122. Hugh Schwartz, "The Consumer Point of View on Imitation Dairy Products," p. 9, in *Proceedings of the Seventh National Symposium on Dairy Market Development*, October 16, 1967, Binder "ImitationFood1_1923–1967," PB Hutt Archives.

123. "Substitute Milk," *Consumer Reports*, January 1969, 8–11.

124. "Interviewee: William W. Goodrich, Interviewers: Ronald T. Ottes and Fred L. Lofsvold, Date: October 15, 1986, Place: Rockville, MD," FDA website, https://www.fda.gov /media/87084/download, last visited April 17, 2023; "Interviewee: Dr. James L. Goddard, Interviewer: Dr. James Harvey Young, Date: April 30 to June 19, 1969, Place: Atlanta, GA," FDA website, https://www.fda.gov/media/123411/download, last visited April 17, 2023.

125. James L. Goddard, "Health and the Consumer," delivered at the annual meeting of the Food Industries of the Nutrition Foundation at Skytop, PA, June 8, 1967, "FDA Speeches" files, PB Hutt Archives.

126. Eugene H. Stevenson, "What Is an Informative Label?," *Journal of the American Dietetic Association* (April 1968): 304–7.

127. "November 22, 1967 Letter from Malcolm R. Stephens (President of the Institute of Shortening and Edible Oils) to Ancel Keys," Binder "4. Polyunsaturates, 1966–1967," PB Hutt Archives.

128. Sanchagrin, "Battle of the Brands," 23.

3. MALNOURISHED OR MISINFORMED?

1. Horowitz, *Anxieties of Affluence*. On the overlooked importance of health and hunger in civil rights scholarship, see Laurie Green, "Saving Babies in Memphis: The Politics of Race, Health, and Hunger during the War on Poverty," in *The War on Poverty: A New Grassroots History, 1964–1980*, ed. Annelise Orleck and Lisa Gayle Hazirjian, 133–58 (Athens: University of Georgia Press, 2011).

2. "Shock of recognition" is Herman Melville's phrase. I thank Leo Marx for bringing it to my attention.

3. On institutionalized forgetting, see Robert N. Proctor and Londa Schiebinger, eds., *Agnotology: The Making and Unmaking of Ignorance* (Stanford, CA: Stanford University Press, 2008).

4. Citizen's Board of Inquiry into Hunger and Malnutrition in the United States, *Hunger, U.S.A.* (Boston: Beacon Press, 1968).

5. Norwood Allen Kerr, "Drafted into the War on Poverty: USDA Food and Nutrition Programs, 1961–1969," *Agricultural History* 64, no. 2 (Spring 1990): 154–66.

6. Annelise Orleck and Lisa Gayle Hazirjian, eds., *The War on Poverty: A New Grassroots History, 1964–1980* (Athens: University of Georgia Press, 2011).

7. Marisa Chappell, *The War on Welfare: Family, Poverty, and Politics in Modern America* (Philadelphia: University of Pennsylvania Press, 2010).

8. Martin Luther King, Jr., "Beyond Vietnam—A Time to Break Silence," speech, April 4, 1967, https://www.americanrhetoric.com/speeches/mlkatimetobreaksilence.htm.

9. Chappell, *War on Welfare*.

10. Robert O. Herrmann, "Consumerism: Its Goals, Organizations and Future," *Journal of Marketing* 34, no. 4 (October 1970): 55–60; Twarog, *Politics of the Pantry*, 71–79.

11. Chappell, *War on Welfare*, 35–50.

12. Annelise Orleck, "Introduction: The War on Poverty from the Grass Roots Up," in Orleck and Hazirjian, *War on Poverty*, 20.

13. Increasingly unable to prevent black voter registration, by the 1950s white segregationists were deliberately using hunger as a weapon to disenfranchise blacks in the South. In response, black activists in regions like the Mississippi Delta created "freedom farms" to feed blacks. Historian Monica White argues that growing food through farm cooperatives ensured their economic autonomy, which provided the political independence needed to challenge black exploitation and white supremacy. Monica M. White, *Freedom Farmers: Agricultural Resistance and the Black Freedom Movement* (Chapel Hill: University of North Carolina Press, 2019), 65–87.

14. Hannah Findlen LeBlanc, "Nutrition for National Defense: American Food Science in World War II and the Cold War" (PhD diss., Stanford University, 2019), 167–69.

15. Larry Brown, "Hunger USA: The Public Pushes Congress," *Journal of Health and Social Behavior* 11, no. 2 (1970): 119.

16. Janet Poppendieck, *Free for All: Fixing School Food in America* (Berkeley: University of California Press, 2010), 47–64. For the history of local and state-level movements in school lunches, which culminated in the National School Lunch Act at the federal level, see Andrew R. Ruis, *Eating to Learn, Learning to Eat: The Origins of School Lunch in the United States* (New Brunswick, NJ: Rutgers University Press, 2017).

17. Poppendieck, *Free for All*, 47–64.

18. *Their Daily Bread* report noted: "The 'Other America' is with us, but not in our midst. . . . It is possible for a suburban family to live its entire life without ever meeting a poor person." Jean Fairfax, Chairman, Committee on School Lunch Participation, *Their Daily Bread* (Atlanta: McNelley-Rudd Printing Service, 1968).

19. CBS, "Hunger In America: The 1968 CBS Documentary That Shocked America," https://www.cbsnews.com/video/hunger-in-america-the-1968-cbs-documentary-that-shocked-america/, last visited April 17, 2023.

20. For example, the documentary avoided the "iconic black female-headed households" that were much maligned in Moynihan's 1965 "culture of poverty" report, and showed "hungry children as American citizens and as members of nuclear families." Laurie B. Green, "'Hunger in America' and the Power of Television: Poor People, Physicians, and the Mass Media in the War against Poverty," in *Precarious Prescriptions: Contested Histories of Race and Health in North America*, ed. Laurie B. Green, John Mckiernan-González, and Martin Summers (Minneapolis: University of Minnesota Press, 2014), 227–28.

21. On the hunger lobby as an example of how public interest groups shape USDA policies, see Jeffrey M. Berry, "Consumers and the Hunger Lobby," *Proceedings of the Academy of Political Science* 34, no. 3 (1982): 68–78.

22. As quoted in Marjorie L. DeVault and James P. Pitts, "Surplus and Scarcity: Hunger and the Origins of the Food Stamp Program," *Social Problems* 31, no. 5 (1984): 552. On the civil rights movement in a Cold War context, see Mary L. Dudziak, "*Brown* as a Cold War Case," *Journal of American History* 91 (June 2004): 32–42.

23. Senate Resolution S. 281 of July 30, 1968, established a thirteen-member select committee to "study the food, medical, and other related basic needs among the people of the United States."

24. On the role of "epistemological fragmentation" in limiting the FDA's responsiveness to new science, see Kirchhelle, *Pyrrhic Progress.*

25. Biltekoff, *Eating Right in America,* 49–54. In 1989 RDAs would be replaced by "Reference Daily Intakes" (RDIs). Suzanne P. Murphy, Allison A. Yates, Stephanie A. Atkinson, Susan I. Barr, and Johanna Dwyer, "History of Nutrition: The Long Road Leading to the Dietary Reference Intakes for the United States and Canada," *Advanced Nutrition* 7, no. 1 (2016): 157–68.

26. "FDA Fact Sheet: Regulations for Foods for Special Dietary Uses," Binder "9. SpecialDietaryFoods5–1967–1969," PB Hutt Archives. On the crepe label, see Apple, *Vitamania,* 131–40.

27. Michael Ackerman, "Interpreting the 'Newer Knowledge of Nutrition': Science, Interests, and Values in the Making of Dietary Advice in the United States, 1915–1965" (PhD diss., University of Virginia, 2005), 241.

28. LeBlanc, "Nutrition for National Defense," 169; Ackerman, "Interpreting the 'Newer Knowledge of Nutrition.'"

29. CDC, *Ten-State Nutrition Survey, 1968–1970—Highlights* (U.S. Department of HEW, 1972). The survey is known today as the National Health and Nutrition Examination Survey (NHANES).

30. Kraut, *Goldberger's War*; Carpenter, "Short History of Nutritional Science."

31. Apple, *Vitamania,* 128; Milstead, "Food and Drug Administration's Program," 5.

32. "FDA Says New Drug Clearance May Be Necessary for High-Level Vitamins," *Food Chemical News,* June 24, 1968, 34.

33. These included: Abbott, AMA, California Canners and Growers, Cereal Institute, Carnation Co., Corn Products Co., National Association of Frozen Food Packers, Mead Johnson, Quaker Oats, Federation of Homemakers, General Foods, General Mills, Hoffman LaRoche, Milk Industry Federation, Kellogg Co., Sugar Association, Merck & Co., Miles Laboratories, National Canners Association, Kraft Foods, National Health Federation, National Soft Drink Association, Nutrilite Products, Inc., Sunkist Growers, Swift & Co., Tropicana Products, Inc., and Vita Foods Company. "Dietary Food Pre-Hearing Conference Enters Argument Stage," *Food Chemical News,* May 13, 1966, 20.

34. "Second Week of Pre-Hearings Conferences at FDA's Vitamin Mineral Reg," *F-D-C Reports,* May 20, 1968, 15.

35. George P. Larrick, "Report on Quackery from the FDA," delivered to the AMA / FDA National Congress on Medical Quackery, October 6, 1961, p. 6, in "FDA Speeches," PB Hutt Archives; Young, *American Health Quackery,* 97.

36. *Nutrition Reviews,* August 1968, 229.

37. Herbert Pollack, "Hunger USA 1968—A Critical Review," pp. 11, 15, W Darby Papers, Series 1, Box 12; "'Hunger, USA' Lacks Scientific Standing, Says MD-Witness at Vitamin Hearings, Dr. Pollack Sees No Evidence of Significant Nutritional Deficiencies in U.S.," *F-D-C Reports,* September 2, 1968, 8.

38. "Pollack Returns to Vitamin-Mineral Hearings, Defends Previous Testimony Opposes 'Super-Saturating' Foods with Nutrients," *F-D-C Reports,* March 3, 1969, 7;

"Lawyer Asks FDA to Make Revisions in Dietary Food Regulations," *Food Chemical News*, September 2, 1968, 12–13; "'Hunger, USA' Lacks Scientific Standing, Says MD-Witness at Vitamin Hearings. . .," *F-D-C Reports*, September 2, 1968, 8–9.

39. "Lawyer Asks FDA to Make Revisions in Dietary Food Regulations," *Food Chemical News*, September 2, 1968, 23.

40. Michael C. Latham, "The Hunger U.S.A. Debate," October 29, 1968, W Darby Papers, Series 1, Box 12, Folder "U.S. Select Senate Committee on Nutrition Hearings 1968."

41. "Pollack Returns to Vitamin-Mineral Hearings, Defends Previous Testimony Opposes 'Super-Saturating' Foods with Nutrients," *F-D-C Reports*, March 3, 1969, 7.

42. Jean Hewitt, "Inadequate Nutrition: A Classless Problem," *New York Times*, May 31, 1969, 10.

43. Alfred D. Klinger, Robert Mendelsohn, and Jaqui Alberts, "A Reply to Dr. Herbert Pollack Re: *Hunger USA*," *American Journal of Clinical Nutrition* 23, no. 6 (June 1970): 677–83.

44. Klinger et al., "Reply to Dr. Herbert Pollack."

45. Klinger et al., "Reply to Dr. Herbert Pollack."

46. Popkin, *The World Is Fat*; Julie Guthman, *Weighing In: Obesity, Food Justice, and the Limits of Capitalism* (Berkeley: University of California Press, 2011).

47. Mark Hegsted's speech at first day of Symposium, "Food Standards," DM Hegsted Papers.

48. Shane Hamilton, *Supermarket USA: Food and Power in the Cold War Farms Race* (New Haven, CT: Yale University Press, 2018).

49. Brown, "Hunger USA."

50. "Text of President's Message to Congress on Proposals to Combat Hunger in U.S.," *New York Times*, May 7, 1969, 50.

51. Patricia Cohen, "Scholars Return to 'Culture of Poverty' Ideas," *New York Times*, October 17, 2010, sec. U.S., http://www.nytimes.com/2010/10/18/us/18poverty.html, last visited April 17, 2023.

52. Meg Jacobs describes the negative impression that the poorly managed Office of Price Administration had on Nixon's father's business during the New Deal. Jacobs, *Pocketbook Politics*, 196.

53. Marjorie Hunter, "Nutrition Conference Organizer," *New York Times*, December 1, 1969, 54. Johanna Dwyer, senior nutrition scientist in the NIH Office of Dietary Supplements, former participant in 1969 White House Conference on Food, Nutrition and Health (assistant to Jean Mayer), phone interview with author, November 20, 2009.

54. John Herbers, "Nixon Aide Builds Nutrition Crusade," *New York Times*, June 29, 1969, 31.

55. "Javits Bids Nixon Consider Major Hunger Drive," *New York Times*, May 2, 1969, 48.

56. According to Johanna Dwyer, "the FDA at that time . . . was really sort of the J. Edgar Hoover of food." Dwyer, phone interview with author, November 20, 2009.

57. U.S. White House, *White House Conference on Food, Nutrition, and Health: Final Report* (Washington, DC: U.S. Government Printing Office, 1970).

58. WHCFNH Nixon Library, Series 2, Conference Working Files, 1969–1971, "White House Conference on Food and Nutrition [1969–1970]," Folder "WHCFNH: Subject Files—[Draft—Geographical List and Task Forces Assignments of Members and Consultants of

the WHC on FNH c. 1969]," Box 35 ([Draft—Geographical List and Task Forces Assignments of Members . . .] to GSA Form 1354 (Job Order) [July 1969]).

59. LeBlanc, "Nutrition for National Defense," 187–89.

60. The conference was also a veritable Who's Who of nutrition scientists, including panels chaired by William Sebrell, George J. Christakis, Mark Hegsted, William Darby, Nevins Scrimshaw, Theodore Van Itallie, Phillip White, Stanley Gershoff, to name just a few.

61. *White House Conference on Food, Nutrition, and Health*, 103.

62. This panel was a Who's Who of executives from food industry giants, including Robert L. Callahan of Coca-Cola; Daniel Gerber of Gerber Products Co., and Harold Mohler of Hersey Foods Corp.

63. *White House Conference on Food, Nutrition, and Health*, 280.

64. *White House Conference on Food, Nutrition, and Health*, 51.

65. Hutt would ease up on the repeal of the "jelly bean rule" when he took on the office of FDA general counsel.

66. *White House Conference on Food, Nutrition, and Health*, 312–13.

67. Fredrick J. Stare, *Adventures in Nutrition: An Autobiography* (Hanover, MA: Christopher, 1991), 127.

68. Jack Rosenthal, "4 Panels Bid Nixon Declare a Hunger Emergency," *New York Times*, November 30, 1969, 74.

69. Sandra Blakeslee, "Food Parley Exposes a 'Trust Gap,'" *New York Times*, December 7, 1969, 85.

70. See, for example, DeVault and Pitts, "Surplus and Scarcity," 554.

71. Jack Rosenthal, "Nixon and Hunger," *New York Times*, December 2, 1969, 49.

72. Poppendieck, *Free for All*, 63.

73. Jack Rosenthal, "Nixon and Hunger," *New York Times*, December 2, 1969, 49.

74. The ISEO compiled a booklet containing all the quotes from different panels indicating the need for changes in food labeling. "1969 White House Conference Report Labeling Recommendations—Prepared by ISEO (March, 1970)," Binder "8. FoodLabelingAdvertising1_1957–1970," PB Hutt Archives.

75. *White House Conference on Food, Nutrition, and Health*, Section 3, Panel 3, "Food Safety," 139; P. M. Boffey, "Nader's Raiders on the FDA: Science and Scientists' Misused,'" *Science* 168, no. 3929 (1970): 349.

76. U.S. FDA, "History of the GRAS List and SCOGS Reviews," https://www.fda.gov /food/gras-substances-scogs-database/history-gras-list-and-scogs-reviews, last visited April 20, 2023.

77. David Hoffman, "Diet Drink Sweetener Controversy Is Reheated," *NY Herald Tribune*, October 3, 1965, 12.

78. "Say Artificial Sweeteners in Large Dose Harm Rats," *Supermarket News*, October 11, 1965, 23: Harold M. Schmeck, "FDA Is Studying Artificial Sugars," *New York Times*, January 31, 1967, C-52.

79. "Cyclamates Safe as Used Now: FDA," *Supermarket News*, May 24, 1965, 18. For a detailed timeline of regulatory events on cyclamate from 1958 to 1974, see "Cyclamates: A Chronology of Confusion," in Vernal S. Packard Jr., *Processed Foods and the Consumer: Additives, Labeling, Standards, and Nutrition* (Minneapolis: University of Minnesota Press, 1976), 332–37.

80. "FDA Geneticist Raise New Doubt on Cyclamate," *Medical World News*, November 15, 1966, 25–27; "Pressure Grows on FDA to Do Something about Cyclamates," *Food Chemical News*, November 25, 1968, 4–5.

81. "Statement by Herbert L. Ley, Commissioner of Food and Drugs" and "Dr. Ley's Press Conference on Cyclamates," April 3, 1969, Binder "22. Cyclamates1_1964–1972," PB Hutt Archives.

82. "Misuse of Artificial Sweeteners Statement Led to New Dietary Regs," *Food Chemical News*, September 15, 1969, 23–25.

83. "Bitterness about Sweets," *Time*, October 17, 1969; Morton Mintz, "Bittersweet Saga: The Rise and Fall of Cyclamates," *Washington Post*, October 26, 1969, 1.

84. Mintz, "Bittersweet Saga." This was a period of growing public interest in cancer and the role of environmental factors. In 1971 Nixon declared a "War on Cancer." Robert N. Proctor, *Cancer Wars: How Politics Shapes What We Know and Don't Know about Cancer* (New York: Basic Books, 1995).

85. Elizabeth Whelan, "The Bitter Truth about a Sweetener Scare," "The Cyclamate Bandwagon," *Nature*, 224, no. 5217 (1969): 298–99.

86. Joshua Lederberg, "Food Additives and Contaminants Committee," *Nature* 224 (November 15, 1969): 734.

87. FDA, "Herbert Ley," https://www.fda.gov/about-fda/fda-leadership-1907-today/herbert-ley, last visited May 12, 2022.

88. Ley's subsequent criticism of the FDA resulted in his being added to Nixon's infamous master list of political opponents.

89. "'Special Dietary Foods' Coverage Pared Down," *Food Chemical News*, January 19, 1973, 19–24.

90. The hearings commenced June 20, 1968, and concluded on May 14, 1970. The transcript of the hearings comprised over 32,000 pages of testimony plus the thousands of additional pages of documentary exhibits.

91. David E. Nye, *Consuming Power: A Social History of American Energies* (Cambridge, MA: MIT Press, 1999), 226; Meg Jacobs, *Panic at the Pump: The Energy Crisis and the Transformation of American Politics in the 1970s* (New York: Hill and Wang, 2016).

92. Warren Belasco, *Appetite for Change* (Ithaca, NY: Cornell University Press, 1993).

93. Francis Sandbach, "The Rise and Fall of the Limits to Growth Debate," *Social Studies of Science* 8, no. 4 (November 1978): 509; Walter Sullivan, "The World Is Running Out Of Raw Materials," *New York Times*, June 22, 1969; "To Grow or Not to Grow," *Newsweek*, March 13, 1972, 102–3.

94. Tom Wicker, "The Nation: Population, Hunger and Oblivion," *New York Times*, May 4, 1969, E15. On how these claims linked to political debates about the "green revolution," see Nick Cullather, *The Hungry World: America's Cold War Battle against Poverty in Asia* (Cambridge, MA: Harvard University Press, 2010), 239–52.

95. Belasco characterizes it as a recurrent cultural battle of "faith" versus "doubt," which takes the dialectical form of technological utopians, or "cornucopians," pitted against dystopian Malthusiasts. Warren Belasco, *Meals to Come: A History of the Future of Food* (Berkeley: University of California Press, 2006).

96. Anthony Lewis, "Affluence and Survival II," *New York Times*, April 22, 1974.

97. The article described Quaker Oats' limited success in Colombia with Incaparina, due to the fact that it resembled a local gruel (colada). Jean Hewitt, "Progress—and Obstacles—Erasing Malnutrition in U.S.," *New York Times*, November 11, 1969, 50.

98. Kenneth Carpenter, *Protein and Energy: A Study of Changing Ideas in Nutrition* (New York: Cambridge University Press, 1994), 161–79. For a critique of development policymakers' focus on protein as a "charismatic nutrient," see Aya Hirata Kimura, *Hidden Hunger: Gender and the Politics of Smarter Foods* (Ithaca, NY: Cornell University Press, 2013), 23–27.

99. Hewitt, "Progress—and Obstacles," 50.

100. "June 26, 1969 Letter from Charles A. Krause (Krause Milling Co.) regarding CSM" and reply from JM, in Box 6, "White House Conference 1969," J Mayer Papers.

101. Kimura, *Hidden Hunger*.

102. *Food Chemical News*, July 14, 1969, 2.

103. Jean Mayer, "Toward a National Nutrition Policy," *Science* 176, no. 4032 (April 21, 1972): 237–41.

104. Mayer, "Toward a National Nutrition Policy," 176.

105. Patricia Allen, "The Disappearance of Hunger in America," in *Culture: A Reader*, ed. Caroline Counihan et al., 4th ed (New York, Routledge, 2019), 441–42. In 2022 the Biden administration held another White House Conference on Hunger, Nutrition and Health. Organizers of the 2022 conference directly evoked the legacy of the 1969 conference and emphasized the continued problem of hunger in America. The 2022 White House report, however, barely mentioned poverty as a root cause of malnutrition, and among its calls to action were integrating nutrition and health through "food is a medicine" initiatives, and empowering consumers through "front-of-package labeling scheme for food packages." The White House, *Biden-Harris Administration National Strategy on Hunger, Nutrition, and Health*, September 2022, 17, 22.

106. J.M. Fitchen, "Hunger, Malnutrition, and Poverty in the Contemporary United States: Some Observations on Their Social and Cultural Context," *Food and Foodways* 2, no. 1 (1987): 309–33. On the use of dry nomenclature and statistics as a "cover-up" of hunger in America, see Joel Berg, *All You Can Eat: How Hungry Is America?* (New York: Seven Stories Press, 2008), 25–44, 217–34.

107. Charles W. Mills, "White Ignorance," in Proctor and Schiebinger, *Agnotology*.

108. Anne Murcott, "Scarcity in Abundance: Food and Non-Food," *Social Research* 66, no. 1 (Spring 1999): 305–39.

4. THE MARKET TURN

1. Historians have come to see 1973 as a key turning point in American history. Kim Phillips-Fein, "1973 to the Present," in *American History Now*, ed. Eric Foner and Lisa McGirr (Philadelphia: Temple University Press, 2011).

2. Peter Barton Hutt, interview with author, Cambridge, MA, January 16, 2008.

3. Frohlich, "Informational Turn in Food Politics."

4. Bruce Schulman, *The Seventies: The Great Shift in American Culture, Society, and Politics* (Cambridge, MA: Da Capo Press, 2002), 25–26.

5. Daniel T. Rodgers, *Age of Fracture* (Cambridge, MA: Belknap Press, 2012), 8. On the 1970s deregulation movements, see also Mark H. Rose et al., *The Best Transportation System in the World: Railroads, Trucks, Airlines, and American Public Policy in the Twentieth Century* (Columbus: Ohio State University Press, 2006); Richard H. K. Vietor, *Contrived Competition: Regulation and Deregulation in America* (Cambridge, MA: Harvard University Press, 1994).

6. Brent Cebul, "The Antigovernment Impulse: The Presidency, the 'Market,' and the Splintering of the Common Good," in *The President and American Capitalism since 1945*, ed. Mark H. Rose and Roger Biles, 99–122 (Gainesville: University Press of Florida, 2017).

7. Mark H. Rose, *Market Rules: Bankers, Presidents, and the Origins of the Great Recession* (Philadelphia: University of Pennsylvania Press, 2018), 1.

8. For example, the 1967 Freedom of Information Act (FOIA) and the 1976 Government in Sunshine Act. Michael Schudson, *The Rise of the Right to Know: Politics and the Culture of Transparency* (Cambridge, MA: Belknap Press, 2015); David E. Pozen and Michael Schudson, *Troubling Transparency: The History and Future of Freedom of Information* (New York: Columbia University Press, 2018).

9. Schudson, *Rise of the Right to Know*, 21–22.

10. Herrmann, "Consumerism," 55–60.

11. Other books criticizing America's chemical food system and poor FDA oversight include Jacqueline Verrett and Jean Carper, *Eating May Be Hazardous to Your Health: How Your Government Fails to Protect You from the Dangers in Your Food* (New York: Simon and Schuster, 1974); Ruth Winter, *Beware of the Food You Eat* (New York: Crown, 1971).

12. Vinsel, *Moving Violations*, 168–69, 247–48.

13. "Nader's 24 Questions Outline Attack against Food Industry," *Food Chemical News* 11, no. 18 (July 28, 1969): 9–11.

14. P. M. Boffey, "Nader's Raiders on the FDA: Science and Scientists' Misused," *Science* 168, no. 3929 (1970): 349–52.

15. In a 1970 law review, Ralph Nader discussed the "Freedom of Information Act" and his efforts to use it on the FDA. Ralph Nader, "Freedom from Information: The Act and the Agencies," *Harvard Civil Rights–Civil Liberties Law Review* 5 (1970): 1.

16. J. S. Turner, *The Chemical Feast: The Ralph Nader Study Group Report on Food Protection and the Food and Drug Administration* (New York: Grossman, 1970), 49–51, 249.

17. Turner, *Chemical Feast*, 32–33.

18. Turner, *Chemical Feast*, 210–11.

19. Apple, *Vitamania*, 137–38.

20. M. F. Jacobson, *Eater's Digest: The Consumer's Fact-Book of Food Additives* (New York: Doubleday, 1972).

21. CSPI, "The Man behind 'Nutrition Facts' Is Leaving CSPI's Top Job," *Food Safety News*, November 3, 2016, https://www.foodsafetynews.com/2016/11/the-man-behind-the -nutrition-facts-is-leaving-cspis-top-job/, last visited April 19, 2023.

22. Schudson, *Rise of the Right to Know*, 96.

23. On the political significance of the flow architecture of the supermarket, see Deutsch, *Building a Housewife's Paradise*. On the political uses of the supermarket during the Cold War, see Ruth Oldenziel and Karin Zachmann, *Cold War Kitchen: Americanization, Technology, and European Users* (Cambridge, MA: MIT Press, 2009); Hamilton, *Supermar-*

ket USA. On the supermarket metaphor in 1970s market talk, and especially in banking policy, see Rose, *Market Rules*, 39–66.

24. A 1979 textbook on food merchandising listed unit pricing, open dating, food labeling (specifically FDA nutrition labeling), and franchising in convenience stores as important consumer protection developments in regulation affecting food merchandising. Theodore W. Leed and Gene A. German, *Food Merchandising: Principles and Practices* (New York: Lebhar-Friedman Books, 1979), 440–50.

25. Frank Trentmann, ed., *The Making of the Consumer* (Oxford: Berg, 2005). See also "information seekers" in Wimberley and McClean, "Supermarket Savvy."

26. George J. Stigler, "The Economics of Information," *Journal of Political Economy* 69, no. 3 (1961): 213–25; George A. Akerlof, "The Market for 'Lemons': Quality Uncertainty and the Market Mechanism," *Quarterly Journal of Economics* 84, no. 3 (1970): 488–500.

27. Phillip Nelson, "Information and Consumer Behavior," *Journal of Political Economy* 78, no. 2 (1970): 311–29.

28. Phillip Nelson, "Advertising as Information," *Journal of Political Economy* 82, no. 4 (1974): 729–54.

29. Michael Schudson, *Advertising, The Uneasy Persuasion: Its Dubious Impact on American Society* (New York: Basic Books, 1986), 106–8.

30. See discussion of the Robinson-Patman Act of 1936 in Deutsch, *Building a Housewife's Paradise*, 136–38; Mayo, *American Grocery Store*, 107–14. Historian Ann Vileisis argues supermarkets sought a "covenant of ignorance" with their shoppers, discouraging them from scrutinizing their options too closely. Vileisis, *Kitchen Literacy*, 171.

31. Twarog, *Politics of the Pantry*, 92–94.

32. Office of Technology Assessment, *Open Shelf-Life Dating of Food* (Washington, DC: Congress of the United States, 1979), 1.

33. Kent B. Monroe and Peter J. LaPlaca, "What Are the Benefits of Unit Pricing?," *Journal of Marketing* 36 (July 1972): 16–22. See also Schudson, *Rise of the Right to Know*, 83–85.

34. One of the UPC inventors argued that its adoption by the grocery industry in 1973 was one of three "great events" that gave birth to the automated data collection industry. Benjamin Nelson, *Punch Cards to Bar Codes: A 200-Year Journey* (Peterborough, NH: Helmer's, 1997), 7, 55–85. Since 1973 the use of UPC bar codes has facilitated a new level of data-mining for improving stock turnover with significant consequences for market research. Hartmut Berghoff, Philip Scranton, and Uwe Spiekermann, "The Origins of Marketing and Market Research: Information, Institutions, and Markets," in *The Rise of Marketing and Market Research*, ed. Berghoff, Scranton, and Spiekermann (New York: Palgrave Macmillan, 2012), 5; Hans Kjellberg, Johan Hagberg, and Franck Cochoy, "Thinking Market Infrastructure: Barcode Scanning in the US Grocery Retail Sector, 1967–2010," in *Thinking Infrastructures*, ed. Martin Kornberger et al., 207–32 (Bingley, UK: Emerald, 2019).

35. Ben H. Wells, "The Consumer Research Institute's Nutrient Labeling Research," *Food Drug Cosmetic Law Journal* (January 1972): 40–44; J. Mayer, "Nutrition Labeling," in Mayer, *US Nutrition Policies in the Seventies* (San Francisco: W. H. Freeman, 1973), 150–56.

36. D. L. Call and M. G. Hayes. "Reactions of Nutritionists to Nutrient Labeling of Foods," *American Journal of Clinical Nutrition* 23, no. 10 (1970): 1347.

37. Margaret L. Ross, "What's Happening to Food Labeling?," *Journal of the American Dietetic Association* 64 (March 1974): 262–67.

38. Esther Peterson and Winifred Conkling, *Restless: The Memoirs of Labor and Consumer Activist Esther Peterson* (Caring, 1997). See also Twarog, *Politics of the Pantry,* 63–71, 77–79; Schudson, *Rise of the Right to Know,* 77–92.

39. Esther Peterson, "Consumerism as a Retailer's Asset," *Harvard Business Review* 52, no. 3 (1974): 91–101.

40. Schudson, *Rise of the Right to Know,* 85.

41. E Peterson Papers, 1884–1998, MC 450, Folder #1515: "Statement by Joseph B. Danzansky, President, Giant Food Inc., on Nutrition Labeling," Giant Food Inc. News Release (September 6, 1971).

42. E Peterson Papers, MC 450, Folder #1515: Giant newsletter, "Giant Food Is Testing Nutritional Labeling"; MC 450, Folder #1530f+: Giant pamphlet, "You Asked for More Nutrition Information."

43. Jean Mayer, "Labeling," in Mayer, *US Nutrition Policies in the Seventies,* 151–52.

44. Schudson, *Rise of the Right to Know,* 94.

45. Letter from Virgil O. Wodicka to Peter Hutt, July 28, 1987, Binder "FoodNutrition-Labeling3_7_86–6_88," PB Hutt Archives.

46. Letter from Ogden C. Johnson to Peter Hutt, August 21, 1987, Binder "FoodNutritionLabeling3_7_86–6_88," PB Hutt Archives.

47. Letter from Wodicka to Hutt; letter from Johnson to Hutt; letter from Sherwin Gardner to Thomas Scarlett, May 3, 1988, FDA, Binder "FoodNutritionLabeling3_7_86–6_88," PB Hutt Archives.

48. The proposed policy rule changes were: (1) the "information panel" concept, (2) the "nutrition information" disclosure concept, (3) "setting a standard of identity for vitamin-mineral supplements," (4) a "label declaration of ingredients in standardized foods" (i.e., universal ingredients labeling), (5) "food flavor labeling," (6) designated difference between natural and artificial flavoring, (7) a policy change on fortified foods, (8) "special dietary food regulations," (9) "Incidental Food Additives" (exemptions for disclosing trace elements), (10) "Imitation Food Labeling," (11) a "Standard of Identity for Mellorine and Parevine," and (12) a uniform effective date for the labeling changes.

49. "Background Conference: Nutrition Labeling," FDA, February 1973, p. 23, Binder "FoodNutritionLabeling1_1970–1983," PB Hutt Archives.

50. "Background Conference: Nutrition Labeling," 25.

51. "Background Conference: Nutrition Labeling," 22.

52. Scrinis, "On the Ideology of Nutritionism," 43.

53. Merrill and Collier, "Like Mother Used to Make," 611–13.

54. "Background Conference: Nutrition Labeling," 19.

55. For example, the Corn Refiners Association wanting to use "corn sugar," and then "corn syrup," instead of "glucose." Cohen, *Pure Adulteration,* 169.

56. "Economic Impact of Fat Source Labeling Stressed by Institute," *Food Chemical News,* September 15, 1975, 9–10.

57. The marketing concern was over the use of coconut oils, now seen to be unhealthy, versus other vegetable oils. "P&G Notes Consumer Survey on Fat Source Labeling," *Food Chemical News,* November 29, 1971, 10–12.

58. Schudson, *Rise of the Right to Know,* 21–22.

59. Self, *All in the Family,* 422–23; Elizabeth Popp Berman, "From Economic to Social Regulation: How the Deregulatory Moment Strengthened Economists' Policy Position," *History of Political Economy* 49 (2017): 187–212.

60. In practice, after this rule change, the FDA rarely used the imitation label on substandard products. It did sometimes require substandard products to use "alternative" or "substitute," which functioned like the "imitation" label but without the negative stigma. Donna Viola Porter, and Robert O. Earl, *Food Labeling: Toward National Uniformity* (Washington, DC: National Academies Press, 1992), 109–10.

61. "FDA Negotiates with GMA Institute for Consumer Survey," *Food Chemical News,* December 14, 1970, 12.

62. W Darby Papers, letter from Ogden Johnson to William Darby, December 2, 1970, Series 1, Box 12.

63. "Interim Report of the First Two Phases of the CRI/FDA Nutritional Labeling Research Program," CRI Working Paper, August 1972, PB Hutt Archives.

64. Porter, *Trust in Numbers*; Jasanoff, *The Fifth Branch.*

65. While the FDA's emphasis was on precision and quantification and avoiding distinctions between natural and processed, the agency saw fit to build some leeway into its rules. Companies would be afforded an error range of 20 percent to account for natural variability. Ira I. Somers, "Quality Control Problems in Nutrition Labeling," *FDC Law Journal* (May 1972): 293, 296–97.

66. US Government Accountability Office, *Food Labeling: Goals, Shortcomings, and Proposed Changes* (Washington, DC: GAO, 1975).

67. The first FDA-approved Patient Package Insert (PPI) was for the asthma inhaler isoproterenol in 1968. The FDA's rules on PPIs for oral contraceptives led to much more substantial, sustained public debate from 1970 to 1975. In 1974 FDA commissioner Alexander M. Schmidt formed the Patient Prescription Drug Labeling Project to explore a wider use of PPIs as a tool to ensure a "patient's right to know." Final rules for an FDA oversight program for broader use of PPIs was set to go into effect in 1982, but was revoked by the Reagan administration because the mandatory program was considered too costly. Elizabeth Siegel Watkins, "Deciphering the Prescription: Pharmacists and the Patient Package Insert," in *Prescribed: Writing, Filling, Using, and Abusing the Prescription in Modern America,* ed. Jeremy A. Greene and Elizabeth Siegel Watkins, 92–116 (Baltimore: Johns Hopkins University Press, 2012).

68. Cornelius B. Kennedy, "The New Vogue in Rulemaking at FDA: A Foreword," *Food, Drug, Cosmetic Law Journal* 28, no. 3 (March 1973): 172–76; Peter Barton Hutt, "Philosophy of Regulation under the Food, Drug, and Cosmetic Act," *Food, Drug, Cosmetic Law Journal* 28, no. 3 (March 1973): 177–88; H. Thomas Austern, "Philosophy of Regulation: A Reply to Mr. Hutt," *Food, Drug, Cosmetic Law Journal* 28, no. 3 (March 1973): 189–200.

69. Kennedy, "New Vogue in Rulemaking," 174–75.

70. Hutt, "Philosophy of Regulation," 181–82.

71. Mirowski and Nik-Khah argue that the start of the field of "information economics" can be traced back to post-WWII debates about socialism and Friedrich Hayek's 1945 essay "The Use of Knowledge in Society." Hayek argued that nobody could "possess all the relevant information" demanded by classical economics, and therefore markets left alone were

"superior information processors." Philip Mirowski and Edward Nik-Khah, *The Knowledge We Have Lost in Information: The History of Information in Modern Economics* (New York: Oxford University Press, 2017), 60–65; Rodgers, *Age of Fracture*, 45–87.

72. Rodgers, *Age of Fracture*, 82–87. The idea of the "therapeutic state" comes from Christopher Lasch, *The Culture of Narcissism: American Life in an Age of Diminishing Expectations* (New York, W. W. Norton, 1979).

73. Wayne L. Pines, "The Start of *FDA Consumer*," in *FDA: A Century of Consumer Protection*, ed. Wayne L. Pines (Washington, DC: Food and Drug Law Institute, 2006), 106.

74. "FDA Launches Nutrition Labeling Education Program," *FDA Consumer* (July–August 1974): 20. The FDA has posted the historical ad online. US FDA, "Historical PSAs—Read the Label with Dick Van Dyke," FDA YouTube Channel, https://www.youtube.com/watch?v=fo2T2mPIchc, last visited April 19, 2023.

75. *FDA Consumer* 15, no. 5 (1981), special issue commemorating the seventy-fifth anniversary of the 1906 act.

76. O. C. Johnson, "The Food and Drug Administration and Labeling," *Journal of the American Dietetic Association* 64 (1974): 17–18.

77. Scrinis, *Nutritionism*.

78. Johnson, "Food and Drug Administration and Labeling," 16.

79. "The State of Nutrition Today," *FDA Consumer* (November 1973): 13–17. On the politics and history of USDA dietary guidelines, see Biltekoff, *Eating Right in America*; Nestle, *Food Politics*.

80. H. Neal Dunning, "What Do Consumers Know about Nutrition?," in *FDA Consumer Nutrition Knowledge Survey: A Nationwide Study of Food Shopper's Knowledge, Beliefs, Attitudes, and Reported Behavior Regarding Food and Nutrition* (Washington, DC: US Dept. of HEW, Public Health Services, Food and Drug Administration, 1976).

81. Alice Fusillo, "Food Shoppers' Beliefs: Myths and Realities," in *FDA Consumer Nutrition Knowledge Survey*, 71–73.

82. "Final Report: Main Findings," in *FDA Consumer Nutrition Knowledge Survey*, 44, 48, 76.

83. "Exhibit V: Statement of The Federation of Homemakers, Harry G. Shupe, Attorney," September 27, 1978, Binder "5. ImitationFood3_1969–1978," PB Hutt Archives. See Hutt et al., *Food and Drug Law*, 221.

84. The FDA continued to face legal attacks into the 1980s from the dairy industry on proposed nomenclatures for new substitute foods. See Hutt et al., *Food and Drug Law*, 196.

85. According to historian Emily Twarog, housewives "no longer comprised a political interest group. In fact, [for many on the left] 'housewife' had become a dirty word." Twarog, *Politics of the Pantry*, 110–11. Schulman, "Chapter 4. Battle of the Sexes: Women, Men, and the Family," in Schulman, *The Seventies*.

86. Matthew D. Lassiter, "Inventing Family Values," in *Rightward Bound: Making America Conservative in the 1970s*, ed. Bruce J. Schulman and Julian E. Zelizer, 13–28 (Cambridge, MA: Harvard University Press, 2008).

87. For a conservative, traditionalist view of the meal, threatened by snacking, one can read Mary Douglas, "Deciphering a Meal," *Daedalus* 101, no. 1 (1972): 61–81.

88. Stacie Taranto, *Kitchen Table Politics: Conservative Women and Family Values in New York* (Philadelphia: University of Pennsylvania Press, 2017).

89. Vietor, *Contrived Competition*; Shane Hamilton, "The Populist Appeal of Deregulation: Independent Truckers and the Politics of Free Enterprise, 1935–1980," *Enterprise and Society* 10, no. 1 (2009): 137.

90. The result for the EPA, much like for the FDA, was to hide behind ever more complicated models and statistical calculations that disguised the politics of risk decisions. Jasanoff, "Science, Politics, and the Renegotiation," 195.

91. Vogel, *Is It Safe?*, 43–77.

92. Jimmy Carter, "The President's News Conference," March 25, 1979, transcript of speech, UC Santa Barbara, The American Presidency Project, https://www.presidency.ucsb.edu/node/249337, last visited April 19, 2023.

93. U.S. General Accounting Office, *Food Labeling: Goals, Shortcomings, and Proposed Changes, Department of Health, Education, and Welfare, Department of Agriculture, Department of Commerce: Report to the Congress* (Washington, DC: U.S. General Accounting Office, 1975).

94. Bob Earl of GMA, interview with author, September 23, 2009.

95. "Medicine: The High Priestess of Nutrition," *Time*, December 18, 1972; Catherine Carstairs, "'Our Sickness Record Is a National Disgrace': Adelle Davis, Nutritional Determinism, and the Anxious 1970s," *Journal of the History of Medicine and Allied Sciences* 69, no. 3 (2014): 461–91.

96. Peter Hutt, quoted in "Background Conference: Nutrition Labeling," FDA, February 1973, p. 26, Binder "FoodNutritionLabeling1_1970–1983," PB Hutt Archives.

97. Proxmire was famous for issuing "Golden Fleece Awards" between 1975 and 1988, where he singled out examples of what he considered to be wasteful government spending in scientific research. Apple, *Vitamania*, 164–74.

98. The Proxmire Amendments were attached to a larger bill, the Health Research and Health Services Amendments of 1976 (Public Law 94–278). See Hutt et al., *Food and Drug Law*, 255–56.

99. Carolyn de la Peña, "Risky Food, Risky Lives: The 1977 Saccharin Rebellion," *Gastronomica* 7, no. 3 (2007): 100–105; Carolyn de la Peña, "Artificial Sweetener as a Historical Window to Culturally Situated Health," *Annals of the New York Academy of Sciences* 1190, no. 21 (2010): 159–65.

100. Congress continued to reenact the legislation every two years up until 1985, when the FDA formally stated its intention to no longer pursue the ban. Marian Burros, "U.S. Food Regulation: Tales from a Twilight Zone," *New York Times*, June 10, 1987.

101. Troetel, "Three-Part Disharmony."

102. According to Glickman, the attacks on the Consumer Protection Act (CPA) in 1969 were a key turning point in the corporate lobbying against the term "liberal." Glickman, *Buying Power*, 285, 291–93.

103. De la Peña, *Empty Pleasures*, 170–74; Bartow J. Elmore, *Citizen Coke: The Making of Coca-Cola Capitalism* (New York: W.W. Norton, 2014), 276–77; Caroline W. Lee, "The Roots of Astroturfing," *Contexts* 9, no. 1 (2010): 73–75.

104. Glickman quoting anti-CPA opponent Arthur Fatt. Glickman, *Buying Power*, 291.

105. On the "sociology of attachment," see Emilie Gomart and Antoine Hennion, "A Sociology of Attachment: Music Amateurs, Drug Users," *Sociological Review* 47, no. 1 (May 1999): 220–47.

106. Alexander M. Schmidt, "FDA—Social Trend and Regulatory Reform," *Food, Drug, Cosmetic Law Journal* (November 1976): 605.

107. Robert Crawford, "Healthism and the Medicalization of Everyday Life," *International Journal of Health Services* 10, no. 3 (1980), 365.

108. In his 1979 best-seller *The Culture of Narcissism,* Christopher Lasch famously declared it a time of withdrawal from public life: "After the political turmoil of the sixties, Americans have retreated to purely personal preoccupations." Lasch tellingly labeled it the rise of a self-absorbed "therapeutic" culture. As quoted in Phillips-Fein, "1973 to the Present," 178.

109. Crawford, "Healthism," 369–70.

110. Wallace F. Janssen, "The Story of the Laws behind the Labels," *FDA Consumer,* June 1981.

111. Vietor, *Contrived Competition.*

112. Margaret R. Taylor, Edward S. Rubin, and David A. Hounshell, "Regulation as the Mother of Innovation: The Case of SO2 Control," *Law and Policy* 27, no. 2 (2005): 348–78.

113. A 1979 Beech Nut ad, "What You Can Learn from a Label." The ad was brought to my attention by Nadia Berenstein.

114. Lee Vinsel, "The Crusade for Credible Energy Information and Analysis in the United States, 1973–1982," *History and Technology* 28, no. 2 (2012): 149–76.

115. Robert Crawford argues that the turn to this healthism partly explains the subsequent political divestment in national health insurance. Robert Crawford, "Health as a Meaningful Social Practice," *Health (London)* 10, no. 4 (October 1, 2006): 401–20.

116. Schulman, *The Seventies,* xv–xvi.

117. Michel Foucault, "Governmentality," in *The Foucault Effect: Studies in Governmentality,* ed. Graham Burchell, Colin Gordon, and Peter Miller, 87–104 (Chicago: University of Chicago Press, 1991).

118. Joel Spring, *Educating the Consumer-Citizen: A History of the Marriage of Schools, Advertising, and Media* (New York: Routledge, 2003).

119. Ronald Reagan, "First Inaugural Address," January 20, 1981, Ronald Reagan Presidential Foundation & Institute website, https://www.reaganfoundation.org/media/128614/inaguration.pdf, last visited April 19, 2023.

120. Indeed, among the Democratic casualties of the "Reagan Revolution" was Senator McGovern, who lost his seat to Republican candidate James Abnor.

5. A GOVERNMENT BRAND

1. Fred Turner, *From Counterculture to Cyberculture: Stewart Brand, the Whole Earth Network, and the Rise of Digital Utopianism* (Chicago: University of Chicago Press, 2008); Jonathan H. Blavin and I. Glenn Cohen, "Gore, Gibson, and Goldsmith: The Evolution of Internet Metaphors in Law and Commentary," *Harvard Journal of Law and Technology* 16 (2002): 265–85.

2. See, for example, Jacob Jacoby, "Comments: Perspectives on Information Overload," *Journal of Consumer Research* 10 (March 1984): 432–35.

3. Jean Lyons and Martha Rumore, "Food Labeling—Then and Now," *Journal of Pharmacy and Law* 171, no. 2 (1993): 249.

4. Steven D. Lubar, *Infoculture: The Smithsonian Book of Information Age Inventions* (Boston: Houghton Mifflin, 1993); Mark D. Bowles, "Liquifying Information," in *Cultures of Control*, ed. Miriam R. Levin (Amsterdam: Harwood Academic, 2000).

5. This concept of the distributed self is from sociologist Sherry Turkle's studies of computers and identity in the 1990s. Turkle describes how the graphical user interface of windows encourages users to "cycle through" different cognitive states in a way that was distinct from the conventional models of the self as "playing different roles in different settings." Instead, users were distributed across different windows, suggesting multiple selves for multiple contexts. Sherry Turkle, "Computational Technologies and Images of the Self," *Social Research* 64, no. 3 (Fall 1997): 1101.

6. I take the idea of a "plug and play" food economy from Bruno Latour's actor-network theory of social interactions at the supermarket. Bruno Latour, *Reassembling the Social: An Introduction to Actor-Network-Theory* (New York: Oxford University Press, 2005), 210.

7. Herbert Burkholz, *The FDA Follies: An Alarming Look at Our Food and Drug Policies* (New York: Basic Books, 1994), 94.

8. Lucas Richert, *Conservatism, Consumer Choice, and the Food and Drug Administration during the Reagan Era: A Prescription for Scandal* (Lanham, MD: Lexington Books, 2014), 81, 96–97.

9. Dale Blumenthal, "A New Look at Food Labeling," *FDA Consumer* 23, no. 9 (November 1989): 15.

10. *Prevention* (1984–85), iii–iv, USDA NAL, Box 11, "Health United States, Annual Reports, 1984, Dietary Guideline Poster, 1989." *Prevention* was a public outreach series published by the U. S. Department of Health and Human Services, from 1981 into the 1990s, not to be confused with Rodale's much more popular alternative health magazine of the same name.

11. Peter Greenwald, FDA oral history by Xaq Frohlich and FDA Historian Suzanne Junod, Rockville, Maryland, August 26, 2009. In the interview, Greenwald characterized the atmosphere around diet advice and institutions like the NIH, FDA, and FNB as a clash between an older school of nutrition scientists, "traditionalists . . . some from the University of Wisconsin, the dairy state," and "activists," "the younger group [who] really was saying cut down the fat." Greenwald had approached the FDA about changing their standards and labeling system to fit better with a public health message, but Sanford Miller and Commissioner Frank Young told him no, apparently without explaining the FDA's institutional interest in maintaining its food-drug line. When asked whether in hindsight he regretted encouraging Kellogg to run the fiber-cancer health message, Greenwald said no, since he believed it was still the best way to expand the public health message to a broader audience. "Oral History Interview with Peter Greenwald, Director of the Division of Cancer Prevention, National Cancer Institute (NCI) 1981 – 2011," FDA website, https://www.fda.gov/media/133560/download, last visited April 18, 2023. See also Elliot Marshall, "Diet Advice, with a Grain of Salt and a Large Helping of Pepper," *Science* 231 (February 7, 1986): 537–39.

12. Stephen Hilgartner and Dorothy Nelkin, "Communication Controversies over Dietary Risks," *Science, Technology and Human Values* 12, no. 3 (1987): 45; Nestle, *Food Politics*, 239–45.

13. Roseann B. Termini, "Product Classification under the Federal Food Drug and Cosmetic Act: When a Food Becomes a Drug," *Journal of Pharmacy and Law* 2 (1993): 1.

14. Psyllium was also not a conventional fiber in American foods. It came from a plant in India and had become popular in dietetic products and the food industry because its effects for relieving constipation and diarrhea were stronger than most naturally occurring fibers in Western grains. When the NIH opened the National Center for Complementary and Integrative Health in 1998, it signaled the growing interest in nonconventional therapeutics, including non-Western medicines. These therapeutics have generally entered the U. S. market as dietary "supplements" to avoid the stricter premarket approval process for drugs. Marlys J. Mason, "Drugs or Dietary Supplements: FDA's Enforcement of DSHEA," *Journal of Public Policy and Marketing* 17, no. 2 (September 1, 1998): 296–302.

15. Paul R. Thomas, *Improving America's Diet and Health: From Recommendations to Action* (Washington, DC: Institute of Medicine, 1991), 156–58.

16. The 1988 NAS report *Designing Foods* catalogued ways in which the meat and dairy industry had already begun to breed for lean meats and low-fat dairy products. National Research Council (U. S.), Board of Agriculture, *Designing Foods: Animal Product Options in the Marketplace* (Washington, DC: National Academies Press, 1988).

17. Alex M. Freedman, "Heart Association to Put Seal of Approval on Foods—but Will Consumers Benefit?," *Wall Street Journal*, December 13, 1988, B1; Mark Bloom, "Controversy Continues over Food Labeling," *Washington Post*, January 17, 1989, C1. Commissioner Frank Young condemned the AHA HeartGuide Program as a highly problematic "for-profit regulatory approach." "FDA's Young Says Heartguide Program Is Regulation for Profit," *Food Chemical News*, November 13, 1989, 15–16.

18. Carole Sugarman, "What Price Approval?," *Washington Post*, August 30, 1989, E1, E4; "Heartguide Program 'Looks Like an Extortion Racket,' AFI Charges," *Food Chemical News*, August 28, 1989, 11–12. Marion Nestle describes the AHA "heart-healthy" label as one of many examples of how industry was "co-opting nutrition professionals" in the 1980s and 1990s. Another example included the American Dietetic Association's collaboration with McDonald's to develop the "Food FUNdamentals" toys for McDonald's happy meals. Nestle, *Food Politics*, 111–36.

19. Marsha F. Goldsmith, " 'HeartGuide' Food-Rating Program Attracts 114 Applications as Controversy Continues," *JAMA* 262, no. 24 (December 22 / 29, 1989), 3388, 3391; Janet Meyers, "HeartGuide Legacy: FDA May Shoot Down Other Seal Programs," *Advertising Age*, May 2, 1990, 60.

20. U. S. Department of Health and Human Services, Public Health Service DHHS (PHS), *The Surgeon General's Report on Nutrition and Health,* Publication No. 8840210 (1988), 17.

21. *Surgeon General's Report on Nutrition and Health,* 18.

22. Other reports include NAS Board of Agriculture, *Designing Foods: Animal Product Options in the Marketplace* (Washington, DC: National Academies Press, 1988); NAS Food and Nutrition Board, *Diet and Health: Implications for Reducing Chronic Disease Risk* (Washington, DC: National Academies Press, 1989); World Health Organization, *Healthy Nutrition: Preventing Nutrition-Related Diseases in Europe* (Copenhagen: WHO Regional Publication, 1988). See also Nestle, *Food Politics,* 49.

23. Naomi Wolf, *The Beauty Myth: How Images of Female Beauty Are Used against Women* (New York: W. Morrow, 2002).

24. Andrew N. Case, *The Organic Profit: Rodale and the Making of Marketplace Environmentalism* (Seattle: University of Washington Press, 2018).

25. Dale Blumenthal, "A New Look at Food Labeling," *FDA Consumer* (November 1989): 15–17.

26. As quoted in Lyons and Rumore, "Food Labeling—Then and Now," 249. See also Nestle, *Food Politics,* 249.

27. Carpenter, *Reputation and Power,* 390.

28. Perhaps the most striking evidence for this subsequent shared ownership of the Nutrition Facts panel is how all of the people I interviewed about the design and implementation of the label repeatedly framed their recollections of decisions with the subject "we," "we decided to do *x*" or "we ended up with *y* label feature." This was true not only for the FDA CFSAN staff members but also for the USDA collaborator, industry representatives, design firm president, and CSPI advocate with whom I spoke.

29. Congress.gov, "H. R. 3562—Nutrition Labeling and Education Act of 1990" entry, https://www.congress.gov/bill/101st-congress/house-bill/3562/text, last visited April 20, 2023.

30. Exceptions included foods sold in restaurants, infant formula (whose content labeling was covered under the 1980 Infant Formula Act), and packages that were too small to carry the nutrition label.

31. Congress.gov, "H. R. 3562—Nutrition Labeling and Education Act of 1990" entry, S.AMDT 3125 and S.AMDT 3562, https://www.congress.gov/bill/101st-congress/house -bill/3562/amendments, last visited April 20, 2023.

32. Geoffrey Rose, "Sick Individuals and Sick Populations," *International Journal of Epidemiology* 14 (1985): 32–38.

33. Institute of Medicine (U. S.) Committee on Examination of Front-of-Package Nutrition Rating Systems and Symbols; E. A. Wartella, A. H. Lichtenstein, and C. S. Boon, eds., *Front-of-Package Nutrition Rating Systems and Symbols: Phase I Report* (Washington, DC: National Academies Press, 2010), "Chapter 2. History of Nutrition Labeling."

34. In what would prove to be an embarrassing move, CSPI promoted products that used *trans* fats instead of saturated fats as a healthier alternative. David Schleifer, "Reforming Food: How Trans Fats Entered and Exited the American Food System" (PhD diss., New York University, 2010), 70–71.

35. CSPI also practiced a more conventional form of political advocacy. While Congress was drafting the NLEA in 1989 and 1990, Bruce Silverglade at CSPI kept tabs on individual representatives and senators and how they were likely to vote, and made sure to meet with swing voters to move the congressional vote on specific issues toward adopting CSPI positions on the nutrition label format and implementation.

36. "CSPI Survey & Summary," FDA Dockets: 90N-0135, vol. 1, BKG 5.

37. See, for example, FDA Dockets: 90N-0135, vol. 9, C115, C160, C187.

38. CSPI Archives, "Food and Nutrition Labeling Group; April 18, 1990 Letter to the Honorable Louis W. Sullivan," Box "Food Labeling NLEA": Robert Earl, phone interview with author, September 23, 2009.

39. William Robbins, "One Man with a Purpose Takes on Heart Disease," *New York Times,* July 22, 1990, 16.

40. FDA Dockets: 90N-0135, vol. 73, C2823 (Kelloggs); vol. 24, C861; vol. 87, C2952 (General Mills).

41. FDA Dockets: 90N-0135, vol. 23, C849.

42. Coca-Cola's classification of core versus fringe food resembles anthropologist Mary Douglas's famous discussion of a proper meal. Douglas, "Deciphering a Meal."

43. Leading to humorous subtleties in jurisdiction. Pizza, for example, is regulated by the FDA, unless it has pepperoni on it, in which case it falls under the USDA FSIS's authority.

44. Schaffer, "Is the Fox Guarding the Henhouse?," 371.

45. Previously the manufacturer set serving sizes. Since the late 1970s, however, the USDA and FDA had received consumer requests for greater clarity in setting serving sizes. In 1979 the two agencies joined the Federal Trade Commission in concluding that standardizing serving sizes were needed, but they didn't take action. FDA, HHS, "Food Labeling; Serving Sizes," 55 *Federal Register* 29517 (July 19, 1990), FDA Dockets: No. 90N-0165.

46. FDA, HHS, "Food Labeling; Serving Sizes."

47. Food Safety and Inspection Service, USDA, "Nutrition Labeling of Meat and Poultry Products," 56 *Federal Register* 60302 (November 27, 1991), FDA Dockets: 91–006P.

48. "American Medical Association Feb. 25, 1992 Letter," FDA Dockets: 90N-0135, vol. 100, C3860, p. 8.

49. For a description of the design and testing of the USDA Food Guide Pyramid, see Mudry, *Measured Meals,* 91–92. For an insider's history of the Food Pyramid, see Nestle, *Food Politics,* 51–66.

50. USDA Center for Nutrition Policy and Promotion, "Insight 22: Serving Sizes on the Food Guide Pyramid and on the Nutrition Facts Label: What's Different and Why?," *Nutrition Insights* (December 2000).

51. Mike Taylor mentioned how this press not only played in their favor but also inspired groups like Phil Sokolof's Heart Savers to put out ads challenging President Bush to do the right thing. Michael Taylor, FDA Oral History of Michael R. Taylor, Parklawn Building, Rockville, MD, December 23, 1992, p. 27.

52. At the meeting were President George H. W. Bush, Vice President Dan Quayle, Mike Taylor, David Kessler, Secretary Louis Sullivan, Jim Baker, Secretary Edward Madigan, Marling Fitzwater, and Bob Zoellick (Deputy Chief of Staff). Among the props the FDA staff brought with them to make their case was the McDonald's tray liner discussing nutrition and using the 2,000 calorie figure.

53. "February 20, 1992 Letter from William D. Evers, Extension Nutrition Specialist," FDA Dockets: 91N-0162, vol. 1, C52; underlined emphasis in original.

54. On the importance of design in science, see Chris Salter, Regula Valérie Burri, and Joseph Dumit, "Art, Design, and Performance," in *Handbook of Science and Technology Studies,* 4th ed., ed. Ulrike Felt, Rayvon Fouché, Clark A. Miller, Laurel Smith-Doerr (Cambridge, MA: MIT Press, 2017); Bruno Latour, "Drawing Things Together," in *The Map Reader: Theories of Mapping Practice and Cartographic Representation,* ed. Martin Dodge, Rob Kitchin, and C. R. Perkins, 65–72 (Chichester, West Sussex: Wiley, 2011).

55. Unless otherwise specified, much of this section comes from the author's phone interview with Burkey Belser, October 14, 2009.

56. Belser noted that "Congress had mandated that the science change to reflect the new concerns with diets of surfeit rather than diets of paucity," but "the Government had not mandated that it be designed as we consider design, graphic design. They considered the design of the label having to do with the nutrients." Congress reduced label design to content, not aesthetic. When Kessler called Belser, the commissioner worried: "We're going to

launch this new label and no one's gonna know we've even done anything, because it won't look any different."

57. Burkey Belser, "Feeding Facts to America," *AIGA Journal of Graphic Design* 14, no. 2 (1996).

58. Belser noted that his firm had just acquired the new Macintosh computer, which according to him had only just become usable from a design perspective. They had only one Apple in the studio and people had to sign up for it. Belser acknowledged the importance personal computers had on design practices in this period. He also noted the novelty of the fax machine the firm had purchased only six months before: "These two pieces of technology had an interesting bearing on the design of the label, and ultimately I believe the success of the label, because we would do a design, say during the day. We would fax it up to the Hill the next morning. Various groups who were looped in, important constituencies, industry and consumer groups . . . they would comment on the label, and we would respond to their comments with different designs." The computer facilitated rapid digital redesign, and the fax machine provided for a more continuous feedback loop with the firm's client.

59. Belser, "Feeding Facts to America."

60. Belser also consulted with Cheryl Achterberg, then director of the Nutrition Center at Penn State University, who had conducted studies on nutrition literacy and had submitted extensive comments to the FDA that Belser and the FDA staff found useful.

61. Helvetica was chosen over Times Roman font because of its "efficiency and simplicity," and because it was popular at the time due to its association with modernist Swiss "Bauhaus" design.

62. It is difficult to determine whether the black border was David Kessler's idea or Burkey Belser's. FDA staff interviewed attributed it to Kessler, but Belser was clear that he stated at the beginning such a box was crucial for distinguishing the label from other package "territories."

63. Consumers showed a preference for numbers over symbols or adjectives. As Bill Hubbard said in a subsequent oral history: "They wanted real information; they wanted the numbers." FDA Oral History, Michael R. Taylor, Parklawn Building, Rockville, MD, December 23, 1992, p. 13.

64. The six graphic designs were selected from about thirty-five different designs the firm experimented with.

65. Food and Drug Administration, HHS, "Food Labeling," 56 *Federal Register* 60373 (November 27, 1991).

66. "Comments of the Center for Science in the Public Interest," February 26, 1992, FDA Dockets: 90N-0135, vol. 100, C3842, pp. 17–19.

67. "Comments of the American Dietetic Association," February 24, 1992, FDA Dockets: 90N-0135, vol. 90, C2992.

68. By contrast, in his description of the Drug Facts panel Belser noted that legal concerns about giving abbreviated instructions on appropriate use "doomed" the Drug Facts label's usability and clarity, resulting in an extended package insert approach with "too much information."

69. In an interview in 2014 Belser emphasized this point that the Nutrition Facts panel wasn't impartial science, but reflected normative policymaking: "Now, if a label were designed by scientists, it would have no boldface. As soon as we bold something, that's a public-policy

decision. In the old label, you boldfaced fats. In the new version, calories." Ariana Eunjung Cha, "Burkey Belser, Nutrition-Facts Label Designer, Talks about the Future of Food Information," *Washington Post,* March 2, 2014, https://www.washingtonpost.com/politics/burkey-belser -nutrition-facts-label-designer-talks-about-the-future-of-food-information/2014/03/02 /50929ccc-9ffc-11e3-a050-dc3322a94fa7_story.html, last visited April 20, 2023.

70. "August 19, 1992 Letter from the National Food Processors Association," FDA Dockets: 91N-0162, vol. 21, C964, pp. 24–25.

71. Food and Drug Administration (FDA), "Food Labeling: Mandatory Status of Nutrition Labeling and Nutrient Content Revision, Format for Nutrition Label, Part IV," 58 *Federal Register* 2079 (January 6, 1993).

72. Belser believed that the government label's legacy for the design industry was to prove that "design can work in the public interest . . . even for the most humble of uses." Author's phone interview with Burkey Belser, October 14, 2009.

73. Dixie Farley, "Look for 'Legit' Health Claims on Foods," *FDA Consumer* 27 (May 1993). The FDA also set eleven "core" terms of nutrition claims: "free," "low," "lean," "extra lean," "high," "good source," "reduced," "less," "light," "fewer," and "more." There were also clarifications on what foods could be labeled "fresh" or "healthy." Dori Stehlin, "A Little 'Lite' Reading," *FDA Consumer* 27 (May 1993).

74. The publication date was two weeks prior to 1992 president elect, Bill Clinton, being sworn in to office; the Bush administration hoped to have the guidelines set before the new administration took over. Food and Drug Administration (FDA), "Food Labeling," 58 *Federal Register* 2079 (January 6, 1993).

75. Paula Kurtzweil, "Good Reading for Good Eating," *FDA Consumer* 27 (May 1993).

76. Paula Kurtzweil, "Food Labeling Education Serves Many Groups," *FDA Consumer* 28 (May 1994): 6.

77. Kurtzweil, "Food Labeling Education," 8.

78. Kurtzweil, "Food Labeling Education," 8–9.

79. Kurtzweil, "Food Labeling Education," 8, 10.

80. Marian Burros, "F. D. A. Throws Its Best Pitches for Food Label," *New York Times,* May 1, 1994, sec. 1, p. 1, col. 2.

81. Kurtzweil, "Food Labeling Education," 6.

82. Burros, "F. D. A. Throws Its Best Pitches."

83. See, for example, *FDA Consumer* 28 (December 1994): 19; Paula Kurtzweil, "Coping with Diabetes," *FDA Consumer* 28 (November 1994): 20–25; Paula Kurtzweil, "Help in Preventing Heart Disease," *FDA Consumer* 28 (December 1994): 19–24; Paula Kurtzweil, "Better Information for Special Diets," *FDA Consumer* 29 (January–February 1995): 19–25.

84. FDA Press Office, "FDA Food Label Wins Presidential Design Achievement Award," FDA Talk Paper T97-54 (1997).

85. The "Drug Facts" label was also designed by Greenfield / Belser Ltd., and introduced on the market in 1999. Belser saw it as an opportunity to "extend the brand." In 2020 Apple Inc. built on the Nutrition Fact's now iconic status when it released its "Privacy Nutrition Labels," digital pages that informed iPhone users what data their phone apps could access and how it could be used.

86. One study analyzed supermarket purchase behavior pre- and post-NLEA for salad dressings, and noted a decline in the sale of high-fat dressings. A. D. Mathios, "The Impact

of Mandatory Disclosure Laws on Product Choices: An Analysis of the Salad Dressing Market," *Journal of Law and Economics* 43, no. 2 (2000): 651–77. Another study provided mixed results, suggesting nutrition labeling had raised general awareness and comprehension of foods' nutrition profiles, but had "widened consumer differences in terms of how much nutrition information was actually acquired—more motivated consumers and less skeptical consumers acquired more information." C. Moorman, "A Quasi Experiment to Assess the Consumer and Informational Determinants of Nutrition Information Processing Activities: The Case of the Nutrition Labeling and Education Act," *Journal of Public Policy and Marketing* 15, no. 1 (1996): 28–44. On the USDA and FMI surveys, see Elise Golan, Fred Kuchler, and Lorraine Mitchell, *Economics of Food Labeling*, Economic Research Service, US Department of Agriculture, Agricultural Economic Report no. 793.

87. Paul J. Petruccelli, "Consumer and Marketing Implications of Information Provision: The Case of the Nutrition Labeling and Education Act of 1990," *Journal of Public Policy and Marketing* 15 (Spring 1996): 150–53.

88. "Food Labels Limited as Education Vehicles, FDA Study Finds," *Food Labeling News*, March 23, 1995, 36–38.

89. One consumer experiment study suggested health claims fundamentally and detrimentally alter consumers' abilities to interpret the nutrition label. G. T. Ford, M. Hastak, A. Mitra, and D. J. Ringold, "Can Consumers Interpret Nutrition Information in the Presence of a Health Claim? A Laboratory Investigation," *Journal of Public Policy and Marketing* 15, no. 1 (1996): 16–27. Another described the tendency of consumers to "generalize" from health claims, interpret "low cholesterol" specific claims as indicators of the general claim "healthy," suggesting such claims could easily lead to distortions of healthfulness. J. C. Andrews, R. G. Netemeyer, and S. Burton, "Consumer Generalization of Nutrient Content Claims in Advertising," *Journal of Marketing* 62, no. 4 (1998): 62–75. Even more than a decade after its introduction, patients with poor literacy or numeracy skills struggled with correctly interpreting the nutrition label. Russell L. Rothman et al., "Patient Understanding of Food Labels: The Role of Literacy and Numeracy," *American Journal of Preventive Medicine* 31, no. 5 (November 2006): 391–98.

90. J. E. Todd and J. N. Variyam, *The Decline in Consumer Use of Food Nutrition Labels, 1995–2006* (Washington, DC: US Department of Agriculture, 2008).

91. C. L. Taylor and V. L. Wilkening, "How the Nutrition Food Label Was Developed, Part 1: The Nutrition Facts Panel," *Journal of the American Dietetic Association* 108, no. 3 (2008): 437–42; C. L. Taylor and V. L. Wilkening, "How the Nutrition Food Label Was Developed, Part 2: The Purpose and Promise of Nutrition Claims," *Journal of the American Dietetic Association* 108, no. 4 (2008): 618–23.

92. Guthman, *Weighing In*.

93. Several health organizations were concerned over the possible confusion the shift from RDAs to RDIs might cause. American Medical Association, "Statement to the U.S. Department of Agriculture and the Food and Drug Administration," January 31, 1992, FDA Dockets: 90N-0135, vol. 108, TS33, pp. 3–4; FDA Dockets: 90N-0135, vol. 73, C2832, pp. 3–5. "Comments of the American Dietetic Association on the Food and Drug Administration's Proposed Rule on Food Labeling," February 24, 1992, FDA Dockets: 90N-0135, vol. 90, C2992.

94. Food and Nutrition Board, *Recommended Dietary Allowances, 10th ed.* (Washington, DC: National Research Council, National Academy of Sciences, 1989), 1; Nestle, *Food Politics*, 306–7.

95. The FDA derived these quantities from the recommendations of three advisory reports: the Institute of Medicine's 1989 *Diet and Health,* a 1990 expert panel report of the NIH's National Cholesterol Education Program, and the 1988 *Surgeon General's Report.*

96. David Kessler et al., "Developing the 'Nutrition Facts' Food Label," *Harvard Health Policy Review* 4, no. 2 (Fall 2003): 15–16. For an account of the switch from RDAs to DRIs, see Suzanne P. Murphy, Allison A. Yates, Stephanie A. Atkinson, Susan I Barr, and Johanna Dwyer, "History of Nutrition: The Long Road Leading to the Dietary Reference Intakes for the United States and Canada," *Advanced Nutrition* (2016): 157–68.

97. "February 24, 1992 Letter from the American Dietetic Association," FDA Dockets, 90N-0135, vol. 90, C2992. Kessler later described this battle over a 2,000-calorie versus 2,300-calorie baseline as one waged principally against the USDA, who preferred the higher threshold and was generally pro-fat. Kessler wrote that the definitive evidence which settled the matter for him was the discovery that McDonald's claims of healthfulness on their tray liner cited the National Research Council's nutrition guidelines at a daily intake of 2,000 calories. David Kessler, *A Question of Intent: A Great American Battle with a Deadly Industry* (Cambridge, MA: Public Affairs, 2001), 56–58; Kessler et al., "Developing the 'Nutrition Facts' Food Label," 16–17.

98. Hine, *Total Package,* 210.

99. F. Edward Scarbrough, phone interview with author, September 30, 2009.

100. Lorna Aldrich, *Consumer Use of Information: Implications for Food Policy* (Washington, DC: USDA ERS, 1999), 1.

101. Aldrich, *Consumer Use of Information,* 14, 18.

102. Paul Rabinow, "From Sociobiology to Biosociality," in *The Science Studies Reader,* ed. Mario Biagioli, 407–16 (New York: Routledge, 1999).

103. Latour, *Reassembling the Social,* 210.

104. On the "balanced woman," see Parkin, *Food Is Love,* 66.

105. Bruce A. Silverglade, "The Nutrition Labeling and Education Act—Progress to Date and Challenges for the Future," *Journal of Public Policy and Marketing* 15 (Spring 1996): 148–56.

106. Massimo Vignelli, "A Masterpiece!," *AIGA Journal of Graphic Design* 14, no. 2 (1996): 5.

107. Krista Hessler Carver, "A Global View of the First Amendment Constraints on FDA," *Food and Drug Law Journal* 63, no. 1 (2008): 151–215; Timothy D. Lytton, "Banning Front-of-Package Food Labels: First Amendment Constraints on Public Health Policy," *Public Health Nutrition* 14, no. 6 (June 2011): 1123–26.

108. This corporate legal pushback should be situated within a broader corporate legal movement against risk regulation, including legal campaigns against "junk science" in tort cases and PR campaigns alleging a litigation crisis. William Haltom and Michael McCann, *Distorting the Law: Politics, Media, and the Litigation Crisis* (Chicago: University of Chicago Press, 2004), 183–226; Peter W. Huber, *Galileo's Revenge: Junk Science in the Courtroom* (New York: Basic Books, 1993); David L. Faigman, *Legal Alchemy: The Use and Misuse of Science and the Law* (New York: W. H. Freeman, 2000); Gary Edmond and David Mercer, "Litigation Life: Law-Science Knowledge Construction in (Bendectin) Mass Toxic Tort Litigation," *Social Studies of Science* 30, no. 2 (April 1, 2000): 265–316; Shana Solomon and Edward Hackett, "Setting Boundaries between Science and Law: Lessons from Daubert

v. Merrell Dow Pharmaceuticals, Inc.," *Science, Technology and Human Values* 21 (1996): 131–56.

109. Michael B. Taylor and John B. Cordaro (1993), Michael Taylor of FDA et al., *Fox Morning News*, VHS tape, U. S. National Library of Medicine, Washington, DC.

110. Unless the FDA determines that the supplements cause direct harm. Dietary supplements are the least-regulated product on the market today that fall within the jurisdiction of the FDA. They represent a return to a "buyer beware" model of consumer responsibility. T. L. Beckstead, "Caveat Emptor, Buyer Beware: Deregulation of Dietary Supplements upon Enactment of the Dietary Supplement Health and Education Act of 1994," *San Joaquin Agricultural Law Review* 11 (2001): 107–35.

111. Robert Earl, phone interview with author, September 23, 2009; Joanne DeCandia, "Dietary Supplements and Drugs: Is the Line Blurred?," *Regulatory Affairs Focus,* December 2003, 29–33.

112. Keystone Center, *The Final Report of the Keystone National Policy Dialogue on Food, Nutrition, and Health* (Keystone, CO; Washington, DC, 1996), 36–46. Virginia L. Wilkening, phone interview with author, September 24, 2009.

113. 21 C. F. R. § 101.14, as quoted in the case. *Pearson v. Shalala* 164 F.3d 650 (D. C. Cir. 1999).

114. *Pearson v. Shalala* 164 F.3d 650 (D. C. Cir. 1999). One broader institutional context for the case was that the FTC and FDA at this time had different standards regarding "significant scientific agreement." In 1984 the FTC had published a notice that it would use the "reasonable consumer" standard on most advertisement issues including health claims. In the 1990s the FDA did not accept the FTC's standard. In 2002, however, the FDA announced it would adopt it. Hutt et al., *Food and Drug Law,* 111, 275. The court's decision in the *Shalala* case was indicative of a broader shift in American courts during the 1990s of problematizing the concept of "significant scientific agreement." The most consequential example of this juridical deconstruction of scientific consensus is the 1993 *Daubert v. Merrell Dow Pharmaceuticals* case. Sheila Jasanoff, "Beyond Epistemology: Relativism and Engagement in the Politics of Science," *Social Studies of Science* 26, no. 2 (1996): 393.

115. Nestle, *Unsavory Truth,* 87.

116. "Line between Foods and Drugs Being Blurred by DSHEA, Panel Says," *Food Labeling and Nutrition News,* May 16, 1996, 9–10; Peter Mansell, "Battling over the Boundaries," *Scrip Magazine,* October 2000, 71–75; Nick Hawker, "Food: The Ultimate Delivery System?," *Scrip Magazine,* April 2002, 14–17.

117. The earliest reference to "functional foods" was in a Japanese Ministry of Health and Welfare classification in 1991, which described them as "processed foods containing ingredients that aid specific bodily functions in addition to being nutritious." Japan's ministry later chose to refer to them as FOSHU, "Food for Specific Health Uses," because the word "function" implied such foods should legally be classed as drugs under Japanese law.

118. Frohlich, "Rise (and Fall) of the Food-Drug Line," in Creager and Gaudillière, *Risk on the Table.*

119. Clare M. Hasler, Richard L. Huston, and Eve M. Caudill, "The Impact of the Nutrition Labeling Act on Functional Foods," in *Nutrition Labeling Handbook*, ed. Ralph Shapiro (New York: Marcel Dekker, 1995), 478–79, 485.

120. See Richard L. Abel, "Law as Lag: Inertia as a Social Theory of Law," 80 *Michigan Law Review* 785 (1982); Sheila Jasanoff, "Making Order," in *The Handbook of Science and Technology Studies*, 3rd ed., ed. Edward J. Hackett, Olga Amsterdamska, Michael E. Lynch, and Judy Wajcman, 761–86 (Cambridge, MA: MIT Press, 2007).

121. Hasler et al., "Impact of the Nutrition Labeling," in Shapiro, *Nutrition Labeling Handbook*, 471–93.

122. The phrase "medical foods" was an administrative category that gained statutory authority in the 1988 Orphan Drug Act Amendments. Sanford A. Miller and Edward F. Scarbrough, "Foods as Drugs," *Drug Information Journal* 21 (1987): 221–28; "FDA Plans Separate Document on Medical Foods," *Food Chemical News*, December 9, 1991, 15–16.

123. R. E. Schucker, A. S. Levy, J. E. Tenney, and O. Mathews, " 'Nutrition Shelf-Labeling and Consumer Purchase Behavior," *Journal of Nutrition Education* 24, no. 2 (1992): 75–80.

124. CNN Larry King Live—Interview with David Kessler (1994), "Food Label Launch," VHS tape, U. S. National Library of Medicine, Washington, DC.

125. Taylor and Wilkening, "Nutrition Food Label . . . Part 2."

126. Bruce Bimber, *Information and American Democracy: Technology in the Evolution of Political Power* (New York: Cambridge University Press, 2003), 229.

127. For a broader theoretical treatment of the role of "informational politics" in the crisis of democracy, see Manuel Castells, *The Power of Identity* (Malden, MA: Wiley-Blackwell, 1997), 391–402.

6. LABELING LIFESTYLES

1. Part of a broader political shift, described by Julie Guthman as "rollout neoliberal governance." Julie Guthman, "The Polanyian Way? Voluntary Food Labels as Neoliberal Governance," *Antipode* 39, no. 3 (June 2007): 456–78.

2. A third food policy movement, food allergen labeling was also gaining importance in this period. See Matthew Smith, *Another Person's Poison: A History of Food Allergy* (New York: Columbia University Press, 2015).

3. On "lifestyle politics," see Anthony Giddens, *Modernity and Self-Identity: Self and Society in the Late Modern Age* (Stanford, CA: Stanford University Press, 1991); W. L. Bennett, "The Uncivic Culture: Communication, Identity, and the Rise of Lifestyle Politics," *Political Science and Politics* 31 (1998): 741–61; W. L. Bennett, "The Personalization of Politics: Political Identity, Social Media, and Changing Patterns of Participation," *Annals of the American Academy of Political and Social Science* 644, no. 1 (2012): 20–39; Ross Haenfler, Brett Johnson, and Ellis Jones, "Lifestyle Movements: Exploring the Intersection of Lifestyle and Social Movements," *Social Movement Studies* 11 (2012): 1–20; Laura Portwood-Stacer, *Lifestyle Politics and Radical Activism*, Contemporary Anarchist Studies (New York: Bloomsbury, 2013).

4. Some notable exceptions: Julie Guthman, "Eating Risk," in *Engineering Trouble: Biotechnology and Its Discontents*, ed. Rachel A. Schurman and Dennis Doyle Takahashi Kelso, 130–51 (Berkeley: University of California Press, 2003); Susanne Freidberg, *French Beans and Food Scares: Culture and Commerce in an Anxious Age* (New York: Oxford University Press, 2004); Michelle Phillips and Katherine Kirkwood, *Alternative Food Politics: From the Margins to the Mainstream* (New York: Routledge, 2019).

5. Claude Fischler argued the present "dietary cacophony" of diet advice had the paradoxical effect of leaving people more anxious about the significance of their choices. Claude Fischler, *L'omnivore* (Paris: Odile Jacob, 1990). It is noteworthy that only a few years later, in 1997, Dr. Steven Bratman coined the term "orthorexia" for patients with a medically unhealthy obsession with eating specific foods they considered to be healthy. Historian Joan Brumberg makes the case that the explosion of eating disorders in the 1980s could be attributed to the fact that "eating ha[d] been desocialized." The social structures for eating gave way to anomie that opened individuals to potentially self-destructive "disregulating behaviors." Ironically, "despite the multiplicity of products from which to choose," she argues that "the contemporary eater probably has less (rather than more) individual control over food than ever before." Joan Jacobs Brumberg, *Fasting Girls: The History of Anorexia Nervosa* (New York: Vintage Books, 2000), 257–58.

6. I do not discuss geographical indication labels here, such as the French system of *appellation d'origine contrôlée* (AOC) or concept of "terroir," because it has a much older history. The origins of the AOC system in France, though more processed-based than product-based, resembled the private branding and government standards story told for the U.S. in chapter 1. Alessandro Stanziani, "Wine Reputation and Quality Controls: The Origin of the AOCs in 19th-Century France," *European Journal of Law and Economics* 18 (2004): 149–67. Recent interest in importing the idea of terroir to the United States as a "values-based food label," however, offers a further example of how alternative food movements challenging conventional industrial agriculture become translated into food labeling initiatives. Amy B. Trubek and Sarah Bowen, "Creating the Taste of Place in the United States: Can We Learn from the French?," *GeoJournal* 73 (2008): 23–30.

7. In her analysis of GM-free and organic labeling, Julie Guthman argues that using voluntary labeling to reform confuses "consumer right-to-know with consumer right-to-buy" and important liberal notions of "transparency" with "shallow ideas of purchasing freedom." Guthman, "Eating Risk," in Schurman and Kelso, *Engineering Trouble*, 149.

8. I am grateful to Julie Guthman for bringing this to my attention. Guthman, "Eating Risk," in Schurman and Kelso, *Engineering Trouble*, 132. See also Julie Guthman, "Unveiling the Unveiling: Commodity Chains, Commodity Fetishism, and the 'Value' of Voluntary, Ethical Food Labels," in *Frontiers of Commodity Chain Research*, ed. Jennifer Bair, 190–206 (Stanford, CA: Stanford University Press, 2009). For a counterpoint to the argument that political consumerism leads to a "flight from politics," see Dietlind Stolle and Michele Micheletti, *Political Consumerism: Global Responsibility in Action* (New York: Cambridge University Press, 2013), 93.

9. On the history of niche marketing as a socially fragmenting force in America, see Joseph Turow, *Breaking Up America: Advertisers and the New Media World* (Chicago: University of Chicago Press, 1998). This "opt-in / opt-out" feature of certain labeling campaigns in recent decades is part of a longer, broader history of "political consumerism," including social movements that use "boycotts" and "buycotts" to politicize shopping. See Glickman, *Buying Power*; Michele Micheletti, *Political Virtue and Shopping: Individuals, Consumerism, and Collective Action* (New York: Palgrave MacMillan, 2003); Lisa A. Neilson, "Boycott or Buycott? Understanding Political Consumerism," *Journal of Consumer Behaviour* 9 (2010): 214–27; F. Forno and P. R. Graziano, "Sustainable Community Movement Organisations," *Journal of Consumer Culture* 14, no. 2 (2014): 139–57.

10. On the frontstage versus backstage institutional management of risk, see Stephen Hilgartner, *Science on Stage: Expert Advice as Public Drama* (Stanford, CA: Stanford University Press, 2000).

11. Many scholars in the field consider its starting point to be electrical engineer Chauncey Starr's 1969 article, "Social Benefit versus Technological Risk: What Is Our Society Willing to Pay for Safety?," *Science* 165, no. 3899 (September 19, 1969): 1232–38. See, for example, Adam Burgess, "Introduction," in *Routledge Handbook of Risk Studies*, ed. Adam Burgess, Alberto Alemanno, and Jens O. Zinn (New York: Routledge, 2016), 5.

12. Lars Noah, "The Imperative to Warn: Disentangling the Right to Know from the Need to Know about Consumer Product Hazards," *Yale Journal on Regulations* 11 (1994): 293–400. On this "anti-sectarian" spirit of risk studies, see Jasanoff, "Science, Politics," 201.

13. I discuss "choice architecture" and its use of labeling in the conclusion. A "founding text" for behavioral economics is Richard Thaler, "Toward a Positive Theory of Consumer Choice," *Journal of Economic Behavior and Organization* 1, no. 1 (March 1980): 39–60.

14. Allan M. Brandt, *The Cigarette Century: The Rise, Fall, and Deadly Persistence of the Product That Defined America* (New York: Basic Books, 2009).

15. The FDA became concerned about inconsistent industry standards for food allergen declarations in 1996, when CFSAN director Fred Shank published a notice to manufacturers to raise awareness about the need for clear labeling to avoid adverse reactions to even minute quantities of an allergen. In 2004 Congress passed the Food Allergen Labeling and Consumer Protection Act (FALCPA) to require clear labeling for the eight most common food allergens: milk, eggs, fish, crustacean shellfish, tree nuts, wheat, peanuts, and soybeans. Neal D. Fortin, *Food Regulation: Law, Science, Policy, and Practice* (Hoboken, NJ: Wiley, 2007), 55–56.

16. Susan G. Hadden, "Labeling of Chemicals to Reduce Risk," *Law and Contemporary Problems* 46, no. 3 (1983): 239. Her argument here has the character of ecologist Garrett Hardin's "tragedy of the commons." Susan G. Hadden, *Read the Label: Reducing Risk by Providing Information* (Boulder, CO: Westview Press, 1986).

17. Hadden, *Read the Label*, 148.

18. Aaron Wildavsky, "Views: No Risk Is the Highest Risk of All," *American Scientist* 67, no. 1 (January–February 1979): 32.

19. The phrase "risk-profiteer" is from Beck, *Risk Society*.

20. Aaron Wildavsky, *But Is It True?: A Citizen's Guide to Environmental Health and Safety Issues* (Cambridge, MA: Harvard University Press, 1995), 26–36, 201–22, 236, 400–402, 428.

21. Ken Lee, "Food Neophobia: Major Causes and Treatments," *Food Technology* (December 1989): 62–73.

22. A third political movement centering on risk in the late 1980s was patient advocacy campaigns on HIV / AIDS. The FDA faced significant negative media and public pressure because of its role in the slow drug approval for HIV / AIDS treatments. See Carpenter, *Reputation and Power*, 374–80, 440; Steven Epstein, *Impure Science: AIDS, Activism, and the Politics of Knowledge* (Chicago: University of Chicago Press, 1998), 222–26.

23. Nicholas Buchanan, "The Atomic Meal: The Cold War and Irradiated Foods, 1945–1963," *History and Technology* 21, no. 2 (June 2005): 221–49; Karin Zachmann, "Peaceful Atoms in Agriculture and Food: How the Politics of the Cold War Shaped Agricultural

Research Using Isotopes and Radiation in Postwar-Divided Germany," *Dynamis* 35, no. 2 (2015): 307–31.

24. 51 *Federal Register* 13399 (April 18, 1986), on 13387–88, Food Irradiation: Hearing before the Subcommittee on Health and the Environment of the Committee on Energy and Commerce, House of Representatives, 100th Cong., 1st Sess., H. R. 956 . . . (June 19, 1987), p. 188.

25. Richard J. Bord and Robert E. O'Connor, "Risk Communication, Knowledge, and Attitudes: Explaining Reactions to a Technology Perceived as Risky," *Risk Analysis* 10, no. 4 (1990): 499–506; Spencer Henson, "Demand-Side Constraints on the Introduction of the New Food Technologies: The Case Of Food Irradiation," *Food Policy* 20, no. 2 (1995): 111–27; Sukant K. Misra, Stanley M. Fletcher, and Chung L. Huang, "Chapter 20. Irradiation and Food Safety: Consumer Attitudes and Awareness," in *Valuing Food Safety and Nutrition*, ed. Julie A. Caswell (Boulder, CO: Westview Press, 1995), 435–55.

26. P. L. Stenzel, "Right-to-Know Provisions of California's Proposition 65: The Naivete of the Delaney Clause Revisited," *Harvard Environmental Law Review* 15 (1991): 493; M. Barsa, "California's Proposition 65 and the Limits of Information Economics," *Stanford Law Review* 49, no. 5 (1997): 1223–47; K. W. Kizer, T. E. Warriner, and S. A. Book, "Sound Science in the Implementation of Public Policy," *JAMA* 260, no. 7 (1988): 951–55.

27. W. John Moore, "Stopping the States," *National Journal* 22 (July 21, 1990): 1758–62. The 1990 NLEA ultimately only included a preemption clause for nutritional labeling and did little to shield industry from California's Proposition 65.

28. Steve Woolgar and Daniel Neyland, *Mundane Governance: Ontology and Accountability* (Oxford: Oxford University Press, 2013).

29. The FDA had requested that the terms "Fresh Choice," "Pure Squeezed," "100 Percent Orange Juice," "100 Percent Pure," and "Fresh," and the statements "We pick our oranges at the peak of ripeness, then we hurry to squeeze them before they lose their freshness," "We Don't Add Anything," and "Guaranteed: No Additives," be removed from Citrus Hill because they gave the consumer a false impression of freshness of orange juice squeezed straight after being picked. Warren E. Leary, "Citing Labels, U. S. Seizes Orange Juice," *New York Times*, April 25, 1991, sec. A, p. 18, col. 1. See also Freidberg, *Fresh*.

30. *NBC Today Show*, "Faith Daniels Interviewing David Kessler, Commissioner of the U. S. Food and Drug Administration (FDA)—FDA's Proposal for New Food Labels, the Drug Approval Process, and the State of the FDA," 1991, VHS tape, U. S. National Library of Medicine. On the alliance between HIV / AIDS activists and free market conservatives lobbying against a "drug lag" in FDA approvals, see Richert, *Conservatism, Consumer Choice*, 145–66.

31. On the recombinant DNA debates, see Susan Wright, *Molecular Politics: Developing American and British Regulatory Policy for Genetic Engineering, 1972–1982* (Chicago: University of Chicago Press, 1994); Sheldon Krimsky, *Genetic Alchemy: The Social History of the Recombinant DNA Controversy* (Cambridge, MA: MIT Press, 1982); Raymond A. Zilinskas and Burke K. Zimmerman, eds., *The Gene-Splicing Wars: Reflections on the Recombinant DNA Controversy* (New York: Collier Macmillan, 1986); J. Benjamin Hurlbut, "Remembering the Future: Science, Law, and the Legacy of Asilomar," in *Dreamscapes of Modernity: Sociotechnical Imaginaries and the Fabrication of Power*, ed. Sheila Jasanoff and Sang-Hyun Kim, 126–51 (Chicago: University of Chicago Press, 2015).

32. Kirchhelle, *Pyrrhic Progress*; Hannah Landecker, "The Food of Our Food: Medicated Feed and the Industrialization of Metabolism," in *Eating beside Ourselves*, ed. Heather Paxson, 56–85 (Durham, NC: Duke University Press, 2022).

33. David Barling, "Regulating GM Foods in the 1980s and 1990s," in *Food, Science, Policy and Regulation in the Twentieth Century*, ed. David F. Smith and Jim Phillips (New York: Routledge, 2000), 245; Stephen Nottingham, *Eat Your Genes: How Genetically Modified Food Is Entering Our Diet* (New York: Zed Books, 1998), 28–31.

34. Lorna Aldrich and Noel Blisard, "Consumer Acceptance of Biotechnology: Lessons from the rBST Experience," *Current Issues in Economics of Food Markets*, Agriculture Information Bulletin no. 747-01 (USDA ERS, December 1998).

35. In 1997 the WTO notified the E. U. to drop its "illegal" ban on rBST. Nottingham, *Eat Your Genes*, 30–33; Michael Balter, "One More Hurdle for Biotech," *Science* 252, no. 5011 (1991): 1367; Barling, "Regulating GM Foods," in Smith and Phillips, *Food, Science, Policy and Regulation*, 246.

36. For background on the GMO debates, see Frederick H. Buttel, "Ideology and Agricultural Technology in the Late Twentieth Century: Biotechnology as Symbol and Substance," *Agriculture and Human Values* 10 (Spring 1993): 5–15; Barling, "Regulating GM Foods," in Smith and Phillips, *Food, Science, Policy and Regulation*; George Gaskell, Martin W. Bauer, John Durant, and Nicholas C. Allum, "Worlds Apart? The Reception of Genetically Modified Foods in Europe and the U. S," *Science* 285, no. 5426 (July 16, 1999): 384–87; Jasanoff, *Designs on Nature*; Javier Lezaun, "Creating a New Object of Government: Making Genetically Modified Organisms Traceable," in Schurman and Kelso, *Engineering Trouble*; Rachel Schurman and William A. Munro, *Fighting for the Future: Activists versus Agribusiness in the Struggle over Biotechnology* (Minneapolis: University of Minnesota Press, 2010).

37. Jim Hightower, *Hard Tomatoes, Hard Times* (Piscataway, NJ: Transaction, 1972), 73–87.

38. Goodman et al., *From Farming to Biotechnology*, 2, 60.

39. Goodman et al., *From Farming to Biotechnology*, 141.

40. J. H. Maryanski, "US Food and Drug Administration Policy for Foods Developed by Biotechnology," in *Genetically Modified Foods: Safety Issues*, ed. Karl-Heinz Engel, Gary R. Takeoka, and Roy Teranishi, developed from a Symposium Sponsored by the Division of Agricultural and Food Chemistry at the 208th National Meeting of the American Chemical Society, Washington, DC, August 21–25, 1994, p. 12; Keith Redenbaugh, William Hiatt, Belinda Martineua, and Donald Emlay, "Determination of the Safety of Genetically Engineered Crops," in *Genetically Modified Foods*, 72–87; John Seabrook, "Tremors in the Hothouse," *New Yorker*, July 19, 1993, 32–41; Nottingham, *Eat Your Genes*, 160.

41. On Monsanto, see Bartow J. Elmore, *Seed Money: Monsanto's Past and Our Food Future* (New York: W. W. Norton, 2021).

42. Maryanski, "US [FDA] Policy," in *Genetically Modified Foods*, 12–17. The FDA was mainly concerned with allergens, and it warned companies to be cautious about using genes from known allergenic foods, such as peanuts, milk, legumes, and shellfish. Oscar L. Frick, "The Potential for Allergenicity in Transgenic Foods," in *Genetically Modified Foods*, 100–112.

43. Henry I. Miller, "Substantial Equivalence: Its Uses and Abuses," *Agricultural Biotechnology* 17 (November 1999): 1042–43. For a critical view of the substantial equivalence doctrine, see Marianna Schauzu, "The Concept of Substantial Equivalence in Safety Assess-

ments of Foods Derived from Genetically Modified Organisms," *AgBiotechNet* 2 (April 2000): 1–4.

44. Henry I. Miller, "A Rational Approach to Labeling Biotech-Derived Foods," *Science* 284, no. 5419 (May 28, 1999): 1471–72.

45. Henry Miller, "A Need to Regulate Biotechnology Regulation at the EPA," *Science* 266 (December 16, 1994): 1815–18; Henry Miller and Douglas Gunary, "Serious Flaws in the Horizontal Approach to Biotechnology Risk," *Science* 262 (December 23, 1993): 1500–1501. Following the "Republican Revolution" in Congress of 1994, sound science would be reincorporated into the EPA's existing goal of basing risk analysis and management on "the best available science and technology," and published in the 1997 EPA Strategic Plan. This helped clear the way for further GM crop approvals and the expansion of GM food markets in the United States.

46. Lezaun, "Creating a New Object," 499–531.

47. Carmen M. Bain and Tamera Dandachi, "Governing GMOs: The (Counter) Movement for Mandatory Non-GMO Labels," *Sustainability* 6, no. 12 (December 2014): 9456–76.

48. This process of "manufacturing of ignorance" through "organizational strategies that seek to minimize or conceal certain risks rather than amplifying them" has become its own subfield of science studies, known as "agnotology." Proctor, *Agnotology*; Marc-Olivier Déplaude, "Minimising Dietary Risk: The French Association of Salt Producers and the Manufacturing of Ignorance," *Health, Risk and Society* 17, no. 2 (2015): 168–83.

49. I am grateful to Bastien Soutjis for his not-yet-published research on industry use of digital labeling for GMOs. He found that many QR codes used on food products in U.S. supermarkets directed users to webpages where information about GMOs was buried deep in the website architecture.

50. Julie Guthman, *Agrarian Dreams: The Paradox of Organic Farming in California* (Berkeley: University of California Press, 2004); 5; Robin O'Sullivan, *American Organic: A Cultural History of Farming, Gardening, Shopping, and Eating* (Lawrence: University Press of Kansas, 2015), 12. Where not stated otherwise, much of this section draws heavily from Guthman, *Agrarian Dreams*; O'Sullivan, *American Organic*; Brian K. Obach, *Organic Struggle: The Movement for Sustainable Agriculture in the United States* (Cambridge, MA: MIT Press, 2015); Andrew N. Case, *The Organic Profit: Rodale and the Making of Marketplace Environmentalism* (Seattle: University of Washington Press, 2018).

51. O'Sullivan, *American Organic*, 185.

52. Case, *Organic Profit*, 8–9.

53. Case, *Organic Profit*, 56.

54. An appeals court would rule against the FTC and in favor of Rodale on due process grounds. Case, *Organic Profit*, 86–95.

55. O'Sullivan, *American Organic*, 56–64, 103–4, 112, 119–20.

56. Guthman, *Agrarian Dreams*, 3–13.

57. On the push for organic certification, see Obach, *Organic Struggle*, 47–79; O'Sullivan, *American Organic*, 102–3.

58. O'Sullivan, *American Organic*, 132.

59. Case, *Organic Profit*, 202–4.

60. Guthman, *Agrarian Dreams*, 117.

61. O'Sullivan, *American Organic*, 208.

62. Guthman, *Agrarian Dreams,* 115; O'Sullivan, *American Organic,* 171.

63. I thank Julie Guthman for pointing me to this direct connection at the time between GM and organic labeling policies. Guthman, "Eating Risk," in Schurman and Kelso, *Engineering Trouble,* 139.

64. On this market bifurcation of big and small organic producers, and the watering down of certification standards to "organic lite," see Guthman, *Agrarian Dreams*; Julie Guthman, "The (Continuing) Paradox of the Organic Label: Reflections on US Trajectories in the Era of Mainstreaming," in *Alternative Food Politics: From the Margins to the Mainstream,* ed. Michelle Phillips and Katherine Kirkwood, 23–36 (New York: Routledge, 2019).

65. Guthman, *Agrarian Dreams,* 21–22; O'Sullivan, *American Organic,* 172–82, 186–202; Michael Pollan, "How Organic Became a Marketing Niche and a Multibillion-Dollar Industry. Naturally," *New York Times Magazine,* May 13, 2001, http://www.nytimes.com/2001/05/13/magazine/13ORGANIC.html, last visited April 20, 2023.

66. Case, *Organic Profit.*

67. Guthman, "The (Continuing) Paradox"; Guthman, *Agrarian Dreams.* The "conventionalization thesis" originates with Daniel Buck, Christina Getz, and Julie Guthman, "From Farm to Table: The Organic Vegetable Commodity Chain of Northern California," *Sociologia Rural* 37, no. 1 (1997): 3–20.

68. As quoted in O'Sullivan, *American Organic,* 174.

69. Rachel Laudan, "A Plea for Culinary Modernism," *Jacobin Magazine,* May 22, 2015, https://www.jacobinmag.com/2015/05/slow-food-artisanal-natural-preservatives/. For a similar argument about the foodie movement, see Josée Johnston and Shyon Baumann, *Foodies: Democracy and Distinction in the Gourmet Foodscape* (New York: Routledge, 2015). In the last two decades, food industry analysts have repeatedly identified both the opportunities of high-tech novelty foods, such as functional foods, and natural and unprocessed foods as top consumer trends for the food industry. See, for example, the "Top 10 Food Trends" annual report, which the Institute for Food Technologist publishes in spring issues of *Food Technology.* A. Elizabeth Sloan, "Top Ten Food Trends for 2015," *Food Technology,* April 15, 2015, https://www.ift.org/news-and-publications/food-technology-magazine/issues/2015/april/features/the-top-ten-food-trends, last visited April 20, 2023.

70. Guthman, "Eating Risk," in Schurman and Kelso, *Engineering Trouble.*

71. Paul Duguid, "Information in the Mark and the Marketplace: A Multivocal Account," *Enterprise and Society* 15, no. 1 (2014): 1–30.

72. A. Gil-Juárez, "Consumption as an Emotional Social Control Device," *Theory and Psychology* 19, no. 6 (2009): 837–57.

CONCLUSION

1. David Schleifer, "Categories Count: Trans Fat Labeling as a Technique of Corporate Governance," *Social Studies of Science* 43, no. 1 (2013): 54–77; David Schliefer, "We Spent a Million Bucks and Then We Had to Do Something: The Unexpected Implications of Industry Involvement in Trans Fat Research," *Bulletin of Science, Technology and Society* 31, no. 6 (2011): 431–517.

2. In other ways the two scares were distinct. In 2002 the FDA had a ready-made tool, the nutrition label, with which to intervene. It also had a shared language, negative nutri-

tion and dietary risk, that both experts and the public could draw upon to make sense of the threat. Another difference was that trans fats were a risk introduced by a system of industrial tinkering with food, and were just one category of ingredients, partially hydrogenated oils, rather than entire sectors of traditional foods. Advocates of low-fat diets in the 1960s had to contend with pushback from traditional food producers. With trans fats, the artificial and the taboo converged. Readers looking for trans fats on the label treated it like a toxin to avoid, much the way Susan Hadden had observed in the 1980s that people tended to read nutrition labels as risk labels rather than diet guides. The 2000s trans fat scare also seemed to mark a partial reversal of the 1960s negative nutrition. In the years since, butter sales have risen and journalists have promoted a return to natural fat foods, arguing that artificial foods explain the rise in health problems.

3. Andrew A. Rooney, *Andy Rooney: 60 Years of Wisdom and Wit* (Waterville, ME: Thorndike Press, 2010), 210.

4. On the growing influence of food writers on Americans' diets, see Molly O'Neill, "Food Porn," *Columbia Journalism Review* 42, no. 3 (2003): 38. On the shift in TV cooking shows from educating to entertainment, see Michael Pollan, "Out of the Kitchen, Onto the Couch," *New York Times*, August 2, 2009.

5. FDA standards of identity continue to exist, and in a few product markets still play an important role. For example, of the more than 280 FDA food standards in 2023, approximately two-thirds are dairy standards. John Allan and Sharon Balhorn, "A Tale of Two Products: Standardized Yogurt and Yogurt Parfaits," paper presented at the International Dairy Food Association (IDFA) Yogurt Cultured Innovation and Ice Cream Technology Joint Conference, Austin, TX, April 18, 2023.

6. Schudson, *Advertising, the Uneasy Persuasion*, 126.

7. On the mid-twentieth century roots of our "disclosure culture," see Schudson, *Rise of the Right to Know*.

8. Self, *All in the Family*, 369.

9. Kevin M. Kruse and Julian E. Zelizer, *Fault Lines: A History of the United States since 1974* (New York: W. W. Norton, 2020), 4, 159.

10. Jefferson Cowie and Nick Salvatore, "The Long Exception: Rethinking the Place of the New Deal in American History," *International Labor and Working-Class History* 74, no. 1 (Fall 2008): 3–32; Frohlich, "Rise (and Fall) of the Food-Drug Line."

11. Krista Hessler Carver, "A Global View of the First Amendment Constraints of FDA," *Food and Drug Law Journal* 63, no. 1 (2008): 187–88. The 1910 case was *Florence Mfg. Co. v. J. C. Dowd & Co.*, 178 F. 73 (1910).

12. Bimber describes an acceleration of interest group pluralism since the 1990s, an evolution from "interest groups" to "issue groups" to "event groups," in *Information and American Democracy*, 22.

13. Twarog, *Politics of the Pantry*.

14. On the rise of health as a super value, see Jonathan M. Metzl and Anna Kirkland, eds., *Against Health: How Health Became the New Morality* (New York: NYU Press, 2010).

15. Cohen, *Pure Adulteration*, 227.

16. Richard H. Thaler and Cass R. Sunstein, *Nudge: Improving Decisions about Health, Wealth, and Happiness* (New Haven, CT: Yale University Press, 2008), 1–3.

17. Tim Wu, *The Attention Merchants: The Epic Scramble to Get Inside Our Heads* (New York: Knopf, 2016). On the rise of "decision fatigue" research since the 1990s, see Weber, "Cult of Convenience," 623n5.

18. Thaler and Sunstein, *Nudge*, 7–9.

19. On the concept of "rationally irrational," see Bryan Douglas Caplan, *The Myth of the Rational Voter: Why Democracies Choose Bad Policies* (Princeton, NJ: Princeton University Press, 2007); Dan Ariely, *Predictably Irrational: The Hidden Forces That Shape Our Decisions* (New York: Harper Perennial, 2010).

20. Mirowski and Nik-Khah, *Knowledge We Have Lost.*

21. Taubes gets the concept "informational cascade" from fellow science skeptic journalist John Tierney. Gary Taubes, *Good Calories, Bad Calories: Challenging the Conventional Wisdom on Diet, Weight Control, and Disease* (New York: Knopf, 2007); John Tierney, "Diet and Fat: A Severe Case of Mistaken Consensus," *New York Times*, October 9, 2007, F1.

22. Brian Wansink, *Mindless Eating: Why We Eat More Than We Think* (New York: Bantam, 2010); Brian Resnick and Julia Belluz, "A Top Cornell Food Researcher Has Had 15 Studies Retracted: That's a Lot," *Vox.com*, October 24, 2018, https://www.vox.com/science-and-health/2018/9/19/17879102/brian-wansink-cornell-food-brand-lab-retractions-jama, last visited April 20, 2023.

23. Paula B. Ford and David A. Dzewaltowski, "Disparities in Obesity Prevalence Due to Variation in the Retail Food Environment: Three Testable Hypotheses," *Nutrition Reviews* 66, no. 4 (2008): 216–28; Guthman, *Weighing In.*

24. Berg, *All You Can Eat,* 118–26.

25. David A. Kessler, *The End of Overeating: Taking Control of the Insatiable American Appetite* (Emmaus, PA: New York: Rodale Books, 2010).

26. David Harsanyi, *Nanny State: How Food Fascists, Teetotaling Do-Gooders, Priggish Moralists, and Other Boneheaded Bureaucrats Are Turning America into a Nation of Children* (New York: Broadway, 2007).

27. Julie Guthman, "Can't Stomach It: How Michael Pollan et al. Made Me Want to Eat Cheetos," *Gastronomica* 7, no. 3 (August 1, 2007): 75–79.

28. On the old roots of diet skepticism, see Shapin, "Expertise, Common Sense, and the Atkins Diet." On the pure food movement's search for food authenticity, see Cohen, *Pure Adulteration.*

29. Barry Schwartz, *The Paradox of Choice: Why More Is Less* (New York: HarperCollins, 2004). This anxiety is a deliberate product of consumer capitalism. Advertisers know that consumers "shopping around" for the best services or products have two options to reduce risk on a purchase: (1) they can seek out information, or (2) they can fall back on information-limiting tools such as brand loyalty. Schudson, *Advertising, Uneasy Persuasion,* 97–98.

30. Nadia Berenstein, "Clean Label's Dirty Little Secret," *The Counter*, February 1, 2018, https://thecounter.org/clean-label-dirty-little-secret/.

31. Schudson, *Rise of the Right to Know.*

32. Despite the feasibility of pushing toward "radical transparency" using blockchains to map supply chains, Jeremy Brice has argued retailers are pressured to "not know" about extended supply chains in order to not be held liable, an example of the "cultivation of strategic ignorance." Jeremy Brice, "The Legal Construction of Ignorance: Risk, Trust and

Food Supply Chain Governance in the Shadow of the 2013 Horsemeat Scandal," paper presented at the Law and Society Association annual meeting, Washington, DC, June 1, 2019.

33. Or as Jessie Coles put it, "Who Shall Certify the Certifiers?" Coles, *Standards and Labels for Consumers' Goods*, 272–73.

34. Not to be confused with Manuel Castells's notion of "informationalism," which replaces industrialism. Manuel Castells, *The Rise of the Network Society* (Malden, MA: Wiley, 2009).

35. See Nestle, *Unsavory Truth*.

36. Brandt, *Cigarette Century*.

37. Drawing from "reader response" theory, this also means readers bring values and information with them to the label.

38. Charlotte Biltekoff calls this "reform working" and argues that "dietary literacy" should involve recognizing that dietary facts are also cultural constructions with an embedded ethos. Biltekoff, *Eating Right in America*, 153–55.

39. Here I am using economic sociologists' notion of "performative." On the distinction between performativity and misrepresentation, see Mitchell, "The Properties of Markets."

40. Kjærnes, Harvey, and Warde also argue labels are a translation, and not just about transparency. Unni Kjærnes, Unni, Mark Harvey, and Alan Warde, *Trust in Food: A Comparative and Institutional Analysis* (Hampshire, UK: Palgrave Macmillan, 2007).

41. Bastien Soutjis, "The New Digital Face of the Consumerist Mediator: The Case of the 'Yuka' Mobile App," *Journal of Cultural Economy* 13, no. 1 (2020): 114–31; Bastien Soutjis, Franck Cochoy, and Johan Hagberg, "An Ethnography of Electronic Shelf Labels: The Resisted Digitalization of Prices in Contemporary Supermarkets," *Journal of Retailing and Consumer Services* 39 (2017): 296–304; Sarah Lyon, "The GoodGuide to 'Good' Coffee," *Gastronomica* 14, no. 4 (2014): 60–68.

42. See Cohen, *Pure Adulteration*, 222–27.

43. Taylor and Wilkening, "How the Nutrition Food Label . . . Part 2."

44. Brice Laurent and Alexandre Mallard, "Introduction Labels in Economic and Political Life: Studying Labelling in Contemporary Markets," in *Labelling the Economy: Qualities and Values in Contemporary Markets*, ed. Laurent and Mallard (Singapore: Palgrave Macmillan, 2020), 8.

45. Hadden, *Read the Label*, 261–62.

46. Norah MacKendrick, *Better Safe Than Sorry: How Consumers Navigate Exposure to Everyday Toxics* (Oakland: University of California Press, 2018), 104–8.

47. Soutjis, "New Digital Face"; Natasha Dow Schüll, "Data for Life: Wearable Technology and the Design of Self-Care," *BioSocieties* 11, no. 3 (2016): 317–33.

48. On "contextual commerce," see Roy Erez, "Contextual Commerce: What It Really Means and 3 Reasons You Should Care about It," *Forbes*, May 2, 2019, https://www.forbes.com/sites/royerez/2019/05/02/contextual-commerce-what-it-really-means-and-3-reasons-you-should-care-about-it/. On "convergence culture," see Henry Jenkins, *Convergence Culture: Where Old and New Media Collide* (New York: NYU Press, 2008).

49. Javier Lezaun and Tanya Schneider, "Endless Qualifications, Restless Consumption: The Governance of Novel Foods in Europe," *Science as Culture* 21, no. 3 (2012): 265–391.

SELECTED BIBLIOGRAPHY

Abel, Richard L. "Law as Lag: Inertia as a Social Theory of Law." *Michigan Law Review* 80 (1982): 785–809.

Ackerman, Michael. "Interpreting the 'Newer Knowledge of Nutrition': Science, Interests, and Values in the Making of Dietary Advice in the United States, 1915–1965." PhD diss., University of Virginia, 2005.

Allen, Patricia. "The Disappearance of Hunger in America." In *Food and Culture: A Reader*, edited by Caroline Counihan et al., 4th ed, 441–42. New York, Routledge, 2019.

Anderson, Oscar E. *The Health of a Nation: Harvey W. Wiley and the Fight for Pure Food.* Chicago: University of Chicago Press, 1958.

Apple, Rima. *Vitamania: Vitamins in American Culture.* New Brunswick, NJ: Rutgers University Press, 1996.

Backer, Kellen. "World War II and the Triumph of Industrialized Food." PhD diss., University of Wisconsin–Madison, 2012.

Bain, Carmen M., and Tamera Dandachi. "Governing GMOs: The (Counter) Movement for Mandatory Non-GMO Labels." *Sustainability* 6, no. 12 (2014): 9456–76.

Ball, R. A., and J. R. Lilly. "The Menace of Margarine: The Rise and Fall of a Social Problem." *Social Problems* 29, no. 5 (1982): 488–98.

Balleisen, Edward J. "The Prospects for Effective Coregulation in the United States: A Historian's View from the Early Twenty-First Century." In *Government and Markets: Toward a New Theory of Regulation*, edited by Edward J. Balleisen and David Moss, 443–81. New York: Cambridge University Press, 2009.

Balogh, Brian. *The Associational State: American Governance in the Twentieth Century.* Philadelphia: University of Pennsylvania Press, 2015.

Barling, David. "Regulating GM Foods in the 1980s and 1990s." In *Food, Science, Policy and Regulation in the Twentieth Century*, edited by David F. Smith and Jim Phillips, 239–55. New York: Routledge, 2000.

Beck, Ulrich. *Risk Society: Towards a New Modernity.* Thousand Oaks, CA: Sage, 1992.

Belasco, Warren. *Appetite for Change.* Ithaca, NY: Cornell University Press, 1993.

Belasco, Warren. *Meals to Come: A History of the Future of Food.* Berkeley: University of California Press, 2006.

Beniger, James R. *The Control Revolution: Technological and Economic Origins of the Information Society.* Cambridge, MA: Harvard University Press, 1986.

Bennett, W. L. "The Personalization of Politics: Political Identity, Social Media, and Changing Patterns of Participation." *Annals of the American Academy of Political and Social Science* 644, no. 1 (2012): 20–39.

Bennett, W. L. "The Uncivic Culture: Communication, Identity, and the Rise of Lifestyle Politics." *Political Science and Politics* 31 (1998): 741–61.

Bentley, Amy. *Eating for Victory: Food Rationing and the Politics of Domesticity.* Urbana: University of Illinois Press, 1998.

Bentley, Amy. *Inventing Baby Food: Taste, Health, and the Industrialization of the American Diet.* Berkeley: University of California Press, 2019.

Berenstein, Nadia. "Designing Flavors for Mass Consumption." *Senses and Society* 13, no. 1 (2018): 19–40.

Berg, Joel. *All You Can Eat: How Hungry Is America?* New York: Seven Stories Press, 2008.

Berghoff, Hartmut, Philip Scranton, and Uwe Spiekermann. "The Origins of Marketing and Market Research: Information, Institutions, and Markets." In *The Rise of Marketing and Market Research,* edited by Hartmut Berghoff, Philip Scranton, and Uwe Spiekermann, 1–26. New York: Palgrave Macmillan, 2012.

Berman, Elizabeth Popp. "From Economic to Social Regulation: How the Deregulatory Moment Strengthened Economists' Policy Position." *History of Political Economy* 49 (2017): 187–212.

Bettencourt, Clare Gordon. "Bread and Butter Policy: Food Identity Standards in the United States, 1938–2022." PhD diss., University of California Irvine, 2022.

Bettencourt, Clare Gordon. "Like Oil and Water: Food Additives and America's Food Identity Standards in the Mid-Twentieth Century." In *Proteins, Pathologies and Politics: Dietary Innovation and Disease from the Nineteenth Century,* edited by David Gentilcore and Matthew Smith, 165–68. London: Bloomsbury Academic, 2019.

Biltekoff, Charlotte. *Eating Right in America: The Cultural Politics of Food and Health.* Durham, NC: Duke University Press Books, 2013.

Bimber, Bruce. *Information and American Democracy: Technology in the Evolution of Political Power.* New York: Cambridge University Press, 2003.

Black, Jennifer M. "The 'Mark of Honor': Trademark Law, Goodwill, and the Early Branding Strategies of National Biscuit." In *We Are What We Sell: How Advertising Shapes American Life . . . And Always Has,* vol. 1, edited by Danielle Sarver Coombs and Bob Batchelor, 262–284. Westport, CT: Praeger, 2014.

Blaszczyk, Regina Lee. *Imagining Consumers: Design and Innovation from Wedgwood to Corning.* Baltimore: Johns Hopkins University Press, 2002.

Block, James E. *A Nation of Agents: The American Path to a Modern Self and Society.* Cambridge, MA: Belknap Press, 2002.

Bobrow-Strain, Aaron. *White Bread: A Social History of the Store-Bought Loaf.* Boston: Beacon Press, 2012.

Bowlby, Rachel. *Carried Away: The Invention of Modern Shopping*. New York: Columbia University Press, 2002.

Bowles, Mark D. "Liquifying Information." In *Cultures of Control*, edited by Miriam R. Levin, 225–246. Amsterdam: Harwood Academic, 2000.

Boyce, Angie M. " 'When Does It Stop Being Peanut Butter?': FDA Food Standards of Identity, Ruth Desmond, and the Politics of Consumer Activism, 1960s–1970s." *Technology and Culture* 57, no. 1 (2016): 54–79.

Boyle, James. *Shamans, Software, and Spleens: Law and the Construction of the Information Society*. Cambridge, MA: Harvard University Press, 1997.

Brandt, Allan M. *The Cigarette Century: The Rise, Fall, and Deadly Persistence of the Product That Defined America*. New York: Basic Books, 2009.

Brinkley, Alan. "The New Deal and the Idea of the State." In *The Rise and Fall of the New Deal Order, 1930–1980*, edited by Steve Fraser and Gary Gerstle, 85–121. Princeton, NJ: Princeton University Press, 1989.

Brumberg, Joan Jacobs. *Fasting Girls: The History of Anorexia Nervosa*. New York: Vintage Books, 2000.

Buchanan, Nicholas. "The Atomic Meal: The Cold War and Irradiated Foods, 1945–1963." *History and Technology* 21, no. 2 (June 2005): 221–49.

Buck, Daniel, Christina Getz, and Julie Guthman. "From Farm to Table: The Organic Vegetable Commodity Chain of Northern California." *Sociologia Rural* 37, no. 1 (1997): 3–20.

Busch, Lawrence. *Standards: Recipes for Reality*. Cambridge, MA: MIT Press, 2011.

Buttel, Frederick H. "Ideology and Agricultural Technology In the Late Twentieth Century: Biotechnology as Symbol and Substance." *Agriculture and Human Values* 10 (Spring 1993): 5–15.

Callon, Michel, ed. *The Laws of the Markets*. Malden, MA: Wiley-Blackwell, 1998.

Carpenter, Daniel P. *Reputation and Power: Organizational Image and Pharmaceutical Regulation at the FDA*. Princeton, NJ: Princeton University Press, 2010.

Carpenter, Kenneth J. *Protein and Energy: A Study of Changing Ideas in Nutrition*. New York: Cambridge University Press, 1994.

Carpenter, Kenneth J. "A Short History of Nutritional Science: Part 3 (1912–1944)." *Journal of Nutrition* 133, no. 10 (2003): 3023–32.

Carstairs, Catherine. " 'Our Sickness Record Is a National Disgrace': Adelle Davis, Nutritional Determinism, and the Anxious 1970s." *Journal of the History of Medicine and Allied Sciences* 69, no. 3 (2014): 461–91.

Case, Andrew N. *The Organic Profit: Rodale and the Making of Marketplace Environmentalism*. Seattle: University of Washington Press, 2018.

Castells, Manuel. *The Power of Identity*. Malden, MA: Wiley-Blackwell, 1997.

Castells, Manuel. *The Rise of the Network Society*. Malden, MA: Wiley, 2009.

Cebul, Brent. "The Antigovernment Impulse: The Presidency, the 'Market,' and the Splintering of the Common Good." In *The President and American Capitalism since 1945*, edited by Mark H. Rose and Roger Biles, 99–122. Gainesville: University Press of Florida, 2017.

Chandler, Alfred D. *The Visible Hand: The Managerial Revolution in American Business*. Cambridge, MA: Belknap Press, 1993.

Chandler Jr., A. D., and J. W. Cortada, eds. *A Nation Transformed by Information: How Information Has Shaped the United States from Colonial Times to the Present.* Oxford: Oxford University Press, 2000.

Chappell, Marisa. *The War on Welfare: Family, Poverty, and Politics in Modern America.* Philadelphia: University of Pennsylvania Press, 2010.

Chessel, Marie-Emmanuelle, and Sophie Dubuisson-Quellier. "Chapter 4: The Making of the Consumer: Historical and Sociological Perspectives." In *The SAGE Handbook of Consumer Culture,* edited by Olga Kravets, Pauline Maclaran, Steven Miles, and Alladi Venkatesh, 43–60. Thousand Oaks, CA: Sage, 2018.

Cochoy, Franck. "Another Discipline for the Market Economy: Marketing as a Performative Knowledge and Know-How for Capitalism." In *The Laws of the Markets,* edited by Michel Callon, 194–221. Malden, MA: Wiley-Blackwell, 1998.

Cochoy, Franck. *On the Origins of Self-Service.* New York: Routledge, 2014.

Cochoy, Franck. "A Sociology of Market-Things." In *Market Devices,* edited by Michel Callon, Yuval Millo, and Fabian Muniesa, 109–129. Malden, MA: Wiley-Blackwell, 2007.

Cochoy, Franck, and Catherine Grandclément-Chaffy. "Publicizing Goldilocks' Choice at the Supermarket." In *Making Things Public: Atmospheres of Democracy,* edited by Bruno Latour and Peter Weibel, 646–659. Cambridge, MA: MIT Press, 2005.

Cochoy, Franck, and Alexandre Mallard. "Another Consumer Culture Theory: An ANT Look at Consumption, or How 'Market-Things' Help 'Cultivate' Consumers." In *The SAGE Handbook of Consumer Culture,* edited by Olga Kravets, Pauline Maclaran, Steven Miles, and Alladi Venkatesh, 384–403. Thousand Oaks, CA: Sage, 2018.

Cohen, Benjamin R. *Pure Adulteration: Cheating on Nature in the Age of Manufactured Food.* Chicago: University of Chicago Press, 2019.

Cohen, Benjamin R., Michael S. Kideckel, and Anna Zeide, eds. *Acquired Tastes: Stories about the Origins of Modern Food.* Cambridge, MA: MIT Press, 2021.

Cohen, Lizabeth. *A Consumers' Republic: The Politics of Mass Consumption in Postwar America.* New York: Knopf, 2003.

Collingham, Lizzie. *A Taste for War: World War II and the Battle for Food.* London: Allen Lane, 2011.

Courtwright, David T. *Forces of Habit: Drugs and the Making of the Modern World.* Cambridge, MA: Harvard University Press, 2009.

Cowie, Jefferson, and Nick Salvatore. "The Long Exception: Rethinking the Place of the New Deal in American History." *International Labor and Working-Class History* 74, no. 1 (Fall 2008): 3–32.

Creager, Angela N. H., and Jean-Paul Gaudillière, eds. *Risk on the Table: Food, Health and Environmental Exposure.* New York: Berghahn Books, 2021.

Cronon, William. *Nature's Metropolis: Chicago and the Great West,* repr. ed. New York: W. W. Norton, 1992.

Cross, Gary S., and Robert N. Proctor. *Packaged Pleasures: How Technology and Marketing Revolutionized Desire.* Chicago: University of Chicago Press, 2014.

Cullather, Nick. *The Hungry World: America's Cold War Battle against Poverty in Asia.* Cambridge, MA: Harvard University Press, 2010.

De la Peña, Carolyn. "Artificial Sweetener as a Historical Window to Culturally Situated Health." *Annals of the New York Academy of Sciences* 1190, no. 21 (2010): 159–65.

De la Peña, Carolyn. *Empty Pleasures: The Story of Artificial Sweeteners from Saccharin to Splenda*. Chapel Hill: University of North Carolina Press, 2010.

De la Peña, Carolyn. "Risky Food, Risky Lives: The 1977 Saccharin Rebellion." *Gastronomica* 7, no. 3 (2007): 100–105.

Déplaude, Marc-Olivier. "Minimising Dietary Risk: The French Association of Salt Producers and the Manufacturing of Ignorance." *Health, Risk and Society* 17, no. 2 (2015): 168–83.

Deutsch, Tracey. *Building a Housewife's Paradise: Gender, Politics, and American Grocery Stores in the Twentieth Century*. Chapel Hill: University of North Carolina Press, 2010.

DeVault, Marjorie L., and James P. Pitts. "Surplus and Scarcity: Hunger and the Origins of the Food Stamp Program." *Social Problems* 31, no. 5 (1984): 545–57.

Dudziak, Mary L. "*Brown* as a Cold War Case." *Journal of American History* 91 (June 2004): 32–42.

Duguid, Paul. "Information in the Mark and the Marketplace: A Multivocal Account." *Enterprise and Society* 15, no. 1 (2014): 1–30.

Dumit, Joseph. *Drugs for Life: How Pharmaceutical Companies Define Our Health*. Durham, NC: Duke University Press Books, 2012.

Dupré, R. "'If It's Yellow, It Must Be Butter': Margarine Regulation in North America since 1886." *Journal of Economic History* 59, no. 2 (1999): 353–71.

Dupuis, E. Melanie. *Nature's Perfect Food: How Milk Became America's Drink*. New York: NYU Press, 2002.

Eden, Sally. "Food Labels as Boundary Objects: How Consumers Make Sense of Organic and Functional Foods." *Public Understanding of Science* 20, no. 2 (2011): 179–94.

Edmond, Gary, and David Mercer. "Litigation Life: Law-Science Knowledge Construction in (Bendectin) Mass Toxic Tort Litigation." *Social Studies of Science* 30, no. 2 (April 1, 2000): 265–316.

Elmore, Bartow J. *Citizen Coke: The Making of Coca-Cola Capitalism*. New York: W. W. Norton, 2014.

Elmore, Bartow J. *Seed Money: Monsanto's Past and Our Food Future*. New York: W. W. Norton, 2021.

Epstein, Steven. *Impure Science: AIDS, Activism, and the Politics of Knowledge*. Chicago: University of Chicago Press, 1998.

Ferguson, Priscilla Pankhurst. "The Senses of Taste." *American Historical Review* 116, no. 2 (April 2011): 371–84.

Feudtner, J. Chris. *Bittersweet: Diabetes, Insulin, and the Transformation of Illness*. Chapel Hill: University of North Carolina Press, 2003.

Fischler, Claude. *L'omnivore*. Paris: Odile Jacob, 1990.

Fitchen, J.M. "Hunger, Malnutrition, and Poverty in the Contemporary United States: Some Observations on Their Social and Cultural Context." *Food and Foodways* 2, no. 1 (1987): 309–33.

Fitzgerald, Deborah K. "World War II and the Quest for Time-Insensitive Foods." *Osiris* 35 (2020): 1–19.

Forno, F., and P. R. Graziano. "Sustainable Community Movement Organisations." *Journal of Consumer Culture* 14, no. 2 (2014): 139–57.

Foucault, Michel. "Governmentality." In *The Foucault Effect: Studies in Governmentality*, edited by Graham Burchell, Colin Gordon, and Peter Miller, 87–104. Chicago: University of Chicago Press, 1991.

Frank, Dana. *Purchasing Power: Consumer Organizing, Gender, and the Seattle Labor Movement, 1919–1929.* New York: Cambridge University Press, 1994.

Freidberg, Susanne. *French Beans and Food Scares: Culture and Commerce in an Anxious Age.* New York: Oxford University Press, 2004.

Freidberg, Susanne. *Fresh: A Perishable History.* Cambridge, MA: Belknap Press, 2009.

Frohlich, Xaq. "The Informational Turn in Food Politics: The US FDA's Nutrition Label as Information Infrastructure." *Social Studies of Science* 47, no. 2 (2017): 145–71.

Frohlich, Xaq. "Informationism in Food Politics: How the U.S. Food and Drug Administration Came to Regulate Food through Informative Labeling." In *Administering and Managing the U.S. Food System: Revisiting Food Policy and Politics*, edited by A. Bryce Hoflund, John C. Jones, and Michelle C. Pautz, 131–46. London: Lexington Books, 2021.

Frohlich, Xaq. "Making Food Standard: The U.S. Food and Drug Administration's Food Standards of Identity, 1930s–1960s." *Business History Review* 96, no. 1 (March 2022): 145–76.

Frohlich, Xaq. "The Rise (and Fall) of the Food-Drug Line: Classification, Gatekeepers, and Spatial Mediation in Regulating U.S. Food and Health Markets." In *Risk on the Table: Food, Health and Environmental Exposure*, edited by Angela N.H. Creager and Jean-Paul Gaudillière, 297–329. New York: Berghahn Books, 2021.

Gabaccia, Donna. *We Are What We Eat: Ethnic Food and the Making of Americans.* Cambridge, MA: Harvard University Press, 2000.

Giddens, Anthony. *Modernity and Self-Identity: Self and Society in the Late Modern Age.* Stanford, CA: Stanford University Press, 1991.

Giebelhaus, August W. "The Pause That Refreshed the World: The Evolution of Coca-Cola's Global Marketing Strategy." In *Adding Value: Brands and Marketing in Food and Drink*, edited by Geoffrey Jones and Nicholas J. Morgan, 191–214. London: Routledge, 1994.

Gieryn, Thomas F. "Boundary-Work and the Demarcation of Science from Non-science: Strains and Interests in Professional Ideologies of Scientists." *American Sociological Review* 48, no. 6 (1983): 781–95.

Gil-Juárez, A. "Consumption as an Emotional Social Control Device." *Theory and Psychology* 19, no. 6 (2009): 837–57.

Glabau, Danya. *Food Allergy Advocacy: Parenting and the Politics of Care.* Minneapolis: University of Minnesota Press, 2022.

Glickman, Lawrence B. *Buying Power: A History of Consumer Activism in America.* Chicago: University of Chicago Press, 2012.

Goldstein, Carolyn M. *Creating Consumers: Home Economists in Twentieth-Century America.* Chapel Hill: University of North Carolina Press, 2012.

Goodman, David, Bernardo Sorj, and John Wilkinson. *From Farming to Biotechnology: A Theory of Agro-Industrial Development.* New York: Basil Blackwell, 1987.

Gomart, Emilie, and Antoine Hennion. "A Sociology of Attachment: Music Amateurs, Drug Users." *Sociological Review* 47, no. 1 (May 1999): 220–47.

Green, Laurie B. "'Hunger in America' and the Power of Television: Poor People, Physicians, and the Mass Media in the War against Poverty." In *Precarious Prescriptions: Contested Histories of Race and Health in North America, edited by Laurie B. Green, John Mckiernan-González, and Martin Summers, 211–36. Minneapolis: University of Minnesota Press, 2014.

Green, Laurie B. "Saving Babies in Memphis: The Politics of Race, Health, and Hunger during the War on Poverty." In The War on Poverty: A New Grassroots History, 1964–1980, edited by Annelise Orleck and Lisa Gayle Hazirjian, 133–58. Athens: University of Georgia Press, 2011.

Greene, Jeremy A. Generic: The Unbranding of Modern Medicine. Baltimore: Johns Hopkins University Press, 2014.

Greene, Jeremy A. Prescribing by Numbers: Drugs and the Definition of Disease. Baltimore: Johns Hopkins University Press, 2007.

Guthman, Julie. Agrarian Dreams: The Paradox of Organic Farming in California. Berkeley: University of California Press, 2004.

Guthman, Julie. "Can't Stomach It: How Michael Pollan et al. Made Me Want to Eat Cheetos." Gastronomica 7, no. 3 (August 1, 2007): 75–79.

Guthman, Julie. "The (Continuing) Paradox of the Organic Label: Reflections on US Trajectories in the Era of Mainstreaming." In Alternative Food Politics: From the Margins to the Mainstream, edited by Michelle Phillips and Katherine Kirkwood, 23–36. New York: Routledge, 2019.

Guthman, Julie "Eating Risk." In Engineering Trouble: Biotechnology and Its Discontents, edited by Rachel A. Schurman and Dennis Doyle Takahashi Kelso, 130–51. Berkeley: University of California Press, 2003.

Guthman, Julie. "The Polanyian Way? Voluntary Food Labels as Neoliberal Governance." Antipode 39, no. 3 (June 2007): 456–78.

Guthman, Julie. "Unveiling the Unveiling: Commodity Chains, Commodity Fetishism, and the 'Value' of Voluntary, Ethical Food Labels." In Frontiers of Commodity Chain Research, edited by Jennifer Bair, 190–206. Stanford, CA: Stanford University Press, 2009.

Guthman, Julie, Weighing In: Obesity, Food Justice, and the Limits of Capitalism. Berkeley: University of California Press, 2011.

Haenfler, Ross, Brett Johnson, and Ellis Jones. "Lifestyle Movements: Exploring the Intersection of Lifestyle and Social Movements." Social Movement Studies 11 (2012): 1–20.

Haltom, William, and Michael McCann, Distorting the Law: Politics, Media, and the Litigation Crisis. Chicago: University of Chicago Press, 2004.

Hamilton, Alissa. Squeezed: What You Don't Know about Orange Juice. New Haven, CT: Yale University Press, 2009.

Hamilton, Shane. "Analyzing Commodity Chains: Linkages or Restraints?" In Food Chains: From Farmyard to Shopping Cart, edited by Warren Belasco and Roger Horowitz, 16–28. Philadelphia: University of Pennsylvania Press, 2009.

Hamilton, Shane. "Cold Capitalism: The Political Ecology of Frozen Concentrated Orange Juice." Agricultural History 77, no. 4 (Autumn 2003): 557–81.

Hamilton, Shane. "The Populist Appeal of Deregulation: Independent Truckers and the Politics of Free Enterprise, 1935–1980." Enterprise and Society 10, no. 1 (2009): 137–177.

Hamilton, Shane. Supermarket USA: Food and Power in the Cold War Farms Race. New Haven, CT: Yale University Press, 2018.

Haushofer, Lisa. *Wonder Foods: The Science and Commerce of Nutrition*. Oakland: University of California Press, 2022.

Hawley, Ellis W. *The Great War and the Search for a Modern Order: A History of the American People and Their Institutions, 1917–1933*. Prospect Heights, IL: Waveland, 1997.

Hilgartner, Stephen. "The Dominant View of Popularization: Conceptual Problems, Political Uses." *Social Studies of Science* 20, no. 3 (1990): 519–39.

Hilgartner, Stephen. *Science on Stage: Expert Advice as Public Drama*. Stanford, CA: Stanford University Press, 2000.

Hilgartner, Stephen, and Dorothy Nelkin. "Communication Controversies over Dietary Risks." *Science, Technology and Human Values* 12, no. 3 (1987): 41–47.

Hine, Thomas. *The Total Package: The Secret History and Hidden Meanings of Boxes, Bottles, Cans, and Other Persuasive Containers*. Portland, ME: Back Bay Books, 1997.

Hisano, Ai. "Selling Food in Clear Packages: The Development of Cellophane and the Expansion of Self-Service Merchandising in the United States, 1920s–1950s." *International Journal of Food Design* 2, no. 2 (2017): 139–52.

Hisano, Ai. *Visualizing Taste: How Business Changed the Look of What You Eat*. Cambridge, MA: Harvard University Press, 2019.

Horowitz, Daniel. *The Anxieties of Affluence: Critiques of American Consumer Culture, 1939–1979*. Amherst: University of Massachusetts Press, 2005.

Horowitz, Roger. *Kosher USA: How Coke Became Kosher and Other Tales of Modern Food*. New York: Columbia University Press, 2016.

Howes, David, and Constance Classen. *Ways of Sensing: Understanding the Senses in Society*. New York: Routledge, 2013.

Hurlbut, J. Benjamin. "Remembering the Future: Science, Law, and the Legacy of Asilomar." In *Dreamscapes of Modernity: Sociotechnical Imaginaries and the Fabrication of Power*, edited by Sheila Jasanoff and Sang-Hyun Kim, 126–51. Chicago: University of Chicago Press, 2015.

Hutt, Peter Barton. "Government Regulation of Health Claims in Food Labeling and Advertising." *Food, Drug, Cosmetic Law Journal* 41, no. 1 (January 1986): 3–73.

Hutt, Peter Barton, and P. B. II Hutt. "A History of Government Regulation of Adulteration and Misbranding of Food." *Food, Drug, Cosmetic Law Journal* 39 (1984): 2–73.

Hutt, Peter Barton, Richard A. Merrill, and Lewis A. Grossman. *Food and Drug Law*. 3rd ed. St. Paul, MN: Foundation Press, 2007.

Jackson, Charles O. *Food and Drug Legislation in the New Deal*. Princeton, NJ: Princeton University Press, 1970.

Jacobs, Meg. *Panic at the Pump: The Energy Crisis and the Transformation of American Politics in the 1970s*. New York: Hill and Wang, 2016.

Jacobs, Meg. *Pocketbook Politics: Economic Citizenship in Twentieth-Century America*. Princeton, NJ: Princeton University Press, 2005.

Jasanoff, Sheila. "Beyond Epistemology: Relativism and Engagement in the Politics of Science." *Social Studies of Science* 26, no. 2 (1996): 393–418.

Jasanoff, Sheila. *Designs on Nature: Science and Democracy in Europe and the United States*. Princeton, NJ: Princeton University Press, 2007.

Jasanoff, Sheila. *The Fifth Branch: Science Advisers as Policymakers* (Cambridge, MA: Harvard University Press, 1994).

Jasanoff, Sheila. "Making Order." In *The Handbook of Science and Technology Studies*, 3rd ed., edited by Edward J. Hackett, Olga Amsterdamska, Michael E. Lynch, and Judy Wajcman, 761–86. Cambridge, MA: MIT Press, 2007.

Jasanoff, Sheila. *Science at the Bar: Law, Science, and Technology in America*. Cambridge, MA: Harvard University Press, 1997.

Jasanoff, Sheila. "Science, Politics, and the Renegotiation of Expertise at EPA." *Osiris* 7 (1992): 194–217.

Jenkins, Henry. *Convergence Culture: Where Old and New Media Collide*. New York: NYU Press, 2008.

Johnston, Josée, and Shyon Baumann. *Foodies: Democracy and Distinction in the Gourmet Foodscape*. New York: Routledge, 2015.

Josephson, P. R. "The Ocean's Hot Dog: The Development of the Fish Stick." *Technology and Culture* 49, no. 1 (2008): 41–61.

Junod, Suzanne [White]. "Chemistry and Controversy: Regulating the Use of Chemicals in Foods, 1883–1959." PhD diss., Emory University, 1994.

Junod, Suzanne [White]. "The Chemogastric Revolution and the Regulation of Food Chemicals." In *Chemical Sciences in the Modern World*, edited by Seymour Mauskopf, 322–55. Philadelphia: University of Pennsylvania Press, 1993.

Junod, Suzanne W. "Food Standards in the United States: The Case of the Peanut Butter and Jelly Sandwich." In *Food, Science, Policy and Regulation in the Twentieth Century: International and Comparative Perspectives*, edited by David F. Smith and Jim Phillips, 167–88. New York: Routledge, 2000.

Junod, Suzanne W. " 'Proscribing Deception': The Gould Net Weight Amendment and the Origins of Mandatory Nutrition Labeling." In *Setting Nutritional Standards: Theory, Policies, Practices*, edited by Elizabeth Neswald, David F. Smith, and Ulrike Thoms, 165–94. Rochester, NY: University of Rochester Press, 2017.

Kaplan, S. L. *The Bakers of Paris and the Bread Question, 1700–1775*. Durham, NC: Duke University Press, 1996.

Karpik, Lucien. *Valuing the Unique: The Economics of Singularities*. Princeton, NJ: Princeton University Press, 2010.

Kerr, Norwood Allen. "Drafted into the War on Poverty: USDA Food and Nutrition Programs, 1961–1969." *Agricultural History* 64, no. 2 (Spring 1990): 154–66.

Keuchel, Edward F. "Chemicals and Meat: The Embalmed Beef Scandal of the Spanish-American War." *Bulletin of the History of Medicine* 48, no. 2 (1974): 249–64.

Kimura, Aya Hirata. *Hidden Hunger: Gender and the Politics of Smarter Foods*. Ithaca, NY: Cornell University Press, 2013.

Kirchhelle, Claas. *Pyrrhic Progress: The History of Antibiotics in Anglo-American Food Production*. New Brunswick, NJ: Rutgers University Press, 2020.

Kjærnes, Unni, Mark Harvey, and Alan Warde. *Trust in Food: A Comparative and Institutional Analysis*. Hampshire, UK: Palgrave Macmillan, 2007.

Kjellberg, Hans, Johan Hagberg, and Franck Cochoy, "Thinking Market Infrastructure: Barcode Scanning in the US Grocery Retail Sector, 1967–2010." In *Thinking Infrastructures*, edited by Martin Kornberger et al., 207–32. Bingley, UK: Emerald, 2019.

Kraut, Alan M. *Goldberger's War: The Life and Work of a Public Health Crusader*. New York: Hill and Wang, 2004.

Krimsky, Sheldon. *Genetic Alchemy: The Social History of the Recombinant DNA Controversy.* Cambridge, MA: MIT Press, 1982.

Kruse, Kevin M., and Julian E. Zelizer. *Fault Lines: A History of the United States since 1974.* New York: W. W. Norton, 2020.

Kumar, V. "Evolution of Marketing as a Discipline: What Has Happened and What to Look Out For." *Journal of Marketing* 79 (January 2015): 1–9.

Landecker, Hannah. "The Food of Our Food: Medicated Feed and the Industrialization of Metabolism." In *Eating beside Ourselves: Thresholds of Foods and Bodies*, edited by Heather Paxson, 56–85. Durham, NC: Duke University Press, 2023.

Lassiter, Matthew D. "Inventing Family Values." In *Rightward Bound: Making America Conservative in the 1970s*, edited by Bruce J. Schulman and Julian E. Zelizer, 13–28. Cambridge, MA: Harvard University Press, 2008.

Latour, Bruno. "Drawing Things Together." In *The Map Reader: Theories of Mapping Practice and Cartographic Representation*, edited by Martin Dodge, Rob Kitchin, and C. R. Perkins, 65–72. Chichester, West Sussex: Wiley, 2011.

Latour, Bruno. *Reassembling the Social: An Introduction to Actor-Network-Theory.* New York: Oxford University Press, 2005.

Laurent, Brice, and Alexandre Mallard, eds. *Labelling the Economy: Qualities and Values in Contemporary Markets.* Singapore: Palgrave Macmillan, 2020.

Lears, Jackson. *Fables of Abundance: A Cultural History of Advertising In America.* New York: Basic Books, 1995.

LeBlanc, Hannah Findlen. "Nutrition for National Defense: American Food Science in World War II and the Cold War." PhD diss., Stanford University, 2019.

Lee, Caroline W. "The Roots of Astroturfing." *Contexts* 9, no. 1 (2010): 73–75.

Levenstein, Harvey. *Paradox of Plenty: A Social History of Eating in Modern America.* Berkeley: University of California Press, 2003.

Levenstein, Harvey. *Revolution at the Table: The Transformation of the American Diet.* Berkeley: University of California Press, 2003.

Lezaun, Javier. "Creating a New Object of Government: Making Genetically Modified Organisms Traceable." *Social Studies of Science* 36, no. 4 (2006): 499–531.

Lezuan, Javier, and Tanya Schneider. "Endless Qualifications, Restless Consumption: The Governance of Novel Foods in Europe." *Science as Culture* 21, no. 3 (2012): 265–391.

Logemann, Jan L. *Engineered to Sell: European Émigrés and the Making of Consumer Capitalism.* Chicago: University of Chicago Press, 2019.

Lubar, Steven D. *Infoculture: The Smithsonian Book of Information Age Inventions.* Boston: Houghton Mifflin, 1993.

Lyon, Sarah. "The GoodGuide to 'Good' Coffee." *Gastronomica* 14, no. 4 (2014): 60–68.

Lytton, Timothy D. *Outbreak: Foodborne Illness and the Struggle for Food Safety.* Chicago: University of Chicago Press, 2019.

MacKendrick, Norah. *Better Safe than Sorry: How Consumers Navigate Exposure to Everyday Toxics.* Oakland: University of California Press, 2018.

Marchand, Roland. *Advertising the American Dream: Making Way for Modernity, 1920–1940.* Berkeley: University of California Press, 1985.

Marks, Harry M. *The Progress of Experiment: Science and Therapeutic Reform in the United States, 1900–1990*. New York: Cambridge University Press, 2000.

May, Elaine Tyler. "Cold War—Warm Hearth: Politics and the Family in Postwar America." In *The Rise and Fall of the New Deal Order*, edited by Steve Frazer and Gary Gerstle, 153–184. Princeton, NJ: Princeton University Press, 1989.

Mayo, James. *The American Grocery Store: The Business Evolution of an Architectural Space*. Westport, CT: Praeger, 1993.

Merck, Ashton Wynette. "The Fox Guarding the Henhouse: Coregulation and Consumer Protection in Food Safety, 1946–2002." PhD diss., Duke University, 2020.

Metzl, Jonathan M., and Anna Kirkland, eds. *Against Health: How Health Became the New Morality*. New York: NYU Press, 2010.

Micheletti, Michele. *Political Virtue and Shopping: Individuals, Consumerism, and Collective Action*. New York: Palgrave MacMillan, 2003.

Miller, Peter, and Nikolas Rose. "Mobilizing the Consumer: Assembling the Subject of Consumption." *Theory, Culture and Society* 14, no. 1 (1997): 1–36.

Mintz, Sidney. *Tasting Food, Tasting Freedom: Excursions into Eating, Power, and the Past*. Boston: Beacon, 1997.

Mirowski, Philip, and Edward Nik-Khah. *The Knowledge We Have Lost in Information: The History of Information in Modern Economics*. New York: Oxford University Press, 2017.

Mitchell, Timothy. "The Properties of Markets." In *Do Economists Make Markets?: On the Performativity of Economics*, edited by D. A. MacKenzie, F. Muniesa, and L. Siu, 244–275. Princeton, NJ: Princeton University Press, 2007.

Mol, Annemarie. "Good Taste: The Embodied Normativity of the Consumer-Citizen." *Journal of Cultural Economy* 2, no. 3 (2009): 269–83.

Moore, Martin D. "Food as Medicine: Diet, Diabetes Management, and the Patient in Twentieth Century Britain." *Journal of the History of Medicine and Allied Sciences* 73, no. 2, (2018): 150–67.

Mudry, Jessica J. *Measured Meals: Nutrition in America*. Albany: State University of New York Press, 2010.

Murcott, Anne. "Scarcity in Abundance: Food and Non-Food." *Social Research* 66, no. 1 (Spring 1999): 305–39.

Neilson, Lisa A. "Boycott or Buycott? Understanding Political Consumerism." *Journal of Consumer Behaviour* 9 (2010): 214–27.

Nestle, Marion. *Food Politics: How the Food Industry Influences Nutrition and Health*. Berkeley: University of California Press, 2002.

Nestle, Marion. *Unsavory Truth: How Food Companies Skew the Science of What We Eat*. New York: Basic Books, 2018.

Nye, David E. *Consuming Power: A Social History of American Energies*. Cambridge, MA: MIT Press, 1999.

Obach, Brian K. *Organic Struggle: The Movement for Sustainable Agriculture in the United States*. Cambridge, MA: MIT Press, 2015.

Okun, Mitchell. *Fair Play in the Marketplace: The First Battle for Pure Food and Drugs*. DeKalb: Northern Illinois University Press, 1986.

Oldenziel, Ruth, and Karin Zachmann. *Cold War Kitchen: Americanization, Technology, and European Users.* Cambridge, MA: MIT Press, 2009.

Oreskes, Naomi, and Erik M. Conway. *Merchants of Doubt: How a Handful of Scientists Obscured the Truth on Issues from Tobacco Smoke to Global Warming.* New York: Bloomsbury Press, 2011.

Orleck, Annelise, and Lisa Gayle Hazirjian, eds. *The War on Poverty: A New Grassroots History, 1964–1980.* Athens: University of Georgia Press, 2011.

O'Sullivan, Robin. *American Organic: A Cultural History of Farming, Gardening, Shopping, and Eating.* Lawrence: University Press of Kansas, 2015.

Parkin, Katherine J. *Food Is Love: Advertising and Gender Roles in Modern America.* Philadelphia: University of Pennsylvania Press, 2006.

Paxson, Heather, ed. *Eating beside Ourselves: Thresholds of Foods and Bodies.* Durham, NC: Duke University Press, 2023.

Phillips, Michelle, and Katherine Kirkwood. *Alternative Food Politics: From the Margins to the Mainstream.* New York: Routledge, 2019.

Phillips-Fein, Kim. "1973 to the Present." In *American History Now*, edited by Eric Foner and Lisa McGirr, 175–197. Philadelphia: Temple University Press, 2011.

Phillips-Fein, Kim. *Invisible-Hands: The Businessmen's Crusade against the New Deal.* New York: W. W. Norton, 2009.

Popkin, Barry. *The World Is Fat: The Fads, Trends, Policies, and Products That Are Fattening the Human Race.* New York: Avery, 2009.

Poppendieck, Janet. *Free for All: Fixing School Food in America.* Berkeley: University of California Press, 2010.

Porter, Glenn. "Cultural Forces and Commercial Constraints: Designing Packaging in the Twentieth-Century United States." *Journal of Design History* 12, no. 1 (1999): 25–43.

Porter, Theodore M. *Trust in Numbers: The Pursuit of Objectivity in Science and Public Life.* Princeton, NJ: Princeton University Press, 1996.

Portwood-Stacer, Laura. *Lifestyle Politics and Radical Activism.* Contemporary Anarchist Studies. New York: Bloomsbury, 2013.

Power, Michael. *The Audit Society: Rituals of Verification.* Oxford: Oxford University Press, 1997.

Pozen, David E., and Michael Schudson. *Troubling Transparency: The History and Future of Freedom of Information.* New York: Columbia University Press, 2018.

Proctor, Robert N. *Cancer Wars: How Politics Shapes What We Know and Don't Know about Cancer.* New York: Basic Books, 1995.

Proctor, Robert N., and Londa Schiebinger, eds., *Agnotology: The Making and Unmaking of Ignorance.* Stanford, CA: Stanford University Press, 2008.

Rabinow, Paul. "From Sociobiology to Biosociality." *The Science Studies Reader*, edited by Mario Biagioli, 407–16. New York: Routledge, 1999.

Rees, Jonathan. *The Chemistry of Fear: Harvey Wiley's Fight for Pure Food.* Baltimore: Johns Hopkins University Press, 2021.

Richert, Lucas. *Conservatism, Consumer Choice, and the Food and Drug Administration during the Reagan Era: A Prescription for Scandal.* Lanham, MD: Lexington Books, 2014.

Rioux, Sébastien. "Capitalist Food Production and the Rise of Legal Adulteration: Regulating Food Standards in 19th-Century Britain." *Journal of Agrarian Change* 19, no. 1 (2019): 64–81.

Rodgers, Daniel T. *Age of Fracture*. Cambridge, MA: Belknap Press, 2012.

Rose, Mark H., et al. *The Best Transportation System in the World: Railroads, Trucks, Airlines, and American Public Policy in the Twentieth Century*. Columbus: Ohio State University Press, 2006.

Rose, Mark H. *Market Rules: Bankers, Presidents, and the Origins of the Great Recession*. Philadelphia: University of Pennsylvania Press, 2018.

Rose, Nikolas. *The Politics of Life Itself: Biomedicine, Power, and Subjectivity in the Twenty-First Century*. Princeton, NJ: Princeton University Press, 2006.

Ruis, Andrew R. *Eating to Learn, Learning to Eat: The Origins of School Lunch in the United States*. New Brunswick, NJ: Rutgers University Press, 2017.

Schleifer, David. "Categories Count: Trans Fat Labeling as a Technique of Corporate Governance." *Social Studies of Science* 43, no. 1 (2013): 54–77.

Schleifer, David. "Reforming Food: How Trans Fats Entered and Exited the American Food System." PhD diss., New York University, 2010.

Schliefer, David. "We Spent a Million Bucks and Then We Had to Do Something: The Unexpected Implications of Industry Involvement in Trans Fat Research." *Bulletin of Science, Technology and Society* 31, no. 6 (2011): 431–517.

Schudson, Michael. *Advertising, The Uneasy Persuasion: Its Dubious Impact on American Society*. New York: Basic Books, 1986.

Schudson, Michael. *The Rise of the Right to Know: Politics and the Culture of Transparency*. Cambridge, MA: Belknap Press, 2015.

Schüll, Natasha Dow. "Data for Life: Wearable Technology and the Design of Self-Care." *BioSocieties* 11, no. 3 (2016): 317–33.

Schulman, Bruce J. *The Seventies: The Great Shift in American Culture, Society, and Politics*. Cambridge, MA: Da Capo Press, 2002.

Schurman, Rachel A., and Dennis Doyle Takahashi Kelso, eds. *Engineering Trouble: Biotechnology and Its Discontents*. Berkeley: University of California Press, 2003.

Schurman, Rachel A., and William A. Munro. *Fighting for the Future: Activists versus Agribusiness in the Struggle over Biotechnology*. Minneapolis: University of Minnesota Press, 2010.

Scrinis, Gyorgy. *Nutritionism: The Science and Politics of Dietary Advice*. New York: Columbia University Press, 2013.

Scrinis, Gyorgy, "On the Ideology of Nutritionism." *Gastronomica* 8, no. 1 (2008): 39–48.

Scrinis, Gyorgy. "Sorry, Marge." *Meanjin-Carlton* 61, no. 4 (2002): 108–15.

Self, Robert O. *All in the Family: The Realignment of American Democracy since the 1960s*. New York: Hill and Wang, 2013.

Shamir, Ronen. "The Age of Responsibilization: On Market-Embedded Morality." *Economy and Society* 37, no. 1 (2008): 1–19.

Shapin, Steven. "Expertise, Common Sense, and the Atkins Diet." In *Public Science in Liberal Democracy*, edited by Peter W. B. Phillips, 174–93. Toronto: University of Toronto Press, 2007.

Shapiro, Laura. *Something from the Oven: Reinventing Dinner in 1950s America*. New York: Penguin Books, 2005.

Sklansky, Jeffrey. *The Soul's Economy: Market Society and Selfhood in American Thought, 1820–1920*. Chapel Hill: University of North Carolina Press, 2002.

Sklar, Kathryn Wish. "Consumers' White Label Campaign of the National Consumers' League, 1898–1918." In *Getting and Spending: European and American Consumer Societies in the Twentieth Century* (German Historical Institute), edited by Susan Strasser, Charles McGovern, and Matthias Just, 17–36. Cambridge: Cambridge University Press, 2013.

Smith, Matthew. *Another Person's Poison: A History of Food Allergy.* New York: Columbia University Press, 2015.

Smith-Howard, Kendra. *Pure and Modern Milk: An Environmental History since 1900.* Oxford: Oxford University Press, 2013.

Solomon, Shana, and Edward Hackett. "Setting Boundaries between Science and Law: Lessons from Daubert v. Merrell Dow Pharmaceuticals, Inc." *Science, Technology and Human Values* 21 (1996): 131–56.

Soutjis, Bastien. "The New Digital Face of the Consumerist Mediator: The Case of the 'Yuka' Mobile App." *Journal of Cultural Economy* 13, no. 1 (2020): 114–31.

Soutjis, Bastien, Franck Cochoy, and Johan Hagberg. "An Ethnography of Electronic Shelf Labels: The Resisted Digitalization of Prices In Contemporary Supermarkets." *Journal of Retailing and Consumer Services* 39 (2017): 296–304.

Spring, Joel. *Educating the Consumer-Citizen: A History of the Marriage of Schools, Advertising, and Media.* New York: Routledge, 2003.

Stanziani, Alessandro. "Wine Reputation and Quality Controls: The Origin of the AOCs in 19th-Century France." *European Journal of Law and Economics* 18 (2004): 149–67.

Starr, Paul. *The Social Transformation of American Medicine: The Rise of a Sovereign Profession and the Making of a Vast Industry.* New York: Basic Books, 2017.

Stoll, Steven. *The Fruits of Natural Advantage: Making the Industrial Countryside in California.* Berkeley: University of California Press, 1998.

Stolle, Dietlind, and Michele Micheletti. *Political Consumerism: Global Responsibility in Action.* New York: Cambridge University Press, 2013.

Strasser, Susan. *Satisfaction Guaranteed: The Making of the American Mass Market.* New York: Pantheon Books, 1989.

Swanson, Kara W. "Food and Drug Law as Intellectual Property Law: Historical Reflections." *Wisconsin Law Review* 2011, no. 2 (2011): 331–98.

Tangires, Helen. *Movable Markets: Food Wholesaling in the Twentieth-Century City.* Baltimore: Johns Hopkins University Press, 2019.

Taranto, Stacie. *Kitchen Table Politics: Conservative Women and Family Values in New York.* Philadelphia: University of Pennsylvania Press, 2017.

Taylor, Margaret R., Edward S. Rubin, and David A. Hounshell. "Regulation as the Mother of Innovation: The Case of SO2 Control." *Law and Policy* 27, no. 2 (2005): 348–78.

Tedlow, Richard S. *New and Improved: The Story of Mass Marketing in America.* New York: Basic Books, 1990.

Thompson, E. P. "The Moral Economy of the English Crowd in the Eighteenth Century." *Past and Present* (1971): 76–136.

Tomes, Nancy. *The Gospel of Germs: Men, Women, and the Microbe in American Life.* Cambridge, MA: Harvard University Press, 1999.

Tomes, Nancy. "The Great American Medicine Show Revisited," *Bulletin of the History of Medicine* 79, no. 4 (Winter, 2005): 627–663.

Trentmann, Frank, ed. *The Making of the Consumer.* Oxford: Berg, 2005.

Troetel, Barbara Resnick. "Three-Part Disharmony: The Transformation of the Food and Drug Administration in the 1970s." PhD diss., City University of New York, 1996.

Trubek, Amy B., and Sarah Bowen. "Creating the Taste of Place in the United States: Can We Learn from the French?" *GeoJournal* 73 (2008): 23–30.

Turkle, Sherry. "Computational Technologies and Images of the Self." *Social Research* 64, no. 3 (Fall 1997): 1093–111.

Turner, Fred. *From Counterculture to Cyberculture: Stewart Brand, the Whole Earth Network, and the Rise of Digital Utopianism.* Chicago: University of Chicago Press, 2008.

Turow, Joseph. *Breaking Up America: Advertisers and the New Media World.* Chicago: University of Chicago Press, 1998.

Twarog, Emily E. LB., *Politics of the Pantry: Housewives, Food, and Consumer Protest in Twentieth-Century America.* New York: Oxford University Press, 2017.

Twede, Diana. "The Birth of Modern Packaging: Cartons, Cans and Bottles." *Journal of Historical Research in Marketing* 4, no. 2 (2012): 245–72.

Veit, Helen Zoe. "Eating Cotton: Cottonseed, Crisco, and Consumer Ignorance." *Journal of the Gilded Age and Progressive Era* 18 (2019): 397–421.

Veit, Helen Zoe. *Modern Food, Moral Food: Self-Control, Science, and the Rise of Modern American Eating in the Early Twentieth Century.* Chapel Hill: University of North Carolina Press, 2013.

Vietor, Richard H.K. *Contrived Competition: Regulation and Deregulation in America.* Cambridge, MA: Harvard University Press, 1994.

Vileisis, Ann. *Kitchen Literacy: How We Lost Knowledge of Where Food Comes From and Why We Need to Get It Back.* Washington, DC: Island Press, 2010.

Vinsel, Lee. "The Crusade for Credible Energy Information and Analysis in the United States, 1973–1982." *History and Technology* 28, no. 2 (2012): 149–76.

Vinsel, Lee. *Moving Violations: Automobiles, Experts, and Regulations in the United States.* Baltimore: Johns Hopkins University Press, 2019.

Vinsel, Lee. "Virtue via Association: The National Bureau of Standards, Automobiles, and Political Economy, 1919–1940." *Enterprise and Society* 17, no. 4 (2016): 809–38.

Vogel, Sarah A. *Is It Safe?: BPA and the Struggle to Define the Safety of Chemicals.* Berkeley: University of California Press, 2012.

Wade, Louise Carroll. "The Problem with Classroom Use of Upton Sinclair's *The Jungle.*" *American Studies* 32, no. 2 (Fall 1991): 79–101.

Wang, Jessica. "Imagining the Administrative State: Legal Pragmatism, Securities Regulation, and New Deal Liberalism." *Journal of Policy History* 17, no. 3 (2005): 257–93.

Wargo, John. *Our Children's Toxic Legacy: How Science and Law Fail to Protect Us from Pesticides.* New Haven, CT: Yale University Press, 1998.

Watkins, Elizabeth Siegel. "Deciphering the Prescription: Pharmacists and the Patient Package Insert." In *Prescribed: Writing, Filling, Using, and Abusing the Prescription in Modern America,* edited by Jeremy A. Greene and Elizabeth Siegel Watkins, 92–116. Baltimore: Johns Hopkins University Press, 2012.

Weber, Margaret. "The Cult of Convenience: Marketing and Food in Postwar America." *Enterprise and Society* 22, no. 3 (September 2021): 605–34.

Weiner, Mark. "Consumer Culture and Participatory Democracy: The Story of Coca-Cola during World War II." *Food and Foodways* 6, no. 2 (1996): 109–29.

White, Monica M. *Freedom Farmers: Agricultural Resistance and the Black Freedom Movement*. Chapel Hill: University of North Carolina Press, 2019.

Wilkins, Mira. "The Neglected Intangible Asset: The Influence of the Trade Mark on the Rise of the Modern Corporation." *Business History* 34, no. 1 (1992): 66–95.

Wilkins, Mira. "When and Why Brand Names in Food and Drink?" In *Adding Value: Brands and Marketing in Food and Drink*, edited by Geoffrey Jones and Nicholas J. Morgan, 15–40. London: Routledge, 1994.

Wimberly, Sara L., and Jessica L. McClean. "Supermarket Savvy: The Everyday Information-Seeking Behavior of Grocery Shoppers." *Information and Culture* 47, no. 2 (2012): 176–205.

Woolgar, Steve, and Daniel Neyland. *Mundane Governance: Ontology and Accountability*. Oxford: Oxford University Press, 2013.

Wright, Susan. *Molecular Politics: Developing American and British Regulatory Policy for Genetic Engineering, 1972–1982*. Chicago: University of Chicago Press, 1994.

Yates, JoAnne. "How Business Enterprises Use Technology: Extending the Demand-Side Turn." *Enterprise and Society* 7, no. 3 (2006): 422–455.

Yates, JoAnne, and Craig N. Murphy, *Engineering Rules: Global Standard Setting since 1880*. Baltimore: Johns Hopkins University Press, 2019.

Young, James Harvey. *American Health Quackery: Collected Essays*. Princeton, NJ: Princeton University Press, 1992.

Young, James Harvey. "The Fielding H. Garrison Lecture. 'This Greasy Counterfeit': Butter Versus Oleomargarine in the United States Congress, 1886." *Bulletin of the History of Medicine* 53, no. 3 (1979): 407–8.

Young, James Harvey. "Historical Aspects of Food Cultism and Nutrition Quackery." In *Food Cultism and Nutrition Quackery*, edited by Gunnar Blix, 9–21. Stockholm: Almqvist & Wiksell, 1970.

Young, James Harvey. *The Medical Messiahs: A Social History of Health Quackery in Twentieth-Century America*. Princeton, NJ: Princeton University Press, 1967.

Young, James Harvey. *Pure Food: Securing the Federal Food and Drugs Act of 1906*. Princeton, NJ: Princeton University Press, 1989.

Young, James Harvey. "Saccharin: A Bitter Regulatory Controversy." In *Research in the Administration of Public Policy*, edited by Frank B. Evans and Harold T. Pinkett, 39–49. Washington, DC: Howard University Press, 1975.

Zachmann, Karin. "Peaceful Atoms in Agriculture and Food: How the Politics of the Cold War Shaped Agricultural Research Using Isotopes and Radiation in Postwar-Divided Germany." *Dynamis* 35, no. 2 (2015): 307–31.

Zachmann, Karin, and Per Østby. "Food, Technology, and Trust: An Introduction." *History and Technology* 27, no. 1 (2011): 1–10.

Zeide, Anna. *Canned: The Rise and Fall of Consumer Confidence in the American Food Industry*. Berkeley: University of California Press, 2018.

INDEX

AARP (American Association of Retired Persons), 143

Abbott Laboratories, 61, 62, 63 (fig.), 64, 73, 98, 99, 100

Achterberg, Cheryl, 239n60

Ackerlof, George, 111

the "active consumer," 6, 111, 156, 192

ADA (American Dietetic Association), 143, 149, 155, 236n18

added sugars, on Nutrition Facts label, 200

additives. *See* food additives; *specific types*

the administrative state, 10, 22, 30–31, 45, 126. *See also* anti-government/anti-regulatory sentiment; government regulation

adulteration and food fraud, 13, 16; economic adulteration, 25, 38, 123, 195; the embalmed beef incident, 23; the Pure Food and Drug Act and food forensics, 23–26, 208n11. *See also* food additives; food standards; substitutes and imitations

advertising: FDA false advertising regulation authority, 31; Sokolof's ads in support of the Nutrition Facts label, 143. *See also* health claims; marketing

affluence, 16, 50, 56, 60–61; debates about population growth and limits of, 101–2; "diseases of affluence," 16, 59, 90, 94, 139, 154. *See also* poverty

Affluence in Jeopardy (Park), 101

African American civil rights activism, 81, 82, 83, 84, 222n13

African American communities: poverty and hunger in, 82, 222n20; the Watts Riot, 82

agnotology, 249n48

agriculture: chemical use and residues, 61, 167, 177, 178; civil rights–era "freedom farm" cooperatives, 222n13; commodities distribution and use programs, 81, 83; GMOs in, 170–72, 175–76, 249n45; industry participation in the White House Conference on Food, Nutrition and Health, 92; "nutrition myths" related to, 51; organic farming and the USDA organic label, 139, 163, 167, 176–80, 181, 190–91, 198–99. *See also* dairy industry; meat industry; *specific crops*

agriculture policy, 6, 83, 97

AHA. *See* American Heart Association

AIDS/HIV activism, 170, 245n22

airline industry deregulation, 126

Alar apple scare, 167, 178, 179, 198

Alcoholic Beverage Labeling Act, 166, 198

Aldrich, Lorna, 155

All-Bran, 136, 137 (fig.), 198

allergens: allergen labeling, 166, 199, 244n2, 246n15; in GM foods, 174, 248n42

alternative medicine and therapeutics, interest in, 60–61, 236n14. *See also* dietary supplements; healthism

271

digital labeling, 176, 191, 200; UPC codes, 113, 197, 229n34

digital platforms and information environments, 135, 193–94, 235n5, 239n58

disease. *See* diet and health; dietary risk; diet-heart thesis; health and disease; *specific conditions*

the "distributed consumer," 155–56, 185

the distributed self, 135, 235n5

doctors. *See* medical professionals

Douglas, Mary, 205n36, 238n42

drug industry, 72, 76, 87. *See also specific companies and products*

drugs and drug regulation, 13; consumer reliance on expert authority, 15–16; drug and supplement retailing and marketing restrictions, 54, 58, 156, 216n53; the Drug Facts label panel, 152, 239n68, 240n85; during Goddard's FDA tenure, 76; FDA's regulatory approach, 17–18; FDCA classifications and requirements, 15, 33, 34, 54–55; generic drugs, 206n54; HIV/AIDS drug approvals, 246n22; industry and medical establishment reactions to FDCA passage, 15–16, 33–34; informative package inserts, 55, 121, 197, 215n30, 231n67, 239n68; patent medicines, 8, 195; patient advocacy for HIV/AIDS drug approvals, 170, 245n22; pre-market requirements for manufacturers, 31, 33, 34, 41, 54–55, 196, 215n30; Pure Food and Drug Act requirements, 24; safety scares and their impacts, 33, 54–55, 196. *See also* dietary supplements; food-drug distinction

drug stores, 216n53. *See also* pharmacies

DRVs (Daily Reference Values), 145, 154, 242n95

DSHEA (Dietary Supplement Health and Education Act), 157, 199

Dubos, René, 101

Duguid, Paul, 181

Dunbar, Leslie, 83

Dunbar, Paul, 54

DV (Daily Values), on the Nutrition Facts label, 142, 143, 147, 154–55

D vitamins, 53

Earth Day, 101

Eater's Digest (Jacobson), 109–10

eating disorders, 245n5

eating less. *See* negative nutrition

economic adulteration, 25, 38, 123, 195. *See also* substitutes and imitations

economic citizenship, 5; economic rights as civil rights focus, 81, 82, 83, 84, 222n13

economic concerns and conditions: economic implications of FDA policy decisions, 107; food cost increases, 82, 89, 104; healthcare costs, 105, 107, 152; 1970s stagflation, 113; population growth and food scarcity concerns, 101–2. *See also* affluence; poverty

Economic Opportunity Act (1964), 81

Economics of the Coming Spaceship Earth (Boulding), 101

Edelman, Marian Wright, 82

Edwards, Charles C., 110, 113

Edwards, Gordon, 93

Ehrlich, Paul, 101

Eisenstadt, Benjamin, 62

Elixir Sulfanilamide, 33

Elwell, Richard D., 44

embalmed beef incident, 23

"empty calories," 64–65, 160

Emerson, Gladys A., 94

emulsifiers, 52

The End of Overeating (Kessler), 188

enriched foods. *See* fortified and enriched foods

Environmental Defense Fund, 169

environmentalism, 101

Environmental Protection Agency (EPA), 12, 126, 175, 233n90, 249n45

European law and markets: cyclamate bans, 100; GMO foods and policies, 171, 174, 175–76; the precautionary principle in, 167

experience goods, 111

experts and expertise: consumer reliance on/trust in, 2, 15–16, 17, 192–93, 216n42; differences of opinion among, 77, 88, 100; expert endorsements of product health claims, 136–39, 137 (fig.), 158, 159, 190, 236nn17, 18; expert/non-expert divides, 80, 95, 97; expert participation in 1969 White House Conference on Food, Nutrition and Health, 91–92, 94, 95, 97, 225n60; FDA's reputation for expertise, 10–11, 45; industry access to and uses of, 48, 73–75, 77, 217n57, 236n18; roles and influence of, 4–5, 6–9, 48. *See also* certifications and endorsements; gatekeepers/intermediaries; medical professionals; nutritionists and nutrition science

Fair Packaging and Labeling Act (1966), 56–57, 112, 121, 196

fair trade certification labels, 164 (fig.), 198

White House Conference on Food, Nutrition
and Health (1969), 91–97, 197; framing and
purposes of, 91, 92, 93, 101, 105; participants
and panels, 91–94, 95, 97, 98, 116, 225nn60,
62; reactions to, 95, 96 (fig.), 97, 103, 105;
recommendations, reports, and policy outcomes, 93–94, 97, 98, 116, 225n74
White House Conference on Food, Nutrition
and Health (1971), 104
White House Conference on Hunger, Nutrition
and Health (2022), 227n105
White, Philip, 60–61, 225n60
whole foods: FDA assumptions about diets
based on, 52, 77; market disadvantages of
labeling, 117–18. *See also* packaged and proc-
essed foods; traditional foods
Why People Buy (Cheskin), 57
Wildavsky, Aaron, 166–67
Wiley, Harvey W., 23–24, 195
Wilkening, Virginia, 161
Wilkinson, John, 173
Wisconsin Alumni Research Foundation
(WARF), 98
Wodicka, Virgil, 94, 116
Wolf, Naomi, 139
women and women's organizations: African
American women and "cultures of poverty,"

82, 222n20; gender differences in daily calorie needs, 154–55; housewives as consumer
activists, 38, 82, 125–26, 185, 232n85; at the
1969 White House Conference on Food, Nutrition and Health, 93, 95, 105; warning labels
intended to protect pregnant women, 166;
women as marketing targets, 57, 59, 139, 185
Woodruff, Robert, 43
World Trade Organization (WTO), 171, 175–76,
199
World War II: margarine consumption and,
68; military foods and purchasing, 42, 52;
wartime food and packaging technology innovations and their market impacts, 41–44,
45, 50, 57, 213n94
Wright, Marian, 82
WTO (World Trade Organization), 171, 175–76,
199

Yates, JoAnne, 45
You Can Do It! (Proxmire), 129
Young, Frank, 236n17

*Zauderer v. Office of Disciplinary Counsel of
Supreme Court of Ohio*, 156–57
Zeide, Anna, 32
Zoellick, Bob, 238n52

CALIFORNIA STUDIES IN FOOD AND CULTURE
Darra Goldstein, Editor